# GOOD GOD BUT YOU SMART!

# GOOD GOD BUT YOU SMART!

*Language Prejudice and Upwardly Mobile Cajuns*

**NICHOLE E. STANFORD**

**UTAH STATE UNIVERSITY PRESS**
*Logan*

© 2016 by Nichole E. Stanford

Published by Utah State University Press
An imprint of University Press of Colorado
5589 Arapahoe Avenue, Suite 206C
Boulder, Colorado 80303

All rights reserved

 The University Press of Colorado is a proud member of
The Association of American University Presses.

The University Press of Colorado is a cooperative publishing enterprise supported, in part, by Adams State University, Colorado State University, Fort Lewis College, Metropolitan State University of Denver, Regis University, University of Colorado, University of Northern Colorado, Utah State University, and Western State Colorado University.

ISBN: 978-1-60732-507-9 (paperback)
ISBN: 978-1-60732-508-6 (ebook)

Library of Congress Cataloging-in-Publication Data

Names: Stanford, Nichole, 1977–
Title: Good God but you smart! : language prejudice and upwardly mobile Cajuns / Nichole Stanford.
Description: Logan : Utah State University Press, [2016] | Includes bibliographical references.
Identifiers: LCCN 2015044264 | ISBN 9781607325079 (pbk.) | ISBN 9781607325086 (ebook)
Subjects: LCSH: English language—Dialects—Louisiana. | Sociolinguistics—Louisiana. | English language—Dialects—Social aspects.
Classification: LCC PE3102.C35 S73 2016 | DDC 427/.9763—dc23
LC record available at http://lccn.loc.gov/2015044264

Cover photographs courtesy of the author

# CONTENTS

*Foreword by Suresh Canagarajah*   vii

Introduction   3
1. Sexy Ass Cajuns: The Complicated Reasons We Comply   31
2. Bas Class: Cajuns and the US Class System   74
3. "I Will Not Speak French. I Will Not Speak French": The Grand Dérangement de la Langue   119
4. Don't Blame Teachers (Not Too-Too Much): The Limits of Classrooms   160
5. Beyond Classrooms: Debunking the Language Myths   213

*Acknowledgments*   256
*Appendix: Survey on Cajun Vernacular English in Classrooms*   258
*Notes*   290
*References*   294
*About the Author*   304
*Index*   305

# FOREWORD

Suresh Canagarajah

Since the Students' Right to Their Own Language resolution was passed in 1974, the field of rhetoric and composition has developed diverse ways to address minority languages and English varieties in the classroom. Though much more can be done to promote these languages in more broad based and agentive ways, it is inspiring that teachers and individual writing programs are developing their own initiatives to transition multilingual students to academic norms; feature their languages in materials for study; affirm the communicative values and norms they bring with them, treating them as having a structure and logic of their own; and, in more radical cases, help strategically mesh these languages in academic texts framed around dominant institutional conventions. Recent theoretical orientations such as postcolonialism, identity politics, and resistance studies have also helped to affirm the transformative possibilities in localized contexts such as classrooms and texts. The changes in these contexts for providing spaces for voice and diversity are perceived as defying the power of the larger social and discursive structures, and having the potential to reconfigure power relations at the broader societal level.

However, we have to be careful not to exaggerate this micro-level orientation to resistance and change. Social structures cannot be constructed or reconfigured from the ground up. They have a solidity and materiality all their own. They always have the power to appropriate the changes wrought in local contexts for their dominant interests. In fact, the motivations of students, parents, and their communities are affected by the power structures. The agentive work we do in classrooms may not be welcomed when minority communities perceive that the institutions outside may actually penalize them for such writing and language practices. Moreover, it is important to understand the experiences and attitudes of students as they grow and live in the context of inequality and discrimination if we are to develop more effective ways of addressing their concerns, voices, and language resources in classrooms.

Nichole Stanford's *Good God but You Smart!* rectifies this imbalance of orientation in rhetoric, composition, and language studies. She rightly shifts the attention of teachers and policy makers to life outside the classroom. We are allowed to visit the homes, neighborhoods, workplaces, and villages our minority students come from. Her book provides a complex but embodied and passionate insight into the mechanism of language politics in the United States. It brings out the effects of language discrimination and oppression on students and communities. It helps us understand the unfair world our students come from in order to address their needs and concerns better.

As the history and experiences of each community are different, Stanford opens a window into the language biases relating to her own community. In addressing the challenges relating to Cajun English, Stanford performs an important service to the academic community. We don't know enough about the concerns of this community and its variety of English. While some other ethnic Englishes and postcolonial varieties have received a lot of attention in US educational and writing circles recently, there is still limited awareness of Cajun English. It is important through this book to examine how the status and history of Cajun English are both similar to and different from those of other ethnic varieties.

It is also valuable that Stanford provides a personal rendition of this language politics by including her own life experiences in this book. In speaking for her own language community and engaging with dominant scholarship from her personal experiences, she joins many other eminent scholars in our field—from Richard Rodriguez to Gloria Anzaldúa, Keith Gilyard, Minzhan Lu, Morris Young, and Vershawn Young—who have provided us a window into their communities through their narratives. Thus the book powerfully personalizes the exploration of critical literacy and education. It touchingly reminds us why we need to understand the painful experiences of our students that stem from language inequality, empathize with the concerns and aspirations that arise from these experiences, and collaborate with students in constructing better alternatives in writing and in society.

This book—with its perceptive and complex analysis of the processes of language domination and prejudice in an unequal and unfriendly world—inspires me to recommit myself to working for changes in classrooms and writing alongside Stanford's efforts to reach those outside classrooms.

# GOOD GOD BUT YOU SMART!

# INTRODUCTION

*Our culture of literacy functions as though it were a plot against the spoken voice, the human body, vernacular language, and those without privilege. That is, our pervasive cultural assumptions about speech, writing, and literacy—especially as they are communicated through schooling—seem as though they were designed to make it harder than necessary for people to become comfortably and powerfully literate.*
—Peter Elbow, *Vernacular Eloquence*

*Writing theory must move beyond composition studies' neurosis of pedagogy, must escape the shackles of classrooms, students, and management.*
—Sidney Dobrin, *Postcomposition*

Growing up Cajun, one of my favorite compliments was being mistaken for non-Cajun. My upwardly mobile Cajun friends and I identified with mainstream white US culture, and we rarely lapsed into our Cajun accents, except to make fun. Our linguistic work was praised by family members. "Good God but you smart!" my grandfather once exclaimed after reading a lengthy paper I wrote. I lapped it up, but I knew a huge factor in his praise was that, to him, use of standardized English was a sign of intelligence, whereas even deft use of Cajun English (CE) or Louisiana French was a sign of illiteracy and backwardness. My grandfather, born to uneducated sharecroppers, did his best to hide the fact that his first language was Louisiana French because he worried that it would prevent him from climbing the ranks at his insurance job and providing for his family. That anxiety is so entrenched among Cajuns that many of us have resisted progressive policies designed to honor and preserve our home languages, Louisiana French and CE, even though these languages are virtual treasure troves for linguists. I certainly did throughout my schooling, and then in retrospect I wondered why. Why do we comply with language inequality? Why do we help enforce language prejudice by self-censoring and even by policing each other's speech? Why do we, like my grandfather did, buy into the idea that someone's way of speaking can determine his or her intelligence, employability, and even social worth?

As I answer these questions, I'm balancing between the reproduction model of sociopolitical inequality and the resistance model, between Robert Phillipson's assertion in *Linguistic Imperialism* (1992) that language inequality is unilaterally imposed on marginalized people (forced assimilation) and A. Suresh Canagarajah's reply in *Resisting Linguistic Imperialism in English Teaching* (1999) that marginalized people actually choose to appropriate and subvert the dominant language for their own purposes (a form of resistance). In this theoretical space, marginalized people do choose to comply with language prejudice—but not quite voluntarily. It's a clever choice made in the interests of getting a leg up, per Canagarajah, kind of like working the system. But the choices have been predetermined by the center, which designed the system to be quite unequal: conform linguistically or face failure in some form.

Phillipson theorizes the sociopolitical "might is right" dynamic that says nations have languages, while tribes have only dialects or vernaculars, building on the work of Tove Skutnabb-Kangas, who coined the term *linguicism* in *Linguistic Genocide in Education* to describe language discrimination. As she puts it, "Linguicism is a concept which describes more sophisticated forms of racism . . . I have defined linguicism as ideologies, structures, and practices which are used to legitimate, effectuate, and reproduce an unequal division of power and resources (material and immaterial) between groups which are defined on the basis of language" (Skutnabb-Kangas 1988, 40). She argues that English is a "killer language," choking out the "necessary diversity" of other languages, and that English language teaching (ELT) is fraught with ethical concerns because it poses a threat to local communities and languages: "If you are an ESL [English as a second language] teacher and/or you teach minority children through the medium of a dominant language, at the cost of their mother tongue, you are participating in linguistic genocide. You are killing the necessary diversity and the prerequisites for life on our planet" (25).

In response to the idea of linguistic biodiversity embraced by Skutnabb-Kangas and others, Salikoko Mufwene in *Language Evolution: Contact, Competition and Change* is more cautious about portraying all processes of language change and loss as negative, since these processes have been common to all linguistic history. He further points out that "the rhetoric has been less about the rights of speakers than about the *rights of languages* to survive [and] . . . about the benefits of *linguistic diversity* to linguistics (especially the extent to which the research on language universals and typology is negatively affected by the lost languages)" (Mufwene 2008, 226). Languages do change over time, and it's important not to conflate them with the people who use them, but language domination is inevitably linked to sociopolitical domination. Phillipson consequently argues that ELT is a tool of imperialism and, listing three types of colonial power—"sticks (impositional force), carrots (bargaining), and ideas (persuasion)"—he writes that ELT belongs in the third category, which he later expands as part of cultural hegemony (Phillipson 1992, 53, 72).

I take up this third category, but not from the perspective of someone in the center thrusting ideas upon unsuspecting periphery students, as ELT is generally understood. I'm more interested in the perspective from which Canagarajah writes—a periphery user of English making decisions about how to use the empire's language. Canagarajah maintains that Phillipson is limited by his "center" position, and he criticizes Phillipson for focusing on the reproductive function of ELT without representing "the subtle forms of resistance to English and the productive processes of appropriation inspired by local needs" (Canagarajah 1999, 3). He proposes instead a "resistance perspective" in which periphery communities neither conform unthinkingly to center values nor reject English but find ways to "*reconstitute* it in more inclusive, ethical, and democratic terms," something he argues that many of his fellow Sri Lankans and others from former colonies already do very well (2). He goes on to examine the ways periphery teachers and students negotiate intersections of the mainstream and the local in their daily classroom experiences. Vinay Dharwadker offers a helpful phrase for understanding this nuanced view of language politics when he calls for the "decolonization of English" in "The Historical Formation of Indian-English Literature" via intermixing Indian languages and English, instead of rejecting English (Dharwadker 2004, 262). This periphery perspective of English allows for language change, something Mufwene argues is a normal process, while still acknowledging the politics of language use and contesting inequalities in gatekeeping standards. Canagarajah also espouses this kind of language intermixing as a form of resistance to linguicism.

Ngũgĩ wa Thiong'o, another periphery writer, is famous for his decision to totally reject English because language domination is so inextricably connected to political domination. But another important difference in perspective is between those of the first generation, who were forced to speak English in school, and the following generations, who are often monolingual native English speakers. As is the case for many other marginalized and colonized groups, Cajuns initially had to be strongly persuaded to give up Louisiana French, and that persuasion came via ELT. The experiences of the first generation of Louisiana French speakers to learn English in school were similar to what Ngũgĩ describes in *Decolonising the Mind: The Politics of Language in African Literature* (Ngũgĩ 1981) as a physically and psychologically violent tension between his home Gikuyu culture and the British culture in school. In the same vein as Phillipson, Ngũgĩ writes that ELT is a weapon of imperialism, a "cultural bomb": "The effect of a cultural bomb is to annihilate a people's belief in their names, in their languages, in their environment, in their heritage of struggle, in their unity, in their capacities and ultimately in themselves" (3). Ngũgĩ sees no way of redeeming English from its imperialist past and has since made the decision to write only in his native Gikuyu, which he later translates for English readers, in contrast to writers like Chinua Achebe, who write in English but mark it with their home languages. But things are different three and four generations after the cultural bomb, when the local culture has been rebuilt around a French-inflected English, and most Cajuns no longer have the option to resist by speaking only Louisiana French.

I appreciate Canagarajah's spotlight on the agency of periphery speakers, not just their automatic consumption of the center's language and ideas. Models that blame only the center for inequalities, ignoring the agency of periphery speakers, tend also to propose solutions from only the center, and the end result is that people at the periphery are once again acted upon instead of acted with. But in my experience, Cajuns don't appropriate the dominant language and use it as a savvy form of resistance against the center. Unlike Canagarajah's experience in Sri Lanka, the bulk of the periphery speakers I know and grew up with decide to conform to the center as much as they are able, consciously censoring any influence of Louisiana French and CE from their public and especially school- and job-related speech performances. They seem to have the same mindset I grew up with, more along the lines of conforming than resisting. So, like Phillipson, I'm looking at the hegemonic reproduction of language inequality but, like Canagarajah, I do so from the perspective of periphery speakers, and I'm asking why many of us—who could resist—don't resist.

Overwhelmingly, my research has revealed that Cajuns believe they must appropriate standardized English for the sake of socioeconomic success and, in many cases, for mere financial stability. Linguistic assimilation is no longer forced—at least not in school—but resisting it doesn't seem to be a responsible option to most Cajuns. I was genuinely surprised to find in my survey that Cajuns usually learned to self-censor their Cajun linguistic markers from their mamas, not their schoolmarms. For these Cajuns, speaking standardized English is part of a good work ethic, like being on time for work or dressing appropriately. Because the motivation to self-censor is not pedagogical in the case of most Cajuns today, as well as many other internally colonized groups, the implications are that even the most progressive pedagogy will not help them resist linguistic assimilation. Sometimes the most ardent supporters of monolingual and monodialectal language policies are actually the people against whom the policies most discriminate.

Perhaps an important factor in Cajuns' linguistic compliance is their status as an internally colonized group within the United States. Though the United States is a "center" nation, many native-born Americans speak forms of what Canagarajah calls "periphery Englishes." As Victor Villanueva has argued in *Bootstraps: From an American Academic of Color*, the process of internal colonialism (an idea developed in Hechter 1975) has created multiple groups of minorities within the United States whose languages are subject to domination by English. He describes, for example, a cultural erasure among Puerto Ricans living in the United States. Referencing the work of John Ogbu, he explains "the essential differences between immigrants and minorities": "The immigrant enters; the minority is entered upon . . . The difference between the immigrant and the minority amounts to the difference between immigration and colonization" (Villanueva 1993, 24, 29).[1] Villanueva argues that English-only policies are a form of language discrimination for these internally colonized communities, leading to the academic lag of minority children (who internalize their failure) and linguistic insecurity among academics of color. This insecurity can in turn prompt academics of color, on the one hand, to espouse patriotism and monolingualism and, on the other hand, to resist progressive language policies and pedagogies even more ardently than their white peers. Other examples of internally colonized groups are Mexican Americans, Native Americans, Hawaiian Americans, African Americans and, of course, Louisiana Cajuns and Creoles.

Though language has been and continues to be an extremely important educational concern in South Louisiana, this is the first book-length study of those language issues in the field of composition and rhetoric (comp/rhet), which has a strong history of considering "students' rights to their own language" and the nonprivileged dialects of native English-speaking minorities. Geneva Smitherman (1986) gave a groundbreaking analysis of African American English in *Talkin and Testifyin: The Language of Black America*, and Victor Villanueva (1993) introduced the idea of Puerto Rican rhetoric in English in *Bootstraps: From an American*

*Academic of Color*. Malea Powell (2002) presented American Indian forms of written English in "Listening to Ghosts: An alternative (Non) argument," and Kathy Sohn (2006) brought Appalachian English to the attention of comp/rhet theorists in *Whistlin' and Crowin' Women of Appalachia: Literacy Practices since College*. Other theorists have written about the nonprivileged Englishes of native English speakers from former colonies. For example, A. Suresh Canagarajah (2006) introduces Sri Lankan English in "The Place of World Englishes in Composition: Pluralization Continued," Vaidehi Ramanathan (2005) discusses Indian Englishes in *The English-Vernacular Divide: Postcolonial Language Politics and Practice*, and Caroline Macafee (2004) writes about Scottish English in "Scots and Scottish English." LuMing Mao (2002) discusses the influence of Chinese discourse on English in "Re-clustering Traditional Academic Discourse: Alternating with Confucian Discourse," and Min-Zhan Lu (1994a) contrasts the rhetorical traditions of Maoist Chinese essays with western English essays in "From Silence to Words: Writing as Struggle." CE has been heavily documented in applied linguistics, and it merits a stronger presence in comp/rhet, a field that has long recognized the tensions between center and periphery discourses within the United States.

So in this book I investigate the hegemonic language exchanges that reproduce inequalities in US educational sorting practices, particularly the factors that lead to individual compliance with language inequality. I offer the history of the linguistic assimilation of the Cajuns of Southwest Louisiana as a case study, presenting new data from archival records, previously unpublished interviews, and my own survey of Louisiana teachers in four colleges. I weave history, sociolinguistics, politics, socioeconomic theories, Cajun studies, pedagogical and educational theory together with family memoir. I have an enormous family—six siblings, six more stepsiblings, and dozens of aunts, uncles, cousins, nieces, and nephews; this is a book stressing the role of family in institutionalized language inequality, so they show up a lot. The lens I use to discuss the role of individual consent is Pierre Bourdieu's (1991) theory of the legitimate language in *Language and Symbolic Power*, which he developed after studying the language dynamics in his own internally colonized group in France as well as other historical cases of language inequalities. Exploring his theory, I describe the language hierarchy that was established during US nation building, the sociohistorical background of Cajuns that predicted their low linguistic status even before their US assimilation, the English-only educational policies that all but eradicated Louisiana French, current educational practices that relegate the newly emergent Cajun English to the status of a slang, and the cultural myths that justify institutionalized language inequality. My depiction of Bourdieu's theory and terms is accurate but maybe a little tidier than in his original text; I systematized some of his discussions on language inequality into a framework upon which I drape my case study. His main argument is that language functions as a form of capital in a nationalist, capitalist economy; people's access to power tends to be determined by how much of the legitimate language they inherit from their parents. After examining the reproductive function of language hegemony among Cajuns in this framework, I conclude by discussing alternative forms of organization for normalizing counterhegemonic ideas about language equality, specifically in working-class family social structures.

Composition scholars have lobbied for policy changes in primary, secondary, and postsecondary schools—focusing mainly on educational changes to push back against linguicism. Smitherman has lobbied to institutionalize multilingualism in schools, most notably in *Talkin and Testifyin* (Smitherman 1986) and "Toward a National Public Policy on Language" (Smitherman 1987). She argues that standards are too narrow in US education when they deem only one version of English "correct," and she envisions a multilingualism that includes nonprivileged Englishes such as African American English (AAE) and other languages. Bruce Horner and John Trimbur, in "English Only and U.S. College Composition" (Horner and Trimbur 2002), build on Smitherman's vision by imagining ways to institutionalize multilingualism rather than monolingualism (for instance, making use of more diverse research to lobby for changing university policies). They argue that, just as English only has been institutionalized in schools over time with the reorganization of college departments (that territorialize other languages as "foreign") and other factors, multilingualism can be reinstitutionalized.

These proposals are geared toward creating policies to implement Students' Right to Their Own Language (SRTOL), a 1974 position statement about students' rights by the Conference on College Composition and Communication (CCCC), an annual meeting created to discuss composition pedagogies:

> We affirm the students' right to their own patterns and varieties of language—the dialects of their nurture or whatever dialects in which they find their own identity and style. Language scholars long ago denied that the myth of a standard American dialect has any validity. The claim that any one dialect is unacceptable amounts to an attempt of one social group to exert its dominance over another. Such a claim leads to false advice for speakers and writers, and immoral advice for humans. A nation proud

of its diverse heritage and its cultural and racial variety will preserve its heritage of dialects. We affirm strongly that teachers must have the experiences and training that will enable them to respect diversity and uphold the right of students to their own language. (Smitherman 1995, 21)

Since the resolution's acceptance, some of its tenets have come under criticism. The editors of *ALTDis* point out, for example, that SRTOL encourages ethnic inequality and the assimilation of less privileged groups: "'The Students' Right to Their Own Language,' whatever revolutionary sentiments may have animated its framers, turned out to espouse methods to make assimilation to the dominant culture easier, at least in theory, for students from politically marginalized social groups" (Schroeder, Fox, and Bizzell 2002, vii). Canagarajah (2011) further points out that some of its ideology is based on nationalism and unnatural language processes (which I explain in chapter 4). SRTOL has also lacked institutional support since its acceptance, revealing the economic interests of the field in preserving the linguistic status quo.

In spite of its lack of institutional support and ideological problems, SRTOL has spurred more pedagogical responses. Min-Zhan Lu writes in "Professing Multiculturalism: The Politics of Style in the Contact Zone" about "how to conceive and practice teaching methods which invite a multicultural approach to style, particularly those styles of student writing which appear to be riddled with 'errors'" (Lu 1994b, 442). As Lu writes in "From Silence to Words: Writing as Struggle" (Lu 1994a), her perspective on multiple discourses is informed by her own background, having been raised with a tension between the home language and literacy practices of her family and the nationalist policies and pedagogies she encountered at school. At home, Lu's Chinese family favored a Western humanist discursive upbringing, featuring the power of the individual and economic success, while her teachers at school stressed the values of Maoist China, featuring the strength of the collective and the virtue of common labor. She long kept these discursive voices separate according to context but later decided to merge them. Lu concludes by encouraging educators to let students "see themselves as responsible for forming or transforming, as well as preserving the discourses they are learning" (175). Expanding on this idea of multicultural style later in "Professing Multiculturalism," Lu asks why students are not permitted the same stylistic deviations as "real" writers, and she poses the student construction *can able to* as a discussion piece in the contact zone of the classroom, urging her students to feel confident in making stylistic decisions in their own work and in assessing the decisions of others (Lu 1994b, 446).

Canagarajah has similarly worked on creating practical pedagogical strategies that accommodate both multilingualism and college language standards. Building on his earlier work in *Resisting Linguistic Imperialism* (Canagarajah 1999), Canagarajah writes in "The Place of World Englishes in Composition: Pluralization Continued" (Canagarajah 2006, 613) that teachers can support multilingualism by teaching what Vershawn Young (2004) calls *code meshing*, the practice of interweaving linguistic contributions from home discourses and the conventions of academic discourses in writing done for school. In Canagarajah's conception of code meshing, multilingual students write neither entirely in their home languages and vernaculars nor entirely in standardized English. Rather, he proposes appropriating "the high-brow activity [of] inserting Greek or Latin without translation into English texts" and practicing it with untranslated bits of nonprivileged languages and Englishes (Canagarajah 2006, 598) or merging rhetorical styles of home and academic discourses. He stresses that he encourages code meshing even for final products, in contrast to Peter Elbow's allowance for multilingualism in rough drafts only, because, as he writes, "The editing of the other Englishes in the final product may also lump these varieties into the category of 'errors' to be avoided" (598). He proposes teaching code meshing to students as a substantial form of resistance to unequal language policies and also as a way to begin implementing equal policies: "The classroom is already a policy site; every time teachers insist on a uniform variety of language or discourse, we are helping reproduce monolingualist ideologies and linguistic hierarchies" (587). Canagarajah's proposals on the use of code meshing are an important development for creating usable pedagogies that address the very real pressures of language inequality while allowing for and even teaching student resistance.

A more recent collection of essays, *Code Meshing as World English: Policies, Pedagogy, and Performance* (Young and Martinez 2011), builds on the idea of code meshing in the directions of pedagogy and policy. The volume, which includes chapters on Hawaiian Pidgin, CE, AAE, Appalachian English, and Spanglish, hosts important scholarly discussions of what are acknowledged to be language inequalities. In the introduction, the editors (with Julie Ann Naviaux) write, "We wonder why, in the forty-odd years since NCTE adopted the *Students' Right to Their Own Language* resolution, something like code-meshing has not been instituted, remains a wish, and is still not a fact of practice" (xxii). They conclude with a "charge" to teachers of English to consider implementing code meshing. In his afterword, Canagarajah proposes that code meshing is valuable not only for its political function but also because it is a more normal state for languages than discreteness: code meshing "is the basic process by which language appropriation and localization has always taken place in English and other lingua franca" (276). Canagarajah writes that code meshing is not only a form of world English but a process of world Englishes.

These examples of attention to the Englishes of minority, immigrant, and working-class students in the United States illustrate the concern for language equality in the field of comp/rhet. Like most of the discourse surrounding language inequalities in comp/rhet, these authors' arguments generally focus on changing pedagogies and policies. This focus makes sense because the heart of the field is pedagogy. But there has been less discussion in an area I'm particularly interested in, the hegemonic values in the United States that push back against these progressive policies and pedagogies. In Canagarajah's (2011) afterword to *Code Meshing as World English*, he concludes that, in order to transform pedagogies and policies, there must also be challenges to hegemonic values about language, particularly the ideas of language purity and change. Along those lines, my hope is that *Good God but You Smart!* contributes to the work already done in comp/rhet by addressing the hegemonic values about language that reproduce inequalities *outside* of classrooms.

Peter Elbow also argues for the importance of publicly challenging inaccurate ideas about language correctness in his nonacademic volume *Vernacular Eloquence: What Speech Can Bring to Writing* (Elbow 2012). Elbow's main argument is that writing will benefit from the directness and clarity of speech. Writing tends to get convoluted—specifically because there is an unspoken rule that the less likely we are to utter something, the more academic and proper it is (and this is because of class distinctions, as he points out)—whereas speech helps us get to the point more clearly. Like other writers in comp/rhet, he concludes with pedagogical suggestions—the same pedagogical stance, in fact, that Canagarajah previously criticizes him for in "The Place of World Englishes in Composition" (Canagarajah 2006). Elbow recommends having students edit multilingual or multicultural influence from their final products (unless it is "hidden" meshing, something I explain in chapter 4) until language standards have changed to allow vernaculars in formal writing.

Elbow also makes a conscious effort to influence hegemonic beliefs about language inequality so that we can begin to move in the direction of accepting vernaculars in formal writing. He writes, "My main goal is to change how everyone *thinks* about writing and literacy" (Elbow 2012, 8). He works toward this goal by making it a point to include nonacademics in the conversation about language standards and change their minds about "correctness" by writing to a public audience. He explains the classed and raced origins of language inequalities; literacy standards that function more as gatekeepers than social mobilizers; and the hegemonic values that uphold these standards, through the lenses of pedagogy, theory, history, politics, and public opinion. As he addresses beliefs, he also encourages every English speaker, novice and expert, to take ownership of the English language and help it evolve to more closely reflect spoken Englishes by "speaking onto the page" (though not in gatekeeping moments like final exams). In the end, he hopes that writing will not only benefit from speaking, but that the gap between improper speech and proper writing will disappear as the laws of language divergence kick in, as people follow his guidelines and get more comfortable with the idea of democratic language (and in the process actually democratize language), and as the Internet increases our comfort with "talkiness" and decreases our need for formality. Parts of Elbow's model are problematic, as I discuss later, but it's a significant move in comp/rhet scholarship in that it addresses the hegemonic values that reinforce discriminatory pedagogies and policies concerning language.

### THE LIMITS OF PEDAGOGY

Like Elbow and Canagarajah, I think it's important to change societal definitions of correctness and proper language behavior. Throughout my research, I have found many discussions of classroom-based solutions for addressing language prejudice, but very little attention to the language prejudice in families and home communities that can foil the best progressive attempts at language equality in classrooms. A major reason that policies and pedagogies haven't been entirely effective in creating language equality is that it's not only teachers and administrators reinforcing these unequal standards, but also just about everyone else. There is a network of forces *outside* schools that pressure individuals into complying with unequal language standards. These forces are connected to what happens in school, but they can operate apart from school as well, so that people who don't go to school or who have finished their schooling are constantly reminded and compelled to abide by the language hierarchy and even enforce it on others.

Working-class families often resist "liberal" educational policies designed to create an equal playing field for their children in the classroom, striving instead to gain the same educo-linguistic capital as people from the middle and upper-middle classes (what Bourdieu 1984 calls usage of "high distinction," already controlled by the affluent as a class-based privilege). The parents of the children and their communities, whom these educational policies are intended to benefit, are often the most vehement detractors. In *Your Average Nigga: Performing Race, Literacy, and Masculinity*, Vershawn Ashanti Young cites, for example, the work of Mary Rhodes Hoover on this contradiction among African American parents, who are resistant to allowing African American English in schools as a valid language choice (Young 2007, 2). Chatting together at a convention in 2011, Young and I discussed the incredible levels of resistance to—and sometimes ridiculing of—progressive language ideas that we've heard from our own families. Young and I veer slightly on how to teach code meshing, but we agree emphatically that people's learned beliefs about language standards are one of the greatest impediments in the struggle for language equality.

Some of the most famous texts in the comp/rhet canon illustrate the pressures that students feel to censor their home languages, pressures that circulate in classrooms but aren't pedagogical in nature. The coming-to-literacy narratives of Richard Rodriguez (1982), Mike Rose (1987), Keith Gilyard (1991), Victor Villanueva (1993), and Vershawn Young (2007) relate the academic biographies of minority scholars who must negotiate home and academic discourses. Generally, the authors narrate their experiences going through the US school system, beginning in a working-class family and ending with a "successful" writing or academic career. They debate the meaning of success in light of their lost or compromised connections with their home communities and personal identities. Along the way, the authors also describe the *nonacademic* pressures to censor their home discourses—pressures from important individuals and even their entire communities. These pressures are portrayed as leagues more important and motivating than pedagogical pressures.

Richard Rodriguez (1982), for instance, describes in *Hunger for Memory: The Education of Richard Rodriguez* a class tension that prompted both his well-known critique of language-based diversity policies and his linguistic disidentification with his own family. Unlike other writers who grew up bicultural, Rodriguez rejects Spanish and embraces English only. He concludes by criticizing affirmative action, ethnic studies departments, and the practice of allowing other languages and Englishes in schools. Changes to college policies are too little, too late. A true left reform, he writes, would be concerned with early education, housing, nutrition, and other social factors: "The revolutionary demand would have called for a reform of primary and secondary schools" (162). It was his attention to class differences that also led Rodriguez to distance himself from his family and their language. As a child, he hoped to identify with middle- and upper-class people who spoke English instead of what he calls "los pobres" (the poor) who spoke Spanish. The same desire prompted him, as a "scholarship boy," to seek the praise and attention of his teachers instead of his parents early on in elementary school. He stayed after school to "help" and devoted pretty much all his free time at home to reading the books recommended by his teachers. Familial intimacy gave way to alienation as he mastered English and his academic identity. One summer in college, after meeting and utterly failing to relate to a group of los pobres, he realized that he had achieved middle-class status. After that, he celebrates the fact that, unlike his parents at his age, he is part of the middle class: "I wear double-breasted Italian suits and custom-made English shoes . . . I register at the Hotel Carlyle in New York and the Plaza Athenée in Paris" (146–47). In the prologue to his book, which he calls "Middle-Class Pastoral," he concludes that he has arrived: "I write this book as a middle-class American man. Assimilated" (1). Rodriguez's drive to master the dominant literacy values of the United States and distance himself from his family was fueled by class pressures woven into the economy and pushed on him by teachers and parents alike.

In response to Rodriguez's narrative, Keith Gilyard also discusses the pressures he felt to self-censor his home discourse. He alternates chapters of narration with chapters of analysis, also alternating between AAE and standardized English as he explores the tension between his two identities and his two languages in *Voices of the Self* (1991). Unlike Rodriguez, who wanted to impress teachers, Gilyard was driven by a desire to impress his classmates and feel a sense of belonging to his community. He writes that he coveted the admiration and affirmation of his fellow students, letting himself be pushed into doing things he didn't even believe in, like brokering a "silly" peace treaty between the boys and girls of the class and almost getting kicked out of school when it ended with his hitting a white girl (47–51). As part of his desire to win his classmates' recognition, he writes that he also "scored highly on all [his] tests and raised [his] hands as vigorously as anyone else" (45). This desire to be accepted and admired by peers conversely led him into crime, drugs, and multiple legal encounters later when he moved to a poorer community, where grades weren't valued but street bravado was. He writes, "I was torn between institutions, between value systems. At times the tug of school was greater, therefore the 90.2 average. On other occasions the streets were a more powerful lure, thus the heroin and 40 in English and a brief visit to the Adolescent Remand Shelter" (160). Gilyard concludes by calling on educators "to successfully challenge current practices that justify eradicationist attempts aimed against African-American identity and the language variety in which that identity is most clearly realized" in schools (165). But in addition to eradicationist pedagogies, Gilyard felt intense class- and race-based pressures from his peers in the middle-class community to excel at standardized English. It was ultimately the approval of his peers, which he sought through academic success, that drove him to censor his language, not the pedagogy or feedback of his teachers. Gilyard and the students around him had absorbed cultural messages about language, possibly from their parents and other educational encounters.

Mike Rose similarly traces his journey from a working-class, Italian American neighborhood to a professorship at UCLA in *Lives on the Boundary: A Moving Account of the Struggles and Achievements of America's Educationally Underprepared* (Rose 1987). What pushed him from being a mediocre, "just wanna be average" student to working his tail off to excel in literacy was not pedagogical, policy-related, or even class-driven: he was trying to win the approval of his new father figure, Mr. McFarland, who initiated his students into the mysteries of the classics. His biological father had slipped into a coma during his junior year, never to wake again, and the inspiring English teacher "couldn't have come into [his] life at a better time" (32). Rose writes, "I must tell you that venal though it might have been, I loved getting good grades from McFarland" (34). Rose immediately began striving for the best grades and eventually decided to go to college upon his new father figure's urging. Examining his experiences as a minority student and educator later in the book, he asks other educators to reconceive the dynamics of language, failure, and poverty in their pedagogies by rethinking literacy crises, error, and the "canonical approach to education" (237). Striving to orient and assimilate working-class students like himself into the language protocols of the elite academy, he proposes close tutorial mentoring in academic usage and disciplinary canons for working-class students who are lost in a sea of academic expectations. He recommends this kind of mentorship because the father-son bond he felt with McFarland was so influential, whereas standard schooling had failed. It was a form of family pressure that compelled him to depart from the working-class lifestyle he had been prepared to inherit from his own parents and instead spend long hours outside school cultivating his grasp of literacy so he could go to college.

Another landmark coming-to-literacy story is *Bootstraps*, in which Villanueva (1993) narrates his struggle to belong to both his family's world and the academic world, beginning with his experiences in his working-class Puerto Rican neighborhood in Brooklyn and winding up with his position as tenure-track assistant professor at Northern Arizona University. He writes that his academic success was due to a natural facility with language but then compounded by his desire to be accepted racially and nationally in the United States: "I have never stopped trying to assimilate," he writes (xiv). In spite of his family's patriotism and his commitment to learning English, he was considered "foreign" at his new high school in East Compton and ultimately became, as he writes about himself, "the only portorican rhetorician he knows" (5, 13). He strove to speak standardized English as part of working out his national identity and later came to understand that cultural rhetorical differences are often viewed as illogical or inferior instead of simply different. Examining his own desire to assimilate and that of other internally colonized groups, Villanueva argues that national language identification is the reason members of minorities are often the most ardent defenders of English only and standardized English policies. Hegemonic beliefs that link nationalism and language compel people to excel in the nationally recognized language. He explores theories of changing the hegemony so that one need not be ethnically either/or but both/and, and he concludes by suggesting an exercise for teaching students to question hegemonic "common sense" in fairy tales. These hegemonic beliefs that Villanueva discusses circulate both inside and outside classrooms—from homes to jobs to the military—leading both insiders and outsiders of the US economy to comply with stereotypes and language standards that reinforce prejudice.

Vershawn Young discusses the challenges faced by young black males who want to do well in school but still be perceived as sufficiently masculine in their home communities in *Your Average Nigga: Performing Race, Literacy, and Masculinity* (Young 2007). Like other comp/rhet writers who examine their literacy narratives, Young began life in a low social position and in a nonwhite family. Born to a single mother in a ghetto of Chicago called the Governor Henry Horner Homes housing projects, he struggled with choosing between performing black masculinity or white masculinity throughout his childhood. His interest in books and the literacy practices he learned at home, he writes, made him appear to be "acting white" to his peers. Though the behavior worked well for him in school, it constructed him as a "fag" in his home community, where he needed not only to "act black" but also continually to perform his masculinity "less as a faggot and more as a nigga" (54). This dilemma followed Young throughout life, and he usually settled on performing whiteness because it was easier: "I'm a dark-skinned black man who spent a good deal of his youth wishing he were white because he believed he was failing miserably at being black" (1). Looking back, he writes that he longed to be white not because he had internalized the oppressor and not because of self-hatred, but just because "race-switching" was so taxing. It seemed easier to perform whiteness most of the time and make brief gestures toward black masculinity only when he felt it necessary. "I was tired" is a refrain throughout the book. Three hours at his brother's house, for example, exhausted him so much that he pretended not to hear people calling him gay at a nightclub later that night (70–71). As an educator with a PhD, he writes that he is still confronted with the dilemma, but he wants to create pedagogical choices for students, choices that aren't so polarized. Young argues that the pedagogical practice of code switching amounts to the same thing as race switching: students must perform either whiteness or blackness, and are rarely given any other options. Instead, he proposes code meshing: students can represent themselves linguistically somewhere between black and white, something he argues is closer to reality anyway. Interestingly, neither pedagogies nor teachers seem to have influenced his academic performance and awareness of racial prejudice. As a seventh grader, he was so confident that he "marched straight to [his] class" to challenge a teacher and later a principal about the racial expectations and limitations they put on him (31). What drove him to embrace standardized English—to perform whiteness through language, as he puts it—was his older brother's dogged taunts that he was a "fag." He grew so tired of having to prove his black masculinity that he began to ignore his brother, treat him as invisible. Likewise, he began to live as if there were no dilemma, and he avoided having to prove his gender identity as much as possible by simply performing whiteness.

The perspectives and suggestions that these theorists bring to the field of comp/rhet have been critical for furthering discussions of US language inequalities and influencing pedagogy and policy decisions. But I'm focusing on these texts because they are actual stories of minority children who learned to censor their home discourses and appropriate standardized English so well that they earned the ultimate achievements in English composition—doctorates, tenured professorships at reputable institutions, publications that are amply cited, keynote status, and high gatekeeping positions in some cases. In these narratives, which might be the most famous success stories in the composition field, the reasons the authors excelled in school rarely had anything to do with classroom policies or pedagogies. They were motivated by the desires to get good jobs and provide for their families, to feel a sense of belonging with a community and peers, to win the approval of family members, and to earn political, gender, and racial legitimacy. There is no question in my mind that these are completely valid motivations. But they are all extrinsic to school, though they are tied to and enforced by schools, and they cannot be addressed by pedagogy or policy changes alone.

My own literacy experiences were similarly most heavily influenced by things happening outside the classroom. Like other Cajuns in my generation, I was born into the cultural assumption that I would pursue "good" English, a solid education, and various elements of the American dream. I was happy—proud—to be Cajun, but I worked as hard as anyone else in my class to learn to speak standardized English for school and professional settings. Code switching seemed to be part of being Cajun. I can recall feeling ashamed of my Cajunisms only when I was making an effort to code switch and didn't pull it off too well. Like Villanueva, Rose, Gilyard, Rodriguez, and Young, I was already exceptionally good with language, and I became an outlier after I devoted myself to learning to use English well. In my case, though, it wasn't in an effort to identify with a certain gender, nationality, socioeconomic class, or family figure. I clung to literacy a little more tightly than most of my Cajun classmates because it became an escape for me from abuse and a resulting social anxiety that I couldn't physically escape. I preface this by saying that I've made peace with everyone in this story, and I have a deep sympathy for the difficult things they were dealing with in their own lives that spilled over into mine. My family is very dear to me, so it's with great care that I share our stories. It's not my intent to sensationalize or expose anyone, but I feel compelled to be as transparent as Villanueva, Rose, Gilyard, Rodriguez, and Young have been about the struggles that pushed them to excel in language.

Raised by a single mother on welfare in one of the poorer areas in Louisiana, I turned to literacy as an alternative to running away from home. I was my mother's second teenage pregnancy, born a couple months before my father left. My mother's parents were financially stable and lived on the next block, but they believed their children would learn best from hard work, so they tough-loved my mom by trying not to help too much. They pushed her to go back to school for nursing and, meanwhile, they became a second set of parents for my brother Jade and me while our mother worked days and studied at night. It was a pretty good life; I was happy and outgoing. But I dreaded going to my father's house, where my stepmother taunted and tormented me. She had a special hatred for me—I guess because I looked like my mother, whom my father happened to admit he was still in love with about a week or so into his new marriage. My stepmother kicked my brother and me, with our tiny floral-print suitcases, out of the house on the first weekend we came over for our court-appointed visit. I was three and Jade was five. On another visit she tried to run us over in her little green car, a Datsun. Physical violence was normal. All five of us kids—my brother, me, and her three children—would pile on my stepsister's bed to cry and hold each other while our parents crashed and yelled in the next room. When I could make out the yelling, it was usually about Jade and me. My father explained that my stepmother was a little moody because of a hysterectomy due to uterine cancer, and he stayed with her because divorce is a sin. He tried to make it easier on Jade and me by telling us that his wife loved us very much but didn't know how to show it, and he made us promise not to tell my mother about anything that went on at his house because she would stop our visits. We were very good at keeping secrets. I didn't tell anyone about the time I came inside for a drink of water and found my stepmother pointing a rifle at my father. He was very still, like someone approaching a feral cat, softly asking her to put the gun down. I watched for a while, then went outside to play again. I didn't tell my other siblings.

Keeping secrets took a toll on me. I developed a stomach condition (spasms) in the third grade—"Stress," the doctor said—then boils on my legs, like Job from the Bible. When the boils appeared, my stepmother, a nurse, "applied a warm compress" to the back of my leg by laying plastic bags filled with boiling water directly on my skin. She had stretched me out on kitchen chairs and told my father to hold my hands and help me stay still while she burned me. Every time the bags cooled enough for me to stop shaking, she'd put them back into the microwave until they reached a rolling boil and reapply them. Again and again. I can't remember how many times; I just remember digging my fingernails into my father's hands and focusing on the microwave with its giant red sticker proclaiming, "JESUS HEALS CANCER." Since she was a nurse, I'm guessing she knew her ministrations would make my skin blister, ooze, and finally settle into shiny, mangled burn scars. But she said at the time that what she did was "necessary"—the same thing her youngest son, my half brother, would say a few years later as he pointed a pistol at my face, preparing to shoot me and then the rest of the family, shortly after my stepsister's boyfriend shot and killed his own parents, who had been our pastor and Sunday school teacher. While my legs healed, my stepmother wouldn't let me sit on any of the furniture in the house because I "might infect" her. I was allowed only to sit on the floor. I think she needed to humiliate me that way to make up for her own humiliations and losses in life. She seldom spoke directly to me, but often made announcements to the rest of the family that I—"Princess Di," as she called me—thought I was better than everybody else because I was sitting quietly or because I wore a dress to church or because my hair was thick. Once, as I stood washing dishes at the sink, which came to my chin at the time, my stepmother walked in and said, "You wash dishes like a nigger. Get out of my kitchen." My father explained that she was sick, so I loved her and told her so, but I think she hated me more for it.

Maybe I was an unwanted stepchild at my father's house, but I was still a pretty happy and balanced kid at my mom's house. I was very close to my grandparents and brother, and I was Mom's "cuddle bunny," lying in her lap every night after supper. But things changed when I was eight: my mom fell in love, married a nice man named Pat who yelled a lot (but insisted he wasn't yelling), moved us to his house in a new town but continued to commute to her old job and work overtime, and enrolled Jade and me in separate schools. In all the shuffling, I lost my deep connections with anyone who had made my life stable. Between my mom's new romance and her long commute, we rarely spoke anymore, and I only saw my grandparents on occasion. Jade and I grew apart, keeping to ourselves except to vent our frustrations on each other in loud, physical fights during the long hours we were home alone. I continued to keep my father's secrets, which leaked into the rest of my life as a pretty bad lying problem, so even when I tried to reach out to my mother—like about my stomach spasms—only the emotions came out, not the words. My mother became frustrated with me for having meltdowns for no apparent reason and would often walk away irritated, calling me "Miss Priss." She says in retrospect that she saw me drifting away, that she knew she was neglecting me when I needed her, and she kept promising herself she would make time for me soon. I remember watching her cuddle with my stepfather on the sofa every night after supper and wishing she would hold me. I began to feel like a stepchild in my own home.

Things worsened when my mom switched Jade and me to a new school, a private school that she was proud to be able to afford with a great deal of sacrifice. It was a college-prep school with a demanding classical curriculum and homework load, quite a contrast from my public school experience. Most of the students in my sixth-grade class had been together since pre-K, so, once again, I recognized the feeling of being a stepchild. One of the last things I remember confiding to my mother was that nobody at school liked me. "Why do you think that? Are they mean?" she asked. "No, they're all nice. I just *know* they don't like me," I said. My grades bottomed out, and I developed extreme social anxiety.

I dreaded having to see other kids; I panicked knowing I had to interact with them between classes, at recess, or waiting for the bus. What would we talk about? I exhibited classic signs of child abuse but, since nobody at the new school knew I had been happy and extroverted before, nobody could tell the difference. To them, I was just odd. I tried lying to my teachers about being sick in order to go home. After getting several sick calls about me, my mom started showing up with her stethoscope and interrogating me on my symptoms: "Loose stool? Fever and chills? No? You're not sick." Thinking I needed a little help making friends, she enrolled me in after-school activities. More panic and terror. I was a disappointment to every coach because I was too scared to do anything productive. I knew what kind of well-adjusted student I was supposed to be—I was surrounded by them—but I was terrible at faking it. I wanted to escape, to rest, to be somewhere alone, not required to lie and pretend anymore. I couldn't focus on anything going on in church or class or various sports matches because I was always fantasizing about running away—literally running out the door and maybe knocking a few people down in the process. I was nervous, and my nervous system was set for flight at all times. I became obsessed with exits and escape routes. I kept a suitcase packed in my closet with my favorite white jeans and looked for opportunities to run away from home. I thought a lot about dying.

And then my great escape presented itself. If I put a book between the world and me, the world left me alone. I didn't have to lie or pretend or watch people wince at my bad acting anymore. Reading was safe. All the words and story lines were spelled out there in black and white, third-person omniscient. I was still stuck in the same school and situation, but I finally had an escape. It was like I just disappeared. Not only did people leave me alone, but I went somewhere else in my head. If it's true that the mind can't tell the difference between books and reality, I had a pretty stable childhood from then on (except for *Alice in Wonderland*, a terrifying story about angry and violent adults, unclear rules and expectations, and a young girl who is barely staying alive). I already liked reading, and it soon became one of the only things I did. I read almost every series known to children (and completed many), everything I could afford from the Scholastic book order sheet, every book in my library that looked interesting, every bulletin board in the classroom, the backs of shampoo bottles—anything to keep from being wherever I was at the moment. Other "book nerds," as they called themselves, gravitated toward me, and after a while I let them sit with me during those stressful unstructured play times. Somehow, they were fine with how cold and awkward I was.

It's worth noting that in all my reading, nobody was Cajun. The canon of preteen literature and classics available to me was based on an already structured hierarchy of languages that I recognized from the cultural code-switching practices I had been born into. And my new school, a Christian private school, embraced a strictly classical curriculum based on the greatest hits of past empires. Run by reformed Presbyterians with libertarian leanings and severe cases of anglophilia, my school was like something out of *Dead Poets Society*. We studied Latin, memorized entire psalms from the Bible, and read Augustine's *Confessions* and other "great books." Imagine a bunch of Cajun kids practicing Shakespearean recitations. That was us. Meanwhile, we learned the glories of capitalism, the US flag code, and all the verses of "The Star-Spangled Banner." We had to copy the Bill of Rights for detention. We were told at least once a week how depraved and despicable and about six other adjectives starting with *d* we were without God by this one Lutheran teacher who was kind and jolly but tended to spit a lot. My history was rewritten. I still feel as much kinship with John Calvin as with my great-great-grandpa Omar Vizinat (who was, incidentally, the only man my Paw-Paw Jeff was ever afraid of). My school's administration specifically recruited teachers from the North, maybe because there weren't enough Calvinists in the South, so we learned their northern accents. All these things combined, and people in my hometown began mistaking me for not Cajun. I was still proud to be Cajun, especially when the northern teachers joked about our Cajunisms. But I was also honored years later when my coworkers at McDonald's said they thought I was from the North. In all this, I never felt any dissonance. I was doing what Cajuns in my generation most wanted, learning to code switch very well. Family members, especially my grandparents, who remembered the terrible stigma of being Cajun during early assimilation, were very proud of how American I sounded.

After a couple years hiding behind books, things got easier. I began imitating other girls in my class, and I grew more confident in my social performances. When I got to high school and met the senior boys (who were notoriously interested in freshman girls), I didn't even need to talk, just giggle. And once again I had Jade by my side, since the entire high school—just shy of seventy-five students—lunched together. Our group of friends formed around our rigorous involvement in a coed Boy Scouts troop, our appreciation for Monty Python, and a fair amount of teen angst. Those were good years. But my group graduated a year ahead of me and I found myself alone and nervous again, ready to dart, my senior year. I still didn't tell my mother what went on at my father's house, not even about the pistol incident. Two days into my senior year, my younger half brother ambushed me with a gun, weeping and telling me he loved me but had to kill me. He would kill the rest of the family when they came home. We had always had a deep connection, so I didn't know why he wanted to kill me. I was confused and sad. There were murmurs later implicating violent video games and a change in his attention disorder medication. I remember staring at the pistol, inches from my face, and deciding not to repent for making out with the hot guy at the party the night before. I was sorry, but it seemed more respectful to both God and myself to own my actions than to weasel out with a deathbed confession. I was ready to die.

My dear brother never pulled the trigger—I snatched the gun from him at one point when his eyes were forced shut with a strong sob—but the incident triggered something in me, like the pistol shot that sets free all the runners from their marks. I had faced death with not a drop of fear. I shook and shook afterward, watching our other brother wrestle him down like a calf in one of his rodeos and hold him till our parents returned. But I hadn't been afraid to die; I had bigger balls than anyone I knew. I could do anything I wanted. And what I wanted most was to escape my family, my school, Cajuns, Christians, Louisianans, Americans, almost any group of people I found myself in. So I did. I reverted to being cold to everyone I didn't give a damn for anyway, and now I really did escape school, skipping much of my senior year and secretly doctoring the attendance records so that I could pass. I began using literacy as my escape in a new way. With all that reading and maybe an eye for detail I already had, I had become pretty good at reading, writing, punctuation, grammar, spelling—all things literate. I landed in gifted programs, tested at college levels, rocked the ACT with a 33 in English, and graduated at the top of my senior English class (though my teacher threatened to fail me because I had missed so many classes). In college, I chose English as my major because I knew I could travel with it.

Like the authors of other literacy narratives in comp/rhet, I'd need an entire book to give a proper analysis of my childhood, but I want to focus on the fact that virtually none of my pivotal language decisions happened in or as a result of a classroom. My story may be more extreme than most other Cajuns' language experiences, but I think it serves to illustrate more starkly the way other pressures are involved in most people's decisions to assume the hegemonic perspective on language inequality. In terms of the rags-to-riches narrative, I am now a "successful" academic in English, having gone from welfare to a PhD, and it took a lot more than pedagogy in my language classes to cause me to disidentify with my home community enough to (again, scare quotes) "succeed." For me, the factors were abuse and isolation, a debilitating social anxiety, a near-death experience, a natural propensity for language arts, an exceptionally rigorous college-prep school, an already existing widespread cultural decision to reject Cajun languages, and the pride and support of my family in my code switching. My family was key in my literacy decisions; I code switched because they urged me to learn standardized English, along with other important aspects of employability, and I excelled at it because I wanted to be financially independent of them.

The literacy narratives of Rose, Gilyard, Villanueva, Rodriguez, and Young are also tied strongly to family and other circumstances, more so than pedagogy in many cases. But changing family dynamics alone can't undo linguicism; likewise, the entire burden of change doesn't belong to schools. To that end, I use the next few chapters to look at the network of pressures involved in language inequalities to understand why upwardly mobile Cajuns self-censor cultural linguistic markers and why many of us like people in other minority groups, balk at progressive language policies. Canagarajah touches on this complexity when he argues that periphery language speakers often assimilate the dominant language as a tool for their own benefit (not just because they're brainwashed), but I want to look at why periphery language speakers also assimilate dominant language attitudes. Though I am drawn to classroom practices—something I'm trained in and very much enjoy—I strive in this book to balance educational considerations with socioeconomic and family pressures in order to more fully understand linguicism and the complicated reasons we comply.

**WHAT'S IN THIS BOOK**

In chapter 1, "Sexy Ass Cajuns: The Complicated Reasons We Comply," I explain the stereotypes surrounding Cajuns and, consequently, Cajun ways of speaking, especially in pop culture contexts like movies and TV shows. Pop culture representations, which are pretty accurate reflections of hegemonic values, consistently depict Cajuns as buffoons, murderers, mystics, and sex objects—all standard postcolonial roles. I introduce the two most common Cajun languages, Louisiana French and CE, and I discuss language attitudes inside and outside South Louisiana that bring down the "market value" of CE and increase the value of standardized English. As in the case of other internally colonized groups, the ethnic label *Cajun* helps sell foods and promote tourism, but it works against folks who want the American dream. This chapter also introduces my methodology (a case study) and my framework (Pierre

Bourdieu's theory of the legitimate language in *Language and Symbolic Power* [1991]).

Chapter 2, "Bas Class: Cajuns and the US Class System," details the origins of stereotypes about Cajuns and the illegitimate status of their languages by describing how the legitimate language was selected during codification and why Cajuns were destined to speak something illegitimate before Louisiana was even ratified as a US state. Because class position is so important in determining the status of languages, I explain the history and position of Cajuns in the US socioeconomy—from their ethnic cleansing in present-day Nova Scotia to the way that the label *Cajun* has been used in Louisiana as an insult. I discuss the differences between Acadians, Cajuns, and Creoles as well as past and present racial ambiguities. Today, Cajuns have mostly assimilated to capitalism, with some lingering precapitalist, clan-based traditions that are, like their persisting Cajun linguistic markers, considered "quaint" but not "American" by surrounding communities. I also report current understandings of how a standardized English was selected during US nation building and its connections to the capitalist economic system that was established. As a result of early socioeconomic and language planning, the lines between class, race/ethnicity, nationalism, and mastery of the legitimate language tend to be blurred in US education.

I turn to reports from Cajuns who endured the 1921 French ban in chapter 3, "'I will not speak French. I will not speak French': The Grand Dérangement de la Langue," to illustrate the level of influence that schools have on language decisions. After the legitimate language is codified, which I described in the previous chapter, it must be normalized by state institutions (the most important being the educational system) so that individuals learn to self-censor. In that vein, I describe the shaming and punishments from the 1920s to the 1960s of Cajun children who were forced to quit speaking French and normalize to standardized English. As children, they were physically and psychologically punished until they learned English, and then many pretended not to know Louisiana French as adults. The sometimes shocking reports from these previously unpublished interviews and letters reveal the normalizing power of schools, but they also demonstrate how self-censoring became a required practice in Cajun families, an institution that is equally powerful in normalizing the legitimate language.

In chapter 4, "Don't Blame Teachers (Not Too-Too Much): Code Censoring in Classrooms," I caution that any pedagogies and policies, no matter how progressive, that help prepare students for job markets will reinforce US linguicism. Since schools exist to integrate youth into the US economy, pedagogies—or *sociopedagogies*—generally follow the economy, so there is a contradiction between promoting language equality and equipping students for gatekeeping moments in an economy that is structured on race, class, and gender inequality. Economic shifts have prompted national reorganization and, consequently, changes in sociopedagogy that correspond to new worker-training needs. The first part of the chapter paints a picture of the landscape that prompted a shift from eradication to bidialectism. I report, based on survey responses, the pedagogical decisions of college English teachers in Southwest Louisiana, the Cajun and Creole regions of the state. All the teachers write that they mourn the loss of Louisiana French and reject the eradication practices I describe in chapter 3, yet almost all of them report that when it comes to CE they teach code switching, a practice that many scholars have argued is equivalent to eradication. Next, I address "translingual pedagogies," which have emerged recently as an answer to SRTOL and a shift to transnationalism. While I strongly support these translanguaging pedagogies, I caution that, in light of the current economic shift to global capitalism, they can be used sociopedagogically in the same ways that code switching has been used—to integrate students unthinkingly into their current sociopolitical layout—and I stress the importance of layering them with critical pedagogy.

I conclude by reporting in chapter 5, "Beyond Classrooms: Debunking the Language Myths," some optimistic stories of Cajuns who came to value Cajun languages. Based on their experiences and the writings of resistance theorists like Paulo Freire, I consider ways to introduce counterhegemonic ideas to people who are beyond the reach of classrooms. Pervasive myths underlie the values and practices of the "language markets," which in turn determine the economic potential of all language users. I propose that, in addition to pedagogy and policy, the collection of language myths is an important site for addressing language inequalities because these myths help define the language markets and ultimately the job markets toward which education is geared. Because schools exist to integrate students into these language markets, it's difficult to work solely within schools to debunk the language myths circulating in US cultural hegemony. I suggest that it's possible to network within the family social structures of minority and working-class groups, especially when our increasingly polarized economy is forcing many families to depend on each other even more. Finally, I ask anyone who was interested enough to pick up this book to quit consenting to language inequality in small, daily ways. After all, hegemony is based on mass consent, so mass dissent can change it.

This is a timely study in several ways—first, because we're at a pedagogical juncture in comp/rhet. *Good God but You Smart!* bridges and anticipates a transition regarding vernaculars from code switching to translanguaging. Because of that transition and because the debates about vernaculars are often circumscribed by the ways people outside comp/rhet (for instance, composition teachers with no composition training) talk about it, I present a complete body of literature and analysis about both code switching and the newer translanguaging pedagogies. This is also a timely study because of what's happening in Louisiana and the Cajun community right now. Governor Bobby Jindal cut education budgets by more than 50 percent and took extreme measures to undermine faculty governance and tenure. Former US assistant secretary of education Diane Ravitch (2013) writes that Jindal, backed by major out-of-state corporate leaders, was intentionally defunding public education in order to privatize it, and she warns that Louisiana is intended to be a test case for other states seeking to dismantle public services. On a different note, this study is also timely because the first Cajun generation of English speakers is aging and disappearing, so it's becoming more and more difficult to gather firsthand accounts of events that are not thoroughly documented.

This book is geared toward two audiences: scholars in comp/rhet and local Louisianans who are interested in learning more about language issues in Southern Louisiana. Because I think this is an important public and political issue, and because I think that internally marginalized groups have traditionally been excluded from decisions made about them, I've made it a point to create a conversational bridge between Cajuns (with about a high school education) and experts in the field of comp/rhet in several ways. I've avoided jargon as much as possible and I was a little more explanatory than I may have needed to be if writing for only an academic audience. Also, because a primary Cajun teaching strategy is telling stories, I've designed the anecdotes in my chapter introductions and conclusions to embody the important points from my more opaque theoretical sections, so that Cajun nonacademics can skim the theoretical sections but still understand my arguments. Finally, I include local Louisiana voices in my discussions, not just the "experts." Academic conversations often exclude nonexperts, and the result is the creation of policies and pedagogies that ignore their needs and preferences. This dynamic is similar to past forms of ideological domination in which the dominant make decisions for the subordinated, based on the idea that the subordinated are incapable of ruling themselves. So I strive to make Cajuns heard by the people making policy decisions, and I strive to help Cajuns understand the arguments of policy makers. I quote the experts in my discussions, and I quote Cajuns right alongside them.

A few caveats. I'm cautious about codifying CE because once language is standardized, there can be a right and wrong way to use it, whereas CE (like other dialects) varies by region, audience, and context—in accents, phrases, register, even vocabulary. That's normal behavior for a language. Similarly, I'm cautious because it's difficult for languages to remain fluid and living once they've been codified. There's museum culture, and then there's living culture. But that puts me in a mess because I need to be able to explain it and give examples for the sake of this book. So I'm "defining" it from the research of sociolinguists, but not all other Cajuns will be able to relate to everything, and that's fine. In fact, in my research of CE literature, I found that some of what has been documented as CE in general was actually specific to only certain regions of Louisiana (not mine), but that's an inevitable problem with trying to codify a living language. There's no way to represent all parishes (Louisiana is organized by parishes instead of counties), neighborhoods, and families here. Not all Cajuns will relate to my personal Cajun experience either. I grew up in Opelousas, where it's common to pronounce *striped* and *checked* with two syllables, like *blessed*, but that's probably more southern than Cajun. Opelousas, one of the larger rural Cajun towns, is also 80 percent African American. In my language studies, I've sometimes had a hard time discerning AAE from CE because of the language mixing in my town. That's also normal behavior for a language. And I want to emphasize that CE will continue to evolve and possibly transition into something very different, as all languages do. I'm not fighting to preserve it, just fighting for the rights of the people who currently speak it, as well as anyone else who speaks a nonstandard English.

Another reason I'm not interested in codifying and/or standardizing CE is that standards can be used to measure people's Cajunness—whether or not someone is truly Cajun. Young has explored the problem of conflating ethnicity and language; he writes that he isn't "ghetto enough for the ghetto," but he's also not "white enough for white folks," leaving him in some "liminal" space he has to figure out (Young 2007, xvi). Villanueva has also spoken about not being able to totally fit into his worlds. The conflation of language and cultural identity is becoming prevalent in Louisiana; one strand of Cajun activists argues that one is not really Cajun if one doesn't speak Louisiana French. Me, I don't speak the Louisiana French—*je comprends just un p'tit peu*—but I'm still Cajun. What makes a Cajun and what constitutes Cajun talk are things that are ever evolving due to context and experiences. I think it's all right to be Cajun and speak a little Spanish or AAE in there too—or even a little Academese—just like it's fine to be Cajun and cook Lebanese food. After all, this linguistic and cultural integration is what produced Cajuns in the first place, as I'll explain in chapter 2. There is no such thing as "pure Cajun." Our culture and language have been mixing for centuries. Might as well keep going with it, eh?

I also don't want to love on CE too-too much because languages are usually defined for the sake of nationalism. I'm critical of the United States' (and other empires') use of nationalism to persuade the poor within the nation's borders to work and die for the rich's causes and wars, and, while I understand that smaller groups and ethnicities want to protect their languages and cultures, I disagree with trying to compete with the bully by imitating the bully.[2] There has been a movement among members of the Acadian diaspora to create an Acadian nation, so there have been multiple attempts to codify Acadian and Cajun French in service to this movement. I support the efforts of minorities and disempowered folks to preserve their language and culture in the face of forced assimilation (though I'm cautious of the word *preserve* because of my concerns expressed above about what happens when culture is put in a museum), but not for the sake of another nationalism and not at the expense of keeping languages and cultures from continuing to evolve in contact with other languages and cultures. That said, though, I do support native language movements that push against colonial and nationalist impositions of legitimate languages, such as the efforts of the Council for the Development of French in Louisiana (CODOFIL) to keep French public in Louisiana.

My one regret is that space and time permitted me to answer only one of the questions I began with: Why do we comply with language inequality? I've concluded that Cajuns' compliance is largely due to socioeconomic pressures that filter down into our families, but I've only just begun to think toward my other questions: How do we resist? How do we change the hegemonic language myths that our families believe and push on us? And, maybe more pressing, how do we change the socioeconomic circumstances that require us to sort ourselves and each other by language into distinct social classes? I hope *Good God but You Smart!* creates productive conversations in academic and Cajun contexts that invite people to think with me toward solutions.

# 1
## SEXY ASS CAJUNS
*The Complicated Reasons We Comply*

*I have done accents before, and we did study American accents in drama school. But I had to hold back a little bit on the Cajun accent so people can understand me. It doesn't sound American at all.*
—Tom Payne, English actor portraying a
Cajun character in HBO's *Luck*

*[T]he language of authority never governs without the collaboration of those it governs, without the help of the social mechanisms capable of producing this complicity.*
—Pierre Bourdieu, *Language and Symbolic Power*

*No one can make you feel inferior without your consent.*
—Eleanor Roosevelt (attributed)

Even when it came out that he was the killer, I found blog posts and comments all over the Web saying that René the Cajun was the hottest, sexiest thing ever to hit HBO. These were conversations about the TV show *True Blood* (premiering in 2008), a series several of my New York friends insisted that I needed to watch. There was a character on there, one friend told me over drinks at a pub near our grad school, who sounded just like me. This was the same friend who told me I should meet Frank, who is now my husband, so I took her advice and rented season 1. True, René had the best fake Cajun accent I've ever heard on TV (the actor had hired his own dialect coach, a Cajun), but what surprised me was the sexualization and exoticization of Cajuns and Cajun Louisiana. *True Blood* is set in non-Cajun North Louisiana but consistently borrows images from South Louisiana to create an exotic setting—the moss and swamps, for example, alligators, and Cajun-style homes. There is also a fair share of displaced French names like Bons Temps (the town) and Lafayette (one of the characters), which may come from either the Cajun area or New Orleans (from whose legends vampires are also borrowed) but definitely not from North Louisiana. Meanwhile, even though it turns out René was only faking his Cajun accent (he was really a southern boy named Marshall, posing as a Cajun), you can hear a clip of his speech on YouTube; it's called "Rene's sexy ass cajun accent."

Cajuns are used to being portrayed as dimwitted and drunk, as in Adam Sandler's 1998 *Waterboy*, and even crazy and murderous, as in *Southern Comfort* (1981) and *Green Mile* (1999) (see Bernard 2003). So when we heard that Disney was going to feature a Cajun character in *The Princess and the Frog* (2009), we were braced for the same old same old. Ray the Cajun firefly did not disappoint. Granted, he's probably the most lovable character in the whole movie, and it certainly was a moving moment when he—spoiler alert—died, but he was also the most illiterate, stupid, toothless, and backward character in the movie. Disney made it seem endearing that Ray was hopelessly in love with a star, which he took to be a fellow firefly with not much to say. Discussions of the movie have mostly centered on stereotypes of African Americans (deservedly, since Tiana is the first African American Disney princess), but it was disconcerting to see Ray and his family characterized as "low class" with telltale signs like obesity, laziness, bad or no teeth, an unusually large family, and clap-on lights (okay, the clap-on lights were kind of funny). And, of the dozen or so accents in the movie, the Cajun accent alone is discussed onscreen, when another character, Prince Naveen (whose own "Maldonian" accent is a Disney invention), calls Ray's accent "funny." Ray's accent actually isn't too shabby—his actor knew Cajuns in the Merchant Marines—and it was a welcomed improvement on Sandler's Cajun Man, who francized (inaccurately) any word ending in *-on* (like *inebriation* and *onions*). But if Prince Naveen had called Tiana's African American accent "funny," meaning "not normal," it probably would have sparked massive discussions online. It turns out that it's fine to portray Cajuns as not normal, though, because we're magical. Ray happily explains that his accent is funny because he and his family are from the bayous of Southwest Louisiana, whereupon the Cajun fireflies break into song and change the formerly scary, ugly swamp into a mysterious, surreal, and romantic interlude for Naveen and Tiana.

Another magical film about Louisiana was *Beasts of the Southern Wild* in 2012. There was a lot of local support for the film, especially since it's based on several real fishing communities in Louisiana that have been continually threatened by coastal erosion. But I wondered if locals, many of whom were in the movie, were surprised upon first viewing the movie to see their livelihoods portrayed like a magical adventure in a faraway land. I wondered if they could even recognize the area with all the sparklers and shaky cams. It was emotional and sublime, but it was so—foreign. The upside was the attention to environmental and political issues in South Louisiana; the downside was the otherization of the people in the film: the happy buffoons, the sex objects, and the noble savages. It's unclear who is Cajun, Creole, or whatever else (I'd say the characters that seem the most Cajun are the chubby, nice, drunk ones), but it doesn't really matter because Cajun/Creole/Louisiana/New Orleans is kind of all the same thing for most Americans at this point. I actually loved the movie, but I felt like I would have to do a lot of explaining to keep my parents and grandparents from guffawing at it.

I'm bringing these recent media representations of Cajuns up because they reflect how my people are currently defined outside of our area. First of all, it comes as a surprise to many Cajuns that people are even interested in us. This goes back to long before Hurricane Katrina brought Louisiana into the media. Thomas Dolby, most known for his hit "She Blinded Me with Science," released a 1992 song set in Louisiana called "I Love You Goodbye." Collaborating with some of our locally known musicians like Wayne Toups and Michael Doucet, Dolby actually sang about my hometown, Opelousas. It was cute to me that he mispronounced it with a long *o*, and that he sang about a "county sheriff" (we have parishes, not counties), but I wondered to death how this musician in England had even heard of Opelousas, kind of like how I couldn't comprehend why we had a hotel in our town. "Under a Cajun moon," he sings, "I lay me open. There is a spirit here that won't be broken." Curiously, he's not the only celebrity interested in Cajun music. Gordan Gano of the Violent Femmes and even Scarlett Johansson recently collaborated with the Lost Bayou Ramblers on their 2012 release *Mammoth Waltz*. There's nothing quite like a live Cajun version of "Blister in the Sun," fiddles and all.

Second surprise, people think we're sexy/magical/clownish/intimidating or any other adjective to indicate we're somehow so different we should be admired, laughed off, or feared. Cajun characters are generally so obscured by stereotypes in popular representations that it's easier for me to relate to the mainstream characters than the ones who are supposed to be Cajun like me. The stereotypes of Cajuns in these movies and TV shows aren't exactly unique; they're pretty much the same as the stereotypes assigned to other postcolonial communities (peoples who were folded into an empire without their consent). Edward Said developed a list of the characteristics the British attributed to Indian colonials in his book *Orientalism*: they were presumed to be criminal, sexual/exotic, mystical, illiterate or uneducated, sometimes feeble-minded—all the things that make it necessary to rule the people of the colonies since they're incapable of ruling themselves (Said 1978, 12). Empires generously intervene in other groups' and countries' politics in order to save the inferior people from themselves. They need education, religion, civilization, progress, and/or (the latest fad) democracy.

One writer, Dave Thier (2014), recently wrote that Louisiana has fallen prey to a form of Said's orientalism, "Southern orientalism." He was responding to the current trend of depicting Louisiana as exotic in *Beasts* and other recent Louisiana-set shows like *Treme*, *True Blood*, *True Detective*, and *American Horror Story*: "Louisiana, we learn from these shows, is something else. It's not like whatever state you're watching it from. Dangerous, primal, magical and otherworldly. It's quaint, honest and unapologetic. Darkness lurks in every hazy corner, uncommon beauty just behind it. Some people down here are sort of French, which is the most magical of all nationalities, except maybe Tibetan." Thier, who claims an insider view of Louisiana, says it's no different from Cleveland, and this magic is simply an invention of the film industry, which is happy to cash in on the state's whopping tax credits. True, Louisiana became the film production capital of the world in 2013, but Thier rolls over to the other proverbial ditch by arguing that Louisiana is not exotic at all but is in fact pretty boring. He admittedly mostly played video games and watched Netflix during his three years in New Orleans. Also, he has never lived in Cleveland. Thier's article "Sorry, Louisiana Is Not Actually Made of Magic" prompted a slew of local comments and response articles defending the things that are to be celebrated about Louisiana. I gravitate toward the defensive side because I do think Louisiana has magical qualities—just like every other environment and culture. Different doesn't have to be better. Or worse. Different is just different. But he's right when he says these over-the-top depictions, even the "positive" ones, "leave the realm of celebration and move wholeheartedly into fetishization—Southern Orientalism, an obsession with an imaginary other."

Postcolonial depictions of Cajuns in pop culture are directly related to Cajuns' status as, essentially, a colony of the US empire—in this case, as a result of what Michael Hechter (1975) called "internal colonialism" in his theorization of British empire. The same way England annexed and colonized what became Great Britain, the United States colonized Cajuns and dozens of other groups into its nation. In the Louisiana Purchase of 1803, Cajuns, who had already undergone British exile from present-day Nova Scotia and ethnic cleansing during Le Grand Dérangement beginning in 1755, were transferred from one colonial power, France, to another upcoming one, the United States. Cajuns remained insular and uninterested in modernization or southern capitalism (sometimes called "plantocracy"), operating outside the US economy until they were forced to assimilate educationally in the first half of the twentieth century (more on that later). So Cajuns and many other French-speaking communities in Louisiana are literally colonies that the United States bought and later forcibly Americanized.

At the time of their forced assimilation, Cajuns (as Said explains about Indian colonies) did not have the privilege of representing themselves in the United States' hegemony; instead, the empire renamed them (*Acadians* became *Cajuns*) and created stereotypes of their inferiority. Illustrations in magazines from the nineteenth century depict licentious Cajun washerwomen—legs spread-eagled, exposed to the thigh (Brasseaux 1992, 88h)—and raggedy Cajun men in some display of laziness or low moral character (88c, h). Travel journalist William Henry Sparks made no attempts to disguise his disdain for Cajuns in his 1882 memoirs: "A sallow-faced slatternly woman, bareheaded, with uncared-for hair, long, tangled, black, with her dress tucked up to her knees, bare-footed and bare-legged, is wading through the mud from the bayou with a dirty pail full of muddy Mississippi water" (quoted in Istre 2002, 34). Current depictions, like the ones in *The Princess and the Frog*, *The Waterboy*, and *Beasts of the Southern Wild*, still represent Cajuns as drunk, illiterate, dimwitted, poor, and low class. But even the "positive" depictions of Cajuns in these films as "magical" or "sexy" are disturbing because they relegate Cajuns to the status of others. These postcolonial stereotypes in pop culture references to Cajuns are instrumental for understanding what I really want to talk about: the status of Cajun ways of speaking and current language tensions.

## LOUISIANA FRENCH AND CAJUN ENGLISH

In South Louisiana, the French part of Louisiana sometimes called "the northern tip of the Caribbean" (Gaudet 2003, vii), Cajuns and other francophone populations are still struggling with issues of linguistic permission as a result of language policies and prejudices. Louisiana French was legally banned in 1921 during a wave of English-only policies, and public schools were designated as the sites that would implement this prohibition. Children were physically punished for speaking French— even on the playground—and eventually French was almost completely shamed out of public spaces (Ancelet 1996). My grandfather was one of those kids on the playground, and he must have learned his lesson really well, because he practiced oratory alone in his bedroom to learn nearly flawless English, then hitchhiked his way through an MBA and raised his own children in an English-only household. By the time I came along, the older folks in my family spoke "Cajun" (as we called it) only when they didn't want us to understand them—to fuss about us, or to whoop and holler about whatever it was they whooped and hollered about.

Louisiana Cajun French is the variety of French spoken by descendants of the Acadians who immigrated to Louisiana and people who assimilated into Cajun culture. It's commonly described as seventeenth-century "folk French," incorporating vocabulary influences from surrounding Native American, European, and African languages as well as English. Several Frenches came to Louisiana in three waves of immigration, according to the *Dictionary of Louisiana French: As Spoken by Cajun, Creole, and American Indian Communities* (Valdman et al. 2010). The first wave consisted of colonists from Quebec and different parts of France (1699–1762), the second wave was the influx of Acadians from Nova Scotia during the Grand Dérangement (1764–1785), and the third wave were elite French speakers from St. Domingue (now Haiti) and France who were attracted to the "flourishing plantation economy" (xi–xii). The Frenches meshed to different degrees to produce a variety of Louisiana Frenches, also absorbing some Spanish and Native American vocabulary for things local to Louisiana—fishes, plants, and mosquitoes, for instance. Because Frenches local to Louisiana were separated from continental French, they evolved in different directions, so Cajuns and other Louisiana francophones still use older words like *char* (cart, carriage) for "car" instead of the Parisian *voiture*. A Cajun soldier in World War II, for instance, said he encountered a French officer abroad who told him he spoke seventeenth-century French "that had been forgotten in France" (Bernard 2003, 9).

Self-identification and ethnicity are complex arrangements in Louisiana, but in general the state is divided into North Louisiana, encompassing a variety of Anglo communities, and South Louisiana, encompassing a variety of "ethnic" communities (Cajuns, Creoles, Native Americans, Isleños, and many more). North Louisiana tends to identify with other southern states in what is often called "the Bible Belt," like Arkansas, Alabama, and Mississippi, whereas South Louisiana has been called the "Catholic pocket of the Bible Belt" or "south of the South." It's not entirely accurate to divide the state geographically because there are pockets of French-speaking communities as far north as Natchitoches, but most Louisiana locals have settled on the north/south divide, describing Louisiana as almost two different states. When I was still very young, my father moved up to a tiny town just outside

Alexandria, which is part of Central Louisiana (CenLa) but identifies mostly with North Louisiana. As I visited his family every other weekend, it was fascinating to hear my stepsister's accent change from a liquid Avoyelles Parish French inflection to a southern staccato; our three younger brothers grew up identifying completely with North Louisiana and still sort of talk out of the sides of their mouths.

Another cultural and geographical division is the line between Southwest Louisiana and Southeast Louisiana, usually demarcated by Baton Rouge's central and almost neutral position. A lot of locals say that everything west of Baton Rouge is Cajun and everything east is Creole, so the two areas have been divided into, respectively, Acadiana (named after the original settlement of Cajuns' ancestors in present-day Nova Scotia before their exile) and the greater New Orleans area, or NOLA (short for New Orleans, Louisiana), but this also isn't entirely accurate. The areas are indeed very different culturally, but it's not just a difference between Cajun and Creole. There are plenty of Creole French and Spanish speakers in Southwest Louisiana, and there are plenty of self-identifying Cajuns in Houma, just south of New Orleans. Since the name "Acadiana" excludes a lot of people who don't identify as Acadian or Cajun but who live in Southwest Louisiana and are integral to local culture, I prefer to stick to the geographical state associations, acknowledging that there are pockets of variations: North Louisiana is grouped in with the other southern states, with similar accents, foods, and culture; and South Louisiana (or SouLa, pronounced "so-la") encompasses the variety of non-Anglo communities, generally including NOLA (but not always) and generally excluding Baton Rouge, which most locals acknowledge to be a pocket that better suits North Louisiana. Incidentally, many locals informally prefer the older postal abbreviation "La." because the newer "LA" is inevitably confused with Los Angeles.

As people in these different communities struggle with our similarities and differences, discussions around language have been similarly complex. Though it's increasingly more common to label Englishes separately, the trend in Louisiana language studies is to consolidate in order to emphasize not the common heritage of SouLa but the common diversity. So all these different Frenches now fit under the heading "Louisiana French," even though some are very different from each other, historically, structurally, and culturally. For example, the French spoken by Cajuns exists locally alongside Louisiana Creole, which is based on a different grammatical structure, but both are now considered Louisiana French. Personally, I don't identify as French, since I was raised monolingual English (albeit a French-inflected English). I identify as Cajun because I was raised culturally Cajun, but I'm also ethno-racially Isleño (from the Canary Islands), German, French Creole, Spanish Creole, Scots-Irish (hence the name Stanford), and whatever mysteries have been lost or hidden, just like any other family in SouLa. For the sake of clarity, I sometimes use the more specific term *Cajun French* (which is now identified as a variety of Louisiana French) when discussing the dialects common to Cajuns instead of the broader *Louisiana French* (which also includes the varieties spoken by Native Americans, Creoles of color, French Creoles, Spanish Creoles, black Creoles, and a number of more recently arrived communities like Vietnamese, Laotian, and Lebanese).

In the United States, Cajun French has traditionally been viewed not as linguistically interesting but as a sign of being "low class" (in contrast to Parisian French, also spoken in Louisiana, and Plantation Society French, another variety of Louisiana French that evolved from elite French speakers and has now all but disappeared). One *Chicago Times* reporter in 1880 wrote, "The educated people [in Louisiana] speak the bona fide Parisian, but the 'Cagin' patois is deemed good enough for the 'low-down folks'" (quoted in Bernard and Bernard 1999). Barry Jean Ancelet writes in "A Perspective on Teaching the 'Problem Language' in Louisiana" that the language was stigmatized as "not the real French, just broken Cajun French" (1988, 346) because people didn't understand basic linguistics principles—namely, the way languages evolve and borrow from each other. Critics of Louisiana French argued that it had no grammar, and it was only an oral (thus, illiterate) language (347). Linguistic prejudice toward Cajuns was already well established when the ban took effect in 1921.

The French ban was enforced in schools well into the 1970s, when what came to be known as the "Cajun Renaissance" prompted resistance to the denigration of Cajuns and Louisiana French. According to Shane K. Bernard in *The Cajuns: Americanization of a People* (2003), the Cajun Renaissance began as a result of several factors. First, during World War II, Cajuns who went off to fight discovered that knowing French was a valuable skill, and they returned with a new fondness for their culture. Second, when oil was discovered on their land in the 1950s, Cajuns began to interact with mainstream culture on a higher economic level, providing the option of a semi self-sustaining community once again. Third, the economic stability enabled a wave of Cajun academics to work to preserve cultural literature and traditions as well as to begin to correct false assumptions about and stereotypes of Cajuns. As a result, universities began to codify and even teach Louisiana French; Cajun authors began writing novels and children's folklore; and Festival International was established in Lafayette, Louisiana, as an annual invitation to all francophone countries to share music, clothes, food, and other cultural aspects. The Cajun Renaissance also corresponded to a general interest in ethnic groups and multiculturalism at the time.

Since the Cajun Renaissance, there have been many attempts to revive Louisiana French, which suffered a serious blow in circulation during the period the ban was enforced. A "safe" language (not in danger of extinction) requires a minimum of 100,000 speakers (Skutnabb-Kangas 1988, 24). According to some estimates, though, Louisiana French is spoken by about 17,000 people, most of whom are over the age of sixty (Omisore 2010). The Council for the Development of French in Louisiana (CODOFIL) was formed in 1968 to promote the public use of French—in advertisements and official speeches, for example. Louisiana was declared a de facto bilingual state (French and English), as a result of the efforts of CODOFIL and other activists in 1974. Later, in 1980, Cajuns were deemed a minority group protected from discrimination by Title VII's ban on national origin discrimination (under the Civil Rights Act of 1964) in the lawsuit of *James Roach v. Dresser Industries*. The SouLa area also instituted multiple French-immersion programs in elementary schools during the 1980s and 1990s (they continue today) in an effort to counter the forced English immersion of Cajun students during the first half of the twentieth century. Many monolingual English-speaking Cajuns have decided to learn Cajun French as adults, even traveling in large groups to Nova Scotia for French-immersion programs. These efforts have not restored the use of Louisiana French to its former levels of circulation, but they have had a huge impact in renormalizing French in SouLa.

Fewer Cajuns are speaking Louisiana Cajun French, but that doesn't mean fewer people are speaking Cajun languages. What has emerged in the last few decades is a new linguistic way of expressing Cajunness—a blend of English and Louisiana French that parallels the locals' blended identities as American and Cajun. In a 1992 special issue of the *Louisiana English Journal*, a group of linguists and linguistics students compiled eight papers on this variety of English with Cajun linguistic markers—what they called Cajun English. They wrote that this variety of English could be identified immediately by Cajuns and non-Cajuns alike, but there was no documentation of it in professional literature yet: "A preliminary review of available literature on the dialect we termed Cajun English (CE) revealed a complete absence of published work. Tracking down occasional references to *the Cajun language*, we found that in all cases *Cajun* turned out to be Cajun French" (Scott 1992b, i).[1] The group documented much of the phonology, morphology, syntax, and lexicon of CE. Since this special issue on CE, Sylvie Dubois has done considerable work on CE, coauthoring dozens of publications with Deborah Horvath and Megan Melancon, among other linguists. Dubois uses the term *Cajun Vernacular English*, but I prefer *Cajun English* because, though *vernacular* literally means that the language arose locally, the connotation is that it isn't a "real" language (see Phillipson 1992, 40–42, for a discussion of language labels).

Along those lines, Dubois and Horvath confirmed that CE is not a transitory phase between French and English but a rooted dialect prompted by a generation-wide resistance to cultural identity loss. Unlike "border dialects" that arise to enable communication temporarily between speakers of two different languages, CE emerged *after* most people had already pretty much mastered English. It arose in response to a need for cultural identity, not communication. Dubois and Horvath identified what they call a "V-shaped pattern" that illustrates the resurgence of Cajun linguistic markers after there was no longer a need for a temporary border dialect: the first generation of Cajuns to switch to English spoke with a high level of typical ESL features, the next generation followed a common immigrant pattern in speaking virtually error-free English, but the English of the third generation returned to something more like that of the grandparents (Dubois and Horvath 2003b, 53). The V-shaped pattern is the level of "errors" or influence from Cajun French that disappeared in the second generation and returned in my generation. As is arguably the case for most "involuntary" minority groups, Cajuns maintain their cultural identity with linguistic markers that distinguish them from what they perceive as mainstream or other cultures. The result after three generations, according to Dubois and Horvath, is a nonstandard dialect of English similar to today's African American English and, I would add, similar to what was once English's status as a vernacular of Latin.

Briefly, here's a layperson's overview of the linguistic and sociolinguistic features of CE (see the original texts if you're interested in more precise linguistics codings). First, the Cajun accent and cadence is one of the most immediately recognizable aspects of CE; it sounds like what's spoken in the south of France with a mixture of (most notably) West African and Spanish, as well as the many surrounding cultures that influenced and combined with Cajuns over the years. Megan Melancon sums up the phonetic features of third-generation English speakers in "American Varieties: Cajun English" (part of a PBS series): "vowel pronunciation, stress changes [to the end of the word], the lack of the

/th/ phonemes, non-aspiration of /p/, /t/, and /k/ . . . The use of these features has resulted in no Southern drawl at all in Cajun English. Cajuns talk extremely fast, [and] their vowels are clipped" (Melancon 2005, 2). Words with aspirated consonants like *pollution* and *Cajun* can sound like *bollution* and *Gajun*. And, rather than the Parisian /r/ in the back of the throat, Cajuns use the tip of the tongue like West African French speakers or Spanish speakers with a slight trill. What Melancon calls "clipped" vowels is lack of diphthong, as Ann Martin Scott writes in "Some Phonological and Syntactic Characteristics of Cajun Vernacular English," so that English words *I* and *time* (which have "bendy" vowels in standard English) sound like /a/, as in *father* or *pot* (Scott 1992c, 27). As a result, *boiled eggs* can sound like *bald eggs*. There is no /th/ sound in CE; it is replaced by something similar to regular /d/ and /t/, as in *dis* for *this* and *tink* for *think* (29). The cadence of CE, like its morphology, derives from Cajun French. Scott writes, "In French, all syllables are held for approximately the same length of time regardless of stress, and the last syllable of a word, phrase, or sentence is normally stressed" (28). The effect in English, she writes, lends a "musical quality" to CE that is impossible to show on paper without convoluted symbols (or a musical staff).

Next, CE regularly mixes in French vocabulary and grammar. Some common French words are *lagniappe* (a little something extra), *coulee* (large ditch), *honte* (embarrassed), *canaille* (mischievous), *envie* (craving), *frisson* (a chill, goose bumps), *couillion* (roughly, an idiot), and many, many others. Specifically, many of the phrases that the second and third generations heard often as children are persistent: *do-do* (sleep), *touché pas!* (don't touch!), *cher* (dear), *ta-ta* or *cher-cher* (there, there), *viens manger* (come eat), *ça c'est bon* (that's good), and so on. A minor scrape or bruise is a *bo-bo* (not to be confused with *boo-boo*, a small mistake). These words and phrases are woven into English with results like "Don't ta-ta me" (Don't baby me) and "I caught a frisson" (I got a chill). Many food items are still called by their French names as well, such as *sauce picante, courtbouillon, fricassee, étouffe, pain perdu,* and *boudin*. In addition, *bayou* and *gumbo* are examples of words that Louisiana French borrowed from surrounding cultures and passed on to CE—*bayou* from the Choctaw Indian word *bayuk* and *gumbo* from *gombo*, a Bantu word for 'okra'; *colombo*, a West Indies word for a kind of chicken soup; and *kombo*, an Amerindian word for a soup-like dish thickened with filé (ground, dried sassafras leaves commonly used in gumbos)" (Cheramie and Gill 1992, 44, 47). And *mais* (but) is a culture-wide language filler for adding emphasis, as in "Mais, yeah, cher" and "Mais, no"—so prevalent that one old joke says it's possible to identify the Cajun baby in the nursery by listening for "Mais, wah!"

In addition to French vocabulary, Deany M. Cheramie and Donald A. Gill wrote in "Lexical Choice in Cajun Vernacular English" that French calques (literal translations that are nonstandard in English) are common in CE. Some French verbs that make their way into a lot of English constructions are *pass, make,* and *catch*. Speakers of CE pass the broom (sweep), pass by someone's house to say hey (visit someone's home), pass a good time (have a good time), catch a headache (get a headache), catch a frisson (get a chill), ask someone to please catch them the salt (pass the salt). In addition, they make a B+ (earn a B+), make the groceries and save them (buy groceries and put them away), get down from the car (get out), and ask their companions to come see (come here, from a meshing with the French *vien ici*) (1992, 39–41). CE calques also include nonstandard usage of the preposition *for*—"when I was pregnant for Marie" (with Marie) and "Who's this jacket for?" (Whose jacket is this?), among others (42–43)—and the article *the*—"speak the French" and "go to the Walmart." Speaking of the word *the*, Cajuns tend to francize its pronunciation: rather than elongating the *e* before vowels, they drop it altogether and append the article to the next word, as in "th'apple" or "th'entire thing." This is similar to French constructions like " l'école."

CE also commonly anglicizes French words like *bouder* (to whine) with constructions like "He boudé-ed all morning" or "Quit your boudéing" (Cheramie and Gill 1992, 45). Another syntactic calque is double-referencing a noun for stress: "I got the envie for some gumbo, me"; "That Pat, he's a couillion"; and "Me, I don't know," similar to the French construction, "Moi, je ne sais pas." Cheramie adds the usage of "went" as a form of past tense, as in "We went see the movie" (Cheramie 1998b, 113). Functionally, it's the opposite of using *go* in the future tense, as in "We're going to see the movie." Another nonstandard syntactic feature of CE is creating interrogative constructions, as in French, by simply "tagging" declarative sentences with a *no* or *hein* (pronounced *ahn* or *eh*) at the end—for example, "Y'all not leaving, *hein*?" Canadian patterns of speech in some regions are similarly known for this kind of tagging. Another Cajunism is doubling up on adjectives and adverbs to create emphasis—like "not too-too much" or "love you big-big"—instead of adding intensifiers like *really* or *so much*.

Finally, a very important feature embedded in the deep structure of CE, and probably one of the most persistent crossovers from Louisiana Cajun French to English, is the rhetorical strategy of storytelling as a means of passing on oral history. Important lessons and cultural identity are usually taught in stories by the community raconteurs at family gatherings and public venues like the Liberty Theater in Eunice, and the knowledge of elders is privileged, regardless of documentation. Storytelling is so embedded in Cajun culture that Sherri L. Condon and Pamela T. Pittman report in "Language Attitudes in Acadiana" that one difficulty they have with objectively comparing language samples of speakers of CE with other speakers is the "colorful style that provide[s] much more detail and convey[s] much more enthusiasm than the other speakers" (Condon and Pittman 1992, 71). The authors debate whether the style of narration could skew the results of a survey they conduct on language attitudes, but they conclude that "the colorful quality of Cajun speech is an important, natural characteristic, and any attempt to eradicate it could lead to an underrepresentative sample of speech" (71). In contrast to the "bland" style of "the other two speakers [who] sounded like they were reading [the same anecdote]," (71) Cajun storytelling is an engaging way of passing on cultural information.

As part of this tradition, joke telling is an important part of the culture, and Cajun jokes are almost always long stories, rarely clever one-liners. Joke tellers using CE usually relate stories about Cajun characters in the process of assimilation who seriously convolute—and simultaneously critique—dominant American customs. Here, Tommy Joe Breaux, a well-known storyteller and the grandson of a Cajun Frenchman from Breaux Bridge, Louisiana, illustrates many of the phonological features of CE in a partially phonetic rendering as he introduces a story told by his grandfather:

> De folks who have read my first book, *Cajun Humor from the Heart*, or listened to any of my six cassettes, or watched my videos, know de numba-one hungout in Breaux Bridge, Louisiana, for granpa an' his frans was T'Bub's Barroom. It was a place where men could talk 'bout fishin', huntin', sports and women, an' everybody was interested an' agreed wit' wat was say, 'specially 'bout women. Some of my favorite stories Granpa tole me as a kid came out of T'Bub's an' by far, de one 'bout old Amos Bordelon goin' to one of dem nudist camps is one of my favorites. Granpa tole me Amos got back from his nudist camp trip an' naturally he had everybody's full attention an' center stage to tell dem all 'bout de camp. Amos say, "Well, befo I got start tole y'all 'bout camp, I wanna got one tang clear—it ain't all it's crack up to be, I could garontee you dat."
> Averybody say, "Wat you mean by dat, Amos?"
> Amos say, "Well, to tole y'all de trueff, it's kinda' embarrasin'."
> Averybody say, "Wat's de matter, Amos, you ashame of you birthday suit?"
> Amos say, "No, I'm not ashame of my birthday suit at all, I'm jus' sayin' it's hard to look you bess wan you walkin' 'round wit' you pocket change

an' you wallet in you mouth all de time." (quoted in Dubois and Horvath 2002, 279; bracketed insertions deleted)

This phonological transcription is an example of a third-generation speaker purposefully stressing his Cajun accent. Tommy Joe Breaux grew up outside SouLa, but he still demonstrates the differences between a first-generation speaker (the text in quotations) and a third-generation speaker (the rest of the text).

The collision of standardized English in classrooms with the CE spoken in SouLa can lead to interesting writing results. Our local pronunciations combined with the standard phonics I learned at school led me to spell *pecan* as *becan* and *Bataille* (a card game meaning "Battle") as *Battie* in elementary school. I was stumped when I tried to write a thank-you note to my godfather, whom I knew as *Parrain* (French for godfather). I was pretty sure it began with *p-a-d-*, but couldn't figure out the ending, the French nasalized /n/. We didn't have any sounds like that at school. No one else in my family knew how to spell it either, so I think I just didn't include a greeting in the note. Even now, as I intentionally use more CE in my writing, I'm often unsure of how to write what I say. When I was in grad school, a Canadian French student in my dissertation workshop graciously pointed out to me that I was using feminine endings incorrectly. Later, it was extremely difficult to find out how to spell *canaille* for an article I was writing because I didn't know if it was a word from French or some other language that Cajuns had francized. Every Cajun I asked knew how to use the word, but almost all thought it was just the first two syllables of *conniving*. As I finally found out from a Canadian French teacher, it has an entirely different etymology, and it's spelled like that other problem word from my childhood, *bataille*. The fact is most Cajuns are English literate, not CE literate, and this can cause problems from kindergarten to beyond terminal degrees. Even now, as I reenter the world of phonics with my young daughter, I am jarred to read in one of her books that the first syllable in *envelope* is supposed to be pronounced with a short *e*, like the other *e* words it's next to—*egg* and *elevator*—instead of the French way we say it in my family.

Cheramie has studied several of these linguistic intersections that are read as "errors" across college classrooms in SouLa. In her dissertation "Cajun Vernacular English and the Influence of Vernacular on Student Writing in South Louisiana" (Cheramie 1998a), she analyzed 431 writing samples from students of all backgrounds in developmental classes at the University of Southwestern Louisiana (which has since been renamed the University of Louisiana at Lafayette), Louisiana State

University at Eunice, and Nicholls State University "for spelling (as a likely reflection of phonology), morphosyntax, and lexical usage that differed from standard usage and could be traced to spoken dialect features" (104). She concludes that "characteristics of CE do appear in the writing of CE speakers. In fact, both CE and AAE speakers produced features in their writing that are dialectical" (22). The students who were identified as Cajun (as opposed to African American or southern) "produced 89% of the CE phonology features, 82% of the CE morphosyntax features, and 84% of the CE lexicon features" (142). Cheramie breaks it down further: 51 percent of the features found were morphosyntactic, 32 percent were lexical, and 17 percent were phonological (143). She recommends that both teachers and students be educated about dialect influence to change any negative attitudes toward nonstandard varieties and to raise awareness of possible rhetorical decisions. Meanwhile, Cheramie's study demonstrates not only that dialect influence is an important consideration in classrooms, but also that CE is prevalent in SouLa classrooms.

## THE PROBLEM

Cajuns are becoming more prominent in mainstream media, as well as prouder, and CE is prevalent in SouLa schools, as Cheramie demonstrates, but that doesn't mean that Cajuns have progressive attitudes about nonstandard Englishes. It's a complicated affair. Dubois and Horvath have noted that, similar to Cajun French in the first half of the twentieth century, CE features disappear according to level of education. The more education, the less CE. Rather than becoming bidialectical, most upwardly mobile Cajuns shed CE linguistic markers altogether (Dubois and Horvath 2003b, 40–41). In other words, Cajuns who want more socioeconomic status try not to sound Cajun. The results of my own survey of English teachers across four colleges in SouLa confirm their finding (I describe the survey in detail in chapter 4). Eleven of the forty respondents identified as Cajun, and ten of those eleven Cajuns report that they censor their language (whereas only 70 percent of the non-Cajuns report that they self-censor).[2] This finding seems to be at odds with the cultural pride that arose in the Cajun Renaissance, resulting in multiple Cajun festivals, a new wave of Cajun music bands, and even efforts to create an Acadian nation. This trend of CE loss is especially peculiar considering that schools have now embraced French and generally abandoned the harsher policy of linguistic eradication in favor of the more permissive policy of "code switching," in which students are required to use what has come to be known in composition and rhetoric as "academic discourses" in school settings but are free to use "home discourses" everywhere else.

In fact, a substantial number of my survey respondents report that they weren't taught to censor the Cajunisms from their language in school at all but picked up the practice somewhere else. In creating the survey, I (admit that I) expected to gather loads of sad school stories so that I could come down on bad teaching practices, but only one report involved direct instruction from a teacher. The rest of the responses to my questions about if and when my Cajun participants learned to censor their CE focused on class, privilege, and position, as the excerpts below show. In the longer quotations, I've italicized the sections I find most telling:

> When I entered college, my freshman year, I realized that most professionals (in this case, my professors) pronounced the "th" sound, and I often did not. I remember hearing myself say, "I'm going to da store," and thinking, *"My professors would never say 'da store.'"* That's when I really began to force myself to remove "Cajun-speak" from my writing and speaking.

This respondent also reported self-censoring for the sake of social position:

> Since becoming a teacher of composition, I am more careful [about Cajun linguistic markers] when writing.

Other participants reported similar experiences of learning to censor themselves for the sake of academic success, but they don't connect it with their teachers:

> Throughout school, engaging in extracurricular activities that often involved *public speaking made me acutely aware of how Cajun accents affected attitudes* toward those speakers. *Many people believe that the Cajun accent sounds unintelligent and uneducated,* so I fought to develop a more "Anglicized" accent, especially in professional and public matters.
>
> As a child, I didn't realize that the accent was different; I was living within a society that consisted of nothing but Cajun accents. As I became a young adult, I did become a bit more ashamed of my accent and those of my family members, but only because *I was learning that people associated that accent with a lack of intelligence.*

All the respondents above report that their censoring is motivated by the desire to seem intelligent and professional, to distance themselves from negative stereotypes associated with Cajun linguistic markers. Only one Cajun in my survey reported learning to alter his or her language for the mere sake of being understood instead of some socioeconomic reason:

Times when I realized someone didn't know what I was talking about because they weren't from here.

A few other responses revealed a degree of ambivalence toward CE. Though they are proud of their Cajun linguistic markers, they still recognize the associated stigma and censor themselves just as much as the respondents who said they were ashamed of their accents. The following respondent, who reports self-censoring in another response, writes:

> My personal attitude toward the accent and features of the Cajun language is still one of pride, *but I do recognize the stigma associated with those features.*

Another writes similarly that, despite a sense of cultural pride, he or she also self-censors in relation to job or economic considerations:

> I was never embarrassed, really, about my Cajun accent. And as I grow older, I am more and more proud of it. *I'm just careful to keep some of the "Cajun slang" in check when I'm in a professional setting.*

In these instances, the Cajun respondents didn't learn to self-censor in school. But if CE is not being forcibly silenced by any educational or legal policies, why do upwardly mobile Cajuns stop using it? I should add that, by "upwardly mobile," I mean pretty much everyone who wants a better income, so this is very broad. Why do we comply with the disappearance of our languages? The long answer has to do with the way the economy has been engineered, and that's what the rest of this book is about. But the short answer is that Cajun ways of speaking aren't worth much in this economy. The pop culture representations of Cajuns I described earlier reveal hegemonic attitudes toward Cajuns as—well—not exactly CEO material. Not really middle management either. As the respondents in my survey put it, Cajun linguistic markers invoke ideas of unprofessionalism at best and incompetence at worst. If they sounded Cajun, they were likely to be written off as having other stereotypical Cajun characteristics like drunkenness, lower intelligence, maybe some magic and sexiness too, but nothing very hirable. So trying not to sound Cajun, especially in high-stakes situations like job interviews and writing exams, winds up being the responsible thing to do, like dressing nice and being punctual. A fascinating survey on language attitudes in South Louisiana confirmed this idea, but before I get to that, I want to explain my theoretical framework, Pierre Bourdieu's theory of legitimate languages, which shows the close link between language capital and financial capital.

## THEORETICAL FRAMEWORK

This project, which is a case study and analysis of the educational and linguistic assimilation of the Cajuns of Southwest Louisiana, situates the language conflicts and practices of the Cajun community within Pierre Bourdieu's theory of the emergence, circulation, and suppressive function of what he calls the "legitimate language" in *Language and Symbolic Power* (1991). In short, languages are like money. With enough of the right kind of currency (the standard language), one can buy a pretty good lifestyle. But the legitimate language, like paper money, has worth only because we believe in it and comply with it. This compliance, however, is never really voluntary because the language "market" (like the financial market) is upheld by intimidating forces (like the threat of losing a job) and people's own normalized beliefs (for example, people who speak nonstandard Englishes deserve to be poor). In the same way that Cajuns are stereotypically represented as too foreign (exotic, magical) and/or too inept (drunk, illiterate) for standard American jobs, their languages have a very low exchange rate in the American economy.

Bourdieu explains his work on language prejudice and discrimination in terms of socioeconomic relationships—pertinent in this case since the issue of language ownership for Cajuns hinges largely on class position and mobility. Both Cajuns and non-Cajuns in my survey and in other surveys articulated their positions overwhelmingly in terms of class and economy; teachers, students, and parents routinely observed that Cajuns occupy a low class position and that Cajuns need to sound *not* Cajun to have access to higher working positions in the economy. Race and gender are equally important factors in these constructions of linguistic identity and economic opportunity, especially since talking in terms of economy is often a screen for gender- and race-based prejudices that are actually programmed into the economy. I hope somebody will take up these other considerations at some point, but I'm starting the conversation with a sociopolitical analysis of language because of its centrality to Cajuns' and non-Cajuns' own consciousness about Cajun languages as a hindrance to economic mobility.

Bourdieu writes in the introduction to *Language and Symbolic Power* that modern linguistics has earned the label "scientific" by studying only the internal structures of language to the exclusion of the sociopolitical ways that languages are used, as if language were "a game devoid of consequences" (1991, 34). But it is necessary to look at linguistic exchanges in the context—political, historical, and even geographic—of the people who use them. Bourdieu proposes that language dynamics are determined by a network of unequal social forces, which create a *market* that determines the high worth of some dialects and languages, with the most powerful group in society installing its own usage as the *standard*. These more prestigious codes or *legitimate languages* become national or official languages, and the process of language legitimation also *delegitimates* all other codes (the languages and dialects of subordinated groups), rendering them "vernaculars," "slangs," or "broken" Englishes (or "broken" Frenches and so forth). He is known for developing the ideas of *social capital, cultural capital,* and *symbolic capital* in *Distinction: A Social Critique of the Judgement of Taste* (Bourdieu 1984) to explain how inequalities are maintained without direct coercion, something that is integral to his analysis.

Bourdieu's work is also particularly helpful because he gives equal attention to the external imposition of language prejudice and the seemingly voluntary compliance of individuals who internalize and reinforce prejudiced beliefs about language, likely because of his own experience growing up in France speaking the politically subordinate dialect Béarnese. In brief, he holds three major agents responsible for language inequalities: *nation builders, institutions,* and *individuals.* The legitimate language is selected as a function of nation building (by the "founding fathers"), then programmed into the nation's educational and legal systems (institutions), and finally enforced by individuals who consent (though not entirely voluntarily) to it. Periodically, the legitimate language is refined through the financial and ideological efforts of the powerful elites who function as nation builders during periods of national reorganization (during times of war, for example). In the beginning, during the founding of the nation (and again during periods of national reorganizing), a legitimate language is *codified*. This process of *codification* could mean creating an entirely new language, but it usually entails selecting a linguistic code already in use and elevating it from the status of dialect or vernacular to *language*. Codification of a legitimate language creates a unified market for language distinction just as selection of a singular currency does for commerce. In this sense, owning a substantial amount of the legitimate language is almost like being wealthy or, as Bourdieu would say, like owning a lot of "symbolic capital."

After the founding of the nation and its corollary language selection, Bourdieu writes, this now "legitimate" language must be *normalized*. Normalization is the process of getting everyone else to learn and recognize the legitimate language, even if they can't use it well. Within Bourdieu's paradigm of the legitimate language, there are two kinds of forces that help reproduce whatever linguistic structures were put in place at the founding of the nation: *coercive* forces and *intimidating* forces. The coercive forces are self-explanatory—physical and immediately punitive threats that lead to direct reproduction of the language hierarchy in place. Examples of coercive forces are legal and educational institutions, which can directly enforce use of the legitimate language or enforce consequences for not using it. Physical punishments can directly penalize children's language use, as in the case of Cajuns' educational assimilation, and grades can protect class hierarchy, as I explain in chapter 3. In the tradition of Louis Althusser's theory of ideological state apparatuses that protect the status quo, Bourdieu writes that schools are the primary institutions enforcing the legitimate language.

In addition to the ways in which educational policies and pedagogies lead to social reproduction, individual compliance is a major factor—and the one in which I am most interested in this study. Bourdieu categorizes individual compliance under *intimidating* forces. Though coercive forces can monitor language use in classrooms and other institutional settings, they can't control what happens at home or in social settings. The institutions and mechanisms of coercive forces, he writes, "can at best impose the acquisition, but not the generalized use, and therefore the autonomous reproduction, of the legitimate language" (Bourdieu 1991, 50). Intimidating forces take over where coercive forces leave off. They are things like jobs, social pressures, and myths about language that circulate among people and compel them to censor their own language. This not-quite-voluntary consent to the legitimate language happens at the levels of teachers, students, politicians, and the media, as well as seemingly uninvolved people sitting next to you on the subway. The network of legitimating forces pervades every area of life, leading Bourdieu to describe the process of language legitimation in terms of markets. This idea is important for my analysis of Cajuns and CE, since CE is disappearing among the most educated Cajuns in spite of the fact that code switching ostensibly allows them to speak in any way they wish outside the context of school and in spite of the cultural resurgence of Cajunness since the Cajun Renaissance.

Though he didn't use the term *hegemony*, Bourdieu's theory of the market is very similar to Antonio Gramsci's theory of cultural hegemony developed in his *Prison Notebooks* (1971). I borrow from Gramsci here because his theorization is already well known and can make the relationship between markets and individual compliance a little more accessible. Cultural hegemony is a pervasive cultural network of knowledge and practices that, even allowing for differences and disagreements, somehow always affirms the current order of things. Gramsci proposed cultural hegemony as the reason that workers cooperated with increasingly unequal conditions in nineteenth-century industrial Europe when they weren't being forced to; he argued that they complied because they came to hold the perspective of the ruling class and made decisions accordingly. Though Gramsci is sometimes criticized for portraying people as unthinking conformists, his theory of cultural hegemony actually allows for a great deal of resistance, something I explain further in chapter 5. Under cultural hegemony, however, their efforts at resistance are subsumed and appropriated by the hegemony.

One helpful expansion on the idea of effective and ineffective forms of resistance is James C. Scott's (1990) *Domination and the Arts of Resistance: Hidden Transcripts*. Though Scott is not writing specifically about cultural hegemony, his analysis of different forms of resistance demonstrates how inequalities can be upheld in Gramsci's cultural hegemony in spite of individuals' and groups' efforts to resist it. The ruling class controls what he calls the *public transcript*, the official story, while the oppressed or the ruled go along with it—officially. All participants perform and endure the public transcript until they get a chance to escape to private transcripts with no boss or other authority figures present and let it all hang out. Scott calls this use of the private transcript "venting." Think of the pressure safety valve on a machine; as long as that vent exists, the machine can keep going, but remove the valve and the machine will self-destruct. Scott writes that venting includes any practice that helps folks blow off steam—complaining, gossiping, spreading rumors, sneaking, stealing, even praying for divine retribution—and enables them to return to the public transcript, refreshed and renewed, ready to comply with the inequality. To change the public transcript, writes Scott, the dominated should use their private transcripts for organizing events of mass public resistance instead of venting, because any resistance occurring in the private transcript in the form of venting just winds up reifying the status quo. In cultural hegemony, people either take the perspective of the ruling class and reify inequalities, or they *perform* as if they do, which amounts to the same thing in the public transcript (conformity) and similarly reifies inequalities.

Bourdieu's theory of market pressures operates like Gramsci's cultural hegemony, but Bourdieu prefers economic terms to support his theorization of language as a form of capital. Using Marx's analysis of capital and labor, Bourdieu theorizes language as a form of what he calls symbolic capital, which produces and determines the user's status in a capitalist economy. Language use (that is, our recognition of other people's grasp of the legitimate language) helps sort people into the class to which they belong. This function of language is particularly important for a capitalist economy, Bourdieu writes, because capitalism operates as a "competitive struggle" in which there must be winners and losers (1991, 64). The winners wield the legitimate language properly; the losers, who must serve as the working class, speak the legitimate language "incorrectly" and understand that they do not deserve to make national decisions as a result of their inadequacy (they recognize the legitimate language even if they can't access it). In Bourdieu's theory, the language market was created during national codification as a result of coercive forces and then operates as an intimidating force that persuades people to comply with unequal language standards even when no one is monitoring.

Within this language market, Bourdieu portrays language as symbolic capital that can be commodified: bought, exchanged, measured, and sold. The price of this language capital, like the prices of gold and oil, is subject to fluctuation according to supply, demand, and artificial inflation: "Utterances receive their value (and their sense) only in their relation to a market" (1991, 67). The linguistic standard of this market determines what jobs and social standing people can qualify for, so people, aware of what "sells" in the market, comply in order to "buy" the lifestyle they want. They self-censor and even censor one another for the sake of marketability, or acceptability: "It is this sense of acceptability . . . which, by encouraging one to take account of the probable value of discourse during the process of production, determines corrections and all forms of self-censorship—the concessions one makes to a social world by accepting to make oneself acceptable in it" (77). One may not like money, but one probably likes what money can buy. Likewise, one may not like the legitimate language, but one probably likes what it can buy. Thus, as in hegemony, we individually uphold unequal language standards that we may not like but that we *want* for the sake of what the legitimate language can get us.

Bourdieu's use of financial terms also makes it easier to understand why the people who comply with language inequalities are generally people who are upwardly mobile, people who are also complying with— "buying into"—socioeconomic inequalities. In trying to accumulate more wealth, they also try to accumulate more linguistic-cultural capital. These pressures don't necessarily apply to people who are unconcerned with the "American dream," many of whom may already be politically aware enough to consciously resist linguistic and other forms of conformity. So, though there are rich forms of language resistance worth studying, Bourdieu's model is limited to language compliance in connection with attempts to rise in class status. His theory explains why Cajuns who choose upward mobility also commonly choose to censor linguistic traces of their ethnicity—usually not because anyone forces them to, but because they find that Cajun ways of speaking simply aren't worth much in most markets. In fact, I explain later that there are few economically viable options that require Cajun linguistic capital.

As he describes intimidating forces, Bourdieu writes that individuals consent to language inequality but, as I noted earlier, it's never quite voluntary: "All symbolic domination presupposes, on the part of those who submit to it, a form of complicity which is neither passive submission to external constraint nor a free adherence to values" (1991, 50–51). For one thing, the threat of losing one's livelihood or being ostracized from one's community hardly leaves space for objective or aesthetic decisions about language. But another reason that individuals' compliance is "not quite" voluntary is that they often don't recognize the language inequalities they are complying with and upholding. In addition to the market that pressures individuals to censor themselves and one another, there are pervasive ideas that reinforce the illegitimacy of other dialects and vernaculars. Individuals often comply with unequal language standards because they have been persuaded that the standards are equal.

Bourdieu's theory of *habitus* explains why postcolonial and other marginalized groups sometimes unknowingly comply with language inequalities. He writes that "*intimidation*, a symbolic violence . . . can only be exerted on a person predisposed (in his habitus) to feel it, whereas others will ignore it" (1991, 51). The habitus is the environment that shapes our tastes and values, which in turn lead us to reproduce our environment. He sums up his model as "the relation between linguistic habitus and the markets on which they offer their products" (37–38). In *Distinction: A Social Critique of the Judgement of Taste*, Bourdieu describes habitus as something based on and reinforcing class hierarchy:

> The habitus is not only a structuring structure, which organizes practices and the perception of practices, but also a structured structure: the principle of division into logical classes which organizes the perception of the social world is itself the product of internalization of the division into social classes. Each class condition is defined, simultaneously, by its intrinsic properties and by the relational properties which it derives from its position in the system of class conditions, which is also a system of . . . differences, differential positions, i.e., by everything which distinguishes from what it is not and especially from everything it is opposed to; social identity is defined and asserted through difference. (1984, 170–72)

Having been normalized to an unequal set of conditions, one may actually feel more comfortable with inequality than with equality. Going against one's habitus is like swimming upstream. The speaker of an illegitimate language might comply with language inequalities simply because one can't imagine any other way.

Further, the "structuring" of the habitus can lead people to judge themselves and others according to an unfair standard (which they don't recognize as unfair). Bourdieu writes, "The 'choices' of the habitus . . . are accomplished without consciousness or constraint, by virtue of the dispositions which, although they are unquestionably the product of social determinisms, are also constituted outside the spheres of consciousness and constraint" (Bourdieu 1991, 51). He cites William Labov's research with the working-class *r* in the New York City metro area. When listening to recordings of speech, even poorer people discriminated against their own *r*. They identified the upper-class *r* as "correct" (52). They still regularly use the working-class *r*, and maybe they prefer the company of other people who also use the working-class *r* and even ridicule the upper-class *r* when not in earshot of elite speakers. But because of their habitus-formed "tastes" in language, Bourdieu writes, working-class speakers are willing to accept their lower class position; they don't deserve to be equal.[3]

Bourdieu's "market pressures" are composed of a number of factors that intimidate individuals into complying with the legitimate language and condoning the delegitimation of all other codes. Inaccurate "commonsense" ideas about language combined with the pull of the habitus result in something similar to Gramsci's cultural hegemony, in which the dominated take on the perspective of the dominant and help maintain the status quo, even to the point of judging their own speech and that of their peers to be "low class," as Labov demonstrated in his experiments with the working-class *r*. Finally, even if individuals don't take on the perspective of the dominant regarding language, the worth of an utterance in what Bourdieu calls the market is a great factor in determining when and where it will be spoken. When speakers restrict a code to Scott's private transcript—not quite voluntarily but because they recognize its sociolinguistic worth—they reinforce its position as an illegitimate language. The market value of languages, dialects, and other linguistic markers is determined by the sociopolitical status of the speakers—that is, the market value of the speakers. If the code represents an unprivileged group, the code will not win any privileges in the language market. According to Bourdieu's market theory, then, Cajun ways of speaking will have the same status and reputation as Cajuns.

## THE MARKET VALUE OF CAJUNS

Since the language's status is intertwined with the status of the speakers (due to the codification process during nation building, which privileged the linguistic codes of the dominant over the codes of the dominated and colonized), it's helpful to understand the sociopolitical situation of Cajuns. Cajuns' postcolonial status as an internally colonized group, which I described earlier, is compounded by the postcolonial relationship between the state of Louisiana and the rest of the United States. Two hundred years after achieving statehood in 1812, Louisiana still operates a lot like a colony. Louisiana supplies 80 percent of US offshore oil (and offshore oil accounts for one-third of all national oil), ranking first among states in crude oil production and second in natural gas (Sasser 2010). Louisiana's gross state product for 2010 was $218.9 billion, twenty-fourth in the nation, according to usgovernment revenue.com ("Comparison of State and Local Government Revenue" 2010), yet Louisiana has the seventh-highest poverty rate in the United States ("Poverty on the Rise in Louisiana" 2011). Like a colony rich with resources and cheap labor, we mine and send the raw materials to the empire, which sells it back to us at an inflated cost. Unlike every other oil-producing state, which takes a 50 percent share of the revenues, Louisiana gets 0 percent. State representative Mary Landrieu successfully lobbied in 2006 to divert 37.5 percent of the royalties from the federal treasury to the Louisiana state treasury, but it finally takes effect only in 2017 (and it is still being contested by representatives from other states—particularly Arizona, which takes 50 percent of revenues from its gas and oil production as well as 40 percent of revenues from land-based oil exploration set aside for western states' water projects). Meanwhile, offshore laborers—often locals—are underpaid, overworked (sometimes without sleep for days), and aggressively prohibited from collective bargaining.[4] And locals living in the "Cancer Alley" or "Allée du Cancer," the area along the Mississippi between Baton Rouge and New Orleans with more than 150 industrial facilities, have one of the highest rates of cancer in the United States (Cart 2013).

In addition to the cheap labor and commodities we supply, Louisiana's land is exploited. South Louisiana is recognized as the fastest eroding ecosystem in the world, according to Mike Tidwell (2004) in *Bayou Farewell: The Rich Life and Tragic Death of Louisiana's Cajun Coast*. The coastal delta is disappearing for the sake of Big Oil profits as the silt deposits in the lower Mississippi are regularly dredged out into the Gulf to accommodate commercial transport, and canals are forged in the wetlands for transport to the Gulf oilrigs. According to Landrieu,

"Every 30 seconds we lose a football field of land; we are in a desperate race against time to save our coast" (quoted in Alpert 2011). And as the delta disappears, so does Louisiana's shield from major hurricanes. Tidwell warned economic planners in 2004 that the loss of these lands would exponentially multiply any weather or industrial catastrophes, and his predictions proved devastatingly true. Today, Louisiana is still staggering from the 2005 ravages of Katrina (combined with the Army Corps of Engineers' neglected and failed levees), which resulted in 1,836 deaths and an estimated $108 billion in total damages (Knabb, Rhome, and Brown 2006), and the 2010 BP oil spill, which federal officials estimate at 200 million gallons and whose impact on the fishing industry and local ecosystems is yet to be determined (Vergano, Jervis, and Weise 2011). Early evidence of mutations in Gulf harvests, which supply more than 40 percent of the continental United States' consumption, includes "shrimp with tumors on their heads; fish that lack eyes or are missing flaps over their gills; fish with oozing sores; crabs with holes in their shells; crabs that are missing claws and spikes, or are encased in soft shells instead of hard ones," as well as second-generation shrimp with no eyes ("BP Oil Spill" 2012). Scientists attribute these abnormalities to exposure to oil as well as the 2 million gallons of chemical dispersants used by BP. These chemicals were known in advance to have "mutagenic" properties but were used in spite of local Louisiana lobbying efforts to use straw, an eco-friendly alternative that would float on the surface of the water, where it could be harvested after being saturated with oil, as opposed to the chemical dispersants, which bind oil in great bubbles that sink to the bottom of the Gulf (and can later be "popped" by bottom-dwelling fish and oil pipeline workers). The Katrina and BP catastrophes were awful enough on their own, but federal neglect has been impressive. Louisiana has received just enough aid to get corporations back on their feet and mining the raw materials again—the inhabitants and their livelihoods, not so much.

An interesting aside—this corporate exploitation goes back to Henry Ford, who weaseled countless cypress trees from the inhabitants of SouLa for the dashboards and paneling of his cars for free, according to an exhibit at Vermilionville (a historically precise re-creation of a Cajun village, like Virginia's Williamsburg) on Louisiana's moss harvesting. Ford purchased moss from the bayous for the stuffing in the seat cushions of his cars. Back then, moss was more than abundant, and Cajuns often made a living by harvesting, drying, and selling it. At the time, Cajuns weren't aware of what a commodity cypress wood was. In fact, Cajuns often built their homes out of cypress, a close relative of redwood that can withstand extreme weather conditions (including underwater submersion), but they tried to disguise it as pine, like their neighbors to the west and the north. Ford stipulated that Cajuns were to send the moss to him in boxes built of cypress, yay long by yay wide. Cajuns were happy to oblige, especially since Ford was only asking for that cheap, common wood. Which he then had sanded and converted into luxury paneling for his cars.

Another chief export from Louisiana that profits big business but not Cajuns is "Cajunness." Cajun branding has taken off since the oil bust of 1984, when the state of Louisiana, finding it necessary to diversify its revenue, decided to sell Cajunness as part of its tourism industry. The very same year as the oil bust, the Louisiana Chamber of Commerce pushed for the creation of the Bayou Vermilion District to clean up the Vermilion River in Lafayette and to head the tourist center Vermilionville. The chamber of commerce created a taxing district to finance the center, and voters approved it in 1985. Since then, the Cajun brand has helped Cajuns to achieve a nationally recognized group identity, but it has relied on stereotypes and misunderstandings of actual Cajuns. As Barry Jean Ancelet, a local Cajun activist, put it when he was interviewed for a *National Geographic* feature, "The good news is that Cajun is hot. The bad news is that Cajun is hot" (Smith 1990, 1). The four primary marketing terms—*Cajun, Creole, Louisiana*, and *New Orleans*—have since become so conflated with one another that tourists often travel to New Orleans, which is specifically not Cajun, to find Cajun food. In fact, when new acquaintances find out I'm Cajun or that I'm from Louisiana, they almost inevitably ask if I'm from New Orleans. As if everyone in Louisiana probably mashes into that one city. Besides confusion, the state's marketing plan has created an estimated $5.2 billion tourism/cultural industry and 87,000 jobs ("About Louisiana" 2012).

The state of Louisiana profits immensely from Cajuns in spite of historically treating them as an inconsequential, periphery group—a political dynamic that reemerged during the serial flooding of the Mississippi in the summer of 2011. Massive rains and snowmelts coming from northern Mississippi River states caused the river to rise to levels that endangered major cities downstream in Louisiana like Baton Rouge and New Orleans. The areas settled by Cajuns weren't endangered by the Mississippi but, to save the larger cities, the Army Corps of Engineers decided to open the gates of the Morganza Spillway (along the Atchafalaya Basin Bridge) and flood Cajun farming and residential areas to lower the river. In articles and blogs circulating around this time, Cajuns came under criticism for living knowingly in a floodplain, but what's interesting is that when

Cajuns settled that land 250 years ago, it was not a floodplain. Congress turned it into one with a 1928 decision to build the Morganza Spillway and several other structures to protect the more economically significant downstream cities from flooding.[5] Cajuns were notified that they now lived in a floodplain, and that they should move.

Problem was, first of all, I don't even know if any of them spoke English at the time and could understand what was going on. Second, at that time, Cajuns existed almost entirely outside the US capitalist economy. They used no money but relied instead on an intricate precapitalist system of communal shares. There were communal labor pools (for harvests and home projects) and food shares (like cow and pig slaughters) that rotated by family. Cajuns had very limited possibilities in 1928: either relocate to a safer location without the cash, labor training, or even language required for an entirely different kind of economy, where they were sure to encounter social and job discrimination; or remain with their families and take their chances with the physical consequences. Many of the Cajuns who chose to stay in spite of flooding risks would have lost not only family ties but an entire local economy (jobs, local food sources, and in a lot of cases free childcare from extended family) if they tried to relocate.

Lots of folks criticized them when the floodgates were opened—why don't those people move? It's their own fault if they get flooded. But how many rich folks are forced by national policy planning to choose between family/community cohesion and physical survival? Cajuns were disregarded in state and national decisions because they have been essentially an internally colonized group. As in the cases of other postcolonial populations, the center made policy decisions for and *to* Cajuns, regardless of their preferences or rights.

Now that Cajunness sells, it's worth the most in markets that have traditionally exploited other postcolonial groups for marketing—cuisine, for instance. Following the success of chef Paul Prudhomme, who made blackened redfish and popcorn crawfish famous at his New Orleans restaurant K-Paul's, and Tony Chachere, who created a popular Creole seasoning blend, there have been many spin-offs of Cajun restaurants and flavoring—for example, the Popeye's chain and the McDonald's spicy Cajun chicken sandwich (Bienvenu, Brasseaux, and Brasseaux 2005, 33–47).[6] Living away from Louisiana, I've taken a few gambles and tried my fair share of "Cajun" restaurants, which have turned out to be interesting (but not Cajun). Now that the Cajun label has market value, there are a great many things that are Cajun in name but unfortunately not in reality. At one establishment, my gumbo was red (gumbo is brown) with chunks of sliced lunchmeat and raw celery, and it liked to burn my tongue off (I think it was made of pure Tabasco—this is a common error in faux Cajun cooking). At another, my gumbo (which was sufficiently brown) tasted uncannily like French onion soup. There are "Cajun" restaurants all over the United States with items on their menus that pass for Cajun, like "crawfish macaroni and cheese," "Louisiana breakfast tacos," and "lamb sausage po-boys." These dishes sound tasty, but they are remarkably unrecognizable as Cajun food. And that's not even to mention those "Cajun" fast-food places in mall food courts with "bourbon chicken." (I gave one a shot; I laughed out loud when I found myself looking for where I had laid my chopsticks.) These restaurants profit from the Cajun label, which has high market value in terms of cuisine.

In addition to food, Cajunness can sell music, tourism, cars, and a little onscreen comic relief—things that consumers in the United States are very comfortable buying with postcolonial labels. Americans eat Mexican food, listen to jazz music, vacation in Hawaii, drive Jeep Cherokees, and laugh at the *Beverly Hillbillies*. (And these are only cultural exports, not actual labor exports like clothes made in Vietnam and coffee from Indonesia or—more locally—tomatoes picked by immigrant labor and coal mined by Appalachians.) Cajun boucheries and cuisine are frequently featured on travel and food channels, while Cajun music and dancing have become increasingly popular in *New York Times* articles. Even Porsche is cashing in with its latest SUV: the Macan, nicknamed "the Cajun." It's meant to be the little buddy of the larger Cayenne. In addition to the film industry's profit from postcolonial stereotypes of Cajuns that I mentioned earlier in this chapter, the producers of *Jersey Shore*, a reality series that raised concerns about the use of *guido* to refer to Italian Americans, are banking on the marketability of Cajuns. There will probably soon be discussions of the word *coonass*, a derogatory name for Cajuns, because the same producers recently issued a casting call in Louisiana to find the "loudest, proudest and want to party their asses off" Cajuns. From the Baton Rouge Craigslist posting:

> Callin' all Ragin' Cajuns!
> Doron Ofir Casting in association with 495 Productions is looking for 8 guys and gals who are keepin' it Southern, are the loudest, proudest and want to party their asses off on the sickest reality show during one big Crawfish peelin', Poboy eatin', Bourbon drinkin' Dixie lovin' Bayou summer
> If you call 'gators your neighbors, reckon Mardi Gras should be a national holiday, your daisy dukes fit just right and are ready to make your Maw Maw and Paw Paw proud, we are looking for you!

> Kegs, muddin' and cook-outs, can only mean one thing . . . it's summertime y'all!
> 
> Now casting the hottest and proudest Gulf-Coast Southerners who are at least 21 years old who can prove that the party down South will rise again . . . Screw sippin' champagne, let's make it a six pack summer!
> 
> Oh Lawdy, it's time to Party! Apply now: www.partydownsouth.com

Apart from terribly confusing Cajun, New Orleans, and southern cultures (crawfish, bourbon, and daisy dukes), the writers of this casting call demonstrate their awareness of what aspects of Cajunness sell. As in other markets in which Cajunness has high worth, the producers of *Party Down South* will capitalize on the postcolonial status of Cajuns. In this case, they will do so by selecting the individuals who most closely fit the best-selling stereotypes of Cajuns, which match the colonizer perspective Said (1978) describes—exotic, sexy, dimwitted, illiterate, infantile, and drunk.

And find those Cajuns they will because, since the beginning of the Cajun marketing industry, Cajuns have learned that a small investment of mimicking the culturally perceived Cajun identity can yield some returns. Bernard writes that Cajuns have been willing to put on a show, behaving like "court jesters," in situations where cultural differences can make money or win other forms of positive reinforcement, such as media attention and tourist visits (2003, 120). One researcher found similar results regarding Cajuns cashing in their language capital for various forms of social clout, including sex appeal: "Male college students have told me that they consciously exaggerate their accents when vacationing at resorts outside Acadiana, in order to attract the attention of non-Cajun women, who are allegedly fascinated by the Cajuns' unconventional style of speech" (quoted in Walton 2004, 107). If those male college students received anything like the attention that René's character on *True Blood* did, the exaggerated accent probably paid off.

When it comes to jobs, though, Cajunness can buy notoriety in only a few markets—as a chef, a musician, or maybe a character on *Party Down South*—but not a whole lot of the American dream. A number of local Cajun artists and musicians (like Louis Michot of the Lost Bayou Ramblers) have opted to speak Louisiana French almost exclusively at home, even though some of them actually learned it as adults. Like the market value of other postcolonial and marginalized brands, Cajunness can't buy upward mobility or a good-paying job unless the job specifically calls for Cajunness—and that's a very limited array, which is sadly often satisfied by non-Cajuns annoyingly imitating Cajuns. To be "competitive in today's job market," Cajuns often find that it's best to mimic mainstream America instead.

Sherri L. Condon and Pamela T. Pittman found something along these lines when they conducted a study of language attitudes about CE in "Language Attitudes in Acadiana" (1992). Their results confirm that Cajuns generally recognize the market value of CE and have adjusted to it in their habitus. Condon and Pittman list as their precedents Labov's study of working-class attitudes toward working-class speech and another study among French Canadians, who consistently rated English speakers as "better looking, taller, more intelligent, more dependable, more ambitious, and more respectable than the very same person speaking French" (56). Condon and Pittman asked 280 participants from eleven parishes in Louisiana to rate four different language samples according to knowledge, reliability, honesty, friendliness, attractiveness, and desirability as a friend. The four speaker samples were Standard English, Cajun French, Cajun Accented Standard English, and CE. Overwhelmingly, all participants (46 percent of whom identified as Cajun) judged "the Standard English speaker as Caucasian (88%), better educated, and in a higher economic bracket than the other three speakers" (60). The CE speaker was ranked the lowest in terms of education and socioeconomic status, even lower than the speaker of Cajun French: "62% of the informants ranked him as having an elementary education and 54% ranked him as lower-class" (60). Significantly, the fact that the CE speaker was ranked fairly high "in the areas of reliability, honesty, friendliness, and desirability as a friend" indicates that the survey respondents don't dislike speakers of CE; they just don't think they make much money (61).

One particular trend in the survey responses supports this interpretation: the twenty-one to thirty-nine age group rated the Standard English speaker far higher in the categories of honesty, friendliness, and desirability as a friend than any other age group did. In short, they would rather rub elbows with speakers of Standard English than speakers of CE. Condon and Pittman speculate, "One explanation for these facts might be the association of Standard English with upward mobility. 21–39 is the age group in which people are not only working, but working toward higher positions in their careers" (1992, 66). Because CE doesn't carry much cultural capital in language markets, Cajuns who strive for upward mobility must invest their time in ways of speaking that will yield a better return.

In my survey among teachers, I also asked about the stereotypes that accompany CE. My findings, twenty years later, were consistent with Condon and Pittman's conclusion about the connection between upward mobility and language decisions. Cajuns and non-Cajuns alike often expressed great appreciation for Cajun culture but responded that CE has little academic, financial, or career status associated with it. Respondents were asked to rate their agreement with the statement "The Cajun accent sounds backwards and illiterate," from "strongly agree" to "strongly disagree." Their responses varied, but in most of the additional comments explaining the stigma of CE, they acknowledged that CE has low status when it comes to education and business. Some admitted that they see some elements of CE as signs of illiteracy, as in this careful explanation:

> In the same way that AAE is often accused of sounding "backwards and illiterate," so is CE. I've grown up with SAE [Standard American English], and I'm a strong supporter of proper grammar and conjugation, so at times I feel myself resistant to CE constructions and conjugations, but just because a culture speaks a certain way doesn't make them stupid or illiterate.

And see this succinct assessment. After the respondent disagreed with the statement that the Cajun accent is backwards and illiterate, he or she wrote:

> But it does say "country" doesn't it?

One respondent added that the media reproduce stereotypes of Cajun illiteracy:

> The media has considerable influence on the way accents are perceived. For instance, the Disney Film *The Princess and the Frog* portrays those with Cajun accent as backwards and illiterate. However, this perception is not necessarily accurate, simply commonly reinforced.

Several respondents skirted the issue of prejudice by focusing on the cultural worth of CE:

> I enjoy regional dialects of all types and find them fascinating.
> The Cajun accent is part of what makes this area of Louisiana distinct and interesting.

Others emphasized that they don't think CE is a low-status variety of English, but they are keenly aware that others think so:

> I personally enjoy the local color aspects of it, but I do know that many people would consider it backwards and illiterate (and when used in certain contexts, it could actually create an impression of illiteracy for more than just the individual speaker).

Other respondents similarly made it a point to say that they found nothing wrong with the Cajun accent, but they acknowledge that others are prejudiced toward it, as these simple responses show:

> Maybe to the ignorant.
> I think this is the perception of many.
> How can an accent alone be backwards or illiterate? It seems that it would only be through mistaken association that this could occur.

Throughout the survey, none of the respondents—Cajun or non-Cajun—claimed that Cajun linguistic markers are helpful on the job market. Instead, consistent with Condon and Pittman's conclusion, CE is seen as a handicap at worst and a commonly misunderstood asset at best, neither of which is desirable in a job interview.

In my experience, Cajunness is perceived differently inside Louisiana and outside it, though both views are very much in keeping with Said's orientalism. Within Louisiana, it is a sign of illiteracy and maybe even laziness to both Cajuns and non-Cajuns. This became real to me once in Baton Rouge, which I like to call an outpost of Texas because it's populated with Texans who were transferred there to run oil corporations (whose labor is supplied by Louisiana locals). After living there nearly a decade, my brother Jade had picked up the southern drawl of Baton Rouge, so he generally passed as southern, one step up from being Cajun. We were chatting at the mechanic shop he managed one day when something came up about his being from Opelousas, and one of his regular customers, sitting in the waiting room, asked, "So you're Cajun?" "Yessir, born and raised," Jade replied and resumed whatever he was doing. I watched this guy tilt his head and stare at Jade for a minute, as if he were seeing Jade in a new light. Maybe the man was thinking kind thoughts, but I've been conditioned most of my life to assume he was judging my brother as somewhat less reliable and less intelligent than he had seemed five minutes earlier.

Living outside Louisiana in New York, though, I've been surprised by people's positive (-ish) responses. When they learn that I'm Cajun, they're delighted, even if they didn't previously know that Cajun was anything besides a type of food. They find my accent interesting and—that word again—exotic: "It sounds Jamaican or something!" Even though I consider my accent pretty mild, people sometimes interrupt me to talk about my accent instead of what I'm saying. In Louisiana, I had consciously acquired a southern accent when I was focusing on using helping verbs ("We're studying" versus "We studying") in high-stakes moments like teaching or presenting, because people from North Louisiana and Texas were the only people I knew who regularly used them. I quickly learned that people in the Northeast really look down on southerners, though, so for a while I consciously tried to revert back to my Cajun accent because I got a better reaction. But being exotic or magical is still being marginalized. Consistently, like people from other US subcultures, I've been pigeonholed into writing and talking about my ethnicity; in fact, my PhD dissertation prospectus was rejected for a year until I finally agreed to foreground Cajuns. I certainly don't mind talking about Louisiana, but I've wished I could write about "white" things like Emerson and argumentative essays too.

Along the same lines, racial interpretations of Cajuns seem to vary between how people in the SouLa area and people in the rest of the United States perceive Cajuns, and this has led to debates about Cajuns' racial identity. Outside of SouLa, there is a lot of honest confusion about what Cajuns are. Race is a touchy subject in the United States, so many people have turned to anonymous online discussions to figure out what color Cajuns are, with forum titles like

> What ethnicity are Cajuns?
> Is Cajun an ethnicity?
> Are Cajuns black? What race are they?
> Are Cajuns considered Hispanic?
> What race do u list louisanan creoles and cajuns?

One curious person seems to have been intrigued by the Cajun mystique in pop culture depictions:

> What are cajuns really like? Not personality just culture, looks, accent, etc.? I have seen them a little before, and silly as it sounds I would like to go to New Orleans to meet some Cajun men. I know they are French, a rare group of Indians and something else but that is it.

Another querent seems honestly confused, even as he or she actually interacts with Louisiana locals:

> Is Cajun a race? (light-skinned people from Louisiana)? I visited Louisiana, I met some native families here and they look like light-skinned African American without strong features . . . with long straight or curly dark black hair . . . are these people Cajun or of some other mixed decent?

Several other discussions were begun by people living in other states who had learned they had Cajun ancestors and wanted to know if that made them black or white. In response, lots of kind people from Louisiana patiently explained that Creoles are black—though sometimes light-skinned black—and Cajuns are white—even if some appear dark-skinned. Similarly, in recent canonical Cajun scholarship like that of Carl Brasseaux and Shane Bernard, Cajuns are portrayed as historically and exclusively white. According to Dubois and Melançon, "Creole African Americans without hesitation identify Cajuns as whites, while Cajuns identify Creole African Americans as blacks" (Dubois and

Melançon 2000, 194). Within SouLa, the official story is currently that Cajuns are a poor white or white ethnic community, but scratching at the surface of that story reveals a lot of layers. Part of the confusion about race and ethnicity in Louisiana is due to the tourist industry and state marketing that conflates Cajuns and Creoles, as Brasseaux and Bernard point out. But it's also because many SouLa locals truly were racially ambiguous—at least according to the Old South's standards—as recently as the beginning of the twentieth century.

Christophe Landry, a newer voice in Louisiana francophone studies, suggests that these contrasting interpretations are the results of a racial confusion that was imposed during assimilation, when people who formerly identified as a variety of categories now had to choose either black or white, even when the categories didn't quite fit (Landry forthcoming). Really, this process happened all throughout colonial America, when whiteness was invented to undergird the slave economy, but much of SouLa integrated late in the game, so some of the older ways still hang around in cultural memory. In that vein, Landry argues that people who now fall under the categories of white Cajun, black Creole, and—lesser known—Creole of color were all simply "French" or "Creole" before their class, racial, and linguistic integration into the United States. He cites census reports that reveal a far greater degree of residential integration in what he calls the "Latin" parishes (parishes settled by French, Spanish, Creoles, Isleños, Haitians, and so on) than in the Anglo parishes (which were completely segregated geographically). In other words, Latin Louisiana has an almost entirely different (and mixed) racial history from Anglo Louisiana. Landry also supports his claim with research on food, music, and language (Landry 2011). He argues that these markers of cultural cohesion have evolved in the Latin parishes according to region rather than ethnicity, demonstrating a greater degree of mixing than is evident in the Anglo parishes. It wasn't until US assimilation that these parishes were racially reorganized into "white" Cajuns and "black" Creoles, with corresponding differences between Louisiana French and Louisiana Creole, Cajun cuisine and Creole cuisine, and Cajun music and Creole music. (Creoles of color, unfortunately, have had a hard time proving they exist since assimilation; they are often just lumped in with black Creoles or African Americans, with whom they may or may not identify.)

When I contacted Landry with a few questions, he mentioned the story of the musician Amédé Ardoin (1898–1942) as an example of the mixing in Louisiana's Latin parishes before US assimilation. Ardoin, now generally recognized as "black," played accordion with the famous "white" Cajun fiddler Dennis McGee; together, the two recorded the earliest tracks of Cajun music for Columbia Records. Their recordings sound far more similar to the typical two-steps and waltzes of the Cajun "chanky-chank" (a nickname for Cajun music imitating its rhythm) than the faster, blues-inflected Zydeco (a nickname for black Creole music, based on the West African pronunciation of the French word for green beans, *les aricots*). Ardoin was attacked and run over with a Model A car after one performance in which he purportedly used the handkerchief of a "white" Cajun woman to wipe the sweat from his brow (some claim the handkerchief story is a euphemism for a closer relationship). Details are sketchy, but reports say that Ardoin's attackers were from Alabama, where such mixing in music and society was punishable by death. For Landry, the story of Ardoin demonstrates Latin and American differences in attitudes on race before the French of Southwest Louisiana assimilated into the economy and language of the South, when they also took on dominant US ideas regarding race and separated themselves mostly into white Cajuns and black Creoles.

Interestingly, Bernard paints a picture of cultural mixing that is similar to Landry's claims about foods and cultures evolving together when he describes the famous SouLa gumbo: "Cajuns borrowed the word *gumbo* from a West African word meaning 'okra,' a vegetable introduced to South Louisiana by African slaves and regarded by many as an essential gumbo ingredient. Cajuns obtained filé (powdered leaves of the sassafras tree) from Native Americans, using it to thicken and season gumbo. They adopted red peppers such as cayenne, which gave gumbo its spicy flavor, from the Spanish. And the roux came from the [Acadians'] French heritage" (Bernard 2008, 46). Food fusions are also compatible with racial stratification, which is possibly one reason for the marked difference between the gumbo styles of New Orleans and the prairies of SouLa: in the former, hired or enslaved cooks may well have created the recipes, whereas Cajuns in the latter areas generally cooked their own meals. Yet, in my conversations with him, Bernard holds that Cajuns are and have always been white, with a little Mediterranean and Native American mixing that makes us darker. But still, that's not white—it's just not black.

Scholars in Cajun studies today may be labeling Cajuns white according to the outdated dominant US values regarding race, in which *white* means simply *nonblack*—the same well-known labeling that made Italian, Jewish, and Irish people white. These oversimplified contemporary racial categories are the unfortunate reality, especially in the Deep South, but they don't represent the complexity of Cajuns' and Creoles' preassimilation understanding of race, which was probably more similar to Spanish ideas of creolization. Racism between blacks and poor whites was encouraged and largely established in the South by the 1770s, but Cajuns and Creoles living outside the southern plantation and sharecropping economies wouldn't conform to these new definitions and prejudices, or even necessarily be aware of them, until they began assimilating late in the twentieth century. Even within the areas that were assimilated into the southern economy, there was a separate legal class in Louisiana until 1910 for people "of color," many of whom owned plantations with slaves. People living and operating within the dominant southern economy would recognize Cajuns as "mixed" or, as they were often called, "Acadian niggers." The racially ambiguous, nonwhite past of Cajuns shows up in literature as recently as Dorice Tentchoff's "Ethnic Survival under Anglo-American Hegemony: The Louisiana Cajuns" (Tentchoff 1980), in which she mentions Cajuns mixing with *les gens de couleur libres* (free people of color), Native Americans living in the area, and other surrounding groups (232). She writes that Louisiana Sabines (mixed Native Americans) describe the process of linguistic assimilation to English as "going white" (234–35), presumably because they began to call themselves white when they assimilated. Also, because people have only claimed the term *Cajun* one generation deep (it was an epithet until the 1970s), it's difficult to tell whether their families' former use of *Creole* referred to their country of origin, their class status, or their ethnicity.

But it's not just an issue of outsiders not understanding Cajuns' and Creoles' special heritage; it's tricky for people from SouLa too. Wayne Joseph, a Louisiana native who identified as black Creole, took a DNA test to find out just how many drops of black blood he had and was shocked by the results: none. Joseph had championed African American equality for his entire adult life, writing articles on black issues for magazines such as *Newsweek*, only to find at the age of fifty that he is 57 percent Indo-European, 39 percent Native American, 4 percent East Asian, and 0 percent African (Kaplan 2003). I'm a Louisiana native too, and I've been confused a few times myself, like the time a blue-eyed friend of mine from Opelousas told a joke about Big Bird being black. He saw my appalled look and defended his racial joke, saying, "You know I'm black, don't you?" I didn't. He was fair, with light brown hair and the same yellow undertone as my dad's side of the family that becomes more apparent in winter. Another time, during a discussion of Wayne Joseph's story, one of my students pointed out that she had a whiter nose than I do. She had freckles and an olive/yellow complexion like mine, but she said her family is black. One of her siblings, she said, was still too young to understand race but would one day pass as white.

Moments like these really show the limitations of the old southern standard. I grew up identifying as white Cajun until an aunt on my father's side made a comment about our family's "mixed" features—our hair, our lips, our noses, our hazel eyes. If we weren't white, as far as I knew at that time, we were black. "Are we black?" I asked, turning to my grandmother. "Papa always said we're *creole*," she replied, comfortable being neither black nor white. One of my cousins later traced my grandma's genealogy back to Spain; our ancestors had been exiled to the Canary Islands for a suspected coup in the 1800s, and the papers showed that there was no African mixing. "So we're white after all," my aunt concluded, even though our family is visibly dark-complexioned and almost indistinguishable from some families who identify as Creole of color. I came to understand being neither white nor black after moving away from SouLa and being politely called "ethnic." I am asked if I am Jewish, Latina, Indian, or Italian; I am asked if I speak English. My father and brothers are stopped at borders, assumed to be Mexican or Middle Eastern. When my friend Anne went to Congrès Mundial Acadien (an international annual convention for the Acadian diaspora that facilitates family reunions and features music and foods from other Acadian settlements), she was surprised to note that in contrast to other Acadians, "Cajuns are *dark*."

With increased exposure to areas outside SouLa, more Cajuns and Creoles who formerly identified as black or white are looking for another category. The crude black/white binary that was imposed for the purposes of slavery and then Jim Crow is and has always been overly simplistic. Though we were raised to see ourselves as white Cajuns or black Creoles, many of us in SouLa are finding that we have more in common with each other than with people outside the cultural region who identify as white or African American. Charlene Leger, for example writes in "'White' Doesn't Define Me. I'm Cajun" (2013) that, as she grew up, she was taught that she shared a cultural identity with white, southern women, not the black people next door whom she called "aunt" and "uncle." It was hard for her to identify as white when, as she writes, "I know that only a few hours drive north, east, or west, . . . I will find myself [as a Cajun] the ethnic minority." Like my student who hoped her brother would one day pass as white, it's not uncommon to hear about people seeking to gain more privilege by redefining their ethnicity. Curiously, though, many Cajuns who pass as white are beginning to call themselves "other" (different from passing as "black"), even though they don't stand to gain any social privileges. And, increasingly, Cajuns and Creoles of color are prepared to move past the South's old race standard and be recognized as one of the United States' nonwhite subcultures.

But that growing movement doesn't represent all Cajuns. As I stressed before, the Louisiana French experience varies by region and even by family. In some areas, Cajunness is dark. But in other areas, Cajunness is completely light-skinned—like a couple of my high school girlfriends who turned bright pink during PE. Cajuns aren't monolithically non-white but, in contrast to the assertions of the most recognized Cajun writers, they're also not monolithically white. The main thing is that Cajuns who identify as nonwhite should not automatically be relabeled Creoles if they don't identify as Creole, and vice versa. I like the way the 2010 US Census puts it: whiteness includes French Americans, but only the ones who identify as white—just like Hispanics who are nonwhite if they identify as nonwhite, and white if they identify as white. Since most people in SouLa can probably identify sixteen or more ways when it comes to country of origin or ethnicity, I prefer to honor how people self-identify culturally. The nice thing about the labels *Cajun* and *Creole*—terms that are ambiguous and arguably interchangeable because of their historical mixing—is that they both indicate ethnic fusion instead of purity.

The Louisiana French experience is also circumscribed by an intense racial stratification based on discrimination against African Americans that is still especially pronounced in the Deep South as well as many other parts of the United States. But even before the imposed southern racial standard, people in Louisiana have sought to improve their lot by distancing themselves from lower-classed group in various ways. Ever since the Acadians, from whom many Cajuns are descended, first arrived in Louisiana, the upwardly mobile among them have distinguished themselves from the rabble first by passing as elite French Creoles, then by passing as Anglos whenever possible, later by repackaging themselves as "genteel Acadians" like the characters in Henry Wadsworth Longfellow's (2004) *Evangeline*, and now by disowning Cajuns and Creoles of color who were once part of the same group. In every case, those striving for a higher class position self-removed from the rest of the community. It's possible that white-identified Cajuns are doing the same thing now by self-removing from their darker community members, who are now labeled Creoles.

In spite of this kind of whitewashing, Landry hopes to reclaim the term *Creole* for the whole community and its history, since Acadians/Cajuns are only a small part of the whole culture, but I'm cautious about portraying our past understandings of race as idyllic. Reclaiming the past *creolité* of Louisiana is still subscribing to racial hierarchies, so it's not enough to declare more racial castes without addressing the underlying racism. To be clear, in the history of Louisiana as a colony and state, there have always been "white" people and "black" people whose racial identities have not been contested. It's the third category, people of color, who have had difficulties rearranging themselves along the racial lines of the Deep South. Lobbying for a new (old) way of seeing Creoles may be a way for people of color to self-remove from being grouped with African Americans. After all, being "dark white," "of color," Creole, or "brown" is a level of privilege above African Americans in the Deep South. I continue to use the term *Cajun* because, whether Cajuns are white or nonwhite (or if Cajuns are even a cohesive group apart from Creoles and other groups), Cajuns do exist now as an ethnic group within Louisiana as a result of US assimilation, the 1970s Cajun Renaissance, the efforts of local historians, and the state's tourism marketing. Though many cultural insiders and outsiders recognize that Cajuns often have more in common with Creoles than with other white groups, the term *Cajun* isn't going away anytime soon, considering the community's past and the socioeconomy's present.

As economic repression intensifies in a worsening US economy, so does the tension between people who identify as white and people who identify as black, especially in poorer areas. Skin color in this socioeconomy is another version of cultural capital that is even more apparent and more cemented by birth than language capital. For the most part, in fact, it's the same local artists and musicians who are free about language identity who can also be free about racial identity, because they don't need the cultural capital required for typical US jobs. Upwardly mobile Cajuns in SouLa, however, have no interest in losing the status that being white—even "white ethnic"—affords them. Racial identification has a huge impact on socioeconomic opportunities and living conditions, so many Cajuns readily support local historians' efforts to clean up Cajuns' racially ambiguous past. They are upping their market worth in the US socioeconomy by choosing the best option in a predetermined racial identity hierarchy, just like when they try to clean up their accents. Though some Cajuns and Creoles may have been part of the same group at one time, *Cajun* now denotes whiteness within Louisiana, and Cajuns, even dark-skinned Cajuns, definitely benefit from white privilege. In this sense, Brasseaux and Bernard are right, but the complexity is always right beneath the surface, and there are too many instances of ambiguity for an easy racial demarcation. Cajuns are among the whitest groups in SouLa but, in the broader US context, apart from the black/white binary, Cajuns are a group of color. To indicate this kind of nuance, many white-identified Cajuns readily agree that they are "white but not white-white," meaning there is yet a higher level of white privilege they can't access.

Cajuns may be understood as racially flexible and linguistically interesting outside Louisiana, allowing them to have more freedom to express themselves culturally and linguistically while maintaining a high market worth, but most Cajuns are trying to get jobs within the state, so censoring is more of a compulsory thing. Because the market worth of Cajun ways of speaking corresponds to the market value of Cajunness, many upwardly mobile Cajuns—like the ones in Dubois and Horvath's study, Condon and Pittman's study, and my own study—choose to censor their CE (though not quite voluntarily, as Bourdieu would stress). Aware of the market pressures, individuals aim for the highest linguistic capital they can approximate, even if it means they give up their mother tongue and comply with the disappearance of their own language. Bourdieu writes, "[A] discourse can only exist . . . so long as it is not simply grammatically correct but also, and above all, socially acceptable, i.e. heard, believed, and therefore effective within a given state of relations of production and circulation" (Bourdieu 1991, 76). The "given state of relations" that Bourdieu discusses leaves Cajuns with a difficult linguistic choice. They can, on one hand, continue identifying linguistically with their family and community or, on the other hand, depart from their Cajun traditions and identify more with standardized English for academic success and upward mobility (or, as I argue later, just to avoid downward mobility).

Like the national and state decision to build the Morganza Spillway that forced Cajuns to choose between family cohesion and survival, the relationships between the US national economy and its internally colonized groups forces Cajuns, once again, to choose between family and survival—this time economic survival. This "given state of relations"—the decisions of colonial powers driving Cajuns apart from their families for the sake of survival—has been a recurring theme for Cajuns, as I discuss in the following chapters. Meanwhile, efforts to preserve Cajun languages have not been able to compete with the drive for national language standardization. Applying Bourdieu's theory, if Cajuns continue to self-censor, CE and Cajun French will continue to exist only in contexts that privilege and/or preserve cultural departures from the legitimate language, like museums, musical performances, and TV shows, but not in mainstream use. These acts of linguistic preservation are unfortunately a part of the process of language delegitimation because the languages no longer circulate in the market and change, as spoken languages do. Like car names and exotic foods, museums are places where the legacies of colonized, conquered, and extinct peoples wind up.

### CONCLUSION

I can't stand the reality TV shows *Cajun Justice* and *Cajun Pawn Stars*, which exploit the Cajun name and Cajun people.[7] And I want to hate *Swamp People*, a reality show on the History Channel, which begins with the announcement that this way of living goes back 300 years and some images may be disturbing. I want to hate it because it mostly portrays only the premodern things about Cajuns without representing the way most Cajuns live today. The show documents alligator hunters (some of whom are Cajun and some not), and it's completely complicit with the usual postcolonial stereotypes of Cajuns. The most unnerving thing is the subtitles, even when the people onscreen are speaking English. Like Kathy Sohn's reports of Appalachian reactions to a documentary of "hillbillies," subtitles raise questions about language ownership (Sohn 2011, 79). I also can't stand that the narrator sounds like he just time-traveled from his last gig on *The Dukes of Hazard*, talking about the "good old boys." But I can't help it; I love it, along with 5.5 million other viewers, apparently (Kepler 2011). My favorite is Troy, the one from Pierre Part with the thickest accent of all: "Choot it, Lizbet! Choot it!" Around my place, we call him Nonc Troy (Uncle Troy) because he feels like family. And the show has boosted the Louisiana economy; according to reporter Don Ames (2012), "The interest in swamp tours has increased, and the cost of alligator meat has gone up." *Swamp People* is especially popular among Cajuns, even the CODOFIL board: "After *Swamp People* premiered, the CODOFIL board decided not to take a position on the program. Although it may be argued that the show perpetuates the myth that Cajuns are a malevolent, 'swamp-dwelling' people, it is also apparent that the show did have some very endearing—and real—characters and beneficial aspects, not only to the culture as a whole, but for Louisiana's efforts to promote cultural tourism—one of the CODOFIL's stated missions as prescribed by the legislation that created the state agency in 1968" (Perrin 2012).

But everything comes with a price. Though the show will boost the Louisiana economy, it will also create a more pronounced othering of Cajuns as well as further delegitimate CE by connecting the code with a job (alligator hunting) that occupies a very low rung in the national economy. Within Bourdieu's model, upwardly mobile Cajuns, even the ones who enjoy the show and love the characters, will make an even stronger effort to disidentify linguistically with Nonc Troy.

# 2
## BAS CLASS
### Cajuns and the US Class System

*You know, I was raised in a community where we had black and white together at that time. It was bad to call a white person a Cajun, because if you wanted to fight with another boy, you'd just call him a Cajun. Cajun was a dirty word at one time in the South. That's why I admire them so much now because, the fact that, and even us, they came a long way from being a Cajun. Cajun was considered low class, dirty and that kind of stuff. And, you know, the same as black, Cajun was discriminated against, not like us, but, they was also discriminated against because they were, you know, they were Cajun.*
—Elderly Creole African American man, quoted in
Sylvie Dubois and Deborah Horvath, "Creoles and Cajuns"

*And so we see that the universal [writing] standard is actually set by quite a small group, and a familiar group it is, too: "men" living in "civilized nations" who cultivate the arts and who read science and philosophy. In other words, people just like the people who wrote these textbooks.*
—Sharon Crowley, *Composition in the University*

GrandmaMona calls it love at first sight. "It was just like lights going on," she says about the night they met. Her words crowd together happily when she talks about it. "We couldn't take our eyes off of each other. We were just so in love from the beginning." Mona Ardoin and Jeff Vizinat met on a blind date at the Silver Slipper right outside Eunice, Louisiana. It was "the place to be," according to my grandma. They were engaged and married in the summer of 1950, within the space of one month. Mona's German mother, Winifred—Winnie, as she was commonly called—had always wanted the best for her daughter, so she generously offered to pay for an annulment soon after the wedding.

My great-grandma Winnie had been born into the elite Wilferts, a German family that owned the first filling station in Eunice and half of the now-famous Liberty Theater, but she never recovered from the scandal of her parents' divorce when she was in her early teens. Her father was "running around," so her mother left him and moved to Monroe.

Back then, in the early 1920s, divorce was unheard of in Eunice, and the kids at school shunned her. Just a few years later, Winnie married a good-looking but poor Cajun man who worked at her father's filling station—maybe to get out of a "situation," speculates my grandmother. That good-looking Cajun was my great-grandfather Edovic Ardoin. The Wilfert side of Winnie's family didn't approve of the low marriage, and Winnie's own father—Papa Dutch, we called him—wouldn't even visit after the birth of Winnie's first child, my GrandmaMona. He was extremely wealthy as a result of his involvement with the flourishing oil industry and his stock ventures, but he refused to help Winnie and her family during the Depression. She worked long hours as a seamstress for wealthy families, sewing exquisite clothes for their children as her teeth fell out from malnutrition, nearly all of them before she reached the age of thirty.

Winnie had hoped her daughter would grow up to marry a wealthy German instead of making the same mistakes she made, but Winnie came home from a visit with her ill mother in North Louisiana to find Mona engaged to a Cajun man with no money and a car that wasn't paid for. "If I'da been here," she said, as GrandmaMona recalls, "you'd have never, never gotten engaged."

It was an unlikely match. For his part, Paw-Paw had three requirements for any woman he would consider marrying: she would speak French, she wouldn't smoke, and she would be at least five feet tall. Mona Ardoin met none of these requirements. She is 4 feet, 8 inches, monolingual in English, and she smoked in secret for the first five years of their marriage. She snuck her very last cigarette outside the back door of the hospital, reapplied her red lipstick, and returned to her bed just as the attendant came in to wheel her away for the caesarean section of her first child. Paw-Paw was cocky, she told me, but she was spunky, so when they got engaged he marched over to her uncle's jewelry store and took out credit to buy her the smallest thing that could pass for a diamond. "We never thought twice about the job, the money, where we were going to live, or anything like that," GrandmaMona told me. When Winnie, who had spent all her life trying to accumulate more money, offered to pay for the annulment so that her daughter could marry better, GrandmaMona says she felt shocked: "We were so happy, so in love. Why couldn't she see that? Love and happiness—you can't buy that."

Paw-Paw couldn't buy Granny Winnie's respect either. Until the day she died in 2001, she never approved of Paw-Paw, and everybody knew it. Granny would remind my grandmother that she should have married that nice German boy she had dated at one time. But GrandmaMona said there just wasn't the same spark; she couldn't resist the Cajun man from Pointe Bleu with black curls and blue eyes.

The funny thing is that my grandpa eventually became pretty successful as an insurance salesman. He earned an MBA at LSU in Baton Rouge, then settled down in a house with two bathrooms and two cars to park under the carport—all paid for. He won vacations all over the world for his wife and kids through his insurance company, added on a game room with a pool table and barstools (and a third bathroom), and set aside loads of money in various investments and accounts to take care of my grandmother and himself when they retired. None of it mattered to his mother-in-law because he was still a Cajun. "We were bas class," Paw-Paw explained to me not long before he died in 2010, "the lowest of the low. The worst thing you could be was a Cajun." We were sitting in the new chairs in his recently redecorated kitchen, and I remember how he touched my knees to stress how terrible it felt to grow up Cajun. His brother Lionel, nicknamed Taxi, agreed wholeheartedly. He rolled his eyes as he described the humiliation he felt as a teenager driving the family horse and buggy to town, automobiles whizzing by.

Cajuns, disdained and disregarded, operated almost entirely outside the US capitalist economy at the time of their forced educational and linguistic assimilation in the early 1900s, and even as late as 1950, when my grandparents were married. Carl Brasseaux writes that their socioeconomy at that point "resembled that of modern Third World countries lining the Caribbean rim" (Brasseaux 1987, 150). With no political clout or privilege, they were destined to be at the bottom of the US socioeconomic hierarchy when they assimilated. Likewise, going back to Bourdieu's model of the legitimate language, Cajuns were destined to speak an illegitimate language because of their socioeconomic standing. Bourdieu argues that low class position is the reason minorities always happen to speak "broken" languages or vernaculars instead of the legitimate language. Social prestige determines the authority or illegitimacy of various ways of speaking. This has been true in the cases of both Louisiana French and CE; neither language has been considered legitimate in academic settings—that is to say, the languages are not spoken or written in academic contexts. The declines of Louisiana French and CE are directly tied to their low status in linguistic exchanges of high socioeconomic value.

In the last chapter I explained Bourdieu's theory of language markets to demonstrate the current market value of Cajuns and, consequently, the market value of Cajun ways of speaking, which most Cajuns recognize and comply with by self-censoring Cajun linguistic markers. Put simply, the economy determines the status of language. Here, I delve a little more into the origins of language inequality in the United States by examining the economy planning and language planning of the founding fathers more than 200 years ago. Since, as Bourdieu repeatedly stresses, language legitimacy parallels class position, it's important to understand the historic relationship between Cajuns and the US socioeconomy, specifically Cajuns' resistance to participating in the capitalist model of the South. There are two parts to the Cajun story: their shared history with the rest of the Acadian diaspora and other pockets of former French colonials who experience similar discrimination for their localized Frenches, and their shared history with Creoles and other marginalized groups in Louisiana. First, though, let me nail down the legitimate language I'm discussing and how it came to be. This is difficult since the United States has no official language, just something that goes by various names, like "proper," "correct," "good," "standard," or "white" English.

### WHAT IS THE LEGITIMATE LANGUAGE IN THE UNITED STATES?

When I refer to the legitimate language, I'm talking about the language that's expected in gatekeeping moments like college entrance and exit exams as well as in job interviews and public-speaking events in which markers of race, class, or gender are not desirable. I'm talking about the language the guy sitting next to me in the café refers to when he says, with an eye toward composition teachers, "Students today can't write good English"—even after I've told him that I'm writing about the arbitrariness of our language standards, which serve to reinforce US inequalities. My father, an electrician who never went to college, recognizes the legitimate language when he points out spelling and grammar mistakes in his boss's memos and asks me, "How did this guy get to his position?" Language standards have relaxed in some ways, as professors like to point out in disgust when they receive student emails, but that doesn't mean there isn't a legitimate language.

Academic writers have taken to calling this language names like "Standard English," "Standard American English," "Standard Edited English," and "Standard Written English" to indicate that it is the version of English by which other Englishes are judged. These terms are more neutral than *correct* and *good*, which descend from a moralistic, prescriptivist view of grammar, but I find them still slightly misleading, skirting the political planning and implications behind language discrimination. "White English" is also inaccurate. Race is an enormous issue in how language is judged in the United States because African Americans experience prejudice in such an intense, ever-present way. But to boil down linguistic inequality to "African American English versus White English" is to leave a lot of people out of the conversation. Plus, if it were only an issue of race, Appalachian English would be recognized as legitimate for academic and professional exchanges, since it is spoken primarily by "whites." But, as Kathy Sohn writes in "Language Awareness in an Appalachian Composition Classroom," language prejudice permeates every interaction between the locals and "outsiders" (Sohn 2011). She quotes Michael Montgomery to illustrate the stigma of Appalachian English: "'[F]ive words out of somebody's mouth will completely affect another person's evaluation of their intelligence, their reliability, their truthfulness, and their ability to handle complex tasks'" (83). Boiling it down to the distinction between just black and white also ignores people of color, as Villanueva (1993) writes in *Bootstraps*. He is a "portorican" academic of color who often "passes" for white but, without the same access to cultural capital, has struggled to keep the same footing as cultural elites. Describing himself, Villanueva writes, "He sees himself as essentially of the same race as the majority, and knows that sometimes they do too, and he wonders how it is that what he hears and sees and feels and never seems able to escape is racism nevertheless" (xiii). Linguicism is an issue for many other nonblack groups, too, including Native Americans, Hawaiian Americans, Creoles, and of course Cajuns (who have been considered white ethnic or racially ambiguous).

Suresh Canagarajah avoids terms like *standard* and *correct* by putting language issues in postcolonial terms. He distinguishes between "center Englishes" and "periphery Englishes" to indicate, respectively, ownership and appropriation of language (Canagarajah 1999, 4). Though he is generally discussing world Englishes, I think this terminology is apt in US discussions, considering our history of internal colonization. But it still sort of glosses over the agency and planning behind our language situation. I've come to prefer Peter Elbow's nuancing of the word *standard*: "It might be nice to think of the word 'standard' as merely neutral—like the platinum rod locked away in a Paris safe that is the 'true standard' for what we call a meter . . . So I'm tempted to go along with a custom among many sophisticated scholars to completely avoid the word 'standard.' It's a word that does harm in our culture by silently implying that other varieties of English are inferior or bad or lacking—substandard or 'vulgar.' So I will often use the term '*standardized* English.' Yet I won't run away from the word 'standard' either because it's not the word that does harm; it's the cultural assumption" (Elbow 2012, 214). Elbow's use of *standardized* is helpful in that it stresses the agency involved in the standardizing process. Somebody at some point chose the standard, and then other somebodies updated it (in the process of what Bourdieu calls *dissimilation*). Like Elbow, I find the term *standardized English* most representative for this topic, and I also borrow from Bourdieu's vocabulary to discuss what I sometimes call *legitimate English.*

Each country has its own legitimate language, obviously, but the process of generating a legitimate language is the same in most countries. In the basic process, the people who just finished conquering the land (and conquering any indigenous people or other occupants on it) organize a political system with laws and institutions that help them and their families maintain control over the region. Language is often one of the things they institutionalize. So Bourdieu's view on the origins of the national or legitimate language goes back to the period of nation planning: "Thus, only when the making of the 'nation,' an entirely abstract group based on law, creates new usages and functions does it become indispensable to forge a *standard* language," he writes (Bourdieu 1991, 48). That's why the overarching idea of his analysis is that the legitimate language is tied to national planning of the class-system: "The official language is bound up with the state," he writes, "both in its genesis and in its social uses" (45). He stresses this point repeatedly because the legitimate language often goes under the radar when activists talk about inequalities that are programmed into the political system: "[O]ne must not forget the contribution which the political will to unification (also evident in other areas, such as law) makes to the *construction* of the language which linguists accept as a natural datum" (50). So the origin of the legitimate language (and correspondingly illegitimate dialects and vernaculars) is in the creation of the nation, and the explicit intent behind its codification is to keep power in the hands of the dominant.

Within Bourdieu's paradigm, there are two reasons that the establishment of a legitimate language is linked to the creation of the nation: first, it is the nation builders who explicitly *codify* the language. Codification doesn't necessarily mean inventing a new language. Generally, codification is simply a matter of selecting an already existing dialect (which may have had quite a bad reputation previously) and elevating it to the status of legitimacy. Benedict Anderson writes in *Imagined Communities* (Anderson 1991) that during the process of nation formation, nations prefer to imagine themselves as "antique." Selecting a language that already has a long history helps achieve the illusion of antiquity. For example, the architects of the English nation threw off the French they were required to speak under Norman rule and selected a lowly vernacular spoken by peasants and warriors: thus the political origins of modern English, which was promoted to the status of a language once it had political backing. As the saying goes, a language is a dialect with an army and a navy. The same process happened with Castilian Spanish in Spain, also during empire building, and Chinese during the Cultural Revolution (Elbow 2012, 183–85, 336–39, provides a narrative of these nationalist processes). Conversely, quoting linguist Tore Janson, Elbow points out that languages quickly diverge and evolve apart from empire and nationalism: "Where there is no political unity, the idea of a common standard for a written language is not very close at hand" (368). An important part of creating nationalism is creating a linguistic nationalism.

Something similar happened in the United States under Noah Webster, who strove to politically differentiate American English from British English. At the time, the founding fathers were finding many ways to define the United States apart from England, including driving on the right side of the road (Scotland similarly had plans to switch to driving on the right to declare its independence from Britain if the vote went through in 2014). Webster pursued linguistic independence from Britain by creating superficial differences and arguing that American English variances were superior. In fact, the story of the establishment of US linguistic nationalism is largely about the efforts of Noah Webster to flood language markets throughout the early United States with the dialect of English spoken by the inhabitants of New England. To understand how he accomplished this, though, it helps to understand the second part of Bourdieu's model of linguistic codification.

The second reason that codification is tied to nation building is that it is meant to reflect and reinforce the class system that is concurrently being established. According to Bourdieu, the nation builders create a class system that privileges and is based on the language (as well as the habits and tastes) of the people who will come to comprise the upper classes (themselves). Essentially, the victors wrote the history books, and then they went on to write the grammar books. Linguistic history and correctness are written in favor of the people with the most clout and privilege, both because they have the authority to stack the cards in their own favor and because they need to create a way to distinguish themselves from people with less privilege. As he recounts the standardization of English, Elbow stresses that the codification process deselected a lot of language choices that sounded natural or spoken for the sake of establishing or undergirding class differentiation: "Who *decided* to have a Standard English that made everyone's speech wrong? There was no *Academie Anglaise* in London in the late thirteenth and fourteenth century to make rules (though Norman French was not totally dead yet). We'll never know, but these historical linguists imply a process that's actually not so hard to imagine: the 'better sort of people'—when faced with a choice between forms—tend to opt for locutions that differ from the speech of the masses—even if it means they have to adjust their own speech habits a bit" (2012, 137). Making it difficult to speak and write high English also makes it difficult to achieve high status. In that vein, Elbow cites "the point made by Thorstein Veblen and Pierre Bourdieu: what is hard to learn and takes training to accomplish and causes much confusion turns out to be ideal for showing who has prestige and who can be looked down on" (274). Indeed, many of what are termed "errors" are usually expressions of what Bourdieu calls taste or distinction.

In *Distinction*, Bourdieu (1984) poses the idea that taste is a form of cultural capital into which people generally must be born. Taste, which is determined by one's class, determines choices in fashion, cuisine, residence, and career, and these things in turn identify and reify one's social class. He writes, "[Taste] functions as a sort of social orientation, a 'sense of one's place,' guiding the occupants of a given . . . social space toward the social positions adjusted to their properties, and toward the practices or goods which befit the occupants of that position" (466). Likewise, variances in language usage correspond to and sort people according to class. Popular linguist John McWhorter writes similarly that language errors are "arbitrary fashions of formal language that we must attend to just as we dress according to the random dictates of the fashions of our moment. Remember that what is considered 'proper' English varies with the times just as fashion does" (McWhorter 2008, 84). He cites turns of phrases considered egregious errors in the nineteenth century: *make a choice* instead of *choose*, *have a look* instead of *look*, *first two* instead of *two first*, *the house is being built* instead of *the house is building* (74–75). These "arbitrary fashions" seem trifling now, but they operate like other forms of cultural capital, which serve as powerful tools for social sorting.

Because of my theoretical framing, this book discusses capitalism a great deal. Economic theory is not the only way to understand the assimilation of Cajuns, but because Cajuns consistently understand and portray their own assimilation in classed and economic terms, I find Bourdieu's model useful. One important part of his analysis of the legitimate language relies on the Marxist understanding of class: people born into positions of privilege start out life with more *capital* (money that is invested, not saved or used to buy commodities) than everyone else, and therefore are capable of making greater profits and accumulating more wealth. Likewise, in his discussion of language as a form of symbolic capital, Bourdieu stresses the importance of which family and demographic one is born into, often distinguishing between the *bourgeoisie* (capitalists who are part of the ruling, or most influential, class), the *petit bourgeoisie* (members of the middle class, managers, intellectuals), and the *proletariat* (workers). The Marxist model has its limitations, but many aspects of it are still used in current economic theory, as recent increased attention to capitalism in the United States has shown. Though other systems of class hierarchy have been identified in different versions of capitalism throughout history, the idea of an economy that is built on and *reproduces* social stratification is an important part of Bourdieu's analysis of language within capitalism. One "inherits" the language capital of one's parents, so one will most likely wind up in the same part of the socioeconomic spectrum. As I show later in the chapter, Cajuns barely registered on the class charts because, apart from a few individuals who hired themselves out every now and then, they didn't participate in the capitalist economy established in the South. When they were forced to assimilate, it was at the level of manual labor, and the next generation would remain at the same socioeconomic level because they would inherit the language capital (and other forms of capital) of their parents. The Cajuns whom I have described as upwardly mobile are not exceptions to class reproduction; they must turn elsewhere to acquire the same degree of language capital that other people are born with, often taking on large school loans to pay for it.

Another feature of capitalism that Bourdieu emphasizes is that it is built on a model of *competition* instead of cooperation, pitting workers against one another (instead of, often, the capitalists who are exploiting them). He stresses that the system is designed to require a great number of average-income "losers" in order for there to be a small number of affluent "winners," which is represented by the polarization of the economy ("The rich get richer and the poor get poorer"). Consequently, because the model requires inequality from the very beginning, flunking out of school is not a sign of laziness or ineducability but a byproduct of the smoothly functioning economy that requires losses for the many in order to accrue profits for the few (the actual goal). Likewise, when capitalists "follow" the rules of capitalism, it isn't always a reflection on their character. This type of socioeconomy can extract and reward negative behavior, creating contradictions for some people between their personal ethics and "following" the rules. It's important to emphasize the way the values behind capitalism contrast with the values of the Cajun community (and those of many, many other people in the United States), which will become clearer when I explain later the socioeconomic arrangements of Cajuns. My brother, for example, turned down an offer to open his own tire and mechanic shop locally because the location would have been too near his current place of employment. He didn't want to "steal" customers from his boss, he explained, because he wouldn't want someone to do that to him. In turning down this offer, he was rejecting the most basic tenet of capitalism, competition (which might be said to be built on a philosophy of "Do unto others before they can do unto you"). Instead, he moved his family of eight to North Carolina to open a mechanic shop that wouldn't steal customers from his former boss's business in Louisiana (and that's a *huge* move for a Cajun, as I explain later in this chapter). This discrepancy is important to note because although Cajuns don't entirely support capitalism in practice, they generally buy into it in theory and votes (per Gramsci's cultural hegemony).[1]

Regarding codification of the national language, Bourdieu (1991) draws on Marx's explanation of the *nation*. In Marx's model, members of the *ruling class* form alliances with other members and use their extreme wealth and political clout to lobby for (bribe) and influence (manipulate) policies that the *state* (the centralized government) creates or adjusts in its interests.[2] The state, according to Marx's theory, generally serves the ruling class (not the workers), enforcing the ruling class's biddings on the workers with taxes, the military, and the police. US presidents aren't powerful on their own, just sort of like middle managers between the ruling class and the working class. The ruling class is not monolithic or unified, but its members are often allied. Their alliances and efforts result in arrangements on the national level (or in actually creating *nations*), so even though they aren't the visible royalty of the nation, they in effect rule it by buying their own politicians.[3] In the processes of actual nation building and language codification, according to Bourdieu, the same structure is created in matters of language: the "winners" (the most successful capitalists) select the national language (like the national economy) and create an educational system (a kind of state) to enforce and moderate their decisions.

*Planning the US Class System*

Language codification in the United States followed the same pattern of class hierarchy. Unlike other nations that declared official languages, though, the generally accepted story in the United States is something about a "laissez-faire" linguistic attitude (one that is guided by the "unseen hand of the market") that allowed the strongest language to emerge and beat out the others to control a monolingual market. John Trimbur debunks this myth and demonstrates that US language policy has followed Bourdieu's model, tying together nationalism and codification (Trimbur 2005). He rejects Shirley Brice Heath's claim that the founding fathers chose a wise, progressive linguistic policy of tolerance by never declaring an official language, setting "a historical precedent for bilingualism" in the United States (Trimbur 2005, 577). Trimbur argues that this quite common understanding of the United States' language history is inaccurate—the founding fathers were actually enforcing a specific linguistic hierarchy with the same policy of laissez-faire economics that they used to enforce racism and class structures: through markets and other economic pressures. Though they were presumably letting competition determine both the markets and language, Trimbur points out that they very much controlled the outcomes:

> [A] laissez-faire language policy, despite its ostensible neutrality, may be just as programmatic as overt forms of language policy. The suppression of African languages through the slave trade and the formation of a plantation labor force offers the most revealing evidence of how language policy operated covertly, yet systematically, in the colonial and national period. Slave traders routinely separated speakers of the same African languages as a means of social control, and plantation owners paid particular attention to purchasing slaves who spoke different African languages in order to restrict communication and the possibilities of insurrection. Under threat of harsh punishment, which included having their tongues cut out, slaves were prohibited from speaking their native languages or teaching them to their children. Instead, to manage work relations on the plantations, initially pidgins and eventually creolized versions of English were developed as linguistic innovations that, along with compulsory literacy laws that forbade teaching slaves to read and write, constituted the official and unofficial planning of the planter class. (Trimbur 2005, 576–77)

Trimbur concludes that the "very covert nature [of the founding fathers' laissez-faire language policies] virtually guaranteed the inevitable Anglification of language in the United States through the workings of labor relations, the market, and civil society" (577). The thirteen colonies had an established oligarchy, which controlled the wealth of the colonies and then the early republic; this group of elites was able to set its own language practices as the lingua franca of the dominant. The "unseen hand of the market" suppressed African languages and the literacy of African Americans, resulting in a very unequal opportunity to "compete" with the prevalence of English. That's not even to mention the Native Americans who were killed and geographically isolated from US discourse. Trimbur shows how this covert suppression of languages led to more overt suppression later—for instance, English-only policies in schools at the turn of the twentieth century and a ban on the German language (even in phone conversations) during World War I.

Language selection is just one way to differentiate and to consolidate already existing differences between classes. As a result of this early codification process, Bourdieu writes, the linguistic hierarchy always corresponds to the socioeconomic hierarchy engineered by the builders of the nation. If one is born into a class that is low in the socioeconomic hierarchy, one will likely speak a vernacular that is correspondingly low in the linguistic hierarchy. So, according to Bourdieu, in order to understand the origins of linguistic inequality, it's necessary to note the class system that the nation builders created and engineered into social institutions.

In that vein, then, the political beliefs of the builders of the US nation are as important as any language policies. As I mentioned earlier, the founding fathers' intention was not a democracy but essentially an oligarchy, a society with a few monied elites in power over a dependent mass, as the writings of the most influential nation builders reveal. Noam Chomsky (along with many historians) specifies that, contrary to the commonly accepted story, the leaders of the American Revolution and the following period of policy making were extremely exclusive and undemocratic: "Keep in mind, all of the Founding Fathers hated democracy—Thomas Jefferson was a partial exception, but only partial. For the most part, they hated democracy . . . The major framer of the Constitution, James Madison, emphasized very clearly in the debates at the Constitutional Convention in 1787 that the whole system must be designed, as he put it, 'to protect the minority of the opulent from the majority'—that's the primary purpose of the government, he said" (Chomsky 2003, 315). Elsewhere, Chomsky is more pointed about the founding fathers' exclusivity: "their sense of 'equal participants' included only a small part of the population: white male property-owners. Today we would call that a reversion to Nazism, and rightly so" (267). It's a shocking statement, but Chomsky is emphatically contesting the myth that the United States was built on democracy. Whether or not the founding fathers could rightly be called Nazis, they certainly weren't willing to share control of the new nation or its markets with all of their new fellow citizens (and none of the noncitizens—women, slaves, Native Americans).

Thomas Jefferson, for example, never intended equal opportunity for all. In the collection *Thomas Jefferson and the Education of a Citizen* (Gilreath 1999), Jefferson's vision for democracy emerges as something wonderful but intended for only a few—unfortunate, because his ideas are truly inspiring. In a 1786 letter to George Washington, Jefferson describes a large-scale, state-funded educational system that will teach people how to rule themselves: "It is an axiom in my mind that our liberty can never be safe but in the hands of the people themselves, and that too, of the people with a certain degree of instruction. This it is the business of the state to effect, and on a general plan" (119). In his famous pronouncement that he'd rather have a free press than a government, Jefferson stresses that provisions must be made to ensure everyone has access to newspapers and the ability to read them: "The basis of our government being the opinion of the people, the very first object should be to keep that right; and were it left to me to decide whether we should have a government without newspapers, or newspapers without a government, I should not hesitate a moment to prefer the latter. But I should mean that every man should receive those papers and be capable of reading them" (84–85). Anticipating resistance to the taxation required for a public school system, Jefferson argued in a 1786 letter to George Wythe that it was the cost of freedom: "Preach, my dear sir, a crusade against ignorance; establish and improve the law for educating the common people. Let our countrymen know that the people alone can protect us against these evils [kings, nobles, and priests], and that the tax which will be paid for this purpose is not more than the thousandth part of what will be paid to kings, priests and nobles who will rise up among us if we leave the people in ignorance" (54). Though he lobbied for mass public education, it was intended to preserve class distinctions. Jefferson believed in a "natural aristocracy," to which he belonged, and this aristocracy would identify and select certain promising young men to be trained for leadership positions while assigning everyone else to what we might call today the "vocational track" (86). Historian Richard Brown explains that schools would accomplish this social stratification via a tiered system: "Jefferson's plan aimed to unite mass popular education with the perpetuation of the elite, albeit enlightened, rule. 'The best geniuses will be raked from the rubbish annually,' Jefferson explained, thereby gaining for the state 'those talents which nature has sown as liberally among the poor as the rich, but which perish without use, if not sought for and cultivated'" (Brown 1999, 96). Jefferson's ideas were a form of social planning for the "creation of a progressive, enlightened, and virtuous society" (100). This society, however, was guaranteed to reproduce itself with very little opposition, as the elites were the ones who chose the next generation of elites.

Further, Jefferson's vision for public education would preserve a class hierarchy built on racism, sexism, and xenophobia: "Jefferson's educational hierarchy (and his lack of sustained attention to the marginal status of women, Native Americans, and African Americans) paralleled the existing social inequalities of his era" (Gilreath 1999, 133–34). In Jefferson's view, African Americans were only three-fifths human, Native Americans who failed to assimilate were to be exterminated (Grinde 1999, 195, 208), and "the notion of women, propertied or not, as political actors was almost unthinkable" (Brown 1999, 102). Jefferson never intended education to be the great equalizer of humanity, but instead to ensure general class immobility.

Similarly, Benjamin Franklin, who was extremely influential in the formation of many of our public institutions—including public sanitation, public libraries, and post offices—published several texts on the education of Americans in which he also assumes stiff US class stratifications. Curiously, the idea of social mobility is commonly linked to Benjamin Franklin. In fact, he is upheld (by himself and others) as the ultimate example of social mobility—a poor merchant's son who worked hard enough and sought sufficient education to pull himself up by the bootstraps to become a wealthy and influential statesman and inventor. He is said to have once remarked, in the spirit of the American dream, "I'm a strong believer in *luck*. I find the harder I work, the luckier I get." Franklin's (1993) *Autobiography* has set the tone for hundreds of biographies and inspiring stories of success—enough, in fact, to create a genre: the rags-to-riches narrative.

Franklin, however, intended social mobility—and with it the opportunity to become a cultural leader who shapes political and economic policy—to be available only to a very small demographic: white, propertied males with the potential for aristocracy. In his *Proposals relating to the Youth of Pensilvania*, Franklin (2015) talked about "the public" and "the People" but, as Gerald T. Burns writes, Franklin wasn't necessarily being democratic or inclusive: "the operative audience for his performances likely extended no further than the middle class" (Burns 1990, 107). Specifically, he writes, "The sons of Philadelphia's 'middling people' were to be enabled, through systematic study of their own language and other nontraditional subjects in that language, to progress from relatively 'lowly Beginnings' to 'great Things': positions of leadership, responsibility and power in their society" (117). Franklin excluded "foreigners," the lower classes, and women from the possibility of social mobility (116), greatly restricting the people available to socially mobilize. Like Jefferson, Franklin never intended social mobility to be available to all, just to the people most similar to himself.

Some of the founding fathers were very concerned with socially engineering the population via education in order to bring about the new nation according to their vision, and their writings concerning education were, like much of the writing during the period, very explicit about politics and class considerations. Their writings reveal that the early US founders envisioned and planned a stratified class system wherein the few elites would rule the popular masses. They ardently desired to see equality of opportunity, regardless of birth, for "everyone"—everyone, that is, who was male, white, English speaking, Anglo-Saxon, Protestant, property owning, and capable of imitating the habits of the ruling class. Education for everyone else, for whom social mobility was not an option, would be denied (until a newly trained industrial working class would be required around 1830). Like the "free market" on which our economy is purportedly based, public education was not designed to be a social leveler or "great equalizer" of humankind. Mass public education didn't become a reality until the beginning of the twentieth century, long after the founding fathers, but their plans for stratifying social class and language were built into the nation's institutions and laws. The result has been a rigid class system that favors people born into their demographic.

*Codifying the Legitimate Language*

Enter Webster and his quest to codify an American English. The legitimate language corresponds to and reifies the socioeconomic structure that the ruling class intends to implement and uphold. "[A]uthority comes to language from outside," Bourdieu writes. "Language at most *represents* this authority, manifests and symbolizes it" (Bourdieu 1991, 109). One language isn't inherently correct or right, but someone grants authority to that dialect to become a language—the "correct" language—and this authority derives from socioeconomic structures that are already (or newly put) in place. The language and grammar rules that are selected as "correct" are based on the language habits of the society's elite.

The legitimate language is given high status by those who possess high status. During the establishment phase of the legitimate language, the nation builders grant authority to some to codify the language. It is "[p]roduced by authors who have the authority to write, fixed and codified by grammarians and teachers who are also charged with the task of inculcating its mastery" (Bourdieu 1991, 45). Nationalists select the legitimate language and grant authority to certain authors, teachers, and grammarians deemed "expert." The chosen language can be identified in any formal codifications of language by these "experts." Bourdieu writes, "The dictionary is the exemplary result of this labour of codification and normalization" (48). Certain textbooks and grammar books as well are sanctioned codifications of the legitimate language.

Noah Webster's work is a profound example of Bourdieu's process of codification of the legitimate language. There are many salient moments in US history regarding the selection of the legitimate language, but I focus on what Bourdieu identifies as one of the most important parts of codification: the dictionary. In this vein, Noah Webster was one of the most important figures in the codification of US linguistic nationalism. Author of the first "American" dictionary and probably the most influential spelling book in the early United States, Webster was explicitly concerned with creating a national American character via language. Linguists Albert C. Baugh and Thomas Cable write in *History of the English Language* (Baugh and Cable 2007): "Webster was a patriot who carried his sentiment from questions of political and social organization over into matters of language. By stressing American usage and American pronunciation, by adopting a large number of distinctive spellings, and especially by introducing quotations from American authors alongside those from English literature, he contrived in large measure to justify the title of his work [*The American Dictionary*]. If, after a century and a half, some are inclined to doubt the existence of anything so distinctive as an American language, his efforts, nevertheless, have left a permanent mark on the language of this country" (348). Though Baugh and Cable debate the validity of Webster's title of "father of the American language" (how much did he have to invent, really?), Webster was truly instrumental in *selecting* the legitimate language of the United States and *codifying* it in textbooks and a national dictionary. Maybe Webster was the stepfather of the American language. His indefatigable efforts and considerable influence during the early years of the country were important in creating not an American language but an American linguistic nationalism.

In his publications on the American language, Webster's intention was closely linked to what Bourdieu calls "the making of the nation." A "national language," Webster wrote, "is a band of national union. Every engine should be employed to render the people of this country *national*; to call their attachments home to their own country; and to inspire them with the pride of national character" (quoted in Baugh and Cable 2007, 347). Indeed, Webster sought to create that nationalism. In the introduction to *The American Dictionary*, first published in 1828 and revised today as the *Merriam-Webster Dictionary*, Webster argued:

> It is not only important, but, in a degree, necessary that the people of this country, should have an *American Dictionary* of the English Language;

for, although the body of the language is the same as in England, and it is desirable to perpetuate that sameness, yet some differences must exist. Language is the expression of ideas; and if the people of our country cannot preserve an identity of ideas, they cannot retain an identity of language. Now an identity of ideas depends materially upon a sameness of things or objects with which the people of the two countries are conversant. But in no two portions of the earth, remote from each other, can such identity be found. Even physical objects must be different. But the principal difference between the people of this country and of all others, arises from different forms of government, different laws, institutions and customs . . . the institutions in this country which are new and peculiar, give rise to new terms, unknown to the people of England. (quoted in Baugh and Cable 2007, 348)

Webster was unambiguously concerned with forming a national identity and political system through language, and he was fine with making grand, sweeping assumptions. John Trimbur chuckles, "In a stroke of linguistic nationalism, Webster makes American English historically antecedent to British English. As Webster writes in his *Dissertations on the English Language*, published in 1789, there is a "surprising similarity between the idioms of the New England people and those of Chaucer, Shakespeare, &c. who wrote in the true English stile" (quoted in Baugh and Cable 2007, 582). Webster's appeal to the past is an example of the artificial antiquity Anderson (1991) notes as part of nation building.

This "new" national language would also help unify the nation. According to Harlow Giles Unger in *Noah Webster: The Life and Times of an American Patriot* (1998), Webster traveled through the states shortly after the American Revolution and resolved to codify a national language to unify the citizens: "Instead of the joyous celebrations he expected to hear among a newly independent people, he heard a dizzying cacophony of languages and accents—Dutch, French, German, Swedish, Gaelic, and varieties of English that the Connecticut Calvinist from Yale had never heard before: the muddy drawls of the rural South, the gargled grunts of Philadelphia Negroes; and the clipped utterances of militiamen from the northern reaches of New Hampshire . . . Only four years out of college and a mere twenty-four years of age, Noah Webster believed he could unite the American people by creating a new, common language, or as he called it, a 'federal language'" (Unger 1998, 44). Webster did this largely by creating differences between US English and British English. He once wrote that he hoped for "in a course of time, a language in North America, as different from the future language of England, as the Modern Dutch, Danish, and Swedish are from the German, or from one another" (quoted in Baugh and Cable 2007,

347). So, for example, Webster changed the English spellings of *musick* and *publick* to *music* and *public*, deleted the *u* from words such as *colour* and *glamour*, reversed the *-re* in *centre* and *theatre*, and dropped double consonants in words such as *traveller* and *waggon* (Unger 1998, 105). Further, he made distinctions between American and English usages in his lexicography (308). Webster also changed the way English was taught in classrooms across the country. Unger writes that he set about trying to remedy "the regional accents and speech patterns of the children" by changing textbook pronunciation guides (55). Webster published his first textbook, *A Grammatical Institute of the English Language*, as a three-volume set consisting of a speller (1783), a grammar (1784), and a reader (1785). In 1786, the speller was retitled *The American Spelling Book* and "made every previous speller obsolete and gained a virtual monopoly in American classrooms for more than a century" (54).

Though Webster strongly wanted to define the United States in opposition to Britain, he selected and promoted as the national American language a dialect of the Northeast that was strikingly similar to British English (I'm really understating it here), to the exclusion of the languages and dialects of a large portion of the rest of the US population. This legitimate language was based on what the early leaders of the United States spoke, ensuring that the US educational system would reward anyone who spoke similarly. Like his close friend Benjamin Franklin, Webster believed that the language of US universal education ought to be American English (and by *universal* they meant middle-class males of European decent), while Latin and Greek were reserved for the instruction of Jefferson's "geniuses," who were tracked into higher education and groomed for future leadership positions.

*Protecting the Legitimate Language*

By the beginning of Cajuns' mass forced assimilation in 1921, the legitimate language had hardly changed since the initial codification efforts of the founding fathers. According to Bourdieu's model, this longevity is due to several different undercurrents that protect the language's elite position: cultural distinction or recognition, schools' labors to preserve it, and deliberate continued dissimilation from popular language. Even today, US English is remarkably unchanged, as many composition writers point out. Trimbur writes that language policies in the United States are still based on ideas about language that were formed during nation building, particularly the "Anglo-American dyad Franklin and Webster installed in linguistic memory" (Trimbur 2005, 580). Within comp/

rhet, the legitimate language is sometimes discussed in terms of "academic discourse" or "academic writing," and it takes the shape of the different genres and conventions of different academic fields. The most high-stakes writing we teach is generally an academic essay that's geared toward helping students pass departmental requirements for literacy (before they can get to the classes specific to their majors), so a lot of the comp/rhet literature discusses academic essays.

Sharon Crowley succinctly defines this genre as one still based on the language of white, middle-class males. Describing the class-sorting function of the required freshman comp course in *Composition in the University: Historical and Polemical Essays* (Crowley 1998), she presents a critique of usage standards and correctness that ties into Bourdieu's theory of distinction. Apart from the explicit language plugging of Webster, it is a "pedagogy of taste" that maintains class inequalities built into the United States: "The pedagogy of taste, I would argue, is . . . a policing mechanism . . . Like all ideologies, the ideology of taste works to naturalize that which is culturally instituted" (42–43). Once the legitimate language is culturally ingrained and recognized, it is reified by what people think of as personal preference or good taste. Going a little further, Crowley identifies which groups typically have poor taste: "inevitably non-Anglo or non-European" (40). They are working-class and minority peoples, a dynamic Bourdieu attributes to the codification process during nation building. The upper classes of a brand-new nation deem their own speaking and writing habits "correct" or "legitimate," and their language will be taught in schools, awarded high marks, and preferred in business relations. An ingrained sense of taste or recognition of the legitimate language, consequently, is one reason for its staying power.

The efficacy of culturally ingrained distinctions or the "pedagogy of taste" is evident in the composition course's strong ties to early US nationalism. Discussions of good English and good studentship often refer back to the founding fathers. In fact, literacy in standardized English is often conflated with upright citizenship. Lynn Z. Bloom (1996) writes in "Freshman Composition as a Middle-Class Enterprise" that freshman comp is the one required course because of its nationalist function: it teaches middle-class morality, national character, and the habits of good citizenship—aspects of internalized cultural distinction. Unlike freshman courses in other disciplines, which teach measurable skills or a certain body of knowledge, the composition course doesn't introduce the discipline of English. Instead it inculcates in students middle-class, "Franklinesque virtues" (658). Bloom defines these virtues as self-reliance/responsibility, respectability, decorum/propriety, moderation and temperance, thrift, efficiency, order, cleanliness, punctuality, delayed gratification, and critical thinking; she explains the connections between classroom interpretations of each of the virtues and US nationalism. These values, Bloom points out, are central to capitalism and Anglo culture, meaning they privilege already dominant groups in the United States. This makes sense, Crowley (1998) adds as she explains the pedagogy of taste, since only white, middle-class males were allowed in US colleges for 200 years.

It may make sense, but that doesn't mean it's fair. Higher education is open to women and people of color now, but language requirements still put them at a disadvantage. Feminist writers such as Hélène Cixous (1986) and Lynn Worsham (1991) suggest that the linear structure of academic writing is essentially a male, hierarchal mode of "making a point" as opposed to lateral communication. In *écriture féminine*, or feminine writing, an essay does not always need to prove or conclude something, they argue; it can simply be part of a dialogue. Contesting other aspects of academic writing, composition scholars such as Sondra Perl (forthcoming) and Marianna Torgovnick (2001) propose that first-person creative nonfiction can be a more effective rhetorical approach than the traditional, "neutral observer" persona of academic writing without compromising rigor. They argue that creative nonfiction is more engaging; it creates empathy in the reader, an important element for argument; and, more important, it is more honest in that it admits biases without claiming the impossible human condition of "scientific objectivity."

Academic writing is exclusive in other ways too. In *ALTDis: Alternative Discourses and the Academy*, a collection of authors write about "alternative discourses"—vernaculars, slangs, languages, rhetorics, hybrids, and even texting conventions—that are often perfectly effective yet not legitimate means of communication in academic writing. The editors Christopher Schroeder, Helen Fox, and Patricia Bizzell critique assimilationist pedagogies and policies that require students born into unprivileged demographics to conform to the language habits of privileged demographics. They point out, "The label *alternative* is helpful because it gets at what is perhaps the key feature of the discourses we are discussing, namely that they do not follow all the conventions of traditional academic discourse and may therefore provoke disapproval in some academic readers" (2002, ix). These other writing styles are not wrong, just not privileged. So, even though more diverse populations of students are in college now, there's still a major force working against their success—the fact that they must learn how to write like white, middle-class males from 200 years ago. And because freshman composition is a prerequisite for pretty much every major, there's still not equal access to higher education and higher-income jobs.

The similarity between today's inequalities and the ones established way back then is also due to huge educational efforts to preserve the legitimate language, to keep it from diverging. Bourdieu maintains, like other linguists, that language change is normal—so normal that when languages don't change very much, one must wonder why. As Peter Elbow writes, language divergence is the rule, not the exception: "A single standard for language that differs from spoken dialects is not built into the universe or the nature of language; it's something that has *sometimes* emerged. In cycles. Usually it's been imposed" (Elbow 2012, 364). According to Bourdieu, schools are designed to preserve the legitimate language: "[T]he educational system . . ., charged with the task of sanctioning heretical products in the name of grammar and inculcating the specific norms which block the effects of the laws of evolution, contributes significantly to constituting the dominated uses of language as such by consecrating the dominant use as the only legitimate one, by the mere fact of inculcating it" (Bourdieu 1991, 59–60). Again, he writes, "The legitimate language owes its (relative) constancy in time (as in space) to the fact that it is continuously protected by a prolonged labour of inculcation against the inclination towards the economy of effort and tension which leads, for example, to analogical simplification (e.g. of irregular verbs in French)" (61). Discussions of language purity or crumbling national standards are usually signals of this kind of protection mentality, almost as if language standards were an issue of national defense (and they were treated as such during the Cold War).

Catherine Prendergast (2009) writes in "The Fighting Style: Reading the Unabomber's Strunk and White" that there has been a strong current in writing instruction supporting nationalism, founding fathers–type virtues, and linguistic purity, as she shows in the long-standing popularity of Strunk and White's *The Elements of Style*, whose fifty-year anniversary was celebrated in 2009. William Strunk Jr. revised E. B. White's 1918 guide to style in 1959 to create what is commonly referred to as "Strunk and White," a guide to concise, "correct" writing. Describing a link between linguistic and national purism, Prendergast points out that White's metaphors regarding language relativism are violent, militant ("commands . . . [to his] platoon" [Strunk quoted in Prendergast 2009, 13]), and primitivist ("a gunner . . . roaming the countryside" in contrast to poor writers who drive cars with "automatic transitions" [16]), as he criticizes language changes that are immoral ("permissive" [17]), miscegenated ("crossbreeding" [13]), and signs that modern civilization has lost its way. His language attitudes were consistent with his personal attitudes toward the new, more diverse populations of students entering colleges after World War II and relativist grammarians who condoned their language impurities. White wrote and revised the guide in a tiny cabin in Maine (consciously imitating Thoreau) after fleeing his "materialistic," privileged life in New York (he owned 117 chairs between his country and city houses). Alarmingly, one of Strunk and White's greatest enthusiasts is the infamous Unabomber, Theodore Kaczynski, who also wrote from a tiny cabin in the woods (imitating Thoreau), arguing for a return to linguistic and national purity. Kaczynski's extreme language purism and strict adherence to Strunk and White ultimately identified him as the author of the Unabomber letters, which Prendergast describes as "the stylistic equivalent of a police sketch" (he still compulsively edits police reports about himself and letters he receives in prison) (17). The Unabomber is an extreme example of national and linguistic purism, and Prendergast acknowledges that Strunk and White is not popular in comp/rhet, but she urges compositionists to avoid the still-pervasive platitudes about language change as signs of immorality, impurity, impending doom, or anything else to fight about.

Overall, languages do still naturally evolve over time in spite of efforts to preserve them, not because of top-down edicts but because of usage trends and the tendency toward efficiency and democratization. When these changes make the legitimate language too easy to acquire, it's time for what Bourdieu calls linguistic *dissimilation*. So the third reason the legitimate language still mirrors the class inequalities from the nation's founding is something Bourdieu refers to simply as "strategies of assimilation and dissimilation" (1991, 64). When capitalism, which requires differentiation between the working class and the ruling class, is threatened by an *assimilating*, or rising, working class, the major players in capitalism find it necessary to create new ways to *dissimilate* from the working class. Since, as Bourdieu reminds, this "competitive struggle" requires losers in order for there to be winners, the winners (or people who hope to be winners) need to design new ways for people to "lose." One of the most powerful ways to maintain class inequalities (disparity) is through language inequality, so people in dominant positions in society constantly redefine the legitimate language to make it accessible to only the few.

It's hard to point out exactly who are the people in dominant positions because part of our US linguistic history (written by the victors, of course) is that everyone is equal and there is no ruling class. J. Elspeth Stuckey responds to this misperception in her self-explanatorily titled book *The Violence of Literacy* (Stuckey 1991) that the United States is extremely classed, in spite of a "mythology" to the contrary, and that these class distinctions serve the current economy: "Literacy itself can be understood only in its social and political context, and that context, once the mythology [of classlessness in the United States] has been stripped away, can be seen as one of entrenched class structure in which those who have power have a vested interest in keeping it" (vii). She argues that literacy is an artificial measure that both explains and reifies the status of criminals and the poor as well as that of the dominant and affluent. National literacy (or the legitimate language) is defined according to the literacy habits of those in power so that their demographic continues to be privileged, and everyone else continues to be poor and criminalized. "This is not pessimism," she maintains. "It is system" (126). Crowley, who tends to say it like it is, writes, "Along with J. Elspeth Stuckey, I think that it is absurd and cruel to conflate economic inequality and racial discrimination with a literacy problem" (1998, 234). The freshman composition course exists to measure, sort, and deny most people access to the limited number of higher-paying jobs according to the standards of error and literacy derived from the legitimate language and intended to maintain inequality. She historicizes and contextualizes the function of composition courses as conservative (in the sense that they conserve the unequal status quo from nation building), as opposed to the progressive promises they offer of social mobility via literacy. Crowley writes pointedly, "The myth of the academic essay continues to nurture massive Freshman English programs for reasons other than its salience to writing instruction: it fosters and supports the persistent American belief that universal standards of literacy exist, and it legitimizes and covers over the social and institutional functions of Freshman English" (233).

Elbow similarly suggests that the failed promise of social mobility through literacy is not an unfortunate turn of events but is built into the design of literacy standards: "[O]ur culture of literacy functions as though it were a plot against the spoken voice, the human body, vernacular language, and those without privilege. That is, our pervasive cultural assumptions about speech, writing, and literacy—especially as they are communicated through schooling—seem as though they were designed to make it harder than necessary for people to become comfortably and powerfully literate" (Elbow 2012, 7). Like Stuckey, Elbow argues that this lack of accessibility is based on class inequalities: "Writing takes much more conscious learning than speaking, so the ability to write has been available mostly to people with more advantage, leisure, and better schools. But this 'difficulty' of writing is largely a cultural artifact" (27).

He specifies that it's the unequal standards of literacy (not the mere acquisition of literacy) that block people from democratic participation in literacy-based dialogues.

Dissimilation in the legitimate language means that language errors aren't inherent, just constructs of economic disparities. Mina Shaughnessy famously argues something similar in *Errors and Expectations: A Guide for the Teacher of Basic Writing* (Shaughnessy 1977). Faced with understanding and responding to the writing of nontraditional populations of students as a result of open admissions in CUNY (beginning in 1970), she points out that "most college teachers have little tolerance for the kinds of errors BW [basic writing] students make," interpreting them as "indicators of ineducability" (8). Shaughnessy, however, argues that error is not a signal of low student intelligence but simply a variant of elite "refinements of usage." She writes that teachers should strive to find "the intelligence of their [BW students'] mistakes" and help them develop the writing habits of the more privileged students (9).

In the tradition of Shaughnessy, Mike Rose also seeks to redefine error, arguing that it is a societal problem, not the result of individual student failure or inadequacy. He demonstrates in "The Language of Exclusion: Writing Instruction at the University" (Rose 2008) that error is a changing construction by citing vastly different standards of literacy: "During the last century this country's Census Bureau defined as literate anyone who could write his or her name. These days the government requires that one be able to read and write at a sixth-grade level to be *functionally* literate: that is, to be able to meet—to a minimal degree—society's reading and writing demands" (23). Rose criticizes the model of student error that portrays BW students as cognitively deficient, particularly with words like *remediation, deficits,* and *handicaps*. Rose also argues that these current conceptions of error serve as gatekeepers that parallel social privilege within the United States, a form of institutionalized inequality (26). Low test scores typically spark declarations of national literacy crises, lamentations about student laziness and ability, and accusations about teacher performance. Rose argues that error functions as more of a social marker than an impediment to communication in *Lives on the Boundary*, pointing out that the etymological origin of *grammar* is the same as the root for *glamour*. He criticizes "democratic" attempts to teach all children the "canon," arguing that these calls for higher literacy are actually the same old elitist story (1987, 234). As Rose points out, error and literacy crises are both social constructs.

Language theorists argue that definitions of error and literacy should indeed be constantly changing, but they should derive from the context, not a universally established standard. Sylvia Scribner (1984) argues in "Literacy in Three Metaphors" that there can be no literacy measure to cover all human beings because everybody needs different levels of literacy for different purposes: "[T]he single most compelling fact about literacy is that it is a *social* achievement . . . Since social literacy practices vary in time . . . and space . . ., what qualifies as individual literacy varies with them. At one time, ability to write one's name was a hallmark of literacy; today in some parts of the world, the ability to memorize a sacred text remains the model literacy act. Literacy has neither a static nor a universal essence" (72). With a contextual definition of literacy, error takes on new meaning. Canagarajah (2010) seems to suggest in "Toward a Rhetoric of Translingual Writing" that error can be defined simply as the failure of speakers to negotiate meaning patiently and successfully: "[I]t is not uniformity of meaning but the capacity and willingness to keep negotiating for meanings that interlocutors strive for in translingual orientation" (23). He cites Alan Firth's "let it pass" principle, in which multilinguals look for clues to explain misunderstandings or ask clarifying questions (14). In a paradigm built on contextual understanding of literacy and error, literacy crises would signal the need to redefine literacy instead of the need to toughen up on standards and teaching practices. Sociolinguist William Labov wrote in a report on variants of African American speech that high rates of error or illiteracy should be indicators of language shifts and the consequent need to revise definitions of error: "It is traditional to explain a child's failure in school by his inadequacy. But when failure reaches such massive proportions, it seems to us necessary to look at the social and cultural obstacles to learning, and the inability of the school to adjust to the social situation" (Labov 1972, 208). These failures are actually engineered filters for class mobility via literacy standards.

Consequently, when the language evolves and it still doesn't really favor minority speakers, this is just part of the same old system. Bourdieu calls these modifications to the legitimate language (and simultaneous updates to the class hierarchy) "distinctive deviations" in usage (1991, 64). While the legitimate language is allowed to evolve or deviate, it's inevitably not in a way that reflects minority groups and nondominant subcultures. The language may start to follow them because language evolves to represent anyone speaking it, but then it must be refined: "Thus distinctive deviations are the driving force of the unceasing movement which, though intended to annul them, tends in fact to reproduce them (a paradox which is in no way surprising once one realizes that constancy may presuppose change)" (64). While the legitimate language has evolved to allow for the colloquialisms of white males in dominant (culture-defining) positions, as Elbow shows in *Vernacular Eloquence*, it still doesn't allow for many colloquialisms of minority and working-class groups (unless they are performed tongue in cheek) (Elbow 2012, 348–57). As a result, Stuckey refutes models of literacy that propose educating the lower classes to bring them out of poverty and crime, criticizing, for example, Henry Giroux and Stanley Aronowitz, who argue that changing social conditions will help poor students perform better in school (Stuckey 1991, 17). It's a short-term solution to a long-term planned inequality. As lower classes assimilate to the legitimate language, dominant users will simply dissimilate by creating new usages and standards to maintain class distinctions.

That's how the United States became a monolingual country, according to Bruce Horner and Trimbur, in spite of a history of multilingualism and language hybridity. They argue, based on Benedict Anderson's theory of imagined communities, that the institution of monolingualism in the United States is the result of modernizing forces in the tradition of nationalism: "A unidirectional monolingual language policy that gives primacy of place to English in the modern curriculum is warranted as inevitable, not because English was the only living language available in North America but because the use of spoken and written English forms what Benedict Anderson calls an 'imagined community' and a sense of nationhood" (Horner and Trimbur 2002, 607). They point out that multilingualism is feasible in the university setting, but it has been disallowed because of various nationalist efforts. It has been important to establish the fiction of a monolingual, native speaker of English in the United States for the sake of nationalism, and they list moments when institutions in the country have supported this fiction—decisions, for instance, to declare any language besides English "foreign" and thus the territory of English as a Second Language studies or foreign-language literatures. French, Spanish, Arabic, and so on were moved away from writing courses. These efforts have marginalized "nonnative speakers" (another concept they argue is a fiction) because minority groups don't speak and write the legitimate language, and this monolingual nationalism has been upheld by schools. In our official "linguistic memory" there has been "a systematic forgetting of the multiple languages spoken and written in North America," including Louisiana French, so that US history reports that we are and always have been a monolingual nation (Trimbur 2005, 577).

The legitimate language is inevitably codified according to the tastes of the language codifiers, then programmed into educational institutions, which in turn reify the socioeconomic hierarchy. In addition to codifying national linguistic error and correctness and setting themselves up as experts who can distinguish between what Jefferson called the "laboring and the learned," (quoted in Bowles and Gintis 1976, 29) the founders of the United States socially planned the economy that would create corresponding inequalities in the educational system. From then on, the education system carried out the order of sorting folks into the economy behind a façade of meritocracy. The long-short of it is that, wherever folks are born into the capitalist system, that's where they generally stay. Educational and linguistic inequalities consistently correspond with the class system that the nation builders initially established. Cajuns, who had done their best to stay outside the capitalist economy, were brought in at the bottom of the social hierarchy, meaning that their language—before they even uttered a word—was bound to be a sloppy vernacular with no political clout or privilege.

**SOCIOECONOMY OF CAJUNS**

In the early 1920s, Cajuns were aware of capitalism but maintained something more like an unstratified peasant class rooted in an agrarian economy, a clan society with strong family alliances (like traditional Scottish communities). If an individual chose to rise above the ranks of Cajuns, he or she would self-remove and now claim the title "Creole," while many of the "underclass" from surrounding ethnicities melded with the Cajun community, soon taking on their food and language customs. The result was a community whose identity and coherence were based on social position instead of ethnicity.[4] Though Cajuns were very property centered (valuing their farms in particular), there was a strong tradition of communal labor and assistance. The following brief history of Cajuns demonstrates their position in the socioeconomic hierarchy.

First, a word on sources. In addition to a few other historians, I rely heavily on Carl Brasseaux's books *The Founding of New Acadia: The Beginnings of Acadian Life in Louisiana, 1765–1803* (Brasseaux 1987) and *Acadian to Cajun: Transformation of a People, 1803–1877* (Brasseaux 1992) in this section for a few reasons. In local Louisiana studies, Brasseaux is recognized as one of the most authoritative voices on Cajun history, and his books are the only academic sources for certain periods of Cajun history. Also, Brasseaux is one of the most objective writers of Cajun history, striving to correct past stereotypes, like Henry Wadsworth Longfellow's portrayal of Acadians as Victorian and genteel in *Evangeline: A Tale of Acadie* (2004).[5] In spite of his rigor, even Brasseaux falls into sentimentalizing Cajuns at times in the style of histories about our rugged early American frontiersmen (for example: "Though compelled to tame the wilderness themselves, some Acadian pioneers, by virtue of personal initiative and unflagging industry, nevertheless managed to build modest fortunes. Like biblical patriarchs, these frontiersmen and their descendants measured their wealth in terms of real estate and livestock" [1987, 190]). But his histories, in spite of the frontier talk, are the least sentimental in that they include records and details of some of the less noble things Cajuns have done—for example, the vigilante movement, which I recount later. I also rely on the research of John Mack Faragher, a Yale historian who says he grew curious about the Acadian story upon seeing a poster that depicted the "Acadian Odyssey" after their expulsion. He writes in the introduction to his history, *A Great and Noble Scheme: The Tragic Story of the Expulsion of the French Acadians from Their American Homeland* (2005), that the expulsion is "strikingly similar to events of ethnic cleansing in our own time" (xiii). Like Brasseaux, he uses historical documents and records to reconstruct the events of settlement, community development, and expulsion, since the Acadians themselves were mostly illiterate.

The story of the Cajuns begins far north of Louisiana. French settlers gradually arrived in what is now eastern Maine and Canadian coastal lands at the beginning of the seventeenth century, the same time that England was colonizing the east coast of what is now the United States. They began peaceable trade relations with the indigenous people there. An encampment called l'Acadie (probably a derivation of the Míkmawísimk Indian word *-akadie*, meaning "place of abundance") was established in 1604 in present-day Dorchet Island, Maine, for the purpose of fur trade and populated largely by indentured servants (*engagés*), who called themselves les Acadiens, or "Acadians."[6] After one year and close to 50 percent mortality, the colony relocated to present-day Port Royal, Nova Scotia, where, over the next century and a half, they primarily dwelled, throughout several political skirmishes and repopulations from France.

During this time, the Acadians established socioeconomic and political habits that would last well into their tenure in Louisiana. According to multiple historians, Acadians developed a social structure unlike those of surrounding colonial settlements; it was based on extended kinship ties, communal labor pools, and very little class stratification. Brasseaux writes that this unique socioeconomy arose from a number of unusual factors: common class background (peasants), geographic isolation, and a lack of direct French government (Brasseaux 1987, 3).[7] The vast majority of

Acadians were "drawn from peasant stock, usually in the Centre-Oust provinces [Poitou, Aunis, Angoumois, and Saintoge]," writes Brasseaux (4, 8), where they led agrarian lives under a feudal system and caste structure (5). As a result, Acadians imported their clan-style relations and communal labor pools, with which they invented, constructed, and maintained an elaborate system of dikes to reclaim wetlands as farming land.[8] Their propensity for being "clannish, self-contained" was further enhanced by their geographic location in the marshes, which cut them off from much communication with neighboring settlements (10). Another political feature that set Acadian society apart from the surrounding colonies was its relationship with Native Americans. As Faragher (2005) puts it, "The history of colonization is usually written as the process of native assimilation to European culture. It may be more accurate to think of the men who remained in l'Acadie as assimilated to the customs of the Míkmaq" (36–37). A majority of the first few waves of Acadian men married into the Míkmaw tribe almost immediately, and kinships between the two groups remained strong through the following generations. Acadians lost their colonial ties to France.

Most important to their development as an autonomous settlement, Acadians were largely neglected by France because of France's involvement in various wars and the rapid turnover rate in colonial officials. Because of this governing neglect, Acadians developed a sense of self-government and came to resent any attempts at outside government, including officials sent from France. Brasseaux writes that "the Acadians did not hesitate to protest the actions of local administrators and clergymen to higher authorities in Quebec and France. When appeals proved ineffective, the colonists resorted to procrastination, subterfuge, and other forms of passive resistance to foil unpopular administrative policies" (1987, 7). With the contracts of the engagées expiring and the "chronic" neglect of France, as well as the back-and-forth occupations of the French and English (who were fighting over the land where the Acadians lived), the Acadians developed an independent political stance, refusing to take any side but their own in skirmishes and politics. They came to be called the "French Neutrals" by the surrounding Native Americans, Scots, and English because of this independence.

After the French and Indian War, the 1713 Treaty of Utrecht finally awarded the Acadian French settlement to Britain, which demanded that the "French Neutrals" swear allegiance to the British crown. Most Acadians were willing to comply as long as they were guaranteed neutrality in British skirmishes and wars: "We will take up arms neither against his British Majesty, nor against France, nor against any of their subjects or allies" (Bernard 2008, 15). Brasseaux lists the provisions the Acadians requested: "freedom to exercise their Catholic faith; guaranteed neutrality in the inevitable future Franco-English wars in order to avoid retributive raids by local French-allied Indians; and recognition by the colonial government that the Acadians were, in fact, a distinct community" (Brasseaux 1987, 14). In short, for the next half century, the Acadians were almost content with British rule, even sometimes preferring it to French domination, according to Brasseaux, as long as they could assert their semiautonomy to choose when they would comply and when they wouldn't (19). By 1755, however, a change in colonial administration decisively ended the tenuous relationship between the Acadians and the British. Infuriated by the Acadians' continued negotiations for a conditional oath of allegiance, General Cornwallis, who had overseen the clearances in the Scottish Highlands, told them, "You declare openly that you will be the subjects of His Britannic Majesty only on such and such conditions. It appears to me that you think yourselves independent of any government, and you wish to treat with the King as if you were so" (quoted in Faragher 2005, 254–55). The Acadians had consistently resisted assimilation and subjection to both French and British colonial administrations, but in the eyes of the new officials, the Acadians' independence was especially threatening.

## LE GRAND DÉRANGEMENT

The colony's new governor, Lieutenant Colonel Charles Lawrence, launched an ethnic cleansing that came to be called le Grand Dérangement, a "great upheaval," between 1755 and 1765, during which about half of the 8,000 Acadians died. Longfellow memorialized the tragedy in *Evangeline*, the story of two Acadian lovers who were separated during the Grand Dérangement, even if he fell into romanticizing Acadians. Essentially, the British tricked and captured most of the Acadians, then deported them and distributed them among British colonies all around the Atlantic rim, eventually sending some back to France. Lieutenant Colonel Lawrence wrote a telling memo revealing the English desire for Acadian lands and distrust of Acadian alliances with the Míkmaw: "We are now upon a great and noble Scheme of sending the neutral French out of this Province, who have always been secret Enemies, and have encouraged our Savages to cut our throats. If we effect their Expulsion, it will be one of the greatest Things that ever the English did in America; for by all Accounts, that part of the Country they possess, is as good Land as any in the World: In case therefore we could get some good English Farmers in their Room, this Province would abound with all Kinds of Provisions (*Pennsylvania Gazette*, 4 September 1755)" (quoted in Faragher 2005, x). As in their other campaigns of ethnic cleansing, the British attempted to remove all Acadians and replace them with British peasants. A common tactic in Acadie was to call the men of the villages to a meeting, then take them prisoner. Their wives and children were kidnapped, and their property ransacked to pay for the "cost" of their removal. Many Acadians died during the deportation due to disease and bad conditions, and some died after being denied entrance to coastal colonies because of anti-Catholic and anti-French sentiment, but many others were accepted as indentured slaves. The Acadians who fled their homes and escaped capture either died of malnutrition and starvation (after eating their own moccasins) or eventually surrendered to the British, who brought them back to their own confiscated lands as slaves to teach the newly settled Anglo-Saxon and German immigrants how to operate the complicated dike systems that the Acadians had designed for their farms. Some refugees launched guerilla campaigns against the British and even engaged in piracy along the coast, but they were hunted down by British soldiers or English-allied Natives (Brasseaux 1987, 27–29). Approximately 75 percent of the original French colony was displaced in le Grand Dérangement between 1755 and 1763.

The overriding motive of the English was to destroy Acadian cultural solidarity because that was what most threatened them. Lieutenant-Governor Charles Lawrence wrote in August 1755: "That they may not have it in their power to return to this Province, nor to join in strengthening the French of Canada or Louisbourg, it is resolved that they be dispersed among His Majesty's colonys upon the Continent of America" (quoted in Faragher 2005, 335). In an effort to destroy their cultural solidarity, they were to be removed "in groups not to exceed one thousand persons, in order that 'they cannot easily collect themselves together again' (336). Brasseaux disagrees with the portrayal of forced familial separations. He writes that, "contrary to the Evangeline myth," families or at least communities were often exiled together and "Acadian solidarity consequently remained intact" (Brasseaux 1987, 26). Faragher, however, argues that stories of separations are too strong in Acadian cultural memory to be ignored. Though Governor Winslow instructed his officers that "whole families go together" (Faragher 2005, 359), Faragher writes that the separations probably happened as a result of the language impediments between the English and Acadians and the chaos of the removal.

William Faulkner Rushton's account in *The Cajuns: From Acadia to Louisiana* (Rushton 1979) may explain the conflicting opinions. He writes that the reports of separations are due to the fact that Cajuns had no concept of the nuclear family, just the extended clan ties that structured their communities. By definition, for Acadians, family included not just siblings, parents, and children but also cousins, aunts and uncles, and grandparents (as well as any surviving great-relatives). He cites the experience of one woman who went through the Grand Dérangement: "'Our manner of living in Acadia was peculiar,' recalls the grandmother of a St. Martinville judge, in his 1907 classic oral-history account, *Acadian Reminiscences*, 'the people forming, as it were, one single family.' Such a family . . . forms a community where no one is left out and where institutions like mental hospitals and old-folk homes were never developed" (6–9). In the Acadians' clan society, family was important because of emotional bonds, of course, but also because of social institutions and economic infrastructure. Subsequently, one of the most devastating consequences of the Grand Dérangement was, in addition to familial separations, the destruction of Acadian internal socioeconomic relationships, a cornerstone of cultural solidarity.

From those who survived the deliberate ethnic dispersal, a large Acadian diaspora can be traced all over the world. Brasseaux (1991) writes in *Scattered to the Wind* that Acadians were dropped off all along the eastern American seaboard in British colonies, Saint Domingue (Haiti), Martinique, French Guiana, and St. Pierre and Miquelon (off Newfoundland), as well as the Falkland Islands off Argentina, while some were sent back to France. Countless deportees simply disappeared into British coastal settlements or were imprisoned, indentured, shot on sight (Maryland), or even sold into slavery (North Carolina) because of the English colonies' fierce anti-Catholic and anti-French prejudice. Others died of disease or starvation right outside colonies, as they waited weeks and months to be allowed to disembark from their ships. Some managed to survive and maintain their Acadian identity; several of these French communities still exist along the Atlantic rim. New Brunswick is home to the Acadian population that initially escaped during the Grand Dérangement, and other Acadian locales exist throughout the Canadian Maritimes. There remains a large community of Acadians in the Maine area (Acadian National Park) and other parts of New England. Some trekked further inland into what would become the United States, leaving their mark on a well-known range of mountains along the way: Acadians named the Grand Tetons—roughly, "big titties." Many Acadians who were dispersed throughout North America, as well as those sent back to France, where they found little connection after 150 years' separation, were treated as outcasts and refugees on the dole and became quite a problem for governments.

And this is how they wound up in Louisiana. The Acadians—who were denied entry to many English colonies, unable to return to Nova Scotia, and increasingly discontent in France—began to consider Louisiana, a former French colony now under Spanish rule that was willing to take in Acadians to settle the wilderness. Governor Antonio de Ulloa guaranteed land grants for the approximately 1,000 incoming Acadians between 1757 and 1770, who hoped to reestablish their agrarian lives and be reunited with their families. While the first Acadians to arrive were given generous provision and desirable lands and permitted to settle in their former pattern of widely spaced family clusters, Governor Ulloa created a rigid settling policy for subsequent Acadian immigrants, regardless of their family or preference, in order to create a western border in Louisiana against the English. Many Acadians participated in the Rebellion of 1768 at New Orleans to overthrow Ulloa, who consistently threatened to expel them when they tried to resettle closer to family. Under the administration of the next Spanish governor, Alejandro O'Reilly, however, the Acadians found a more lenient settlement policy and by 1803 were fairly well established. In the end, about 2,600 to 3,000 Acadians settled in Louisiana, some along the Mississippi River west of New Orleans, where they built levees to take advantage of the fertile soil and join the southern agricultural economy, and some in the prairies and bayous west of the Atchafalaya River, where they could be almost completely economically independent (Brasseaux 1987, 115).

Once settled in, Acadians sought to reestablish their semiautonomous neutrality among the colonial powers that took turns running Louisiana—Spain until 1800, then France for a brief three years until finally the United States took over with the Louisiana Purchase in 1803. Though quite independent, Acadians weren't antagonistic toward colonial powers—in fact, they were willing to "soldier up" and fight in the American War for Independence. According to historian Lauren C. Post in "Some Notes on the Attakapas Indians of Southwest Louisiana" (1962), Acadians fought alongside Attakapas Indians, who are native to the Louisiana area, and free men of color in a contingency out of Southwest Louisiana. Historian John Walton Caughey reports, "The militia, particularly the Acadians, who had not forgotten the persecutions they had suffered at the hands of the English, behaved splendidly" (quoted in Post 1962, 230). There are similar reports of Acadians fighting in the Revolutionary War in the Northeast.

After the war, however, Acadians were very serious about returning to their land. Their attitude toward land may have been a reaction to the exploitation they had experienced in feudal France. Brasseaux writes that land acquisition for the newly settled Acadians was based on a desire not for profit but for autonomy: "Products of a precapitalist environment, they sought neither prestige nor affluence through land acquisition, but rather economic independence and a comfortable existence patterned upon their former agrarian life-style" (1992, 4). Unlike their capitalist neighbors in the plantation areas, whose primary goal was to accumulate wealth, Acadians' landownership was important for subsistence farming. Their attitude toward land, which would eventually make trouble for them because they would refuse to assimilate with the southern economy, was passionate, maybe bordering on the absurd. Because land was such a priority, Acadians were quite a lawsuit-happy lot, impressing both their British and Spanish governments with numerous and "petty" legal quibbles. Brasseaux observes, "The intensity and spontaneity of the Acadian defense of property rights is an accurate measure of the prominent position of land in the Acadian hierarchy of values" (1987, 144). He writes that the early civil suits in Acadie usually involved disputed boundary lines (8), and "even the most minor property disputes were brought before the colonial magistrates" (143). Later, in Louisiana, when Acadians became unhappy with the courts' justice, many of them got involved in 1859 with what Brasseaux describes as "the second largest vigilante movement in nineteenth-century America and third largest movement in U.S. history" (1992, 116). The vigilante movement was ostensibly organized to enforce justice on thieves and outlaws who had managed to finagle the notoriously corrupt courts, but it quickly degraded into a racist campaign of the wealthier Acadian men imposing their norms on any deviants, particularly interracial relationships. This class-motivated racial normalization was short-lived, though. With the start of the Civil War, the vigilantes quickly morphed into "Jayhawkers," a group of anti-Confederate men, both black and white, who returned to their dedication to land by guarding local properties from pillaging soldiers, eventually disbanding after the death of their leader, Ozémé Carrière.

Land appears to have been the most important reason the Acadians showed any resistance to their administrators from colonial times on. They demonstrated no concern for state or national interests or the scuffles going on around them because their primary loyalty was to their own farms. In fact, Acadians chose to fight for the Union during the Civil War—what Acadians called "la guerre des Confederes," or "the Confederates' War"—when they got fed up with Southern drafting and pillaging of their farms for Rebel supplies (Brasseaux 1992, 58). The bulk of the resistance to Confederate conscription came from the "insular, poor, nonslaveholding prairie Acadians [who] viewed the war as an elitist cause" and tried often to defect from the Rebels (62). A Union prisoner of war, one Lieutenant George C. Harding, described the deserting tendencies of the Acadians he encountered where he was detained: "Camp Pratt was filled with Acadiann conscripts . . . The wants of the Acadiann are few and his habits simple. With a bit of cornbread, a potato, and a clove of garlic, with an occasional stewed crawfish, he gets along quite comfortably, and for luxuries, smokes husk cigarettes and drinks rum—when he can get it. The Acadiann has great powers of endurance, but not much stomach for fight. Of the herd at Camp Pratt, desertions were frequent, sometimes as many as thirty or forty stampeding in a single night. But they would be caught, brought back, made to wear a barrell for a week or two, and finally broke in" (quoted in Brasseaux 1992, 63–64). Later, when Union soldiers moved into the area, hundreds of Acadians who had fled to avoid conscription or had defected from the Rebel army responded enthusiastically. One Union officer wrote: "The Union feeling in this portion of the state—especially among the poor class of citizens, is very strong. They are coming into our lines by the hundreds, and either volunteering or taking the oath of allegiance. Many of them say they have not been home or inside of a house for eighteen months, but have been hiding in swamps to avoid the conscription. There is now already three hundred of them mounted, and acting as scouts, and they are found to be very useful, as they are acquainted with every part of the country" (66–67). Acadians' willingness to fight for the North, however, changed when Union troops behaved just like Rebel troops, raiding Acadians' crops and livestock and detaining them in a war they didn't give a hoot about. During the Civil War, both Union and Confederate troops noted the Acadian resistance to the war effort and their determination to go home. Lieutenant Colonel Bringier of the Fourth Louisiana Cavalry wrote, "They *all* have excellent reasons to go home . . . Some on whom this home influence is very great, walk as far as 20 & 25 miles to spend only 12 hours at home" (71). An 1863 cartoon in *Leslie's Illustrated Weekly* depicts an Acadian conscript, seemingly on guard duty, shackled and chained to a tree to keep him from running away (88c).

Acadians' intense sense of "home" still exists today—perhaps because of the long journey to finally establish permanent residences, probably also because of the pull of the traditional clan-based economy. Brasseaux researched "early land and conveyance records that provide a nearly comprehensive view of land acquisition and ownership in the predominantly Acadian parishes," reporting that they "reveal a remarkable record of residential stability based on familial cohesiveness. Even in modern Louisiana, it is not uncommon to find Acadian families residing on their ancestral Spanish land grants, and the vast majority of Cajuns currently live within fifty miles of their birthplace" (Brasseaux 1992, 91). One explanation is the difference between urban workers, who control only one asset, their labor (which is exchanged for a money wage), and peasants, who control their labor in coordination with the tools of production and the materials of production (land, animals, seed, and so on), which produces little cash but lots of resources, creating a strong attachment to "place." Cajuns are "one of the most stable populations in the history of North America," and Louisiana is the least transient state, according to the 2000 census, likely because of the localized economies, which rely on local foods and trades (Harden 2002). The economy is not easily re-created because it is not entirely mainstreamed yet, especially in smaller towns, so many Cajuns can't imagine *how* to live somewhere else.

But it's not just the work arrangements; there's something else, and it has to do with the extended family structure in Cajun social arrangements, something I discuss later in the chapter. Cajuns are overwhelmingly no longer subsistence farmers or hunters and are free to move around with their labor, but they are still an unusually static population. Though a long-term trend of leaving the area has emerged among Cajuns with higher education, Brasseaux observes that this development invariably leads to unhappy Cajuns who live elsewhere and complain that they miss the food and their mamas (Harden 2002, 4). Many of them move back to SouLa as quickly as possible. The effect is so common that my friend Dallas Begnaud calls it the bungee cord attached to our backs. "Has Frank discovered it yet?" he asked one night, referring to my then fiancé (now husband). "You can run as hard and as long as you like, but the minute you stop running, it'll snap you back." Dallas had thought he'd never come back to Louisiana after moving away, first to Corpus Christi and then to China, but now there he is, back in Lafayette like the good Begnaud he is, baking bread in the shape of fleurs-de-lis. I tell you what: I don't know exactly what it is, but it's something you got if you're Cajun. The magnetism of home is only one of the many holdovers from early Acadian traditions.

## THE INVENTION OF *CAJUN*

The period after the Civil War marks the emergence of Acadian class divisions and the invention of the Cajun people. *Cajun* is a classed term, as it represents those Acadians who did not assimilate into the southern economy and were disdained as "low class." Though Acadians had remained essentially socially unstratified in Nova Scotia, those who moved to Louisiana quickly developed extreme class divisions, leading to a new system of labels, including *Cajun*. According to Brasseaux, "The fragmentation of the once extremely cohesive Acadian community appears to have taken place between 1790 and 1810, when second- and third-generation Acadians embraced both slavery and the plantation system" (Brasseaux 1992, 5). Other historians agree that the invention of Cajunness coincided with the new class divisions among Acadian immigrants to Louisiana. In "From *Acadien* to *Cajun* to *Cadien*: Ethnic Labelization and Construction of Identity," Jacques Henry (1998) follows the evolution of terminology and cultural identity. Regarding early uses of *Cajun*, he writes, "According to [James] Dormon, the process of exclusion that resulted in the distinction between 'lowly Cajun' and Lordly 'Genteel Acadian'" was achieved by 1865; Brasseaux estimates that the transition from 'Acadian to Cajun' was completed by 1877" (40). Henry writes that Cajuns were a "symbolically discrete" group by the turn of the twentieth century (39).

In short, a difference arose between river Acadians and prairie Acadians. River Acadians, living in close proximity to elite French Creoles and Anglos, found very fertile lands and began to accumulate wealth, with which they copied their neighbors. Many of them acquired slaves and some even climbed into the planter class. Generally, those who assimilated into the southern plantocracy tried to pass as French Creoles and later as Anglo Americans, distancing themselves from their Acadian identity and culture (Brasseaux 1992, 8). Meanwhile, the prairie Acadians established subsistence farms and ranches and, though many acquired a great deal of wealth and sometimes also took slaves (usually wet nurses and domestic labor and later field hands, according to Brasseaux), they remained mostly cut off from the southern economy. River Acadians who did not wish to assimilate into French Creole or Anglo American culture sold their river land and moved out to the prairies and bayous—some historians call this the "second expulsion"—where they maintained their precapitalist economy based on communal labor pools, a sort of a clan system, and very little class stratification.

The word *Cajun* is a derivation of *Acadian* that arose around the time that Acadians became classed. Henry reports, "Most sources agree to award the coining of *Cajun* to *Putnam's Magazine* contributor R. L. Daniels in 1879" (1998, 33–34), but he credits the cementing of the spelling and pronunciation to two factors. First, the pronunciation switch from *Cadian* to the American *Cajun* or the French *cagen* was due to a new consonant sound in Louisiana French: "The introduction of the letters *j* or *g* accurately symbolizes the oft-noted shift in both Acadian and Cajun French from [d] to [dž] when followed by an open vowel [i]. Such a shift is found in *Dieu* [dioe] pronounced [džoe], *diable* [diabl] pronounced [džab]. French spelling has no codified symbol to represent the sound [dž] which is not a French consonant" (36). Second, the spelling of *Cajun* came about as a derogatory Anglo label: "[I]t follows the pattern employed to [create] *Injun*," writes Henry, "the spelling used by American writers to convey scorn and disdain of American Indians" (39). Spellings in literature from the period vary, but the *-jun* suffix became standard.

The word *Cajun* began as an insult, so derogatory that it was avoided in polite company. Henry writes, "[Rebecca] Davis [in 1887] drew a distinction between the good 'Acadian' and the 'wretched Cajans.' *Acadian* is used when positive qualities are mentioned, and *Cajun* is associated with condemnable behavior" (1998, 40). Julian Ralph, a writer for *Harper's New Monthly Magazine* traveling through Louisiana in 1893, reported that "it was strange indeed to hear that we not call them Cajuns to their faces lest they be offended, that the term is taken as one of reproach" (quoted in Henry 1998, 38). Sociological reports from the 1930s and 1940s describe the status of the word: "Cajun became 'a fighting word' . . . and corresponded to the term 'hill-billy' in other sections of the United States" (Trépanier 1991, 164). Henry gives an example of this usage: "Here an old Negro mammy did not say 'poor white trash.' She said 'Cajun'—or 'blue bellied Cajun.' When the old Creoles wished to designate some ignoramus in their midst with whom they were exasperated, they tacked on an adjective . . . '*maudit Cajin*' . . . As another educator, a man from *La Côte des Acadiens*, laughingly puts it, 'Me, I am Creole; the other fellow, he is a Cajun'" (1998, 42). The label *Cajun* was an insult for prairie Acadians well into the twentieth century.

Interestingly, *Cajun* came to designate class position far more than ethnic identity: "[A]n ignorant or poor person, even though Creole in origin, might be called a Cajun, while a prosperous or educated Acadian would be called a Creole" (Trépanier 1991, 164). *Cajun* was a shifting category that covered any poor nonblack (though not always necessarily white) people in the French-speaking areas of Louisiana. A New Orleans Tulane professor tried to pin down the word in 1932: "This name is sometimes used ironically but most often conveys disdain. It does not at all appear to be the abbreviated form of Acadian; it is applied indiscriminately to any Creole who, whatever its origin, smells like the country and looks like a peasant. That's a Cajun!" (Henry 1998, 39). Because the label applied to class status, some people were able to move in and out of the category, depending on their incomes and lifestyles. Consequently, it was also easy to confuse people who identified as Cajuns or Creoles: "[A] Cajun would have been glad to be called a Creole because of the higher status associated with the word, while a Creole would have resented being called a Cajun" (Trépanier 1991, 167). The label was always an insult, and it was always class based.

As it turns out, though the insult was quite unnecessary, the class-based usage of *Cajun* was accurate. Not all Cajuns were Acadian French—or even French—in origin. The insular prairie Acadians absorbed other peoples who also did not participate in the southern economy, and collectively came to be called Cajuns. According to Brasseaux, Italians, Spanish, Germans, Scots-Irish, and some Native Americans assimilated into the Cajun culture, taking on its language, food, economy, and often francophone name spellings. Brasseaux reports that assimilation was so successful in some families that today they don't know they aren't Acadian: "Indeed, the assimilation of the eastern Creoles into the Lafourche Acadian community has been so complete that such families as the Quatrevingts (originally Achtzigger), Chauvins, Himels, Verrets, Cantrelles, and Haydels are generally unaware that their German and French ancestors arrived in Louisiana fully one-half century before the Acadians" (1992, 152). Even today, some of the thickest Cajun accents I've heard have come from the mouths of Laughlins, Romeros, Mesbahs, Snyders, and Sanchezes. My great-uncle Gervis Stanford, who plays a mean Cajun fiddle, said some Scots-Irish guy came down from Kentucky or something and married into the family, so that's how we wound up with an English name. As Brasseaux (1992, 106) argues is typical of Cajuns, the mother passes on the culture, so it doesn't matter what your last name is. The way it all shook out after the Civil War was that those who refused to assimilate into the southern capitalist economy often merged with "lower-class" Cajuns, while those who assimilated took a higher position in the social hierarchy.

So, though Acadians became socially stratified when they came to Louisiana, Cajuns did not, because there was no such thing as a Cajun until well after the migration. And Cajuns are not purely French or Acadian, but they are purely working class. The system of communal labor pools and assistance that had developed in Nova Scotia remained intact in Louisiana. Some were eventually forced to work as day laborers, especially as a result of Reconstruction conditions and a series of natural disasters that reduced almost all working-class groups to extreme poverty and homelessness. But within the community, Cajuns didn't need cash because of subsistence farming and bartering; in fact, Bernard writes that, like many other isolated minority groups, most Cajuns didn't even notice the Depression (Bernard 2003, xxi). They generally didn't participate in the plantocracy or cash economy of the South unless misfortune drove them to. These economic arrangements were functional alternative structures to capitalism, built on cooperation rather than competition.

There were many food-sharing institutions in place among Cajuns, rendering money unnecessary. In addition to personal subsistence farming and bartering with eggs for supplies at local stores, Cajuns held weekly meat slaughters—boucheries (pig slaughters) in the winter and beouf boucheries (cow slaughters) in the summer. Earl Paul Broussard (b. 1931) of Rice Cove, Louisiana, explains the economy of a beouf boucherie:

> Everybody raised a few head of cattle, and they would pick out one calf in the early part of the winter, you know, and set that calf aside for the boucherie in the next summer. And somewhere about the latter part of May or the first part of June, every Saturday morning they would slaughter a calf. One of the farmers in turn—you know, they drew lots, and each Saturday was a different one's turn to furnish the calf. When the calf was slaughtered, everybody was there to help, and the meat was cut up into the different cuts of meat, and it would be stacked on a long table, and everybody had five pounds of meat to bring home. And from week to week your position on the table would move. In other words, this week you might have some of the neck steaks and the ribs, and the following week you would go down and you would hit maybe some of the rib-eye steaks, and then the T-bone steaks, and the rump roast, so every week you had a different type of meat. Some people preferred one type of meat over the others, so there was a lot of exchange. Now, whatever meat was left over after everyone had their five pounds—sometimes there was some meat left over; the calf was too large—some people would buy a few pounds—extra pounds—to bring home if they had a large family, or, then, the person who had the calf this time, he would take this meat and go out and sell it—you know, probably bring it to town, sell it to a butcher. But they tried to select the calf that would just about make the right weight, you know, maybe about a hundred and fifty pounds of meat so that everybody could have their five pounds and there was very little left over. (Broussard n.d.)

With the money they got from the butcher, Cajuns were able to buy dry goods such as sugar and flour or equipment like plows and wrought-iron skillets, which are integral to Cajun-style cooking.

There were different methods of preserving the meat for those without access to the iceboxes that were common in urban areas. Broussard's community kept cooked meat in cages outside, where the meat's grease and the ventilation kept the meat from spoiling for two or three days. My great-uncle Lionel explained to me that they jarred the meat in Pointe Bleu for use in the winter. "We didn't have no refrigerators, no," he said, his voice making a perfect tonal scoop between *didn't* and the last *no* in the Cajun style of stressing something incredible. "You take the meat et un 'tite peu salt, and put them in a jar, and put them in the cistern," located beneath the house where it stayed cool. Nolan M. LeBlanc (b. 1927) writes in a letter that they "salted and/or smoked meat to prevent spoilage" in his community in Morganza, Louisiana.[9]

The community came together for labor projects as well; this type of gathering was called a *coup de mains*, or a "group of hands," for building houses or barns. Particularly for the yearly tradition of chimney maintenance, folks would take turns helping at one another's homes. Chimneys and homes were typically built of *bousillage*, a process combining French and Native American techniques. The homeowner would prepare a mixture of silt and "cured" moss (dead, dried, and shucked) to be shaped into bricks and piled into the wooden structure, then covered in layers of lime wash, or whitewash. Like the food shares, everyone had a turn with the community labor. Other communal events were the house dances, called a *bal de maison* or *fais do-do* (because children slept, or "went do-do," in an adjoining room while the adults danced the night away). The *courir du Mardi Gras*, or "running of the Mardi Gras," was another community event in which men (typically masked and quite tipsy) went from home to home on horseback collecting the ingredients for a gumbo large enough to feed the whole community at the end of the day. In addition to the community food shares and labor pools, community assistance was a given. LeBlanc writes, "On Saturday the grits mill was started and all the neighbors came to get their corn ground into grits—those with no money or gas got their corn made into grits free. No one was turned away. All hobos were fed well also."

The sense of community cohesion was reinforced with the tradition of the shivaree, a nighttime ritual to shame someone for sparking local disapproval. The shivaree, a gentler form of the European *charivari*, usually addressed marital issues like domestic abuse, adultery, or ill-kept mourning periods. Cajuns gathered outside the offender's home after dark and banged pots and pans until they were invited in to have coffee and work out the problem. Whereas the European custom was usually meant to shun someone, Cajuns generally practiced shivaree to bring someone back into the fold (North American accounts in Canada, Louisiana, and other areas influenced by French colonists are similarly mild). Sometimes they demanded some kind of penance like riding a horse backward through town. The pots and pans were brought out again on wedding nights while couples consummated their marriages, many of which were made official by jumping a broom when there were no priests around (as in African American communities). Later, when babies were born, someone galloped a horse through the area, announcing the birth with gunshots—two for a girl, three for a boy. Those babies grew up with stories about the *rougarou* or *loup-garou* (a werewolf-type monster) and Madame Grand Doights (a kind of Mrs. Claus in some parishes and a terrifying witch in others).

Some of these traditions are still integral to the lives of Cajuns, even after we've largely assimilated into capitalism. Not so much the gunshots, but lots of other rituals. I remember devouring cracklins (fried pig skin) at a boucherie hosted by my Pointe Bleu cousins when I was a kid. Boucheries have recently made a tremendous comeback, being featured in several *New York Times* articles and on TV shows like Anthony Bourdain's *No Reservations* (on the Travel Channel). Hunting and fishing are also still enormous sources of food locally. Around my home, we regularly ate fresh fish and venison—even duck, dove, rabbit, and squirrel (but not nutria rat). We had loads of deer sausage from my brother Nathan's first kill (after he was ritually covered in its blood), which my stepdad grilled every Sunday for months. Though nobody really does bousillage anymore (homes are mostly brick and wood), home projects are still often structured around coups de mains; the roof, front porch, and back deck on my mother's home were all constructed in this way. For the roof project, I remember helping my mom make a huge batch of tuna sandwiches to go along with the boudin somebody inevitably brought. The local men came out to help my family for those projects, and of course the men in my family went out to help the other families when it was their turn.

A lot of us also still keep the tradition of the mother's helper from the old days. When someone in the community has a new baby, whoever has a teenage daughter with babysitting experience sends her over to stay for a few days, a few weeks, or a few months to help the new mother. Living in New York, I was extremely disappointed that I would miss out on this tradition for my first baby, especially after having put in my own time as a teenager, but my college-aged sister graciously took a year off school to move up here and be a live-in nanny while I wrote my dissertation. Maybe one of my children will be old enough to stay with her when it's her turn for a mother's helper. Other communal traditions still woven into the lives of many Cajuns are things like organized food assistance during family upheavals (a new baby, surgery, and so on), during which families receive a meal every night for a week or two, and shared child rearing with extended family and even other families (in contrast to "nuclear families"). Children grow up with multiple "parents," who may not be called "mother" or "father" but share in feeding, disciplining, transporting, and housing them. These grassroots social programs are often organized by locals through their churches (Catholic and Protestant), which are still dominant social institutions for many Cajuns.

But these are just fragments of the precapitalist Cajun socioeconomy that existed in the poorest areas of Louisiana in the 1920s when French was banned in schools. As the economy and government changed in Louisiana, especially during industrialization, under which many Cajuns (as well as other ethnic groups across the United States) were assimilated as workers, Cajuns began interacting and intermarrying with outside communities, assimilating to dominant economic and racial values. One Cajun who experienced the transition to capitalism comments in particular on the new preference for accumulation of markers of wealth over former sustenance-based labor: "They've [fellow Cajuns] got big campers, bass boats and swimming pools, but they had to spend half their lifetime offshore [working in the oil industry in the Gulf of Mexico] to pay for them. When I was growing up on the farm, money didn't mean much to us, but oil's changed us. Now, everyone's trying to keep up with the Joneses" (quoted in Bernard 2003, 39). He points out that the new drive for accumulation is fueled by competition—and not just in business but with neighbors—contrasting this with precapitalist Cajun values when "money didn't mean much."

As Cajuns came to value the accumulation of wealth, they also came to value the accumulation of linguistic capital, which they now understood in terms of class value. In the process of their educational and linguistic assimilation, Cajuns recognized that they were seen as "dull-witted, ignorant, slovenly, sexually incontinent and without ambition" (Tentchoff 1980, 229–30). As I explain in the next chapter some of the abusive school conditions under which they were educated, it becomes clear why they would internalize these values. Historian Dave Peyton describes the accompanying stereotypes of Cajun language: "Cajun [French] was considered an illiterate language. In fact, it was; there was no written Cajun language . . . Cajun was so different from standard French that you couldn't write it in standard French. Like a lot of Indian languages, no one had written it down—no one had even attempted to" (Peyton quoted in Deutsch 1979, 82). Though Louisiana French was simply following the natural course of language change apart from standard French, it was deemed illegitimate because of its speakers' class position.

## CONCLUSION

Cajuns' resistance to US capitalism until late in the game would bear great consequences for their children during the period of national reorganization after World War I, when multilingualism became unpatriotic and the inability to speak English became outright un-American. Cajuns' resistance to capitalism wasn't enough to protect them from forced assimilation, especially under the pressures of national economic industrialization at the turn of the twentieth century, but it was enough to keep them from having a say in the decisions about their own schooling and the language that would be taught. The "will to unification" (Bourdieu's helpful phrase) of the founding fathers necessarily excluded minority voices in the planning of the economy, the class structure, and the legitimate language. Only legitimate agents can have legitimate languages, and Cajuns were illegitimate because they rejected the planned economy of the United States, opting instead for social leveling and community living.

After the legitimate language is codified according to class hierarchy, it is enforced and "normalized" through schools, as I explain in the next chapter. This was the period when French was banned in Louisiana schools, and since it was also the same time that Cajuns were being assimilated into the US economy, almost an entire generation of French speakers in Southwest Louisiana internalized the idea that Cajuns and their language were "low class." After being shamed and physically punished for speaking French, as I recount in chapter 3, many Cajuns later attempted to hide their language and background to pass as Anglo Americans and get better jobs. Market pressures, as Bourdieu's model explains, intimidated them into complying with the legitimate language for the sake of upward mobility; the alternative was to accept the stigma and low class position of being Cajun.

My Paw-Paw's parents recognized their place in the socioeconomy during this time. They realized their son was marrying "up" by marrying a quarter-German girl from the city, so they did not attend the wedding. They "didn't feel that they were good enough to be there," recalls GrandmaMona. Paw-Paw's parents were sharecroppers who worked very, very hard to maintain their forty acres and keep their youngest son, my Paw-Paw, in school (the other two sons had to drop out to work the farm). Paw-Paw's mother would eventually commit suicide when I was just a baby; she sat down near the pond, took off her glasses and folded them neatly beside her, then submerged her face until she drowned. I don't know who found her; I didn't even know how she died until my thirties. The story in my family is that she had been diagnosed with a terminal disease, and she was determined not to be a burden for anyone. This doesn't make sense to me, since Cajuns generally had community arrangements for families who needed extra help. She had herself helped her disabled mother-in-law for years. I'm guessing she could see that their community assistance practices were dying as all the local sons and daughters grew up and assimilated into the outside economy instead of staying nearby to continue working the family land. She had raised her boys to be Americans; there was no turning back now. Decades before, when my Paw-Paw got married, she couldn't imagine just how different the world outside her community was. She didn't attend the wedding, but she asked the newlyweds to stop by on the way to their honeymoon at a hotel in Galveston, and she loaded them up with fresh eggs for the journey. "What was I going to do with eggs?" GrandmaMona exclaims.

My uppity great-grandmother Winnie, who died disapproving of my Cajun Paw-Paw, did finally get her wish for a German man in the family when my mother, Paula, remarried—this time to a man with the last name Feucht. Winnie greatly approved of Patrick Feucht's family—all of them blue-eyed, ruddy-cheeked, and fair-haired—and she enjoyed talking at our family get-togethers with his aunt Ella, who raised Patrick and his brother Stanislaus and was known locally as "the German teacher."[10] Now I don't know if Granny ever figured it out, but Pat Feucht is the Cajunest man I have ever known. I'm telling you, he doesn't even have to put on a Cajun accent to tell a Boudreaux and Thibodeaux joke; it's already there. I can't think of a more Cajun family than the Feuchts. Growing up in Mamou, Louisiana—famous for its Mardi Gras celebrations and Fred's Lounge—my stepdad and his siblings were one of the many non-Acadian families to totally assimilate into Cajun culture.

# 3
# "I WILL NOT SPEAK FRENCH. I WILL NOT SPEAK FRENCH."
## The Grand Dérangement de la Langue

> Please let it be known how we were treated for speaking French. This is the first time I have had to write a letter to express my bitterness on this subject . . . I guess after writing this letter I realize that I'm still not completely over my pain and anguish.
> —K. L. Laborde, letter to Shane Bernard

> [T]he night of the sword and the bullet was followed by the morning of the chalk and the blackboard.
> —Ngũgĩ wa Thiong'o, *Decolonising the Mind*

Grandmama Emma, my father's mother, had a quiet job as the principal of a daycare center when I was growing up but, before that, she was involved in different community and political projects—like serving as campaign administrator for some of the first African American politicians in our hometown of Opelousas, and meeting with parents of kids missing school for the Truancy Department. She had only reached tenth grade because her parents didn't see any reason for a girl to graduate, but she didn't like people to know that. After my folks split up, my father moved back in with her until he remarried, so I stayed at her house every other weekend. As a child, I knew her as articulate and stern but with a bottomless candy jar (how I recall that clinking sound). When my brother and I looked like we might be disagreeable, she'd say, "Y'all don't be little shits." As an adult, I moved in with her when she lived alone and began forgetting things shortly before she passed away, and I came to know her as an elegant, gently assertive, and slightly prissy woman. She had two impressively large closets of polyester pantsuits—sized 10 and 12—in every shade of pastel, and she kept tweezers and a mirror near her favorite rocking chair at all times. She was a gorgeous, dark-haired nineteen-year old in my favorite photo who grew up in a Creole family named Hidalgo—"*EE*-dalgo," she'd say clearly. "You don't pronounce the *h*." One of fifteen children, she spoke lovingly of her father, a wealthy businessman who had inherited extensive Hidalgo land grants from the time Louisiana was a French colony.

Having assimilated into the local French community, the Hidalgos spoke only French at home, but my grandma grew up to speak almost solely English, even at home. In fact, she assimilated so well into Anglo culture that I wasn't even aware she still had her French until I was well into my twenties. She had us call her Grandmama Emma, not the typical "Maw-*Maw*" (though we still mangled it into something like GrammmmawEmma), and she nitpicked her children's grammar. Sometimes it was her singing voice and sometimes it was her biting wit that would silence a room bustling with the arguments and reminiscences of all nine of her grown children (and who knows how many grandchildren), but language prejudice was something that could silence *her* real quick. The little-girl bitterness still showed on her face eighty-something years later every time she recalled the humiliation of her first day of school.

The first-grade teacher asked in English who knew their colors, and my grandma, whose parents had begun teaching her at home, was one of only a few students to raise their hands. When the teacher called on her, she proudly gave the names she'd learned—*rouge, bleu, jaune*—but she was interrupted by the teacher. Grandmama's face would twist up in disgust behind her glasses every time she imitated the teacher's hissing reply: "*You* don't know your colors; sit back down!"

Around SouLa, just about everyone has a story about a parent or grandparent who was punished or humiliated for speaking French in school. The 1921 Louisiana State constitution prohibited French in public schools, and children were beaten, shamed, and ignored—even when they asked to go to the bathroom—until they learned English. My Paw-Paw Jeff (my mother's father) said "the worst whooping" he ever got was when he asked a classmate to translate what the teacher was saying. Like many of the other children who were punished and made to write the lines "I will not speak French," Grandmama Emma and Paw-Paw Jeff were persuaded of the illegitimacy of their mother tongue, and they made huge efforts to stop using Louisiana French and learn the legitimate language. All my grandparents raised their children as monolingual English speakers, even though that meant the kids couldn't talk to their monolingual French-speaking grandparents. After three generations, Louisiana French was rarely spoken: "[I]n 1990 only about 30 percent of Cajuns spoke the dialect as their first language, and most of these were middle aged or elderly" (Bernard 2003, xxii). The 1990 census was the last to measure accurately French speakers in Louisiana; twenty-five years later, the number is bound to be far smaller. The French ban has haunted Cajun cultural memory for more than a century now; it has proven to be one of the most effective means of assimilating the notoriously clannish Cajuns into the mainstream US economy, with some exceptions but generally as low-wage manual laborers on dangerous jobs.

The Cajuns' process of internalizing the language standards and then self-policing (and often even policing others) is what Bourdieu describes as *normalization*. He writes that schools are the primary means for normalizing, or enforcing, the legitimate language that nation builders selected. Class inequalities, once established and encoded in the nation's legitimate language, must be perpetuated, or normalized, through a combination of laws, institutional enforcement, and individual compliance. Michel Foucault (1977) explains the process of normalization in *Discipline and Punish: The Birth of the Prison*; experts establish what is normal by issuing judgments or statements (he calls this "expert discourse"), and then everyone adjusts to the new standard or is corrected into a "normal" way of behaving or thinking. The use of normalization corresponds to the societal switch to using institutions to enforce discipline. The two most influential institutions for normalizing "correct" language, according to Bourdieu, are "the family and the educational system" (1991, 62). The educational system has the most weight when it comes to introducing state policies because the legitimate language "acquires the force of law in and through the educational system" (49). But families have equal clout when it comes to internalizing norms and enforcing them on their children outside of the classroom or in preparation for the classroom.

The process of language normalization is always tied to class stratification, so that people who normalize to the dominant view order themselves into appropriate class positions according to their mastery of the legitimate language and culture. As Cajuns took on the language of mainstream Anglo America, they also accepted their position in the economy, like my Paw-Paw Jeff's parents, who understood that they were too "low class" to attend his wedding. Any Louisiana French speakers pursuing the American dream strove to rise above their assigned low positions by renouncing their nonlegitimate home language and imitating the language and habits of the higher classes—by striving to be, essentially, not Cajun—while other Cajuns who maintained their Cajun identities generally adjusted their self-images and life goals to line up with the socioeconomic positions that they came to understand they deserved.

My father's father, Roland Stanford, got just enough education to internalize the dominant view of Cajuns and assume this second approach.

Paw-Paw Roland grew up in an extremely poor Cajun family and left school some time after third grade to work in his family's fields, as was expected of most Cajun sons. He called me Poulette, his "little chicken"—a play on his nickname for my mother, Paulette (her name is Paula). Paw-Paw passed away when I was in my teens, so I never got to ask him all my questions, but I hear he had a rough start, taking on great responsibilities at an early age with his family and their farm after his mother died. My great-uncle Gervis tells me he never knew any other "mama" besides my grandfather, who raised him and the other younger siblings practically alone. I loved watching them play fiddle and accordion when they got together. Paw-Paw tended to hunch over and he always spoke slowly and softly, as if he were translating in his head, but he seemed confident and unselfconscious as he wailed the old French ballads.

My Grandmama Emma, whom my father calls "high class," must have been quite a catch for my grandpa. Roland and Emma met at a dance hall in Lawtell and were married in 1942. From what I hear, she had no shortage of suitors (in fact, she was engaged to someone else), but she liked Roland the best, and she chased him until he proposed. They shared a love of music and dancing. Every Saturday until my grandfather died, to my absolute childhood boredom, they watched the Cajun dance hall channel together: dozens of Cajuns two-stepping and waltzing in a great circle as local musicians wailed and played the chanky-chank. Their version of MTV. Like my Paw-Paw Jeff, Paw-Paw Roland married up when he made Grandmama Emma his bride. But, unlike my Paw-Paw Jeff, he didn't have the education even to try to be upwardly mobile. Accepting his Cajun identity and the cultural assumptions that went along with it, he set a very low bar for his family. After my Grandmama Emma's humiliation in first grade, she made sure her children spoke the legitimate language so that, as she repeatedly told them, they could do anything they wanted. She had learned her lesson, and she wanted to free her children from having to suffer the same humiliations. In contrast, her husband had internalized the same hegemonic beliefs about speakers of Louisiana French but, since he didn't have any hope of improving his lot, he tried to prepare his children for the realities they would one day face by teaching them not to expect too much.

As a carpenter, Paw-Paw Roland was known locally for his high-quality work, but he skimped so badly on his own home that the simplest things were falling apart after he died. Along with his six sons, he built modern homes for families throughout the area, but he had to lose a big argument with his wife before he agreed to install indoor plumbing in the house he built for his own family in 1966. It was like he couldn't imagine a life in which he was financially comfortable—then again, maybe he was comfortable being poor, per Bourdieu's theory of habitus. Though my grandmother begged him to charge his customers a fair price, Paw-Paw consistently charged so little that his family barely got by. Once, when the two worked on the same job together, my father learned that he was making more money than his own father, his superior by decades, simply because Paw-Paw wouldn't ask for more.

He kept his family a notch below others, and he tried to do the same to his wife. One evening, right after they were married, Grandmama Emma went out way back in the fields to find Paw-Paw Roland and tell him it was time for supper. Barefoot for some reason, she picked her way between cow patties the whole way out to meet him. When Paw-Paw saw his well-bred Creole wife daintily avoiding the patties, he asked if she'd ever stepped in one. Of course not, she replied. I guess Paw-Paw Roland thought she could use some humility, because he chased Grandmama and wrestled her till he got one of her pretty feet planted in a pile of cow manure. She stormed back to the house, enraged. Maybe his supper wasn't cold that night, but I bet his wife was. That cow patty story is the story of their marriage, as Paw-Paw sought to create equilibrium between his external reality and his internal beliefs. They loved each other, but the socioeconomic tension was always there.

My maternal grandfather dealt with the financial handicap of being Cajun by trying not to be Cajun, and my paternal grandfather dealt with it by trying to make the best of poverty, which he believed he deserved. Both strategies are built on the assumption that a shaky grasp of the legitimate language (and other forms of cultural capital), for whatever reason, is enough to qualify someone to be poor. As if the way a person wields a language is a reflection of his or her work ethic, morality, or personal worth. In chapter 2, I talked about the origin of the legitimate language and how it corresponds to already existing socioeconomic and sociopolitical inequalities. Here, the process of Cajun educational assimilation demonstrates how, at least in one corner of the United States, this belief gets written onto everyone assimilating into the American economy. The state public school was the initial means of introducing this dynamic, and then families took over the job of normalizing their young ones to the legitimate language.

In this second chapter of Cajun history (1920s to 1950s), I'm focusing on the period of massive educational assimilation of Cajuns into English and, consequently, into the US economy. Drawing on archived records of Louisiana School Board officials (at the University of Louisiana, Lafayette), I report the scant official story of the French ban and reconstruct the events leading up to it. The backstory to the French ban is particularly interesting to Louisiana locals because we haven't been able to figure out who to point the finger at. The teachers blame a policy, but no one seems to know where the policy came from. Meanwhile, there are buildings throughout SouLa named after the men who governed the educational system during the transition, though most of us don't actually know what these names represent. Using firsthand accounts (from historian Shane Bernard's [n.d.] unpublished survey data and UL Lafayette archives) of elderly Cajuns who actually experienced the French ban in schools, I detail the range of punishments and humiliations they underwent. These stories, which are heart-wrenching at times, illustrate the process of normalization leading to self-censoring in Bourdieu's theory of the legitimate language, so that eventually French speakers tried not to let on that they spoke French and self-ordered socioeconomically according to their mastery of "legitimate" English. Equally important, these stories also demonstrate the crucial role of the family in normalizing the legitimate language. Normalization via schools can train an entire generation of students to comply with new socioeconomic conditions but, once the entire family internalizes the hegemonic ordering, it is guaranteed to normalize or at least attempt to normalize generations to come, so that the community eradicates its own home language instead of becoming bilingual.

## BOURDIEU'S THEORY OF LANGUAGE NORMALIZATION IN SCHOOLS

Both educational institutions and familial institutions generally try to assimilate their young smoothly into the economy by normalizing them, but schools are the bridge between the language codification process of the nation builders and families. That means schools are also the bridge between the US social class system and new communities integrating into it (by immigration or internal colonization). Using the legitimate language as a gatekeeper and standard, schools sort people into the appropriate social positions as they enter the job market. English classes and departments, specifically composition courses and programs, are charged with ensuring that everyone adjusts to the linguistic standard or is barred from entering high-level or culture-defining jobs. This happens indirectly as teachers either train students to pass departmental and exit exams (normalize) or allow them to fail those exams, leading eventually to them dropping out of college and getting a working-class job. "Grammar is endowed with real legal effectiveness via the educational system," writes Bourdieu, "which places its power of certification at its disposal . . . [T]his is because, through examinations and the qualifications which [grammar and spelling] make it possible to obtain, they govern access to jobs and social positions" (1991, 258). Specifically within language, Bourdieu identifies concepts of error and correctness in grammar as the primary linguistic-pedagogical means of preserving class hierarchy.

The result, writes Bourdieu, is that the educational system reproduces already existing class structures: "[T]he educational market is strictly dominated by the linguistic products of the dominant class and tends to sanction the pre-existing differences in capital . . . The initial disparities therefore tend to be reproduced" (1991, 62). That is to say schools don't enable upward mobility; they simply help students enter the economy in a job suiting their family's social class. Shirley Brice Heath's (1983) finding in her long-term ethnography *Ways with Words* demonstrates that Bourdieu's theory is applicable in the United States. Heath researched literacy development in three communities in the Piedmont region of the Carolinas and found that only the white middle-class students thrived academically because their home-based literacy events mirrored preferred usage and rhetoric in the schools, while both African American and white working-class kids performed academically at a lower level as a result of their different socializations at home into literacy and rhetoric. Let me stress here that schools aren't pernicious; they're just sort of equal signs between the social standing of families in the dominant economy and the kinds of jobs they can qualify for in that economy.

The role of educational institutions in class reproduction has been well documented in literature on education in the United States. As Samuel Bowles and Herbert Gintis have explained in their landmark *Schooling in Capitalist America: Educational Reform and the Contradictions of Economic Life* (Bowles and Gintis 1976), "[T]he educational system does not add to or subtract from the overall degree of inequality and repressive personal development. Rather, it is best understood as an institution which serves to perpetuate the social relationships of economic life through which these patterns are set, by facilitating a smooth integration of youth into the labor force" (11). Bowles and Gintis describe what they call a "hidden curriculum" in educational institutions that trains students for the appropriate class: "We have emphasized elements of the 'hidden curriculum' faced in varying degrees by all students. But schools do different things to different children. Boys and girls, blacks and whites, rich and poor are treated differently. Affluent suburban schools, working-class schools, and ghetto schools all exhibit a distinctive pattern of sanctions and rewards . . . In important ways, colleges are different [from high schools]; and community colleges exhibit social relations of education which differ sharply from those of elite four-year institutions" (42). Bowles and Gintis have been criticized for focusing too much on the socioeconomic reproductive function of schooling without addressing possibilities for change. In their defense, the topic of the book was social reproduction, not revolution or reform or resistance. Since their study, other theorists—for example, Michael Apple (2009) in *Education and Power* and the contributors to *Bowles and Gintis Revisited: Correspondence and Contradiction in Educational Theory* (Cole 1988)—have written about ways to resist reproduction within educational systems. Meanwhile, despite the gloomy reports of Bowles and Gintis, their findings have been corroborated by subsequent research.

The idea of socioeconomic divides reproduced by pedagogy was strikingly illustrated in Jean Anyon's (1980) study "Social Class and the Hidden Curriculum of Work." Anyon studied the classroom practices of four different types of schools, ranging from schools in lower-class neighborhoods to those in the most affluent areas. She found that the schools, though all in the same economy, equipped the children for different positions on the spectrum of labor, and one of the most defining characteristics of each level was the children's relationship to authority. The lower-class school, for example, rewarded the students for following directions, whether or not they reached the correct answer. These were children of welders, waitresses, and security guards. In the school Anyon called "executive-elite," children were rewarded for creating their own paths to the solutions. Correct answers were based on whether the class reached consensus, not predetermined answer keys and sometimes not even the teacher's approval. These were the children of top corporate executives. Whereas the schools in lower-income areas prepared students for obedience in their future jobs, the schools in the highest-income areas prepared students for leadership and decision making.

In addition to socioeconomic divisions in schools based on neighborhood, class stratification is reproduced within individual schools by means of "tracking." Jeannie Oakes's (1986) study in *Keeping Track: How Schools Structure Inequality* explains the origins of tracking in the beginning of the twentieth century. She writes that tracking, though officially designed for the purposes of more effective vocational training, actually served to preserve class divisions according to subculture, not intelligence or interest. Tracking was a response to a surge of nontraditional students in public schools as a result of new child labor laws, compulsory education laws, a wave of European immigration, and the migration of poor rural families to cities for industrial jobs. In light of these new populations of students, Oakes writes, "a great deal of concern was expressed about preserving dominant WASP culture, eliminating the immigrants' 'depraved' life-style, and making the cities safe" (25). Liberal educators who supported tracking were aiming for the ideal of the "melting pot" but, like many policies designed to manage subcultures, the melting wound up being unilateral. Those who did not "melt" sufficiently were directed into manual labor and wage-based jobs where they would be blocked from participation in hegemonic decisions like policy making, law making, lobbying, and politics. Oakes argues that tracking is a race-based form of discrimination, a "'second generation' segregation" (x).

Most of the foundational literature on educational reproduction is from the 1970s and 1980s, but Peter Sacks (2007) argues more recently in *Tearing Down the Gates: Confronting the Class Divide in American Education* that reproduction is ongoing, all the way up to college. Sacks writes that admissions standards (test scores in particular) ensure that children from well-educated families will land in the most reputable colleges, while children of uneducated parents (these children are Oakes's "second generation") are not properly groomed and consequently land in community colleges or other less prestigious postsecondary institutions. The sorting process is disguised as the social-mobility myth ("if you work hard enough . . . "). In fact, children from affluent families often do work very hard to achieve high scores (enduring private tutoring and test-prep classes during the summer, taking tests multiple times, and so on). A *New York Times* article reports that private tutoring is now a $5 billion to $7 billion industry. Manhattan parents pay $85 to $150 an hour (and up to $400 an hour) to prep their children for Ivy League schools (Sullivan 2010). But Sacks argues that the children of working-class parents aren't lazy, just not aware that they are competing with students who receive private tutoring, take test-prep classes, and test multiple times. They (and their parents) tend to think of standardized tests as accurate measures of intelligence, and they don't question their scores or attempt to supplement state-provided education. They also usually aren't aware that they can appeal most decisions, from grades to class assignments to admissions. The race- and class-based distribution of students in colleges is determined by admissions standards, but Sacks writes that the sorting begins far earlier in the educational process. Annette Lareau (2003) confirms this idea in *Unequal Childhoods: Class, Race, and Family Life*. Her ethnographic study reveals that literacy practices are passed on in home and family encounters, not in schools. Schools do not equalize;

they simply assess already existing literacy practices and sort students accordingly. Once the students are sorted into their (generally) class- and race-based categories, pedagogical differences like the ones Anyon (1980) describes reinforce that categorization as well as the idea that students who wind up near the vocational end of the educational spectrum are either lazy or less intelligent. These studies consistently demonstrate that the US educational system sorts students according to class and reproduces the existing social hierarchy.

This class-sorting process of education relies heavily on control of language and culture. In *Deculturalization and the Struggle for Equality: A Brief History of the Education of Dominated Cultures in the United States*, Joel Spring (2010) demonstrates that one of the most important functions of state schooling is delegitimizing the culture and language of minority groups in the United States. He reinforces Bourdieu's ideas of national codification and dissimilation, writing that school policies and reforms are usually designed to preserve the class (and race) hierarchy established by the founding fathers (10). In *Deculturalization*, Spring documents the educational policies and pedagogies that have paralleled "the legacy of laws and judicial decisions that enslaved, segregated, discriminated against, and attempted to deculturalize Africans, Chinese, Mexicans, Native Americans, Puerto Ricans, and Hawaiians" (1). To this list I add the French-speaking precapitalist communities of Southwest Louisiana.

According to Spring's definitions, the Cajun experience in schools at the turn of the twentieth century falls under the category of deculturalization (what he writes was called "Americanization" at the time). Similar to Villanueva's distinction between those who are internally colonized and those who voluntarily immigrate, Spring writes that the tactics for dealing with minority populations have corresponded to the distinction between dominated and immigrant: "Dominated groups in the United States have primarily experienced cultural genocide, deculturalization, and denial of education. Immigrant groups have mostly experienced assimilation and hybridity" (7–8).[1] Because Cajuns are one of many groups in the United States that have been internally colonized, their experience is more similar to the former category. Within these categories, he defines deculturalization as "the educational process of destroying a people's culture (cultural genocide) and replacing it with a new culture. In the case of the United States, schools have used varying forms of this method in attempts to eradicate the cultures of Native Americans; African Americans; Mexican Americans; Puerto Ricans; and immigrants from Ireland, Southern and Eastern Europe, and Asia. Believing that Anglo American culture was the superior culture and the only culture that would support republican and democratic institutions, educators forbade the speaking of non-English languages, particularly Spanish and Native American tongues, and forced students to learn an Anglo American centered curriculum" (8). This was the experience of Cajun children between the 1920s and 1960s, including being taught Anglo American opinions of Cajuns. One state textbook, *The People of Louisiana* (1951), specifically blames Cajuns for the backwardness of Louisiana. It states, "The educational standing of the population is lowest in those particular parts of the French section in which the Acadian influence has been the greatest," and it faults Acadian values (specifically, lack of Anglo values) for the entire state's failures: "More than any other factor, this contributes to Louisiana's poor national standing, just as the Spanish-speaking population of New Mexico is responsible for that state's low ranking educationally" (quoted in Bernard 2003, 32–33). This state geography textbook, like most textbooks, was likely in circulation for at least a decade before being replaced. This is only one example of the deculturalization that Cajun children, like other internally colonized groups in the United States, were being subjected to.

Studying the educational efforts to dominate minority groups, Spring concludes that an integral part of deculturalization is eradication of the minority's language. He writes, "Forcing a dominated group to abandon its own language is an important part of deculturalization. Culture and values are embedded in language. Educational policymakers in the nineteenth and early twentieth centuries believed that substituting English for Native American languages and for Spanish was the key to deculturalization" (2010, 107). Replacing minority languages with legitimate English was intended to compel minorities to submit more quickly to the socioeconomy of the United States.

Bourdieu distinguishes two roles in this process of replacing minority languages—first, the grammarians who make decisions about the legitimate language and, second, the teachers who enforce the decisions: "[T]his linguistic law has its body of jurists—the grammarians—and its agents of regulation and imposition—the teachers—who are empowered *universally* to subject the linguistic performance of speaking subjects to examination and to the legal sanction of academic qualifications" (1991, 45). The grammarians (meaning the people who write grammar books) adhere to the class system in place (or taking its place) by codifying language norms according to class usage (deemed "correct," "proper," or "standard"), which teachers in turn pass on through various pedagogies. For their part, teachers enforce the legitimate code in any language exchanges, but they also teach hegemonic attitudes about language.

They instill the logic and tastes of the dominant through their teaching philosophy: "[T]he schoolmaster, a *maître à parler* (teacher of speaking) . . . is thereby also a *maître à penser* (teacher of thinking)," a French phrase that denotes someone with disciples (48–49). In this way, even if teachers are unable to teach their students mastery of the legitimate language (and social mobility), they teach values that help students recognize the legitimate language and where people deserve to be positioned in the economy as a result of their level of mastery. "[T]he social mechanisms of cultural transmission," Bourdieu writes, "tend to reproduce the structural disparity between the very unequal *knowledge* of the legitimate language and the much more uniform *recognition* of this language" (62). So pedagogy, in this sense, actually teaches students how to recognize and defer to their superiors in the class hierarchy. The effect of language standards, policy decisions, and classroom enforcement in Southwest Louisiana was to impart a profound consciousness of French speakers' low class status and low-class language.

### EDUCATIONAL ASSIMILATION OF CAJUNS

Though the 1921 French ban was easily the greatest determining factor for the direction of Cajun cohesion and identity since the Grand Dérangement, there is little information in the public record on the pedagogies and policies of Louisiana schools in the 1920s when the French ban took effect. Cultural memory of the French ban is often based on hearsay, like the stories people have heard from their grandparents, and recent literature on it is usually intended to summarize, not give detail. I've had a hard time writing about the French ban because there isn't much information available, and what *is* available seems to leave me with more questions than answers. Some people say the punishments were horrific; others say there weren't really many punishments. Some express a sense of betrayal that it was often Cajun teachers doing the punishing, and others argue that it was for the children's own good. So I'm reconstructing from the extant histories and several archives containing bits of the educational assimilation of Cajuns into English, interpreted in the theoretical framework of Bourdieu's analysis of language and power.

I rely heavily on the research and data of historian Shane Bernard. His account of the assimilation of Cajuns into the mainstream US socioeconomy, *The Cajuns: Americanization of a People* (2003), is the best (and only authoritative) history of this period. He provides the most extensive report of the French ban and punishments to date, but it's still fairly brief because his focus is the overall assimilation of Cajuns into the United States. He recounts the history of Cajuns from early in the twentieth century to the end of the century and writes that World War II was the most important factor in assimilating Cajuns, closely followed by the French ban in schools (5). Many GIs came home, he reports, and announced to their families that they were now American: "The war exerted a profound influence on Cajun GIs, giving them a new sense of national identity and beginning the process of rapid, widespread Americanization. Proud of their wartime contributions, they came home staunch patriots, defenders of the American way of life" (11). Cajun GIs anglicized the pronunciation of their French names, and Cajuns who stayed home involved themselves, like the rest of the country, with communist hunts and victory gardens.

Equally important as the changes wrought by World War II, I suggest, were the changing educational policies of this era, not only because of the role of schools in normalizing and sorting students into the economy but also because education was a far more prevalent experience for Cajuns than the war. Though he does not downplay the weight of the French ban, Bernard concludes that the war was more influential because "census data shows that the use of Cajun French as a first language dropped 17 percent for Cajuns born during US involvement in World War II, the single largest decrease since the beginning of the century" (2003, 5). He speculates on why the influence of the war on language use was greater than educational policies: "Even the practice of punishing Cajun children for speaking French on the school playground or in the classroom, a byproduct of the era's intense Anglo-Saxonist nationalism, did not result in immediate Americanization. Many South Louisiana children did not attend school and so were spared the humiliation of writing lines or being paddled. Those who did experience punishment still tended to use French at home, but when they became parents around World War II, many declined to teach the dialect to their children, viewing it as a shameful impediment to social and economic advancement" (xx). As some of the testimonies of Cajuns in this chapter show, however, they made their decisions not to teach their children French many years before the war, when they were children in school themselves. In addition, the French prohibition was in full effect from the 1920s till well into the 1950s and maybe later (one respondent in my survey from Crowley, Louisiana, reported that she was punished for speaking French when she entered school in the early 1980s), so even the children who dropped out in the beginning and continued speaking French probably saw their own children assimilate to English only. Based on the reports of Cajuns from this period, I think it's safe to say that the war may have been what made Cajuns decide they were American, but education was what made many of them decide they weren't Cajun. Ultimately, World War II and the French ban were two sides of the same nationalist coin; wars and language standardization are both integral to nation (empire) building.

Bernard also generously gave me access to a collection of letters he compiled in response to a questionnaire he posted in newspapers in South Louisiana and east Texas (1997–1998). Personal letters poured in describing the experiences and emotions of Cajuns who underwent the ban in schools. I quote from Bernard's unpublished collection of letters throughout this chapter, marking them with the birth date of each writer. I also mined Bernard's audio interviews in the UL Lafayette Archives, which additionally contain dozens of audio files of interviews conducted by Barry Ancelet and students working on various projects for the Cajun studies program from the 1990s to the present. Many of the respondents are now deceased, but the audio files preserve their stories about their experiences in schools. I was pleasantly surprised to stumble upon bits of my own family in these archives, like the mention of my great-aunt Ella (in chapter 2) and recordings of my great-uncles Vorice and Gervis Stanford playing fiddle. In addition to these records, I studied in the Acadiana Manuscripts Collections the records of T. H. Harris, the superintendent of Louisiana schools overseeing the French ban—his personal letters and memoirs, his public reports of school finances and scores, and a few of his publications in journals. Some articles from the *Journal of the Louisiana Teachers' Association* during the first few decades after the French ban also yielded a small amount of information regarding attitudes and pedagogies concerning French speakers in Southwest Louisiana.

What I've found has been every bit as varied and contradictory as I had originally heard in the oral reports around the community. Like everything else in Cajun culture, there is no monolithic story. Some of the punishments were terrible, while some students hardly even noticed they were being assimilated. Some of the reports, like oral stories I had heard, stress the fact that it was Cajun teachers who helped this process along, and some Cajuns are appreciative of their teachers' efforts—even the physical punishments. I noticed a correlation between this appreciation and the level of Anglo American assimilation: those who eventually assimilated the most successfully into the dominant American culture (speaking with the most Standard English accents and having the highest social positions) were the most forgiving or even defensive of their teachers' punishments. In particular, I noticed that the young

Cajuns who went on to become teachers as adults were the most defensive of their teachers' actions. But those with thick Cajun accents and manual labor jobs often expressed hurt and confusion about their teachers' actions. I include data on this internalization phenomenon, which is consonant with Bourdieu's model of linguistic assimilation. I also include data on the more generalized process of cultural normalizing in which individuals who have learned to self-police according to the legitimate language now insist on the same cultural norm for others. In almost every case, the respondents articulate their decisions to censor their French in terms of class or work, demonstrating the connection between schooling and the economy.

The great exile of Louisiana French in Louisiana actually happened during a time of optimism and hope for social equality, as Deweyan school reforms swept through the United States. These reforms promised the same educational opportunities to the poor as to the rich. As I explain in greater detail in chapter 4, though Deweyan reforms were couched in terms of "opportunity," "social cooperation," and "equality," the tenets of John Dewey's schooling reforms were incompletely appropriated by the educational system to create not democratic citizens but "corporate citizens." Extremely wealthy and influential capitalists who required a new kind of labor for a new kind of industrial economy (as well as more laborers) funded massive changes to schooling at the turn of the century to train people for what I explain later as the "corporate model." These capitalists also directly funded the changes to Louisiana education, something I point out later in this chapter. Just like many other ethnic groups across the nation, Cajuns were assimilated at a time of national reorganization after the Civil War and Reconstruction that required a revised, less tolerant definition of what it meant to be American, and during industrialization, which required a kind of corporate cooperation as well as higher levels of internalization and self-policing (in contrast with previous school models that relied on obedience and punishments). Though most of the key figures involved in ushering in the Louisiana school reform that led to Cajuns' forced assimilation were optimistic and well intentioned as they imposed these top-down programs, they were following in the tradition of other social programs coming from the center that are intended to "help" periphery groups. Education planners were making decisions for Cajuns and other lower-income residents of Louisiana, who were too poor and uneducated to be trusted with decisions about their own governance.

One of the most influential leaders of the Louisiana education reform that led to Cajuns' assimilation was Thomas H. Harris, superintendent of Louisiana schools from 1908 to 1940. It was under Harris's thirty-two-year tenure as superintendent that Louisiana state schools joined the progressive movement. Harris was trained in the Normal School under Thomas Boyd, a huge proponent of progressive education. Edwin Lewis Stephens, a former president of what is now UL Lafayette, gave a glowing account of Thomas Boyd in 1933, as he describes the impetus that led to one of largest school reforms in the history of the state in "Education in Louisiana in the Closing Decades of the Nineteenth Century." The following was written during the height of Deweyan educational optimism in Louisiana; I quote it at length to show the enthusiasm and missionary fervor Stephens associates with Boyd's educational changes:

> I am glad of an opportunity, while that great schoolmaster is still living, to pay to him the sincere tribute of my humble opinion that to him, more than to any other man, is due the credit for that foundation for the cause of public education in Louisiana during the closing decades of the Nineteenth century, upon which has been built the structure of the organization of public education which exists in this State today. Thomas Duckett Boyd, a Virginian, who came to Louisiana in 1868 . . . was educated in Louisiana and became a graduate of the University in the class of 1872. A diligent student and classical scholar, he continued his studies and afterwards became a professor of English in the University. He acquired a reputation with all his students for purity of style, logic of thinking, reasonableness and wisdom of counsel, pre-eminent fairness in "marking" or "grading" of students in class, firmness with kindliness in discipline, and the uttermost cleanness and integrity of character. In 1888 he was called to the presidency of the State Normal School in Natchitoches. And it was here in eight years that he did the great work for public education in Louisiana. He saw and understood the condition of education in the State. He realized that the solution lay in the development of a popular demand for free public schools in every town and village in every parish. He mobilized the support and vigorous assistance of able friends and agencies for public education. He enlisted a large and generous measure of support from the Peabody Fund . . . He organized Teachers' "institutes" and summer normal schools at public expense in every part of the State. He aided in the organization of the Louisiana Educational Association, the forerunner of the present Louisiana Teachers Association . . . He had as a pupil there Thomas H. Harris, destined to become the greatest individual factor in the growth of public education in Louisiana in three decades of the new century. He elevated the public idea of the mission of the teacher and the great work that had to be done in the State, from the dimmest awareness into an enthusiasm like the call to a crusade. In me he inspired the first real appreciation I had had, of the ideal of public education later enunciated by John Dewey—that the culture the wisest and best parents desire for their own children, the Community should desire and should provide for all of its children. (Stephens 1933, 42)

The prodigy of Boyd, Harris was celebrated as the greatest mover and shaker of Louisiana education during the beginning of the twentieth century, as he folded Louisiana into the progressive movement. Another account of early twentieth-century education is from *Louisiana Education since Colonial Days* (1958) by Joel Fletcher, who also served as president of Southwestern Louisiana Institute (now UL Lafayette). Fletcher similarly praises Harris as "the most influential figure in the public schools of Louisiana" (22).

And Harris did vastly change the state of affairs in Louisiana education. The leaders of socialized education in Louisiana were enthusiastic in particular about progress in state schools after a very slow start in education. Raleigh A. Suarez (1971) writes in "Chronicle of a Failure: Public Education in Antebellum Louisiana" (if the title weren't sufficiently self-explanatory) that Louisiana state education was sorely underdeveloped in the pre Civil War period for a number of reasons—mostly state neglect, apathy from all segments of the population, and outright resistance from the French Catholics. State neglect began as a result of military involvement. "In the years immediately following statehood [in 1812]," Suarez writes, "little was accomplished in the field of education partly because of the War of 1812 and the concentration of defending New Orleans against the British in 1814 and early 1815. Public education was not even mentioned in . . . Louisiana's first state constitution [1812]" (112). Finally, in 1845, the state constitution made provision for public education, but funding was greatly reduced by the late 1850s for textbooks, teachers' salaries, and schoolhouse maintenance in order to fund military expenditures.

Meanwhile, Louisianans didn't make much effort to fight the funding cuts to public education. Suarez writes that "as disadvantageous as the above factors were, the program would have had a chance to develop if the people had truly supported it" (1971, 120). Suarez blames the apathy of middle-class Louisianans, who rarely voted, and the outright opposition of the planter and wealthy merchant class, who sent their children to private schools. Like the 1950s Louisiana state geography textbook, Suarez also specifically blames the backwardness of the insular Acadians and Creoles: "The situation was worsened, if possible, because a large segment of the population in South Louisiana was French and Catholic. This group was opposed to any institution that might lessen the power and influence of church and family" (122). Edwin Stephens (1935), in "The Story of Acadian Education in Louisiana," is somewhat kinder is his analysis of French resistance, attributing it to "the natural cause of the difference in language between the colonial settlers in Louisiana and the colonial settlers in the rest of the United States . . . And it should therefore never be taken as a reproach to the French parishes of Louisiana that they remained longest in the high percentage of illiteracy" (20). The long shot, however, is that Louisiana lagged behind other states in education until the 1880s.

During the Civil War and Reconstruction, from 1861 to 1879, education had fallen to a very low position in state interests. In addition to the human and property costs of the Civil War, a series of floods and crop blights reduced a large portion of the state population, of all ethnicities and class positions, to near starvation and homelessness. The state constitution of 1879 again raised the issue of education, and "Anglo-Americans throughout the state began clamoring by the early 1880s for increased educational activity" (Brasseaux 1978, 216). In addition to the interest of the Anglo American sector in Louisiana, wealthy northern philanthropists invested heavily in updating the schools of the South during and after Reconstruction, as this was an excellent opportunity to reengineer the economy and train workers accordingly (more on this dynamic in the next chapter). Louisiana schools by 1921 were largely modeled on Deweyan progressive ideas as a result of the Natchitoches Normal School, established in 1884 (referred to earlier in Stephens's speech about Boyd).[2]

Harris's legacy was guiding Louisiana into the pattern of educational reform that other states were following at this time. In his memoirs, he reflects on the conditions of Louisiana State education at the beginning of his term in 1908:

> Several causes operated in favor of illiteracy in Louisiana. The public system of education was late getting under way, and when a system was inaugurated, public sentiment was apathetic, and in certain sections of the state, antagonistic. Not much was done for negro children anywhere. Due to these and other causes the schools failed to reach many children of both races, with the result that many thousands of our children never attended schools and were unable to read and write. They were illiterates.
> 
> The same conditions prevailed in all of the southern states, and the illiteracy percentages were high in all of them, but Louisiana headed the list for several years, then climbed to second place. She is probably now near the top of the literate states in the south. (n.d.a)

Harris revamped the state's school structure to resemble that of other states. He lobbied for and secured stable funding from the state of Louisiana through taxation as well as from capitalist philanthropists who were interested in reforming education, and he established a broader administration than had previously existed. He explains, "Since 1908 many divisions have been added . . . The various divisions of the state department came into existence in response to the needs and demands of the schools and in the early days of public school lethargy in the south, the General Education Board of New York, a John D. Rockefeller foundation, usually was the friend in times of stress by financing the divisions until such time as public sentiment made possible state financing" (n.d.b). The increased funding for schools allowed for better and more buildings. Harris describes the inferior method that was in place when he came into his position:

> Our older citizens can easily recall when practically all of the country schools were of the one-teacher type. And it was natural that the one-teacher school developed in the country communities and villages. Ten to twenty families living within a radius of a mile or two would become interested in providing at least the rudiments of an education for their thirty or forty children. They would raise among themselves a few dollars and buy the necessary lumber and bricks for a school house twenty-five by twenty-five and for fifteen or twenty double-desks and one or two recitation benches. Certain members of the group would agree to "rive" a sufficient number of cypres, oak or pine boards to cover the house and the work of building the house would be apportioned among the families. In a few days the community would have a school house ready for use. It would be rough and unpainted and the openings would be covered with wooden shutters, but it would answer. (n.d.c)

In contrast, Harris reports in a 1914 letter to *Educational Foundations: A Monthly Magazine of Pedagogy*, "[W]e have been building good houses, consolidating country schools, organizing industrial departments for both boys and girls, establishing high schools, raising the standards of teachers, getting more children into the schools, lengthening the session, and improving the schools generally" (1914, 184). Stephens confirms the immense educational growth under Harris: "Where there were not a dozen high schools in all of southwestern Louisiana in 1900, there were more than 125 in 1930. Where there were less than 50 high school graduates in this territory in 1900, there were more than 1,000 for the year 1930" (1935, 23). Stephens attributes this growth to the fact that the college (where he later served as president) required high school graduation, but it was probably a combination of the new entrance requirement, Harris's activism, and state laws requiring attendance.

It was also under Harris's tenure that the French ban was finally enforced. The French prohibition had been previously written into the Reconstruction-era Louisiana State Constitutions of 1864 and 1868 (Ancelet 1988, 354), and the Louisiana State Board of Education banned French in school as early as 1915 (later, in 1944, Act 239 made provisions "for the punishment of parents who failed to comply") (Bernard 2003, 18, 33). The lynchpin was a combination of the mandatory school attendance law, Act 27, which was passed in 1916, requiring Cajun families (who preferred local Catholic education and/or home education) to send their children to public school, and the Louisiana State Constitution of 1921, which banned French in schools, requiring all instruction in English. These two acts of legislation instituted English monolingualism in schools and changed the lives of hundreds of Cajun children drastically. Yet there is virtually no mention of the French ban in any public or private records. The 1920s saw heightened monolingualism all throughout the United States because of changes in the national economy and resulting worker requirements that were accompanied by changes in how teachers were being trained at their normalizing schools. Because there is so little information in Cajun studies about the official conversations surrounding the French ban, I report here my findings on the status, official policies, and teacher pedagogies regarding French from period documents, demonstrating the state's official silence on the French ban—starting with Harris.

Now Thomas H. Harris, before he became superintendent, had served ten years jointly as principal of high schools in Baton Rouge and Opelousas—the latter of which is my hometown and has one of the oldest, highest concentrations of Cajuns and Creoles—so he was definitely exposed to French speakers. But the only mention in his memoirs and annual school reports that can even be construed as referring to Cajuns is "country schools." Here, he describes the resistance to public education and taxation he found among poor Louisianans:

> In the last quarter of the 19th century there was no demand for public schools in the [primarily Anglo-Saxon] section of rural Claiborne Parish in which I grew up. I think the same may be said of the rest of the parish and the state. Most people were small farmers and while they lived well, they were poor. The boys worked on their fathers' farms, and the girls did the house-work. There was little hired labor, except in the form of renters and share croppers. The older children worked on the farms and could not be spared for much schooling. It was different in the towns, but the towns were too few to affect the conditions. The private pay schools cared for the educational interests of the younger children, and of the few older ones who had in view professional careers.
>
> Then, the people were not accustomed to taxation. There were state and parish systems of government, but they were simple and inexpensive. There were not many public officers, and those in office were paid small salaries. There was no road system . . .
>
> I am also impressed that there was a strong sentiment *against* free schools, except for indigent pupils. "If a parent wishes to educate his

children, let him pay for the instruction," was the generally accepted viewpoint. No justice or fair play in requiring one man to educate the children of another man. This was the attitude of the people generally, and there were no crusaders to present the arguments for the education of all the people at public expense. (n.d.d)

Harris would write in his 1921–1922 annual school report, the very year that public school teachers were required to revise their pedagogies to banish French from their classrooms, that he was proudest of the progress in "country schools." He never mentions the French-speaking population, which I later explain as a function of their class status, and is singularly optimistic about the great changes that year: "If we should select one department of education in which we have made the greatest progress, we should unquestionably choose that of the country schools. The people of Louisiana realized many years ago the importance of providing good schools for the country children . . . Many of the country schools have been organized as state approved high schools which employ the best equipped teachers and are offering educational advantages equal in every respect (and perhaps superior) to those offered in the cities" (1923, 5–6). The 1921 French ban and its implementation in schools were sources of great anxiety, shame, and punishments for Cajun students that would completely change the linguistic landscape of SouLa. Yet, in all the records and archives I searched from the period, I found no mention of the schooling of Acadians or other French-speaking students at the time of the ban. What was a benchmark event for Cajuns barely even registered in the surrounding Anglo American literature.

Two references in scholarly publications from that period may refer to Cajuns, but they are brief, unexplained, and could just as easily be concerned with other local poor subcultures. Four years after the French ban, an article appears in the *Journal of the Louisiana Teachers' Association* with "skills and drills" type pedagogical suggestions to help students learn "the habits, skills, attitudes and ideals essential to the mastery of spoken and written English" (Conniff 1925, 11). The only indication that this pedagogy is intended for ESL students is the editor's note introducing the article with a brief contextualization: "Few engaged in educational work in Louisiana have made a more careful study of spoken and written English, with the idea of improving the language ability of teachers and children, than has Mr. Conniff [member of the State Department of Education]. *He is anxious to assist in the removal of conditions that permit children to enter life with a poor command of the mother tongue and has prepared the following paper with the hope that it will be instrumental in helping the teachers give the high school boys and girls of the state a better working knowledge of the English language*" (11; emphasis mine). It is likely that many of the "boys and girls of the state" are French speakers, but there is still no mention of what the other language is.

The second possible mention of Cajuns is in a 1928 article, "Problems in the Teaching of English" by Albert L. Voss. In this article, Voss discusses the problem of the new population of students he and other teachers are struggling to educate (strikingly similar to opinions surrounding CUNY's open admissions in the early 1970s). He agrees with the progressive Deweyan changes that have come to the state of Louisiana but laments the difficulty of trying "to make some of our students assimilate what is to them totally unassimilable material" (27). He writes that he has no solutions, only problems: "We know what has happened to our educational system within the past two decades. The change that has come about is perfectly well recognized in theory at least. Twenty years ago we admitted into our public high school smaller numbers of students generally from the best environments. Then we commenced to 'sell' education, working on the theory—and rightly in my opinion—that in a democracy the masses should have equal rights educationally as well as in other respects. Higher education ceased to be a class privilege and became a social duty . . . Thus we are immediately faced with the problem of finding different types of pupils in our schools today" (26–27). Writing out of New Orleans, Voss is likely dealing with French-speaking students, though probably not Cajuns.

It was twenty-six years after the French ban before anyone mentioned anything specifically pedagogical about helping French-speaking students learn English. In the *Journal of the Louisiana Teachers' Association*, Archie S. Hollister (1947) published an article titled "The Use of French in the Language Class," in which he stresses the convenience of highlighting cognates between French and English. He writes from Lake Arthur, Louisiana, a famously Cajun area: "Due to the close affinity existing between the English and French languages, those of us who teach in the schools of South Louisiana have an excellent opportunity, by exploiting this relationship, to aid our pupils in solving many of their reading problems . . . [T]he writers of our textbooks, who write for [English-speaking children] often include material that is difficult for [French-speaking children]. However, if an analogy can be established, the new word is often seen to be only the English form of a French word with which the child is perfectly at home" (23, 26). This glossing in the public record during the first two and a half decades of the French ban indicates that Cajuns were a stigmatized minority group that was easy to ignore and override.

As Harris notes of the poor whites in Louisiana, Cajuns were generally unsupportive of public education. Because Cajuns successfully operated outside the southern capitalist economy even as late as the 1920s and 1930s, public education was not appealing to them because it wouldn't train their children for the jobs they would enter. Not surprisingly, before the mandatory school attendance act, Cajuns usually educated their children at home for farm- and housework. Elista Istre (2002) writes that Cajuns also resisted public education because they distrusted dominant Anglo American socioeconomic values. She quotes George Washington Cable, who "reported that many other Cajuns claimed 'My son is rascal enough without an education'" (28). Cajuns perceived dominant US values as dishonest and unequal, but their resistance to education was not well received by the Anglo American community. A travel writer in an 1866 edition of *Harper's Weekly* commented on Cajuns' resistance to public education, using highly charged racial terms (consistent with the US paradigm) to convey his disdain: "[W]ithout energy, education, or ambition, they [Cajuns] are good representatives of the white trash, behind the age in every thing. The majority of all the white inhabitants of these parishes are tolerably ignorant, but these are grossly so—so little are they thought of—that the niggers, when they want to express contempt for one of their own race, call him an Acadian nigger" (quoted in Istre 2002, 31). Cajuns distrusted US socioeconomic structures that encouraged fragmentation over cooperation, but their resistance to educational assimilation was interpreted as laziness, ignorance, and even racial inferiority.

Carl Brasseaux writes in "Acadian Education: From Cultural Isolation to Mainstream America" that even "the few Cajuns who broke with tradition and attended school" were rarely given jobs in "Anglo-American commerce and industry" due to prejudice or what Brasseaux calls "Anglo-American ethnocentricity" (1978, 218). Brasseaux stresses the socioeconomic reasons behind the cultural differences. Cajuns, he wrote, preferred "an education based on practical need (just as the Anglo-American parent sought formal education as a practical need)" (214). The surrounding Anglo American community was a "commercial-industrial class [that] eagerly accepted Horace Mann's concepts of publicly supported education," which required increased taxation for more comprehensive schooling (213). So, due to what Brasseaux calls Anglo American "cultural imperialism," Cajuns were required first to pay taxes for schools they did not attend, then to attend schools they did not want, and finally to dissociate from their family language.

In addition to no official mention of the French ban in the educational documents of this period, there is no official pedagogy for enforcing the ban. At one point, oral histories and local publications (after the Cajun Renaissance of the 1970s) on the French ban report that it was a Louisiana state policy for teachers to punish Cajun students who spoke French. For example, a Jefferson Davis Parish publication states, "In 1921 the Louisiana Constitution prohibited the speaking of any language except English on school property. Legally teachers were required to punish any child who spoke French at school" (Giovo, Turner, and Langley 2000, 38). But there are no documents supporting this kind of edict. It's possible that there were verbal orders but more likely that each school enforced the French ban according to practices it already used for other infractions.

According to Bernard, there was never a centralized school board decision about how to implement the ban, so the consequences for speaking French varied by parish and by school. In my personal communications with him, Bernard said he has also scoured period records to find the "smoking gun" document ordering that all Cajun children be punished for speaking French, but he never came across any. Though, as Bernard tells me, Brasseaux still believes there may have been a centralized "order," Bernard has concluded that the lack of uniform consequences for speaking French and the lack of mention in any state literature of these punishments indicate that individual teachers, principals, and school boards determined their own methods for enforcing the French ban. "Nevertheless," he writes, "by using the classroom as a pulpit for teaching Americanism tainted by Anglo-Saxonism, the Department of Education created an environment that encouraged punishment. It also did little to discourage the practice" (2003, 18). As a result, the practices of each parish and school varied widely. Reports from former students during the French ban indicate that in some parishes there was an unwritten policy that there be only non-French teachers so that the students were forced to learn English more quickly. In other parishes, though, it was the local bilingual teachers who were enforcing these rules and punishments.

The experiences of Cajun children also varied widely. Though there is no official record of the pedagogy teachers used to implement the French ban, there is a great deal of data from older Cajuns who underwent the French ban in schools. According to these reports, there was a general policy of French eradication, consonant with an English-only sentiment sweeping the nation in the first part of the twentieth century. Apart from Hollister's description of his gentle cognate approach in 1947, there are no reports of what we now call code switching, whereby students may use their home languages in all but formal communications. Reports from Cajuns who experienced the French ban through the 1950s indicate that teachers almost universally discouraged students from speaking French at all, even at home. Often they did this by communicating negative messages about the language in various ways, including physical punishments, shame-based punishments, and directly negative statements about Cajuns and/or Louisiana French. A handful of Cajuns reported a fairly positive transition to English, while others were subjected to surprisingly cruel shaming.

### IMPLEMENTING THE FRENCH BAN

I wrote earlier that schools are like equal signs between the family's social standing and the kinds of jobs they can qualify for in the dominant economy, but the detachment of a math symbol can hide what happens in the assimilation process. From the point of view of the dominant culture, nothing really changes about the people who are integrating. They were seen as low before, and they are still low once they assimilate. But a lot changes for the people going through the process. They must internalize the dominant culture's values, including its perceptions of their own culture. It sounds eerily like brainwashing, I know. Maybe that's what it essentially is. Minorities who are integrating may have, like Cajuns, seen themselves and their families as autonomous, hard-working equals, even leaders within their communities, but they must learn to see themselves as the dominant see them: lazy, backward, uneducated, or what have you.

Bourdieu (1991) divides normalization into two primary categories: *coercive forces* and *intimidating forces*. Coercive forces directly and externally enforce the new values or standards, often physically or corporally, and intimidating forces pressure individuals to comply in a way that seems almost voluntary. Compliance is never entirely voluntary, however, when there is threat of shame, social ostracizing, or insufficient income to meet one's perceived needs. Coercive and intimidating forces are so well tied together that it is difficult to separate them, as some of the stories from Cajuns who underwent the French ban later in the chapter demonstrate. Many of the former students follow up their memories of physical punishments immediately with statements about their decisions not to speak French anymore or their decisions not to teach it to their children. Most of the former students report that they strove not only to learn English but also to erase any French linguistic markers. Hilda Richard Breaux, who began school in 1938, reflects on her experiences in a letter to Bernard: "I know that when you read this you will sense the anger and frustration I felt and probably still do. For many years I did not want it to be known that I knew the French language." Coercive forces led Cajuns to internalize dominant values about language so successfully that they came to self-censor French from their own public discourse (something I describe as *code censoring* in chapter 4). Many even opposed efforts to bring French back into schools during the 1970s and 1980s.

Dominique Ryon expands on the concept of normalization in "Language Death Studies and Local Knowledge: The Case of Cajun French" (2005). Drawing on Foucault's theories of discourse and power and building on Bourdieu's theory of the legitimate language, she explains that the dominant view of Louisiana French has been that it should and will die because everyone should speak standardized English, and Cajuns have simply normalized to that pronouncement and complied with language loss as they assimilated. She writes, "The discrepancy between the two versions of linguistic assimilation—one coming from the victor, or dominant group, and the other from the defeated or linguistic minority—should be given a close examination" (70). Ryon's focus is on the ways that linguists portray Louisiana French, but her article is also instrumental in explaining the way normalization has operated in Louisiana schools. She writes that Cajuns' linguistic assimilation to American culture has been achieved largely through the process of normalization in schools. After "decades of repressive measures, institutional intimidation (especially through schooling), and procedures of humiliation," Cajuns have internalized the dominant attitude that Cajunness equals ignorance (62). As an example of normalization to teachers' pronouncements and institutional power, she quotes Jean Arceneaux's poem "Schizophrénie Linguistique," which demonstrates the process of internalization.[3] I include the original, a mixture of French and English, on the left, and Ryon's translation on the right:

| | |
|---|---|
| I will not speak French on the schoolgrounds. | I will not speak French on the schoolgrounds. |
| I will not speak French on the schoolgrounds. | I will not speak French on the schoolgrounds. |
| I will not speak French . . . | I will not speak French . . . |
| I will not speak French . . . | I will not speak French . . . |
| I will not speak French . . . | I will not speak French . . . |
| Hé! ils sont pas bêtes, ces salauds. | Well, they are not stupid, those bastards. |
| Après mille fois, ça commence à pénétrer | After one hundred times, it begins to penetrate |

| | |
|---|---|
| Dans n'importe quel esprit. | In anyone's mind. |
| Ça fait mal; ça fait honte; | It hurts, it brings shame; |
| Puis là, ça fait plus mal. | And suddenly, it does not hurt anymore. |
| Ça deviente automatique, | It is almost natural, |
| Et on speak pas French on the schoolgrounds | And we don't speak French on the schoolgrounds |
| Et anywhere else non plus. | And anywhere else either. (64) |

The internalization of dominant values that Bourdieu, Ryon, and Arceneaux describe is central to understanding how Bourdieu's theory of the legitimate language accounts for the complicity of individuals with dominant policies and practices. Once people have internalized the language standards, they enforce a kind of censorship on themselves, something that is more effective than any coercive force. In this sense, having internalized the values of the dominant, even the subordinated help enforce the same standards. This self-censoring happens both in school and outside school in situations where speakers encounter the same standards, particularly the job market. Bourdieu explains, "It is this sense of acceptability . . . which, by encouraging one to take account of the probable value of discourse during the process of production, determines corrections and all forms of self-censorship" (Bourdieu 1991). He pointedly adds that these are "the concessions one makes to a social world by accepting to make oneself acceptable in it" (77). Linguistic insecurity (as a result of normalizing to dominant standards) leads speakers like my Paw-Paw Roland to silence their linguistic codes, as well as their ideas, because they don't feel authorized to speak. As Bourdieu puts it, "[D]ominated speakers, as they strive desperately for correctness, consciously or unconsciously subject the stigmatized aspects of their pronunciation, their diction . . . and their syntax, [leaving] them 'speechless,' 'tongue-tied,' 'at a loss for words,' as if they were suddenly dispossessed of their own language" (52).

Self-censorship works in connection with ideological submission. In many cases, as these stories of French-speaking children show, the dominated literally are "dispossessed of their own language," but they are also dispossessed of their political autonomy. Ngũgĩ wa Thiong'o illustrates the connection between linguistic domination and political domination. In *Decolonising the Mind: The Politics of Language in African Literature* (1981), Ngũgĩ writes that education is a weapon of imperial warfare for conquering people; it is a "cultural bomb" that "annihilate[s] a people's belief in their names, in their languages, in their environment, in their heritage of struggle, in their unity, in their capacities and ultimately in themselves" (3). He describes the process of the cultural bomb in his own childhood: first, students were punished for speaking their native languages: "[O]ne of the most humiliating experiences was to be caught speaking Gikuyu in the vicinity of the school—the culprit was given corporal punishment" (11). In the process, Kenyan children internalized the stigma of their home languages: "Where his own native languages were associated in his impressionable mind with low status, humiliation, corporal punishment, slow-footed intelligence and ability or downright stupidity, non-intelligibility and barbarism, this was reinforced by the world he met . . . not to mention the pronouncement of some of the giants of the western intellectual and political establishment" (18). Finally, having normalized to the standards of the dominant, the children began to enforce the legitimate language on each other when they were required to turn each other in for linguistic infractions or, as Ngũgĩ puts it, "children were taught to be witch hunters" (11). In the end, Ngũgĩ writes, colonization is complete when the colonized have so well normalized that they identify with their colonizers and prefer their culture: "It is the final triumph of a system of domination when the dominated start singing its virtues" (20). The cultural bomb that Ngũgĩ describes helps explain Cajuns' reactions to their experiences in schools in the first half of the twentieth century.

To say that the reports regarding the Louisiana French ban are remarkable is an understatement. They are informative, moving, and often stunning. As much as possible, I let the stories speak for themselves, adding only introductions and a few additional explanations and analyses where appropriate. Because I want these excerpts to speak for themselves, I've also chosen to adjust nonstandard spelling and grammar. Some of the accounts are handwritten, so they were prone to handwriting mistakes such as using *an* for *am*. Some were typewritten with typos such as *didn'* for *didn't*. Some were transcribed by other people, who also included typos in their transcription (which the participants clearly didn't say), such as *pthe* for *the*. Many others simply had misspellings, nonstandard grammar, or accidental omissions in their letters. My problem was that I directly transcribed many from audio recordings, using standard punctuation and spelling for them and editing out false starts, so some of the participants, even those who were genuinely illiterate, misleadingly seem to have a better grasp of English than the ones who wrote their own letters. None of the mistakes in the handwritten letters were very distracting or unreadable, but it didn't seem fair to clean some up and not the rest. Some people were represented with my grammar, some were represented by others' grammar, and some were represented by their own grammar. Since this chapter isn't an analysis of their writing, I thought it best to standardize grammar and spelling for the purpose of readability while preserving all the language. It's probably still possible to distinguish the oral from the written reports, and that's fine. My intent was simply to include both oral and written reports in a way that would not detract from the fascinating stories and recollections of elderly Cajuns who underwent the French ban.[4] As I explain later, the data I found in these reports confirms that the purpose of these schooling practices was to assimilate Cajuns into the US class and labor system.

Physical punishments were very common in the reported experiences of elderly Cajuns, ranging from being made to kneel to being spanked with shingles:

> If French words were spoken, we were turned over to the principal's office, where this big old man had a set of rubber tubes tied together and we were whipped. The girls caught were punished different, as they were forced to walk around the flagpole with bricks in their hands. (Arlyn Berthier, senior in 1955)
>
> My first-grade teacher would knock me on my knuckles with a wooden ruler for speaking half English and half French. I stood in the back corner of the classroom for what seemed like all day at the time. I had no recess ever. I had to read English books while other children played outside. (Virginia Verret Landry, started first grade in 1946)
>
> You were put on your knees if you spoke French. The impact was to speak English and dream of having an Anglo name. (Cynthia Jones, b. 1939)
>
> The principal would instruct us to go on the shingle pile. There was a pile of shingles, you know (they would reroof the old buildings, and they would stack up the shingles there to burn them in the pot-bellied stove—we had to use wood to fuel up, to heat up the buildings), and we'd go out there and grab a couple shingles and bring them to him, and he'd make us bend over, and he'd spank us. (Richard Nunez, b. 1925 in Lake Arthur)

Many of the punishments were specifically designed to publicly humiliate the students. This kind of consequence for speaking French is a particularly effective form of normalization, because linking embarrassment with language use ensures that students learn negative attitudes toward the language:

> They'd make you kneel on the spot or they'd bring you up to the schoolhouse, which had a long porch in the front facing the highway, and they'd make you kneel alongside that banister for everybody to see going back and forth [on the highway]. (Elvin[?] Soileau, b. 1932)

> I was not punished . . ., but my classmates were punished by being struck with a wooden paddle and having to sit on a stool facing the whole class. (Alice S. Girouard, started school in 1945)
>
> I will never forget my first-grade teacher for making me kneel on two pieces of chalk and putting another chalk between my nose and the blackboard for speaking French to the other boys who were like me. It was humiliating and embarrassing to me and the French kids. The teacher and city kids would laugh at us. Maybe I could not speak English, but being a country boy who had to work on the farm and could throw a punch, that took the laughter out of many after a couple of months. Of course, there again I was punished for fighting. (K. L. Laborde, b. 1946)

Bernard describes one of the most appalling punishments from the interviews. Paul L. Landry reports that one of his teachers locked students who were caught speaking French in a closet and forced them to wear nooses around their necks (Bernard 2003, 33). "Whoever was caught with the noose at the end of the day got a spanking" (Bernard n.d.). Like Ngũgĩ's "witch-hunting" experience with Gikuyu on the playground, this policy encouraged students to turn one another in so that they wouldn't wind up being the one with the noose at the end of the day.

Writing lines was a nearly universal common experience reported by elderly Cajuns. A typical report follows:

> We were punished by writing on the blackboard 100 times: I will not speak French in school. (James M. Sattler, b. 1927)

Writing lines was such a prevalent experience in SouLa that many Cajun homes have reproductions of a painting by the late George Rodrigue, a popular Cajun artist (author of the Blue Dog series), featuring a student writing, "I will not speak French" on the blackboard. A typical common-school pedagogy, writing lines was reported by most Cajuns as more of an annoyance than a normalizing experience. One letter had a surprising ending. Winnie Landry Hebert (b. 1917) writes that she and her girlfriends were assigned lines for speaking French. She was embarrassed and didn't tell her parents; she dutifully wrote her lines and turned them in. Her girlfriends, however, told their parents, and the parents had their daughters drop out of school immediately (in violation of the mandatory attendance law).

What turned out to be a very effective normalizing locale, even with consequences as simple as writing lines, was the playground. Recess was a chance for French-speaking children to try to make heads or tails of what had been happening in the classroom all morning (or simply to let loose), but children were surprised in (often intensely) negative ways when they were punished for using their native language even in the schoolyard:

> When I began school I could not speak a word of English, so when we were outside on the playground, those of us who could speak Cajun French would converse in French to find out what was said by the teacher in the classroom. If the teacher heard us talking Cajun French, we were punished by having our hand whipped with a ruler. I determined that if I had children, I would not teach them to speak Cajun French because of that experience. (Eva Meyers Mooney, b. around 1927)
>
> I knew better than to speak French in the classroom because my sister had warned me about that faux pas. She is seven years older than I am. No one had warned me about the playground . . . We were playing and running and yelling to each other. We made the mistake of yelling in French to each other within hearing of the teacher. She quickly let us know that French was not a proper language to speak at school. We were made to stand quietly at her side during the entire recess. (Billy P. Leonard, b. 1947)
>
> My best friend and I were eating our cold lunch, sitting on the grass behind an old garage and just talking up a storm—of course French—and all of a sudden our algebra teacher sneaked up and caught us. He was very firm and told us to write 400 lines—"I will not speak French on the school grounds." (Hazel M. Thibodeaux, junior high in the late 1930s)

Some students, though, were not so easily deterred:

> When [French] students who were not bilingual asked me (at recess) to explain what the teacher had said during class that morning, I promptly began to explain—in French. The teacher would grab me by the arm, take me to the classroom, hit the tips of my fingers with a ruler, and have me kneel in the corner of the classroom. She told me that French was not allowed on the school grounds. When again asked for an explanation by a French-speaking student I obliged and was punished each time. Unlike other bilingual students I adamantly refused to stop speaking French on the school grounds when a fellow classmate needed help . . . My experience in school made me all the more determined to continue speaking French. Never did I feel inferior. (Camille J. France, began school in the 1940s)

The pressure to normalize also came from peers. In many schools, the message was reinforced by Anglo students who had learned to treat Cajun students badly:

> In 1935 my parents and I moved from Leonville, Louisiana, to Port Arthur, Texas. My father sold our farm and went to work for the Texas Company in Port Arthur. I was five years old and could not speak English. When I started school the other children laughed and teased me. (Jesse Stelly, b. 1930)
>
> I got kidded some about my accent by Texans who naturally called us "coonasses." (James M. Sattler, b. 1927)

> I had a lot of fistfights in school due to the fact I couldn't speak English very well. (Delton J. Menard, finished high school in 1944)

One Cajun respondent writes that she felt pressured to enforce language standards on her peers:

> Although I don't remember being physically punished, the *holy* and *dedicated nuns* of the Most Blessed Sacrament left no doubt in my mind as to *my duty* to help others do away with the French or Cajun language. (J. L. Melancon, graduated high school in 1937)

Eventually, according to Bourdieu's model, some students normalized to the language hierarchy well enough that they learned to apply the same standards to their peers.

In many cases, it isn't direct punishments that Cajuns remember from the French ban but confusion, frustration, and helplessness. Such experiences were written permanently on the developing identities of these very young children:

> We were playing outside and they said the bell is ringing. I did not hear it and didn't understand what they said. I lay down on the ground and fell asleep—and when I woke no one was outside. I felt so alone—and the teacher sent me home for two days, 'cause she said I was real bad. I cried all the way home, 'cause I was bad. I wanted to be good. (Viola Domingue Stevens, b. 1935)
>
> I got caught speaking French and was sent to the principal's office and was spanked. I was very frustrated and angry—really pissed off. (Kermit, b. 1926)
>
> I was spanked and punished for speaking French in school. I was also put in the closet for speaking French. I was slapped, whipped with a ruler, pulled my hair, all for speaking French. I could not speak any English, so I'd speak French. It was hard to be treated this way. I could not understand why I could not speak French. At home we all spoke French. Then I'd go to school and get whipped for speaking it. And now they teach French in school. Very hard to understand. (Chester Abshire, b. 1939)
>
> I remember that in first grade a friend we called "Armadillo" was caught speaking French in the classroom. When the teacher started coming over to his desk to slap his hand with the ruler, he got scared and confused to the point that he stood up on the seat of his desk. The seat came up and his foot got caught in it and he was so scared he started to cry and soiled himself. The teacher whisked him out of the room, I guess to clean him up, because when he did come back, he didn't smell as bad. (Tom, b. 1931)

One of the most common humiliating experiences that the respondents reported was not knowing how to ask to go to the bathroom. Teachers often ignored all requests in French, forcing children to wet and soil themselves. Though the English-only policy was meant to

Americanize subcultures, this kind of treatment wasn't training children to be better citizens, to have better character, or even to speak English. After all, someone *else* had to teach them the English words, perhaps on the playground in secret. This treatment was intended only to humiliate them for speaking French.

> We were not allowed to speak or ask the teacher in French to let us go to the restroom or be excused for personal reasons. (Arlyn Berthier, senior in 1955)
>
> I was so excited about this experience [beginning school] that I did not sleep the night before. Little did I know that I would be going to be in a total world of disbelief. On my first day, the teacher announced that we could not speak French anymore, in French no less. I had no idea how to ask to go to the bath facilities. Therefore my biggest punishment was that I had to return to infancy and use my clothes. I was spanked by the teacher, then by my parents for doing this terrible deed. (A. Grace Guidry Dupuis, b. 1935)
>
> We spoke no English when we started school. If we had to use the bathroom we asked in French and got no answer. Put your hand up—no response. You did it in your clothes because you could not say it in English. (Viola Domingue Stevens, b. 1935)
>
> It was sad to see five- and six-year-olds wet their clothes or worse soil them because they knew not how to ask for bathroom privileges. Eventually one learned, but the process was humiliating and embarrassing. (Hilda Richard Breaux, began school in 1938)

As the most basic literature on potty training explains, toilet behavior is identity-forming for children at this age, so the policy of ignoring requests to be excused to the restroom was probably particularly effective at normalizing students not only to using the English language but also to associating negative experiences with French.

As the respondent Breaux notes above, children eventually learned how to ask permission to be excused, but the learning conditions were harsh and unhelpful, and many students didn't even actually learn the English phrase they were aiming for. Ignoring the children's physical needs didn't help them learn English; it simply humiliated them for not knowing it.

> I remember going to school, having never heard English spoken before. It sounded to me harsh and I thought that by talking in a rougher voice, they'd understand me . . . I first learned the phrase, "May I go out?" I realized that that was what one said to go to the bathroom. My idea how to pronounce those words was far from the way it should have sounded, but soon I was able to make the teacher understand and was able to get that permission. (Tom, b. 1931)
>
> The first thing we learned the first day of school is how to ask to go to the bathroom. We'd raise our hand and we'd say to the teacher, "Be-scue."

We thought it was a word, but we found out later it was a whole sentence, a question: "May I be excused?" (Allen Simon, b. 1937 in Abbeville)

Simon adds that it was years before he and his friends learned the actual English words:

> The school I went to in Meaux, everybody knew what *be-scue* was, and we'd use it on occasion. We'd go to the dance and somebody in the group is missing—somebody would say, "What happened to Houston or Rodney or Curtis?" "Oh, he went be-scue." We were several years in school before we knew exactly what this word meant.

Many Cajuns report that they never suffered any physical punishments for speaking French, but they were specifically taught that speaking Louisiana French was shameful and inferior. Consonant with Bourdieu's theory of the classed status of languages, nearly all of them express their shame in terms of their socioeconomic position:

> What I did experience was probably worse and to me did more harm than any whipping, that is, we were constantly reminded in one way or another that if you spoke French you were "bas class," "low class." So many others believed this, including my own nephews and nieces. (H. C. "Papa" Meaux, grew up during the 1940s and 1950s)
>
> She [the teacher] said all dumb people spoke French and all smart people spoke English. I wanted to be real smart, so by the time I was ten we could speak English real well. But the teachers said we were dumb—'cause we were poor—and that all French-speaking kids were never going to be nothing (Viola Domingue Stevens, b. 1935)
>
> I never remember anyone being slapped for being a Cajun, but we were ridiculed by teachers and students alike because it meant you were "poor, stupid, white trash." (Paul A. Mire, b. around 1943)
>
> I don't recall being punished for speaking French at school, but I do remember being told in no uncertain terms that French on the school grounds was unacceptable. Of course, this made me feel that my Cajun-French heritage made me a "second-class" person. (Sylvia Ann David More, b. 1939)
>
> I really felt humiliated and felt that all the other children were laughing at us for speaking a stupid language. The feeling that Cajun French was less than other tongues was reinforced many times in my childhood. (Billy P. Leonard, b. 1947)
>
> You want to know how I felt? I thought of myself as being below the English-speaking people. (Winnie Landry Hebert, b. 1917)

These socioeconomic associations with Louisiana French and standardized English would eventually lead Cajuns to comply with, as well as reproduce, the language inequalities to which they'd been normalized.

These stories concretely illustrate what—represented in long, Latinate words and dozens of quotations of a translation of French theory—can seem abstract, impersonal, and even trivial. But the strength of reproduction, the forces compelling people to normalize and comply, is almost inescapable for anyone under these kinds of circumstances. As a Cajun, collecting and analyzing these stories was sensitive work for me, because I can now understand the kinds of experiences and emotions that my grandparents must have felt but refused to talk about. For the first three decades of my life, Paw-Paw Jeff denied remembering what happened to him under the French ban. He never spoke publicly about being Cajun until the night of my wedding rehearsal supper, which he and my grandmother proudly hosted in their home with a giant gumbo, potato salad, boudin, and cheesecake. That night, after meeting my husband's parents, who grew up as peasants in southern Italy, he welcomed our Italian American guests from New Jersey and spoke at length to them about the stigma of growing up Cajun, the punishments in school, and the socioeconomic battles he fought to become an independent insurance salesman. It was a really, really long toast, during which my grandmother rolled her eyes multiple times, but it was the first time I heard him open up in public about being Cajun. He was seventy-nine years old. I can also now understand why my other grandma, Emma, rarely let on that she spoke Louisiana French, even though she was never physically punished. To endure the humiliations described in some of these accounts and watch other children being punished must have been sufficient to teach her proper self-censorship.

As a grandchild I'm sympathetic, but as a parent I'm appalled. When I imagine my own children enduring such physical and psychological abuse, I can understand why these Cajun children not only grew up censoring their own ethnicity and language but decided as parents to censor their children's ethnicity as well and later protested bringing Louisiana French back into schools. In the normalization process, the coercive forces of punishments eventually persuade individuals to self-censor and then also to help enforce these standards on the rest of the community. Cajuns who endured the French ban not only internalized the dominant message about Louisiana French as a result of external enforcement; they came to enforce the new standard on themselves, even without teachers around to punish them. This dynamic is an example of what Foucault calls "subjectless subjugation" or "headless subjugation" (Foucault 1980). After the recipient of normalization has internalized the new standard, there is no need for physical enforcement because the forces of what Bourdieu refers to as "intimidation" take over. The normalized student now self-polices, as in the excerpts below illustrating that students denied in public that they spoke French at home:

> This punishment degraded me and all Cajuns. It made me feel like an inferior person, one to be ridiculed by so-called "Americans." It was embarrassing and led me to occasionally lie when asked if my folks spoke French to me at home. (Rodney J. Guilbeaux Jr., b. 1926)
>
> I was never punished for speaking French . . ., but I remember feeling "less than" because I could speak French. I remember denying I could speak French once . . . (I was wrong, but didn't understand). (Willis J. Ducote, b. 1944)

In addition to lying about speaking Louisiana French, some students did in fact stop speaking French at home. The effect of the French ban was to reorganize even the home language practices of students. Not only did the students begin to deny their culture, some learned their lessons so well that they alienated themselves from their own families:

> I would communicate in the class with a very heavy accent and in French. Consequently, I was teased unmercifully, causing me to strike back violently and frequently. It got to the point where I did not want to speak any French, even to my grandmother who could only speak French. I was fussed at by my parents and grandparents for not using the French language. (Ashton J. Landry, b. 1921)

This policy led to other family divisions too, as Cajun children sought to distance themselves from the stigma of speaking French. The following student's older sister had "passed" as a native English speaker until he began to attend the same school as a monolingual French speaker. Evidently, she felt pressured to deny her family rather than admit they spoke French at home:

> To this day I have never forgotten or forgiven her [my sister] for denying to her friends that I was her brother because I was obviously from the second class [the French-speaking class]. I can still see her laughing and making fun of me. (Paul A. Mire, b. around 1943)

Linguistic normalization was effective in SouLa. The practices these students learned in school generally stayed with them throughout the rest of their lives. Interestingly, the following students entered school as monolingual French speakers:

> Being a Louisiana native with a French name, I am not able to speak French. (Arlyn Berthier, senior in 1955)
>
> I can still speak French, but I am not nearly as fluent as I was as a child. My French now is halting and hesitant. I sometimes forget words or can't find the correct French word to express what I really mean. I will speak French to my mother, but my French is so bad that after a couple of sentences we both give it up by some unspoken agreement. (Billy P. Leonard, b. 1947)

Leonard reports that he still feels compelled to censor Louisiana French from his language:

> I quickly learned that having a Cajun accent was something to be avoided. I strove to remove all traces of my Cajun accent from my English vocabulary. Even today, I will sometimes misspeak and pronounce a word with a heavy Cajun flavor and be embarrassed by it.

The result of all this self-policing was a massive loss of Louisiana French in the culture (a 17 percent drop in one generation) because Cajuns were censoring themselves even at home. Many report that they decided not to pass French on to their children, usually because they wanted to protect their children from the shame they had endured:

> I determined that if I had children, I would not teach them to speak Cajun French because of that experience [punishment]. I am the mother of ten children, eight of whom took French in high school, but I did not teach them Cajun French because of my earlier experience—plus the fact that my husband never spoke Cajun French (he only knew English). However, I realize now that I should have taught them Cajun French because there is a definite advantage to being able to speak two languages. (Eva Meyers Mooney, b. around 1927)
>
> My biggest regret is that my wife and I did not teach our five children French. Guess it just wasn't the thing to do then. (Elton P. Bourgeois, b. 1931)
>
> My wife and I still speak Cajun French. But we did not teach the children how to speak French at all. (Dudley Theriot, began school in 1931)

One parent reports that she didn't teach her children English (only Louisiana French), yet she still helped enforce their punishments for speaking French at school:

> They came home and like every week they had lines to write because they were caught speaking French. I *didn't* like it at all but I was always sure that they would do their work. (Mrs. Adam Domingue; her children entered school in 1956, 1957, and 1958)

These reports are examples of a successful normalization campaign. The process begins in schools and leads to self-policing and even further policing in homes. This was the story of my own family, of course; after the shame my grandparents experienced in school for speaking French, my parents and all their siblings were raised as monolingual English speakers, even though most of their grandparents were monolingual French speakers.

That's how families become complicit in the loss of their own language. Schools and families are important sites of normalization, as Bourdieu writes, but the ones who are doing the normalizing are usually doing it with the best of intentions—love, even—because those same inequalities exist throughout the entire socioeconomy. Many of the students who underwent punishments and shaming in schools internalized the stigma of Louisiana French and grew up continuing to censor themselves not only because they had learned their lessons so well but because they encountered the same standards everywhere else too, as a result of socioeconomic norms established during nation building. After all, the schools were only normalizing what already existed in the socioeconomy. Cajuns who assimilated to US culture often found it necessary to deny their ethnicity for the sake of socially fitting in as well as for the sake of a job. Allen Simon (b. 1937), a native Louisiana French speaker who noticed this dynamic, recounts how common it was for Cajuns to lie about speaking French to get and keep a job:

> I have been hanging around Lafayette since 1956, and I had a habit of dropping little hints. I'd go buy some shoes or buy something in a restaurant or leave with a little *merci* when I'd leave, to see if they would bite, and a lot of people in the larger cities have flat told me, "I don't speak that French trash." They were trying in their mind to uplift themselves, which I admire, but they didn't have to be ashamed of their heritage and the language, and I knew better. I knew that they spoke French. But it was so frowned upon, and a lot of them just to get a good job—you could tell that they had a French accent, but they tried and there were some words they couldn't even pronounce—I mean they slaughtered—but still in all, they still wouldn't speak French, because they wanted to be in that upper crust of society. And it always bugged me and it still does—people denying their heritage. (Simon n.d.)

Simon's observations of "upwardly mobile" Cajuns censoring their language illustrate Bourdieu's claim that people will comply with established standards in hopes of acquiring the language capital necessary to participate in job markets. As Cajuns sought jobs outside of Cajun communities, they needed to speak English to fit in with the southern socioeconomy, so the schools' heavy-handed normalization actually did them a kind of "favor" by, as Bowles and Gintis describe the purpose of education, "facilitating a smooth integration of youth into the labor force" (1976, 11). As I mentioned earlier, some Cajuns were thankful for their teachers' diligence, even when it came in the form of physical punishments. The pedagogical linguicism that Cajuns experienced under the 1921 French ban had begun long before they were mandated to attend school; policy and pedagogy just helped the process of cultural domination along.

Similar to Ngũgĩ's description of the cultural bomb, many of the children who endured the French ban normalized so well that they later fought to keep Louisiana French out of schools when it came to the education of their own children and grandchildren. Barry Jean Ancelet documents the struggle to reinstitute French in Louisiana schools in "A Perspective on Teaching the 'Problem Language' in Louisiana" (1988). Under the direction of US congressman James Domengeaux, the Council for the Development of French in Louisiana sought to reintroduce French to the Cajun community from the 1970s on, with a number of French-immersion school programs—a counter to the English immersion of 1921. Yet there was much resistance from the community, as Cajuns who had internalized the illiterate stereotypes "dutifully echoed past criticisms" and adamantly opposed the teaching of Louisiana French: "Older Cajuns, who had written 'I will not speak French on the schoolgrounds' a few thousand times, had learned the lesson well," writes Ancelet, "and avoided inflicting on their own children what was long considered a cultural and linguistic deficiency" (346). After being legally persuaded that Louisiana French was an illiterate dialect, not many Cajuns wanted to pass on a language that "was 'not the real French, just broken Cajun French'" (346). Domengeaux achieved the revocation of the French ban in the 1974 state constitution, but there was no community support for CODOFIL's efforts to bring back Louisiana French to schools.

Linguicism was enforced in Louisiana schools beginning with the 1921 French ban but, as I wrote in chapter 2, it actually originated outside schools and also failed to be redressed in schools, even with progressive policies and state support. Schools play an enormous role in normalization, but the intimidating pressures outside school—families protecting their children, the job market, hegemonic stereotypes, and deeply rooted censorship practices—compelled Cajuns to protest their own language in schools. The response of CODOFIL and its supporters to the rejection of their efforts was bafflement, as this 1984 forward-thinking letter to the editors of the magazine *Louisiana* shows. In response to the local education board's decision not to require foreign languages in high school, one supporter of bilingual education wrote:

> Chers Amis,
> There are a lot of us walking around long-faced today, and just a little puzzled—those of us throughout [bilingual] Louisiana who were waiting expectantly to see foreign language requirements return to our schools. We were sure that the State Board of Education and Secondary Education (BESE) was going to show the rest of the states what a class act we are down here. We were going to be new pioneers, helping to lead our country back out of its insular attitude to the rest of the world. We were going to have youngsters who would be able to communicate with and relate to

our growing numbers of Hispanic citizens. We were going to have happy Cajun grandparents who could look forward to conversations in French with their grandchildren and great-grandchildren. We were going to have a state full of future adults who would one day be able to communicate at least a little with the many foreign visitors who come here and would be confident and articulate travellers abroad. Our children were going to develop an essential awareness of other peoples and other cultures . . .

I suggest that the next issue of *Louisiana* be bordered in black. (McDowell 1984)

The ideas espoused by CODOFIL and its supporters were progressive for their time, but this is an example of a progressive policy decision for schools that lacked community support and consequently failed. When the schools' French-immersion programs were finally instituted, they were conducted in standard Parisian French, as Cajuns had requested, and children still could not speak to their grandparents in Louisiana French. I recently had lunch with a Belgian teacher, my mom's neighbor, who has been heavily involved in the French-immersion efforts in South Louisiana for the past fifteen years. She said standard French might persist in Louisiana, especially because French-speaking countries are projected to control markets by 2050, according to a *Forbes* study (Gobry 2014) (which reports that Chinese students currently study French), but she reluctantly shook her head and said she doesn't think Louisiana French will survive.

## CONCLUSION

Maybe I would have tried harder to communicate with my grandma in French if I had known that she even spoke French. But she had done an excellent job of internalizing dominant values and customs. In spite of her Anglo posturing and successful assimilation, I don't think Grandmama Emma ever forgave her first-grade teacher. "I *did* know my colors," she would insist to us each time she told the story. And she was right; she did know her colors. But knowing that she was in the right didn't keep her from hiding her French later. Her generation's shame has a lot to do with why I don't speak Louisiana French. I was part of the first wave of French classes (nonimmersion) at Park Vista Elementary, and when I learned a few French words—*chat, chien, chapeau*—and tried to talk to my Paw-Paw Jeff, he smiled pleasantly but resumed whatever he was doing. I know he would have pushed me to speak French if he thought I should learn it. He wasn't subtle about suggestions. He was a huge nag about my grades and the career he had planned for me as a nurse, and he seemed pretty comfortable pushing me to do things I strongly disliked—baiting my own fishing hooks, taking tennis lessons, praying the rosary—but French might as well not have existed. And when I came back as an adult from three months in France, finally able to communicate with Paw-Paw in his first language—or so I thought—I was heartbroken. I could understand him, but he couldn't understand my Parisian accent. He smiled apologetically and said, "Je ne parle pas le vrai français." I remember stuttering in my French as I tried to keep this magical moment, keep us talking in French. I knew I could adjust my French to the Cajun accent—it was as natural as relaxing my mouth and letting my Cajun accent out in English—but he had already moved on, and we were officially speaking English only again.

# 4
## DON'T BLAME TEACHERS (NOT TOO-TOO MUCH)
### The Limits of Classrooms

> *Everybody knows it's important to speak English except these knuckleheads. You can't be a doctor with that kind of crap coming out of your mouth. In fact you will never get any kind of job making a decent living.*
> —Bill Cosby

> *[G]reat psychological damage is inevitably done when a student is cut off from the way of life he wishes to lead because he lacks the competencies expected in professional life. For us to shirk the more difficult job of teaching the standard dialect and traditional modes of academic discourse is a serious mistake, for which our students pay the price.*
> —Sarah D'Eloia, "Teaching Standard Written English" (in the first issue of *JBW*)

> *I do require that [Cajun] students write in standard English in their formal writing assignments, but since I teach composition, that's my job.*
> —Louisiana teacher of freshman composition

The first time I experienced a progressive pedagogy as an undergrad, I wrote the teacher off as an airy-fairy liberal. It was Chris Schroeder, the guy who went on to coedit *ALTDis*, one of the best resources available to someone like me, studying the politics of English teaching in the United States. It was my first exposure to a collaborative class—a 200- or 300-level literature course. I hated the peer editing groups. I resisted the revisions and student participation. I just wanted the teacher to tell me the answers so I could tell them back to him on some test, so I could get my degree and get out. But when the students asked questions, he'd pose the questions back to us, then keep a neutral position about however we answered it. Ugh.

Chris was non-Cajun and—I thought—privileged, so relaxed about language and everything else, wearing baggy shorts and Birkenstocks to class each day. I don't remember learning a single thing about grammar or standardized English. I can't even remember the content or course topic, none of the readings. All I can remember is the way he taught. The long, uncomfortable pauses we endured while he waited for someone else to speak up in discussions, his awkwardly respectful replies to my open criticisms of the class, the letters he asked us to write at the end of the semester about what grades we thought we deserved, his easy way of chatting with me when I saw him at the writing center—as if I were an equal. I had never had a teacher let the curtain down before, so to speak, allowing me to see how he made his decisions and requesting my input on the course. He was a grad student in composition and rhetoric at the time, so I figured that was why he didn't know how to maintain the proper teacher distance, how to demand student respect.

I complained to my cousin Angelina, who had grown up in the same extended family and attended the same college-prep private school I had. A grad student in English at the same college, she had become a sort of educational mentor to me, and she had probably shared cubicle space with Chris in the adjunct "quarters" at some point. "Oh, Chris?" she said, raising her permanently skeptical eyebrows. "His problem is that he's a relativist. He completely ignores the way the world works. He would jump off a building and try to fly; he thinks the laws of gravity don't apply to him." An accomplished code switcher, Angelina was as practical about English as I was, and she took me under her wing when I was in college. She prided herself on recognizing and adjusting to absolute truth. In that same vein, Angelina was excellent at identifying unspoken things—for example, the sexual imagery in driving the stake into the vampire's heart in *Dracula*—and explaining them in no uncertain terms to others. No hinting, no stuttering around difficult topics. She did the same thing with the unspoken rules of English composition that sort people into elite and failing categories. She matter-of-factly taught me the five-paragraph essay in about five minutes, and that was the difference between Ds and As for me in freshman comp.

In retrospect, I think Angelina had the right idea. She equipped me with the quick answers I needed to score well on tests and pass all the hurdles. She made elite knowledge accessible to me, and she did it in a way that taught me to identify systems and rules for myself, even if they're unequal or silly. But Chris had the right idea too. He didn't teach me the things I wanted—more code switching, more formulas to impress teachers and make easy As, the inside track—but he introduced the idea that another set of rules was possible. Angelina was an expert on reading the map, choosing the best route, decoding it for others, and navigating students to the end destination. Chris, though, wanted to redraw the map. His way wasn't very practical for me at the time, a

Cajun starving for more linguistic capital. In fact, I thought I learned nothing from him, since I couldn't remember any of the course content, but I'm surprised to note that I remember the course politics, and I remember them very clearly. For all their verbal sparring, Chris and Angelina were actually friends, and they still are. And I'm suggesting that their teaching philosophies—demystifying the map and redrawing it—can be friends too.

I briefly discuss this kind of pedagogy later in the chapter, but let me be very upfront here by reiterating that it's not sufficient to address US linguicism in schools alone. Not even my ideal pedagogy can undo US language inequality because any pedagogical or policy-related changes are limited by the reproductive function of schools, or their *sociopedagogical* function. Schools exist to sort and integrate students into the appropriate place in the socioeconomy (this is the "reproductive" function of schools), and students normalize to language inequalities eventually by internalizing the messages they receive because they receive the same messages from their families and the economy. Pedagogy—at least pedagogy that sufficiently equips students for gatekeeping obstacles and job markets—is limited by the system it's contained in, so the position of any composition teacher who supports language equality (and other forms of equality as well) is sticky. Teachers may not want to reinforce inequalities, but they almost certainly will do so if they want to perform their jobs well and receive good student evaluations. And even if they try—like Chris—to resist, they will be met with the defiance of students like me as well as opposition from the students' families, who often take on great debt to ensure their children's access to the legitimate language. As the epigraphs above demonstrate, teachers' consciousness of the economic pressures of the job market—for both their students *and* themselves—can have an incredible influence on their pedagogical decisions.

This has been the case in the Cajun community, as I report in the results from a survey of teachers of Cajun students in Southwest Louisiana to assess current popular strategies for dealing with language issues in the area. These teachers claim across the board that they are keenly conscious of job markets as they make pedagogical decisions, again demonstrating the connection between pedagogy and the economy. Though a popular strategy called "code switching" (which I argue elsewhere is actually *code censoring*) has replaced the policy of eradication that all but destroyed Louisiana French, composition courses still serve to reinforce the legitimate language by continuing to encourage students to censor all traces of Cajunness. In fact, pedagogies might change drastically, but language prejudice will still be entrenched in the educational system and CE will probably still be near the bottom because changes in pedagogies correspond to transitions in capitalism, which fundamentally requires class disparity. That's because the US educational system is actually underwritten by big-name capitalists. So, before I discuss code switching and a newer strategy called translanguaging for handling language standards, let me provide some context for the meaning of pedagogical shifts.

## US SOCIOPEDAGOGY

There's no such thing as a free lunch, and there's also no such thing as a free education. Whoever is providing the schooling is also getting something out of the deal. That is, they're buying something. "They" in this case are the wealthy philanthropist-capitalists after whom many educational foundations are still named—Rockefeller, Carnegie, and Vanderbilt, for example. The United States has traditionally had its residents pay for their own education with taxes, and most people are content with that system because they generally agree with the idea of nationalized job preparation. But they don't get to decide how much of their taxes go to education versus wars or any other national expenditures. In 2013, the US budget for education was about $70 billion, or 1.9 percent of the total budget (compared to military spending at more than $800 billion), and communities supplemented this figure with box-top programs and fund-raisers (or simply paid for private or home schools). Though we fund our own public education, we don't have much say about purchasing decisions, and we also don't get to set the literacy standards or choose the curricula. When the foremost US philanthropist-capitalists step in and offer contributions, however, that money is usually earmarked for specific changes in pedagogies, classroom layouts, technologies, and curricula. The Bill and Melinda Gates Foundation, for example, has invested hundreds of millions of dollars in public schools, with a specific agenda that includes "charter schools, high-stakes standardized testing for students, merit pay for teachers whose students improve their test scores, firing teachers and closing schools when scores don't rise adequately, and longitudinal data collection on the performance of every student and teacher" (Barkan 2011). These strategic contributions carry a special kind of clout that supersedes the rest of the people paying into the educational system.

The difference is that taxpayers are not "sponsors of literacy," a term Deborah Brandt offers for people who set the standards and stand to benefit in a grander way from those standards. She explains in *Literacy in American Lives* (Brandt 2001) that sponsors of literacy are "any agents, local or distant, concrete or abstract, who enable, support, teach, and model, as well as recruit, regulate, suppress, or withhold literacy—and gain advantage by it in some way" (19). Her model is intended to apply to any form of literacy training, from volunteer pamphlet writing to doctorates in English, and it also includes nonalphabetic literacies like computer applications and codes, media marketing, and data analysis. There are different goals and measures of success in each context, but the common denominator is the sponsor who sets goals and creates rules, whereas everyone else can only try to find ways to take advantage of existing training structures. In that sense, taxpayers have a vested interest in K-12 literacy training, but we aren't sponsors of it because we don't create the rules. In fact, many teachers and parents feel helpless and overwhelmed by the changes being forced on their schools as the Gates Foundation, along with the Walton Family Foundation (Walmart founders) and the Eli and Edythe Broad Foundation (founder of two Fortune 500 companies), push their allied education reform plans on public schools.

Sponsors of literacy have traditionally changed standards according to economic needs. Brandt (2004) explains in "Drafting U.S. Literacy" that the military leadership has been an influential sponsor of literacy in the United States, responsible for changing national literacy standards multiple times. During the 1940s, for example, "in the space of five years, what counted as literacy—or enough literacy—changed six times" (486). These literacy fluctuations were prompted not by expert measures of proficiency or intelligence but simply by the number of soldiers needed during World War II. Literacy standards were lowered every time the military needed more men and raised again when there were enough soldiers. (Incidentally, the military has continued to exert great influence on US education, from testing protocols to ESL programs, and more recently with games-based learning.) Job markets work similarly in a market economy. When the demand for labor is high and the supply is low, job (and literacy) requirements are lowered. When the demand for labor is low and the supply is high (because, say, corporations have moved offshore or the United States has admitted more immigrants to artificially force wages down), competition for the few remaining jobs increases, so employers practice "credentialism," or the artificial elevation of job requirements beyond what is needed for the work. "Standards" are a moving target manipulated by the dominant to meet the needs of the moment, from filtering out certain voters to "warehousing" workers in higher ed while the job market is saturated. These changing standards are sort of like a gate that opens and closes according to the needed numbers, while the class system goes untouched.

To hone in more on schools, pedagogy is the main instrument in educational institutions by which inequalities are reified. It's common knowledge that education is never neutral. Information is given out just so—limited this way, spun that way, mistranslated, and so on. But it's not just the content that's not neutral. The pedagogy is also not neutral. Pedagogy models for and teaches students how to behave in their future relationships with authority figures and with their work. If the economy is unequal, then any pedagogy that prepares students to fit into it prepares them for inequality. Bowles and Gintis also emphasize the sociopolitically normalizing role of pedagogy in the educational process: "The heart of the process is to be found not in the content of the educational encounter—or the process of information transfer—but in the form: the social relations of the educational encounter" (Bowles and Gintis 1976, 265). The "form" of the educational encounter is pedagogy, which they define as the triune relationships between the teacher and the information, the students and the information, and the teacher and the students. This aspect of the classroom is more formative to students' future relationships than any of the content. After having practiced these relationships for twelve (plus) years, students have perfected their roles and are ready to join the blue-collar labor force quietly and seamlessly. Those who opt to go on to college encounter slightly different kinds of classroom socialization there, preparing them for gray-collar or white-collar jobs.

This sociopedagogical function of education is present in any form of schooling, whether it is preparing students to mindlessly join the current society or to help create a new utopian one, because education is always sponsored for some kind of outcome. Within the US educational system, the purpose of pedagogy is the smooth integration of youth into their proper places in the planned economy. As Bowles and Gintis put it, "The educational system, basically, neither adds to nor subtracts from the degree of inequality and repression originating in the economic sphere. Rather, it reproduces and legitimates a preexisting pattern in the process of training and stratifying the work force" (1976, 265). Teachers get to "choose" their pedagogies, but that choice is kind of an illusion because they have no control over the conditions and standards they are normalizing students to. Michel Foucault (1977) similarly wrote that teachers are "relays" of the disciplinary gaze in the tradition of the panopticon. As his word *relay* indicates, teachers are simply another link in the chain. They didn't create the inequality; they are merely passing it along. Victor

Villanueva once wrote that teachers are essentially middle managers for "those who are in truly dominant positions" (Villanueva 1993, 134–36). Likewise, when national educational policies and standards change for some reason, teachers scramble to normalize their students accordingly, even if the economy is growing more and more unequal and requires them to normalize their students to correspondingly intense inequalities.

So when pedagogical trends undergo major changes (about once or twice per century), there's a good chance they're corresponding to shifts in the economy that require new labor training. The enormous amount of money that the Gateses, Waltons, and Broads (commonly called the Big Three) are currently investing in education reform is actually a major signal of national reorganization in response to economic shifts that threaten the United States' competitive position in international markets. Each nation, which is an alliance of extremely wealthy and influential capitalists who unite large, heretofore distinct populations to work, fight, and die for them under the guise of patriotism and national duty (the imagined community), is competing for the largest share of wealth. One of the primary ways of beating out other nations in different markets is equipping workers with ever-improving technologies and methods, similar to the military's ongoing quest for better weapons and tactics. When the economy shifts, capitalists respond by updating the educational institutions responsible for training their workers. The Gates Foundation's website states it pretty explicitly: "[O]ther countries are catching up with and even outpacing us. The times have changed—our schools need to change with them." We're in the process of shifting to transnationalism (a more globalized economy), so the US sponsors of literacy are covering the costs for the structural changes in the educational system necessary to equip laborers to be more competitive.

As a result, these sociopedagogical shifts may be improved forms of job training, but they are not necessarily improvements on social equality. Changes in national US pedagogy, even deep changes, are limited by the institutional function of schools. Any sponsors of literacy with the power to make substantial changes in pedagogy, according to Bourdieu, will maintain the inequalities already built into education because those inequalities benefit them: "[T]he logic and the aims of the strategies seeking to modify [the structural constancy of the educational system's inequalities] are governed by the structure itself, through the position occupied in the structure by the agent who performs them" (Bourdieu 1991, 64). So education reforms and even the most seemingly progressive pedagogies are simply more effective forms of normalizing students to inequalities. Redecorating, not restructuring.

When wealthy capitalists, with their fingers on the pulse of the US economy, suddenly begin pouring big money into education reforms, it's because they stand to benefit in some extraordinary way. After all, they've demonstrated throughout their entire careers a shrewd eye for spotting investments with high yields. Need workers who are comfortable freelancing so that you don't have to pay for office space, equipment, or health benefits? Try e-learning; students learn to manage their time without supervision and develop better computer literacy. They also normalize to the idea of covering their own work-related expenses like laptops and Internet providers. In fact, higher education costs are structured like sharecropping now, where students buy their tools (certification) on credit and are then virtually enslaved to the wage system just to keep up with their student loan payments. Not even bankruptcy can free them. Also, until recently, state colleges were free, but higher education has been commodified and is turning out to be a pretty lucrative for-profit venture. New York City subways are plastered with ads for different colleges and vocational training programs as CEOs and college presidents fight for customers to support their enormous salaries. Not surprisingly, K-12 schools are being privatized as well in the charter movement.

There are other signs of national reorganization in response to the needs of capitalism: increased wars and military activity (indicating struggles with the ruling classes of other nations), national upheavals (financial or natural disasters that challenge the strength of patriotism), explicit discussions and critiques of capitalism, and literacy crises. There are ongoing interventions of the legitimate language, or dissimilations, happening behind the scenes at all times, but literacy becomes a national crisis when it makes headlines and shows up in public policy discussions. Antonio Gramsci explains it similarly but in terms of hegemony: "Each time that in one way or another, the question of language comes to the fore, that signifies that a series of other problems is about to emerge, the formation and enlarging of the ruling class, the necessity to establish more 'intimate' and sure relations between the ruling groups and the popular masses, that is, the reorganization of cultural hegemony" (Gramsci 1971, 16). Discussions of language standards and crises are indications that the economy is being reorganized, requiring massive expenditures from philanthropist-capitalists who stand to benefit most from a smoother-operating workforce. As I suggest later, these periods of language and national renegotiation are also opportunities to struggle for more equal standards.

Literacy crises historically correspond with the introduction of new populations into educational contexts, as Chris Schroeder writes in

"From the Inside Out (or the Outside In, Depending)": "[L]iteracy crises have been linked to dramatic increases in enrollment. From this perspective, each time literacies and institutions were challenged by the infusion of cultures, critics would declare a crisis in literacy rather than confront increasing discursive and institutional differences" (Schroeder 2002, 182). Elbow writes that there were similar responses to students' "incorrect" language usage after the Civil War, after World War II, and during open admissions because these were all periods of influxes of nonstandard student populations (Elbow 1999, 360). Schroeder argues that these aren't crises of literacy but of *legitimacy*. People readily conform to the dictates of academic discourse, he writes, because they want to be considered "insiders." If they can't or don't conform to the proper definitions of literacy, they are held indefinitely in "remedial" courses, where they are denied access to the kind of education that jobs with higher salaries and more clout require.

Accordingly, the major changes and reforms in US pedagogy have historically corresponded with the evolution of the economy to better equip workers for the environment of the workplace into which they are to be integrated. The type of training in turn corresponds to the kind of labor the students will likely be performing once they enter the labor force. Bowles and Gintis (1976) describe three major transitions in US pedagogy that have corresponded with three major transitions in capitalism: the common-school reform during early US nation building, the progressive educational movement after the Civil War, and the movement begun in the 1960s. The common-school reform corresponds with a transition to entrepreneurial capitalism during industrialization, which required workers (who were trained separately from capitalists) to normalize to factory labor habits, so I call this a transition to "factory pedagogy." Next, the progressive educational movement corresponded with a transition to monopoly or corporate capitalism at the end of the nineteenth century that relied on increasingly intricate forms of middle management in its large bureaucratic structures, requiring workers to normalize to self-policing and cooperation, so I call this a transition to "corporate pedagogy."[1] Bowles and Gintis don't name the last transition, simply calling it "the movement begun in the 1960s," but they explain that it corresponds with the integration of new populations of workers, which they define as "uprooted Southern blacks, women, and the once-respectable, 'solid' members of the precorporate capitalist community—the small business people, independent professionals, and other white-collar workers" (234–35). This last period of diversification of labor, a result of economic and national reorganization, is where I step off with my analysis later in the chapter. It is the context from which code switching and other elements of what might be called "multicultural pedagogy" emerged. Here, to illustrate the way pedagogy follows the economy, I explain the first two periods, factory pedagogy and corporate pedagogy.

Even before these pedagogical transitions, though, the very genesis of mass public schooling in the United States was a sociopedagogical response to a shift in capitalism. Capitalism began as simple moneylending (usury), and had moved to a system of "early sharecropping" (this is often referred to as "cottage industry" in England) around the time of the founding of the United States. In this particular system, capitalists supplied materials to the workers and collected the products, but they didn't oversee any of the processing, similar to the practice in which the colonies were responsible for procuring raw materials and shipping them to the mother country to be refined and sold back. With a work environment like this, apprenticeships were the main source of job training. Educational requirements were otherwise minimal—a little reading, writing, and arithmetic. As a result, schooling was minimal as well. Apart from classical education for the children of elites, most children received some degree of religious instruction and the three Rs at dame schools, which varied in rigor by the matron's choice.

With a transition to entrepreneurial capitalism, in which nonworkers (production managers) oversaw workers as they processed commodities in factories, educational requirements rose, spurring a transition to factory pedagogy. In addition to factory labor skills, workers needed to be trained how to work in the special setting of a factory; they would need to be obedient and disciplined. The idea of social control may seem a tad conspiratorial, but several literacy theorists have documented it as the inspiration for mass education in the United States. James Donald (1983) reports in his article "How Illiteracy Became a Problem (and Literacy Stopped Being One)" that public education was invented by British elites to help cement class hierarchy during a time of transition to industrial (or factory) capitalism by controlling the already existing widespread literacy and training workers for factory discipline (not skills). Donald demonstrates that the working class already had high (and increasing) rates of literacy, but was using literacy for political purposes like reading Thomas Paine's tract *Common Sense* or for "incorrect" interpretations of the Bible. "What changed at the end of the eighteenth century [after the institution of public education]," writes Donald, "was not the number of people who could read and write (the rise in literacy rates was marginal) but the perception of literacy" (36–37). Similarly, literacy rates were already high in the United States before public education, about 90 percent of white adults. As Bowles and Gintis (1976) point out, "It is particularly difficult to make the case that the objective of early school reform movements was mass literacy in view of the fact that literacy was already very high . . .prior to the common school revival" (228). State-sponsored public education was developed originally not to encourage literacy but to control the already existing circulation of literature, literacy, and interpretations of the working class—that is, to teach how to think, especially on matters of politics.

In addition to controlling literacy, state-sponsored public education was invented to foster not *skilled* laborers but *disciplined* factory workers. There were already plenty of skilled laborers in the working class, but these workers were accustomed to setting their own hours and rates, and this was a problem for overseers. Harvey Graff writes, "[T]he laboring population had to be trained for factory work and taught industrial habits, rules, and rhythms . . . The problem of course was one of discipline, . . . [which was] required to produce goods on time" (Graff 1990, 228). This new public training was intended explicitly to keep the working class "in its place." In response to concerns from the ruling class that education might cause uprisings from the working class, one educator wrote, "It is not . . . proposed by this institution, that the children of the poor should be educated in a manner to elevate their minds above the rank they are destined to fill in society . . . Utopian schemes for an extensive diffusion of knowledge would be injurious and absurd" (quoted in Donald 1983, 39). Another educator replied that only by education "can the workman be induced to leave undisturbed the control of commercial enterprises in the hands of capitalists" (quoted in Donald 1983, 44). Graff writes that North America copied Britain's model of education for similar purposes: "for the efficient training of the masses to the social order and the reassertion of hegemony" and "the additional important task of assuring that manual workers did not aspire to rise above their station in life" (1990, 23, 31). Graff stresses the class requirements for establishing capitalism in the United States.

In order to train people for factory-type labor, factory pedagogy was highly disciplined; it "brought us the chairs-nailed-to-the-floor classroom" (Bowles and Gintis 1976, 254). The curriculum featured memorization and recitation, which came to be criticized as "rote learning" and "knowledge without understanding" during the Progressive Era. Education theorist Paulo Freire (1993) also criticizes this type of education in *Pedagogy of the Oppressed* as what he calls the "banking model": the teacher deposits information in the students' brains, to be withdrawn again for the test (76). "Back to basics" movements like No Child Left Behind also draw from factory sociopedagogical traditions that emphasize heavy testing and close surveillance; they are often met with resistance from teachers and parents because they simply aren't appropriate for the bulk of today's job training.

The next major economic shift, to monopoly capitalism (an early form of corporate capitalism), required workers to internalize the idea of surveillance and police themselves, so schools transitioned to corporate pedagogy. This corresponding pedagogical shift was during "the period from 1890–1920, marking the transition of the U.S. capitalist system from its earlier individualistic competitive structure [under entrepreneurship capitalism] to its contemporary corporate form" (Bowles and Gintis 1976, 18). Monopoly capitalism required a form of cooperation instead of mere obedience because workers were increasingly tiered into middle management positions. The accompanying pedagogy, a cobbling of elements from the Progressive movement, would focus on student normalization instead of coercion. Under corporate capitalism, there are also increasing divisions of labor by group (and even nations) instead of individuals, controlled by a more centralized bureaucracy. Bowles and Gintis write that factory pedagogy became obsolete as a result: "The Progressive Era accompanied the transition to corporate capitalism, in light of which the small decentralized common school was manifestly anachronistic, both in its internal social relationships and in the degree to which it could be centrally controlled through enlightened social policy" (199). Recognizing the need for a more centralized (national) educational system and a new type of laborer, prominent capitalists invested heavily in updating both K-12 schools and teacher-training schools ("normal schools" for normalizing pedagogy). Bowles and Gintis write that J. P. Morgan, John D. Rockefeller, and "a number of leading capitalists" supported the vocational education movement during the 1890s both politically and financially. In addition, "the bureaucratization, tracking, and test-orientation of the school system [was] promoted by seed money from large private foundations, articulated by social scientists at prestigious schools of education, and enthusiastically implemented by business-controlled local school boards" (200). Influential capitalists who understood the need for a new kind of worker were major sponsors of the new version of literacy (or education) because they stood to profit from these educational investments.

John Dewey was one of the most influential school reformers during this period, with his vision for creating a truly egalitarian educational system that would model and foster a democratic consciousness in all students, but his ideas were appropriated into mass public education only insofar as they helped further corporate capitalism. For example, two of the most important features of Deweyan education were integrating schools with communities and giving students equal participation in school governance (Sabia 2011, 4). Educational policy makers in most states adopted Dewey's perspective on treating all the community's children as their own by enforcing mandatory school attendance, but they weren't so keen on letting the students participate in pedagogical and curricular decisions. Teachers, administrators, and parents were often supportive of the transition to corporate pedagogy because it provided better job training for students. Bowles and Gintis write that there were multiple interests in transitioning pedagogies, and workers often got what they wanted, but only when capitalists wanted it too: "[E]xpansion of public education was supported by employers and other powerful people as well as by organized labor. Where the educational demands of organized labor diverged from that of business elites—as in the turn-of-the-century struggle for control of vocational education—labor generally lost" (1976, 228–29). The school reforms of the Progressive Era are an example of the interests of capital beating out the interests of progressive educators, of pedagogy following the economy.

These economic and pedagogical transitions, as Bourdieu predicts, have also corresponded with major language debates and attempts to redefine the legitimate language. The period of US nation building and common-school reform, of course, corresponds to Webster's drive to define a national language. The Reconstruction Era after the Civil War was an important time of national redefinition and reorganization—economically, linguistically, and even in terms of self-identification for states that had seceded. Once again, people needed to be taught how to be American. As I explain in the next section, it was also during this economic and linguistic transition that the freshman composition course was born.

### THE PEDAGOGY SHIFTS IN COMP/RHET

Like pedagogy in general, language pedagogy is intended to integrate laborers into the status quo and sort them according to class. Freshman composition has functioned on different levels to keep students in their classes, foster nationalism, assimilate minorities and subcultures into the mainstream economy, and teach students how to think (maybe even what to think). Teachers of freshman composition help students conform to the demands of the job market; if students can't or don't conform, teachers are generally expected to fail them until they do conform or are sorted into manual labor. The field of composition was invented to manage the marriage of two of the most important points of negotiation during national reorganization, literacy crises and pedagogies. Language pedagogy paralleled the transitions to corporate capitalism with the invention of freshman composition and then with multicultural pedagogical responses to what Bowles and Gintis (1976) call simply "the movement begun in the 1960s."

Freshman composition has always had a strong link with capitalism, as Donna Strickland explains in "How to Compose a Capitalist: The Predicament of Required Writing in a Free Market Curriculum" (Strickland 1998). The universal college requirement was enacted at Harvard in the 1890s, during the shift to corporate capitalism, to serve as a way to sort capitalists from workers (who were trained differently). Strickland describes the change in pedagogy and how it related to composition. Colleges were transitioning to the elective system (as initiated by Harvard and eventually copied by everyone else) because the most desirable kind of capitalist was one who was competitive and unpoliced yet motivated to study. The role of the composition class, the one required course in an otherwise elective system, writes Strickland, was to filter out students who didn't have the right background. "Students needed to enter the college classroom with a certain amount of English capital already acquired," or they could not proceed with their studies (35). In other words, if they had been raised with a language or dialect other than Harvard's standards, there was a good chance that they would not be allowed to study at Harvard and consequently have a Harvard-worthy career. The composition course was an effective (and delicate) way to socially sort students. Sharon Crowley (1998) writes in *Composition in the University* that because the composition course was portrayed as a meritocratic competition, students accepted their failure as their own fault instead of recognizing that the educational system tended to penalize people from the wrong class. "To put this in Foucauldian terms," she writes, "Freshman English was (and is?) a 'political technology of individuals,' a pedagogy designed to create docile subjects who would not question the discipline's continued and repeated demonstration of their insufficient command of their native tongue" (77). Harvard blamed secondary schools for inadequately educating students, and secondary schools subsequently began changing their own composition standards and tracking methods.

Also during this shift to corporate capitalism, monolingualism was instituted in the educational system. Bruce Horner and John Trimbur write in "English Only and U.S. College Composition" (Horner and Trimbur 2002) that attitudes toward modern languages were reorganized at the same time as college departments (and these attitudes are still with us today). By 1897, they write, "English was elevated to its preeminent status in the curriculum, and the other modern languages were, in effect, assigned their limited spheres of influence, territorialized as national literatures in their separate departments, where students encountered them as texts to be read, not living languages to be written or spoken" (602). The boundaries of languages came to be seen as fixed at this time, and to be American was to speak English. Horner and Trimbur explore ways of instituting multilingualism in the educational system and conclude, "This largely unexamined language policy has made it difficult to see that U.S. college composition, from its formation to the present day, operates for the most part within national borders, at worst justifying writing instruction for reasons of economic productivity, cultural integration, and now perhaps homeland security, while at best imagining a more inclusive, pluricultural, and participatory civic life in the U.S." (623)

The attention to public education composition standards and the institution of freshman composition coincided with a shift to monolingualism when it became unpatriotic in the United States to speak more than one language (after huge waves of immigration at the turn of the century and following World War I). Trimbur charts other moments when the legitimate language came to the forefront in connection with nationalism in "Linguistic Memory and the Politics of U.S. English," including anti-German legislation during World War I and Americanization campaigns designed to teach English. These efforts to influence workers' internal linguistic and nationalist values (which were successful among Cajuns, as I showed in chapter 3) corresponded with the transition to corporate pedagogy, which favored self-surveillance and cooperation over obedience.

The next major pedagogical shift that Bowles and Gintis (1976) chart was extremely significant in comp/rhet. They don't explain the shift, but I suggest that the 1960s saw a great deal of national reorganization in response to major national challenges—from both within and without—particularly the Cold War and the space race following the arms race, the Vietnam War, and demands for access to higher education and job parity from populations that had been previously excluded. In *Class Politics: The Movement for the Students' Right to Their Own Language; Refiguring English Studies*, Stephen Parks (2000) describes the influence of counterhegemonic movements like student power, black power, the

New Left, civil rights, women's liberation, and antiwar organizing. At the same time that the United States required increased levels of nationalism to support its military endeavors, a task that already required significant pedagogical changes, workers were demanding new economic arrangements, which would also require pedagogical changes. This convergence led to a rare opportunity of educational integration. Whereas women and people of color had been previously sorted into different educational (and pedagogical) arrangements, the state conceded to their demands for equal entrance and access to schools and jobs. The educational system would need to negotiate simultaneously a new form of nationalism (to organize citizens against "the enemy" as well as to equip them for the space race) and the labor training of new populations of workers. The field of comp/rhet was heavily involved with these tasks, evidenced in the field's conversations about open admissions at CUNY, the resulting emergence of basic writing, the Ebonics debate in Oakland, and SRTOL. These are all important elements of what I categorize under "multicultural pedagogy," or educational responses to the problem of normalizing speakers of new Englishes in classrooms. This period also marked the development of the pedagogical stance that is most popular among teachers of Cajun students in Southwest Louisiana, code switching.

The first part of creating code switching was to define the distinction between the legitimate variety of English and other Englishes. Trimbur writes in "The Dartmouth Conference and the Geohistory of the Native Speaker" (Trimbur 2008) that the Dartmouth Conference of 1966, which was actually titled the "Anglo-American Seminar on the Teaching of English," was instrumental in this process. In addition to being deemed the official start of the process movement, this conference was an important moment for creating a distinction between native speakers and nonnative speakers of English. Composition teaching had already come to be seen as an important way of shaping US citizen consciousness, enough so that the country was willing to fund English departments as a part of the war effort with the National Defense Act of Education (NDEA) in a 1964 decision called "Project English" (150). In fact, long before this conference, Trimbur writes, others had recognized the importance of teaching English for spreading imperialism, including Winston Churchill: "I am very much interested in the question of Basic English. The widespread use of this would be a gain to us far more durable and fruitful than the annexation of great provinces" (146), and for spreading capitalism: "As [Robert] Phillipson's research makes clear, however, there was a consensus among government, foundations, and academics on the value of English in Cold War strategies to counter the Soviet Union in the Third World and to modernize postcolonial nations by opening them to foreign investments, market economies, and the political influence of the West" (147). But now freshman comp was being redefined to impose the same cultural norms (empire and capitalism) on US speakers of English. Like Bourdieu, Trimbur (2008) points out that definitions of legitimate English have been controlled by those with more power: "[T]he means of producing knowledge about English have been unevenly distributed—according to geohistorical location and differential relations ascribed to native and nonnative speakers, metropolis and colony, center and periphery," and the result of this control over definitions has been to grant more legitimacy to those who already have privilege (145). In the end, even native speakers of English could be deemed "nonnative" if they didn't have command of the legitimate usage.

This native/nonnative distinction in comp/rhet provided the basis for code switching. Whereas previous conversations in the field focused on discrepancies in usage, attention shifted around the 1960s to deal with entirely different language systems, as the content from contemporary *CCC* issues shows. In the spring 1957 issue of *CCC*, sentence-level correctness is the primary issue in a great number of articles, indicating that most writers assumed a population of students familiar with standardized English. Though theorists in the linguistics field at the time are beginning to consider the "relativism" of context-appropriate usage, there is a strong current of grammar guardianism in comp/rhet, as evidenced in titles like "Do Illiterate A.B.'s Disgrace Us All?" and "Doctrines of English Usage." The purpose of composition classes is articulated as refinement of manners and mind (unlike today's explicit focus on job training). For example, one submitter writes, "*[G]eneral education* means pretty much what I get from the term *enlargement of the mind* in Cardinal Newman's *Idea of a University* or from the expression *Liberal Knowledge* as Matthew Arnold used it in contrast with Useful Knowledge" (Allen 1957, 33). Likewise, a speech teacher declares in another article that his purpose is "[t]o assist his students to talk as educated and mature men and women" (Burnet 1957, 23). Another writer decries his students' grammar with missionary fervor, writing that he needs "a minor miracle" to convert "the tongues of the philistines" (Timmerman 1957, 51). One article in this journal issue predicts the coming transition. A group of writers explain a new military-invented teaching approach based on the idea that language use is a habit that can be replaced or retrained behaviorally, and they suggest that the approach may aid in teaching the legitimate language to nonstandard students. They write, "The student's use of his native dialects and styles is anchored on firmly established systems of habits . . . He will have to acquire new sets of habits" (Sullivan et al. 1957, 15). In this article, Sullivan et al. are introducing the emerging field of ESL instruction, ignoring the fact that "problem" students are typically native English speakers whose "errors" are simply English dialect differences. The fallacy of treating native English speakers as foreigners has plagued comp/rhet theory ever since.

The native/nonnative distinction also helped enforce a form of cultural purism in comp/rhet studies, leading to pedagogies that confused working-class and minority students with tourists or immigrants. As a result, teachers strove specifically to assimilate or acculturate students to dominant values and habits. Crowley describes this cultural purism as a "function" of freshman composition, explaining that entering students must take on a new cultural identity: "The course is meant to shape students to behave, think, write, and speak as students rather than as the people they are, people who have differing histories and traditions and languages and ideologies" (Crowley 1998, 89). Chris Schroeder, coeditor of *AltDIS*, agrees: "[I]nstruction in academic literacy has always been about acculturation" (Schroeder 2002, 182). Metaphors of assimilation and acculturation to a new country have been used uncritically to undergird the practice of discrediting the language skills students already have. Even Mike Rose, who is very conscientious about depictions of minority and working-class students, compares vernacular-speaking students to travelers in a foreign land who must learn how to communicate with and not offend the locals: "A traveler in a foreign land best learns names of people and places, how to express ideas, ways to carry on a conversation by moving around in the culture, participating as fully as he can, making mistakes, saying things half right, blushing, then being encouraged by a friendly native speaker to try again. He'll pick up the details of grammar and usage as he goes along. What he must *not* do is hold back from the teeming flow of life, must not sit in his hotel room and drill himself on all possible gaffes before entering the streets . . . My students, too, were strangers in a strange land" (Rose 1987, 142). Though Rose argues that there are real class and race inequalities (and also uses the metaphor of an "academic club"), the "traveler" conceit can lead other teachers to treat internally colonized students as if they are voluntary immigrants or, worse, on vacation. The conceit breaks down because vernacular-speaking American students *aren't foreign*. The model of acculturation assumes that the new students are "nonnatives," so they should be the ones to change. But even within the native/nonnative paradigm (which

Canagarajah [2010] argues is inaccurate and outdated now as I explain later), it's the university culture that's nonnative. It's a transplant, an immigration of values and traditions from Europe.

Ten years after the ESL article and one year after the Dartmouth Conference, the topics in *CCC* moved further from sentence-level issues to considerations of the place of grammar in composition instruction with articles like "Sequence of Tenses, or Was James Thurber the First Transformational Grammarian?" and "Some Thoughts on Teaching Grammar to Improve Writing." In "Some Thoughts," Baum concludes that grammar mastery is important but only one element among many that determines good writing (Baum 1967, 4). This was around the time that theorists of contrastive rhetoric entered the scene, proposing that errors in written arguments were usually simply contrasting cultural values in styles of rhetoric, as explained in Robert Kaplan's "Cultural Thought Patterns in Intercultural Education" (Kaplan 1966). He wrote that the rhetoric of English writers was linear, whereas French, Spanish, and other romance language writers were expected to digress before making their points, Asian writers to be indirect (because of cultural manners), and Jewish writers to be repetitive on important points (in the style of "Semitic parallelism" in Hebrew books like Psalms and Proverbs). Kaplan recommended exercises to behaviorally train students to adjust to the standard language. Another new item in 1967 was the beginning of professionalization of composition studies in English in the article "The Careers of English Majors," which traced the career paths of several hundred English graduates.[2] Increased numbers of English teaching careers were due to the massive influx of students at the time, coinciding with Bowles and Gintis's third economic and pedagogical transition.

With new definitions of native speakers and theories on contrastive rhetoric and ESL, this period also saw the birth of what is commonly called "code switching" in comp/rhet. Geneva Smitherman (1986) writes in *Talkin and Testifyin: The Language of Black America* that discussions of the "bi-dialectical model" of black speech originated around this time. Breaking from the tradition of eradicating the "deficient" language practices of African American students, more liberal educators espoused the idea that African American English was simply "different" and AAE speakers should just learn to be "bi-dialectical" for "home talk" and "school talk" (204–6). This pedagogical strategy is now commonly known as *code switching* in Comp/Rhet discussions, though, as I point out later, the usage is not entirely accurate. So-called code switching is the practice in educational circles of disallowing vernaculars in the classroom because school isn't the appropriate context. Students should be aware of their audience (a teacher or group of scholars) and self-censor street slang from their writing (speech would be nice too). Vershawn Young (2007) explains in *Your Average Nigga: Performing Race, Literacy, and Masculinity* that code switching is "a popular concept and approach to language instruction because it appears to be egalitarian. It's supposed to allow students to keep intact their authentic black identity since they are encouraged to speak one dialect and hold one set of beliefs appropriate for the hood (where their dialect and identity are validated) and speak another version of English and adopt thoughts more suitable for school (where they are asked to give up their dialect and identity for a short time in order to achieve the most good in the long run)" (7). Pedagogically, code switching seemed to some teachers like a reasonable solution to eradication, especially in the face of increasing multiculturalization of classrooms, because the teacher could respectfully exclude the student's home discourse and get on with teaching the legitimate one. Race and class inequalities were still structured into the economy, so teachers who hoped to prepare their students adequately for jobs couldn't ignore the demand for standardized English. Though Smitherman was identifying the flawed logic in code switching as early as 1977, code switching is still the most popular way of dealing with dialect influence among Cajuns, as my survey responses of teachers of Cajun students in Southwest Louisiana indicates.

### PART ONE: CODE SWITCHING

Before I get into a critique of code switching, let me introduce my SouLa survey respondents. The participants were all teachers of college freshman composition (in addition to other classes), ranging from graduate student teachers to full professors. I drew my participants from an area where they were sure to have encountered Cajun students. During the spring of 2011, with approval from the CUNY IRB, I sent requests to the English department chairs at four different colleges in the Southwest Louisiana area to post my survey on their departmental listservs. The colleges were the University of Louisiana at Lafayette (UL Lafayette), Southwest Louisiana Community College (SLCC), Louisiana State University at Baton Rouge (LSU), and Louisiana State University at Eunice (LSUE). At each college, the chairs of the English departments agreed to have their faculty participate, and I received a total of forty responses from self-selecting individuals who consented to participate. All survey results are from the spring semester of 2011.

I broke the survey up into several sections to assess different things. The first was a page called "Personal Information" to find out personal and educational background as well as teaching experience. The next section was "Personal Views of Literacy" to assess the teachers' views on the purpose of freshman composition classes (and thus the role of the instructor). The third section was a questionnaire for Cajuns only entitled "Cajuns' Experience with Cajun English." Here, I asked questions about respondents' attitudes and experiences with language. Finally, on the page "Pedagogical Strategies regarding CE," I asked if teachers had encountered CE errors and how they handled them. The survey format was a simple Web questionnaire on surveymonkey.com delivered in a variety of drop-down boxes, multiple-choice answers, and a few short answers. Every question (apart from basic information questions like name and institution) provided room for additional thoughts, so that teachers could qualify their answers, provide an answer that I hadn't included in the multiple choices, or comment on the survey or question. Every teacher added additional comments to at least some responses. The appendix includes all questions, all possible drop-down and multiple-choice options, all survey responses, and all additional comments.

The purpose of the survey was to assess the attitudes and pedagogical strategies of teachers regarding CE in their classrooms. (A secondary purpose was to assess the personal language practices of teachers who identify as Cajuns; I mention those results in chapters 1 and 5.) Seventy percent of the teachers report that they espouse a strategy of code switching in which they assess their students on the ability to conform to dominant stereotypes of class and race and to avoid any linguistic "triggers" of prejudice (the rate is much higher if I include the teachers who reported that they work between code switching and some other strategy). They generally explain that they espouse code switching because of their more sophisticated understanding of language difference, as one response shows: "I wish more instructors knew about code switching and do not tell Cajun students that they 'speak poor English.'" I discuss their use of code switching later in the chapter, but my analysis is not concerned with critiquing their pedagogical methods or improving them. Rather, my most important finding concerns the intentions, attitudes, and motives of the teachers of Cajuns. The survey data I include below demonstrates that the respondents generally had positive attitudes toward CE, were thoughtful and critical of "standard" English and its constructed nature and, as Bourdieu's model would predict, all taught with an eye toward the language inequalities that exist "out there."

Though nearly all of them required students to hide cultural markers in language, not one respondent denigrated Cajun culture or hoped to eradicate CE. Many of the teachers (both Cajun and non-Cajun) in my survey also really hoped to honor CE. In response to a statement that "the Cajun accent sounds backwards and illiterate," several teachers strongly disagreed and wrote that they personally have positive attitudes toward other Englishes:

> I enjoy regional dialects of all types and find them fascinating.
> No one speaks SAE [Standard American English] the exact same way, and I don't think anyone should.
> Language evolves, and part of the way it does that is through vernacular diversity. Plus, cultural diversity is what makes language so interesting.

One respondent argued for CE on the grounds of nationalism:

> Regional dialects are important parts of American culture!

Another respondent, who identified as Cajun, focused on preserving local culture:

> I think we need to protect our [Cajun] language and lifestyle.

One teacher wrote in a later section on pedagogy that he or she values CE enough to actually encourage using it in some student writing:

> I have included assignments specifically to *allow* students a creative space to use their colloquialisms.

The responses in almost every case indicated that the teachers appreciate the vernaculars of their students.

Further, responses indicated that the teachers were without exception thoughtful, intelligent, conscientious instructors with complex views on the language standards they find themselves teaching. This may have been a function of the self-selecting nature of the survey; it's possible that only teachers with complex views about language standards would choose to click on a link about teaching English to Cajun students and volunteer approximately twenty minutes of their day to write responses. The level of engagement of the teachers was best illustrated in the section "Personal Views of Literacy," in which I listed several polarizing statements about language, literacy, and CE and asked for responses ranging from "strongly agree" to "strongly disagree." I intentionally left statements simplified to elicit comments and allow space for the teachers' own nuancing. It was very rare that any of the teachers had uncomplicated views on literacy. As an example of the kind of nuance I'm talking about, here are a few of the responses to the statement "Standard Edited English is correct English."

Most respondents took issue with the word *correct*, arguing that correctness is relative to the context:

> This is entirely dependent upon the context. In some settings, standard English is preferred and advantageous. In others, it is not necessary.

Another writes,

> It is correct in a formal sense, but not in a cultural sense.

Many defined correctness in terms of academic discourse and genre conventions, as these responses show (emphasis mine, here and following):

> Standard Edited English is *the language of the academy*. In the context of a college classroom it is the expected language. Outside of this context, such as spoken English, other forms of English are acceptable.
>
> *Different genres require different language choices.* To tell students that all writing must follow Standard Edited English is a disservice to the students. Teaching them to analyze the writing situation and determine what is appropriate will serve them in and beyond the University.

Two respondents in particular were very critical of the prejudiced statements I asked them to discuss:

> Question does not make sense without defining "correct." I take it that you're looking for prejudices of participants. Not a good question.
>
> I reject the premise of this question, as I understand it.

The writer of the first comment was so upset by my questions about language attitudes that he or she eventually dropped out of the survey, writing, "Here's where I get off." (Both teach in SouLa, but neither is Cajun.) Meanwhile, the rest of the respondents defined "correctness" as standards imposed from outside their classrooms, as this response explaining correctness in terms of hegemonic standards indicates (all emphases mine):

> "Correctness" has been in debate far too long to speak with any certainty now. "Correct" for me is ultimately a judgment claim, the value/assessment of which usually depends on one's audience. However, *it is also a power issue with the people in power determining which usages are "correct."* So, there is some practical sense to the claim that Standard Edited English is the (hegemonic) "correct" version.

Another stressed that language teaching standards are imposed from outside schools:

> The point is not whether it is correct, but whether one's ignorance of it will limit one's future. In other words, the question is not one of correctness, but of *perceptions and expectations over which Academia has very little control.*

The rest explicitly described correctness in terms of the standards imposed by job expectations (again, outside the classroom), as this response demonstrates:

> "Correct" is a dicey word. [Standardized English] is the correct English for business, academics, etc. but as far as the correct English for home use, that can and does vary.

This explanation of correctness was extremely common. In fact, the majority of teachers qualify their understanding of correctness in terms of jobs.

The teachers' overwhelming attention to the US socioeconomy in relation to their classroom practices was surprising to me. I never explicitly asked what teachers thought about their roles when it comes to jobs or the economy (the idea wasn't even on my radar yet when I created the survey, so I don't think I asked it implicitly either), but many volunteered their opinions anyway. When it comes to pedagogy, many of the teachers indicated that they selected the most effective one based on what gives their students the best job opportunities or, to put it in Bowles and Gintis's (1976) terms, the pedagogy that best "facilitat[es] a smooth integration of youth into the labor force" (11). This sociopedagogical link came up unambiguously in many survey comments with language like *jobs, workers, business, commerce, upward mobility, corporate community, employment, professional world*, and so on. These quotations come from the additional comments to several different questions that were unrelated to anything political or economic for example, "Have you ever addressed any of the above features in your students' speech? If so, please explain"). Again, emphasis mine:

> I encourage them to use their language verbally, but caution them that when they write, they need to treat CE as they would a second language, because *they will be expected to write in Standard English on their jobs.*
> *Industry* requires its *workers* to communicate in Standard English.
> The *professional world* can be a cruel place to those who do not conform to Standard English, and since many people from Louisiana are often judged harshly based solely on their geographical background, they may have even more difficulty proving themselves to be intelligent, thoughtful individuals. *Poor language and composition skills will only hinder those aiming to be part of a larger corporate or academic community.*
> *Needed for business and commerce.* How they talk is fine in any register if they can carry on life skills, but standard written English is a must.
> I believe SEE [Standard Edited English] or SAE [Standard American English] is *the "standard" that the professional world generally demands for upwardly mobile employees.* Vernaculars are just as "correct" in their context, but *American society demands a uniform language for upper levels of business and*

*academia*, and that language happens to be SAE. *A student who masters SAE has a wider range of options for employment than one who does not.*

There is no correct English. However, I recognize the value in our having a common version of the English language that we use to communicate in *professional situations*, and students need to learn to be competent in this English. Students from the South really need to master this English as their speech patterns (and writing patterns) can cause them to be judged as less intelligent than their northern counterparts.

I encourage them to use their [home] language verbally, but caution them that when they write, they need to treat CE as they would a second language, because *they will be expected to write in Standard English on their jobs.*

There are many Englishes, as I tell my students. You may not need all of them. *But you need to know how and when to use Standard Edited English (usually for workplace situations and school).*

There is no such thing as "correct" or "perfect" English, but in written English standard form is *preferred for business and commerce.*

These teachers show that they try to keep an eye on job requirements when they make decisions about how to handle language issues in class. This concern is consonant with the fact that schools (thus pedagogy and policy) exist to normalize students to the working conditions they can expect to encounter in the labor force.

In their efforts to prep students for the job market (which they recognize as central to education, as their comments show), the participants' responses indicate that code switching is very popular among the Louisiana teachers in my survey. Some write that the most basic problem in their classrooms is that students aren't code switching well enough between spoken and written language. In the following responses, teachers assume that students aren't aware of the difference:

> There is a clear distinction between written and spoken language and a composition class is the primary location for them to *understand and practice this distinction*. If not in this type of setting, then where?
>
> *They must learn the difference* between academic writing and less formal options.
>
> If I see that it *[CE] carries over into the writing*, then we discuss it and we do discuss code switching. The proper places to use the proper language. But, lately this has been more often because of subject-verb agreement problems among my African American students.

The following responses describe code switching in terms of audience awareness, assuming that students need help recognizing different rhetorical situations:

> I work in between code meshing and code switching, encouraging students to consider word choice (in vernaculars and also informal/formal language) *based on audience and context/rhetorical situation.*

> I have explained the validity of spoken CE and also explained "code switching" as when the *language changes, for example, if a group of young men are talking and Grandma or the priest walks up;* we can all, and most of us do, switch codes without even thinking about it. I encourage conscious code-switching into more formal written English and do not correct CE in class, as it is a normal given.

A few respondents argued that code switching is necessary for connecting people from different cultures with different Englishes. Standard English in this case is a sort of "lingua franca," without which people wouldn't understand one another:

> I do think that we need to be able to code switch well enough to communicate across vernaculars, and the easiest way to do that is *an accepted "standard" form of English.*
>
> I recognize the value in our having *a common version of the English language* that we use to communicate in professional situations, and students need to learn to be competent in this English.

But the writer of this second comment goes on to base the selection of a lingua franca not on best communication practices but on avoiding already institutionalized prejudice:

> Students from the south really need to master this English as their speech patterns (and writing patterns) can cause them to be judged as less intelligent than their northern counterparts.

I come back to this point again later. In the end, most teachers require students to filter out vernacular influence for their classroom writing, and this is generally based on their understanding of inequalities that they imagine their students will go on to face. As a Cajun student who underwent educational normalization in SouLa and heard these arguments all my life, I should have predicted these responses. I have also taught with teachers at UL Lafayette and the University of New Orleans who espouse the same beliefs. As a teacher of Cajun students myself, actually, I have argued the same (as I explain in the next chapter). Though I argue that the strategy commonly called *code switching* is a flawed approach to handling language difference, reinforcing linguicism, it is one that is based not on teacher-created inequalities but on social, political, and economic inequalities, as these teachers are careful to point out.

*Code Censoring*

There are several problems with code switching. The name is misapplied, for one thing. Conversations between sociolinguists and composition teachers about code switching may be confusing because the term, which originated in applied linguistics, simply refers to the practice of using multiple dialects or languages *at the same time* within *a single conversation* (and it refers to speaking, not writing). Within composition it now means writing completely in one language or dialect to the exclusion of all other codes (or influence from them) that are allowed in other situations. Educational code switching is the exact opposite of linguistics code switching because it demands absolute compartmentalization of language. And it's in this sense that the standard pedagogical stance regarding language might be called *code censoring*, not code switching. The point is to eradicate illegitimate languages completely from classroom writing (though not necessarily from classroom speaking). As I have argued in "Publishing in the Contact Zone: Strategies from the Cajun Canaille" (Stanford 2011), we generally require code *censoring*.

Another reason I'm differentiating between code switching and code censoring is that the practice doesn't necessarily help students communicate more clearly or effectively; it mostly helps them dodge discrimination. Situational awareness would have the interlocutor wield the language in the way that is most intelligible to his or her audience; this is a reasonable practice, and I wholly support it. I usually speak loudly, slowly, and with a pretty intense Cajun accent to the elderly people I know. This was a completely unconscious switching process until I moved to Jersey City and my ninety-four-year-old downstairs neighbor couldn't understand a word I said. When Beatty was growing up, she told me, the Mafia ran the city ("It was so safe," she says), and she rarely dealt with non-Italians, much less Cajuns. So I tried my "white academic" voice, and that didn't work either. When I imitated the Italian American accent, we got along swimmingly. Most issues corrected or adjusted under code censoring, though, are not questions of being understood but flags that betray the writer's position in the social hierarchy (for example, subject/verb agreement in a simple sentence). Yes, punctuation can make a huge difference, as Lynne Truss (2004), author of *Eats, Shoots and Leaves: Why, Commas Really Do Make a Difference!* pithily reminds us. Spelling variations, slang, and nonstandard grammar, however, are usually understandable; the problem is that they betray the fact that the writer grew up in a neighborhood, country, or social class other than what has been codified as legitimate. And what's wrong with being from somewhere else? Code censoring is not the practice of choosing the language or words that are most intelligible but a strategy to hide nonprivileged cultural markers from the audience.[3] Let me say that one more time: code censoring choices aren't based on communicating well; they are based on accommodating the audience's race-, gender-, and class-based prejudices.

As Elbow points out, learning to dodge discrimination is a valuable lesson. In an email to me, he wrote that he wants to protect his students from unnecessary flack. Referring to an article I wrote, he explained his position on teaching code censoring: "I think you give the most clear and fair-minded statement of the indictment against me . . . So I want to be able to plead guilty to suggesting a teaching practice that does indeed involve 'the desire to be accepted': (great and helpful distinction, again, when you write: 'altering codes is motivated by the desire to be understood, code-censoring by the desire to be accepted' ([Stanford] 2011, 128)." Along with Elbow, a huge number of English teachers (including me) would plead guilty to wanting to teach our students how to be accepted and avoid discrimination. In fact, many teachers in my survey expressed something similar. Their desire to help their students code censor is usually based on their own awareness of other people's perceptions of Cajun linguistic markers. When I asked them if they thought Cajun features in speech are "backwards and illiterate," many replied that they didn't see it that way, but they know that others do. These two responses were typical of the views of many:

> I personally enjoy the local color aspects of it [CE], but I do know that many people would consider it backwards and illiterate (and when used in certain contexts, it could actually create an impression of illiteracy for more than just the individual speaker).
>
> If you are not from the area and have not grown up with this [Louisiana French colloquialisms], then you might think the person saying it is not smart, but this may not be the case.

Another teacher, who identifies as Cajun, admits that educational normalization led to his or her own perception of the Cajun accent as uneducated (yet beautiful):

> I am certainly biased because I grew up surrounded by Cajun accents, but it can sound very beautiful, especially when the speaker uses many French terms throughout their speech. On the other hand, having "learned" how a "proper" accent should sound, [I think that] some Cajun accents can make the speaker sound a bit uneducated.

Even when they personally see nothing wrong with linguistic Cajunisms, they understand other people's perceptions. Concerned with protecting their students from social and job discrimination, these teachers enforce code censoring with CE the same way that Cajun parents who were normalized under the French ban taught their children not to speak Louisiana French.

As I said before, I'm sympathetic to this position. But *mais la*. Does anybody else see a problem with the fact that a major course objective of English composition is to teach students about class-, gender-, and race-based language prejudice and how to accommodate it? Why is this the responsibility of English teachers? And is it even worth teaching students how to avoid linguistic prejudice in writing when there are so many other forms that will sort them according to class, gender, and race? Teaching code censoring is a temporary, shoddy work-around, and it is also the institutionalization of prejudice. We should not grow (or remain) comfortable with code censoring.

Further, even though code censoring is almost always required of Cajuns throughout the entire semester, it isn't taught as a part of the curriculum, just quietly edited out of their drafts. Educational approaches in comp courses are generally things like mostly writing versus a lot of reading; reading student texts versus reading "official" texts; reading essays versus reading novels or stories; allowing revisions versus allowing only one product; teaching the "modes" versus teaching genres—things like that. These approaches are integral to the syllabus schedule, class discussions and/or lectures, and in-class practice writing. But according to the Louisiana teachers who espouse code censoring, they don't usually specifically teach any code-censoring methods; the majority of them reported that they just deal with them as they mark papers. In the survey, I posed the question, "Have you ever addressed any of the above [Cajun English "errors"] in your students' writing? If so, explain as thoroughly as possible your pedagogical strategy for dealing with CE in your students' writing"; the following replies were representative of almost everyone:

> I have just written "nonstandard" or explained that one cannot write as one talks.
>
> *I don't really have a strategy* for addressing these problems. I just identify why they are deviations from standard English and tell them to cut it out.
>
> *No strategy*. My rubric for all writing is based on the same three standards: Form (the essay proper), Function (carry out the assignment as given), and Use (all mechanics). I use Word's comment feature and make corrections/comments on individual issues in balloons to the right. My explanation will be centered on whichever standard applies—assuming Standard English.

Even this very sympathetic response is just an explanation of *why* students should code censor not *how* to:

> I frequently point CE features out because many students don't realize the uniqueness of their idiom or usage. I never represent their vernacular as sub-standard or incorrect—the school system did enough of that two generations ago, greatly aiding and abetting the demise of the language

and, in some ways, the culture. Actually, I would never demean speakers of any regional or ethnic dialect, including BVE or the Southern U.S. Scotch-Irish, but *I do explain to students the reasons for appreciating their language, for understanding levels of usage, and for adapting usage to a variety of audiences.*

It's common to minimize the weight of failing to code censor by refusing to discuss it:

> I simply mark the mistakes without addressing possible reasons for the mistake.
> 
> I don't make a big deal out of it as I understand where it's coming from. I simply correct it as it comes up in papers.

This attitude isn't limited to teachers in SouLa. Like these last couple respondents, many teachers don't want to "make a big deal" of it, so they are purposefully vague. They don't teach it, just flag it. As Lisa Delpit (1997) points out in "The Silenced Dialogue: Power and Pedagogy in Educating Other People's Children," when there is race- or class-based awkwardness, educators grow more and more ambiguous in their directives, and this serves only to further disempower people of color. These students know they have broken some rule, but they don't know what the rule is, and no one will tell them, leading them sometimes to internalize their failure as a sign of personal deficit. Glynda Hull et al. provide a striking example of this dynamic in "Remediation as a Social Construct: Perspectives from an Analysis of Classroom Discourse" (Hull et al. 1991). A minority student they identify as Maria begins the semester enthusiastic about English composition and her own abilities but, after breaching the etiquette of her instructor's style of discussion all semester (because she didn't understand the social structure of her freshman comp class), Maria leaves with a new idea of herself—that she simply is not cut out for success in English. The surprising thing is that Maria's instructor is known in the community as an engaging teacher who uses progressive classroom practices like lots of dialogue and class discussions. Hull et al., however, observe that the instructor's ostensibly open-ended questions in these "dialogues" are not in fact "open" to student interpretations. Like traditional banking pedagogies, the instructor looks for very specific, "correct" responses, but the misunderstandings are amplified because she is vague and misleading in her questioning and instruction style. After describing similar situations, Delpit (1997) urges teachers to be explicit in their discussions of these rules and explanations of language. "Tell them that their language and cultural style is unique and wonderful but that there is a political game that is also being played, and if they want to be in on that game there are certain games that they too must play" (581). Hiding the rules of the game, she argues, is hiding the access to the power.

Delpit writes her article to represent the voices of nonwhite educators, who "have spoken passionately on being left out of the dialogue about how best to educate children of color," in contrast to white educators, who in Delpit's experience assume authority about how to educate "other people's children" (1997, 567). As a Cajun/Creole woman who looks white but often feels like I didn't get the white memo, I agree with Delpit. During graduate school, I had to go to great lengths sometimes to get understandable feedback from my professors (or from people who could interpret their feedback for me) when I didn't understand the reason for scores that were lower than I expected. I created a lexicon for my own reference based on things I'd figured out from trial and error. *Why don't you think about this some more?* for example, does not mean what it sounds like: *Keep thinking in this direction.* It means something more like *Wrong answer; read my mind and get back to me.* In those situations, thinking never helped me, but asking other students who had studied under that professor or reading the professor's publications did help. I copied other students' strategies of apologizing excessively or joking about being slow, so that my clarifying questions weren't taken as challenges or arguments. I have come to understand these communication misses and near misses as a kind of dissonance that is based on a combination of my gendered speech, my Cajun rhetoric, and differences in class habits when relating to authority. So even as I critique the language inequalities in the educational system and argue against code censoring, I understand that I was participating in what Delpit calls a "game" with "rules," and I was thankful for professors from working-class backgrounds who pointed them out to me—for example, the voice modulation characteristic of elite language users (and uncharacteristic of minority and working-class speakers, who can seem belligerent or emotionally uncontrolled in academic settings).

In the same vein as Delpit, several teachers in my survey were far more explicit in helping their students code censor:

> I find the best way is to model the correct grammar/construction for them. I simply re-word their sentence, then they must write it down correctly in their revision. Later, *when we have one-on-one conferences, I discuss the error with the student in greater detail.*
>
> It's no different than what I do for students who have other dialects, *explicitly point out the difference between the grammar of the dialect and the grammar of the Standard dialect* and ask that they use the Standard in writing.

> I spend a considerable time *working on sentence structure, particularly subject verb agreement, and proper verb selection.* I also go over *how to use foreign words* within academic language.

Using Delpit's strategy of directly addressing language difference (even if they don't know Delpit's work), these teachers help their students become more aware of instances where they fail to code censor. Had my teachers been this explicit, I would have appreciated their efforts. As long as teachers require code censoring and grade for it, they should do it unambiguously.

Unfortunately, though, even with explicit instruction, code censoring may not be teachable. Patrick Hartwell (1997) famously argues in "Grammar, Grammars, and the Teaching of Grammar" that grammar cannot be taught, period. Familiarity and grammatical dexterity with any given linguistic code is a matter of how much one has used it, not how many rules one has memorized about it. Hartwell builds on W. Nelson Francis's differentiations in meaning of the word *grammar* to discuss problems with the teaching of grammar. He writes, "[L]earners must already have internalized [language knowledge] by means of exposure to the code" in order to make decisions about grammar (201). In fact, the writing of students who memorize language rules has been shown time and time again to decline in quality (he cites the research of Mina Shaughnessy and Mike Rose as examples [200]). Only very long-term exposure to the legitimate language has been shown to be helpful. Explicit grammar and usage teaching may help students better understand the rules of the game, but mere knowledge of the rules has not been shown to help poor students and students of color perform code censoring well enough to pass as "not poor" and "not of color."

The reason for Hartwell's conclusion that grammar is not teachable is that language is, as Bourdieu argues, a form of cultural capital. In the same way that it is impossible to teach cash into someone's pocket, it's impossible to give students a decade or two's worth of another student's linguistic wealth. We can warn students explicitly that people will look down on them if their vernacular leaks in, we can carefully explain grammar rules, and we can provide exercises to help our students practice following the rules, but one or two semesters can't transform the internal grammar of one student to that of another student. Bourdieu writes that "the two principal factors of production of the legitimate competence [are] the family and the educational system"; students who are exposed to the legitimate language in school alone will never perform as well as students who are also exposed to it at home (1991, 62). Level of normalization to the legitimate language boils down to which family the students were born into; students will inherit the literacy practices of their parents, and then they will be sorted into the "proper" curriculum.[4] When some students are unable to sufficiently perform code censoring by the end of the semester, it's often chalked up to laziness or inability; those students must not have deserved to pass. But it's not that they are cognitively unable to recognize changes in the scenery; it's that they don't possess the sociolinguistic capital to make the switch. Better paragraph cohesion and stronger thesis statements are teachable, but language capital must be bought. Since code censoring cannot be taught, though, many of the teachers of Cajun students are unwittingly simply enforcing it. Students are expected to perform it (meaning they come to class already knowing how to do it) or fail.

Ultimately, the policy of code censoring is a justification for continuing to enforce the same standards as before the multicultural shift in pedagogy. In fact, I've heard many teachers invoke *code switching* only to explain why they still teach the same thing composition teachers taught in the 1950s: the legitimate language to the exclusion of all vernaculars and other languages. Teachers of Cajun students respond to multilingualism in classrooms differently from the days of eradication, and these are positive changes—for example, less shaming and of course decreased physical brutality. But the end message is still the same: if you do not write standardized English (betraying no influence from illegitimate vernaculars), you will not make it past the gates that guard the ability to be a culture maker and decision maker in our society. And that's just another form of: Sorry, you weren't born into the right family. And that's aristocracy.

Every now and then, there's a rags-to-riches story, but those "successful" students didn't receive upward mobility for free from their public education. They paid for every cent of cultural-linguistic capital they got. Keith Gilyard describes this price as "psychic costs" and "psychic payments" in *Voices of the Self: A Study of Language Competence* (Gilyard 1991, 11). He writes that he did manage to achieve social mobility, but it wasn't something school provided—rather, it was something he had to pay for himself: "So if I criticize elements of the school system, let it not be said that I am ungrateful. I learned a lot, but I had to *foot the psychic bill* for any success I managed to attain" (70; emphasis mine). Some of these "psychic costs" he talks about are "educational schizophrenia" (163) and "self-annihilation" (161). Richard Rodriguez also acknowledges the price he paid for his upward mobility in *Hunger for Memory* (1982). Envying other Latin students who could still speak Spanish and relate to their families and home communities, Rodriguez resigns to his cultural isolation, explaining, "I had long before accepted the fact that education exacted a *great price* for its equally great benefits" (172; emphasis mine). The great price that Rodriguez paid was, according to Gilyard in *Voices*, "cultural suicide, a conclusion totally unappealing to me, one I rejected as an adolescent" (161). Victor Villanueva (1993) similarly writes in *Bootstraps* that Rodriguez succeeded "at the *expense* of his ties to his family and to his culture. He said this *great expense* is simply the *cost* of becoming American" (xvi; emphasis mine). Villanueva writes that his own academic success was also very expensive culturally: "Choosing to speak the language of the dominant, choosing racelessness, bears a *price*, however. And that *price* is alienation—the loss of fictive kinship without being fully adopted by the white community" (40; emphasis mine). The price of upward mobility is giving up a certain connection to home and creating a connection with the dominant culture. It's unfair that minority and working-class people are put in this position of choosing between family and success, yet another illustration that the educational system does not offer equal opportunities to all Americans.

Not only does social mobility cost family and community ties, it is available for purchase to only a very few people. As Gilyard points out, "Masses and masses of minority students have been unable to use the public school system as a ladder of upward mobility. It is clear that whatever benefits the school can claim to have offered can be matched, if not overshadowed, by a legacy of default" (Gilyard 1991, 63). Villanueva explains this phenomenon in terms of class theory: "Some *must* get through, a matter of ideological credibility in the land of opportunity, the workings of hegemony. Yet internal colonialism remains, never quite equity. How the doctorate? . . . I didn't know what I was getting into, but knew I was getting into something not intended for the likes of me. There are always the contradictions" (Villanueva 1993, xv). Social mobility is the exception to the rule; the US educational system is designed for class reproduction.

Even if it were possible to guarantee the upward mobility and job security of every single student who comes through freshman composition by teaching them to code censor (and even in this terrible economy, which lays off perfect code censorers), we would still be merely "working the system," leaving an unequal educational system unequal. Geneva Smitherman argues in *Talkin and Testifyin*, "Talking about Black English, listing its features and suggesting ways of changing *or* adding to it, without commensurately advocating changes in the sociopolitical system in which black people struggle is not only short-sighted, it amounts to so much pure academic talk, and ultimately, is an implicit acknowledgement that the system is good and valid, and all that need be done is to alter the people to fit into it" (Smitherman 1986, 207). Young also argues that code censoring is based on institutionalized racism, writing that learning it shouldn't "be called education but could be seen as an effect of de facto segregation" (Young 2007, 7). Smitherman points out that the same goes for "other minority groups and lower-class whites as well [who] have had to assimilate the language patterns of the dominant white middle class" (Smitherman 1986, 173)—Appalachians, for example. Code censoring is often an immediate solution for negotiating unfair gates, but it skirts the political inequalities built into our institutions and economy by keeping languages "separate" but definitely not "equal." So teaching code censoring ultimately reinforces the unequal standards outside classrooms that reinforce teachers' decisions to adjust their pedagogies accordingly, which reinforces the inequalities, which reinforces pedagogy, which reinforces inequality, and so on.

But teachers who want to break the cycle can't do it by simply inventing and imposing more language policies and pedagogies, not even extremely permissive ones that affirm students' home identities and languages—not as long as there are unaddressed prejudices everywhere else. Some liberal educators, including Young, have argued that they cannot in good conscience teach code censoring because it's such a blatantly unequal policy, so they choose to completely ignore outside standards in their classrooms. I understand the pull of conscience, but isolated acts of teacher dissent can also reinforce unequal standards by failing to effectively challenge them. Permissive language policies can create positive experiences in classrooms, and it's possible that they can give students the impetus to go on and assert language difference in other contexts and even lobby for equality. In most cases, though, students won't make it very far, failing the next departmental exam or class or some other gatekeeping hurdle. And, chances are, students who were raised in working-class homes like mine will accept their failure as their own. I don't think the main argument here is which is the best pedagogy regarding vernaculars, but which *sociopedagogy*.

### *The Sociopedagogy of Comp/Rhet*

As in Bourdieu's theory of the *maître à penser*, what is reproductive about schools is not just the content that the teachers pass on but also the relationships they create with their students. And, as I've established using Bowles and Gintis's model of pedagogical transitions, the educational system exists to convince people to comply with socioeconomic conditions. The conditions that need to be normalized to change all the time, but the demand for compliance does not. So I want to look at compliance. When teachers impose top-down policies on their students, even with the best of intentions, they are continuing the traditions of colonization and domination by denying their students' rights to make their own decisions. Edward Said (1978) writes in *Orientalism* that past efforts from the center have often been top-down imposed ideologies that were ostensibly benevolent but that actually supported imperialism and conquest. Programs geared at spreading mass civilization—Christianity, education, and progress (and I add democracy)—were usually foreign to the communities being "aided," and they only created or reinforced dependence on the center. Center perspectives, limited by postcolonial attitudes toward colonized and internally colonized groups who are "naïve" at best and "bad" at worst (both meaning they need someone to step in and govern them), can lead to paternalistic solutions that reproduce domination instead of resisting it. So I'm wary of any top-down policies or pedagogies to "help" minority and working-class groups, especially if the decisions are made *for* these populations—even in "their best interests" or to "liberate" them—because these are still dominating practices. Kathy Sohn (2006) writes in *Whistlin' and Crowin' Women of Appalachia: Literacy Practices since College* that the Appalachian region has been subjected to a "plethora of programs designed by missionaries and politicians since the late 1800s to shape this region into step with the rest of the country" (168). These well-intentioned efforts to aid Appalachians have only reinforced Appalachians' marginalization and socioeconomic inequality. I like how Villanueva puts it: "Authoritarianism is authoritarianism, no matter what the authority is espousing. To dictate is not to liberate" (Villanueva 1993, 62). Likewise, in matters of linguicism the problem isn't just that teachers need to affirm students' rights to their own languages. Teachers also need to affirm students' rights to think critically about issues and make their own decisions.

As Min-Zhan Lu categorizes basic writing (BW) approaches in "Conflict and Struggle: The Enemies or Preconditions of Basic Writing?" (Lu 1992), she creates a model that I find helpful for understanding the sociopedagogical limitations of conversations in comp/rhet. Though her analysis is concerned with BW courses, it also applies to the vernacular issues in freshman composition because she argues that pedagogical discussions have been limited by their normalizing function. She compares the old-school thinking of *assimilation* with newer ideas of *acculturation* and *accommodation* and argues that they are all essentially the same thing but with varying levels of kindness and understanding on the teacher's part. Under the policy of assimilation, students were expected to conform "or else." Under acculturation (Lu lists Irving Howe, James Baldwin, and W.E.B. Du Bois as examples), students understandably have a difficult time dealing with the new culture of the academy, so teachers should affirm their content and *gently* help them conform "or else." With accommodation (which she most strongly links with Mina Shaughnessy and Mike Rose), students have the right to resist assimilation and the difficult feelings that accompany this identity transition, but teachers, sympathetic to their students' resistance, find ways to teach them painless ways to *perform* conformity "or else." Lu criticizes the narrow scope of pedagogical responses to student vernaculars, arguing instead that educators need to make pedagogical decisions that take into account and build on student agency.

To put the vernacular debate in the terms of Lu's analysis, code censoring is a gentler form of eradication, as acculturation and accommodation are gentler forms of assimilation, even when we allow (celebrate, even) the students' vernaculars but still require them to "clean it up" for the test or final draft or the departmental exam over which we have no control. Shaughnessy was far kinder about student error than some of her contemporaries, as Lu explains, but she was still doing the same old same old: sorting students according to linguistic capital. Likewise, the policy of eradication literally banned free speech in public spaces (with physical punishments of children who spoke Louisiana French on state property), and the message of code censoring is strikingly similar: "You have the right to freedom of speech, but only at home." Even in the kindest, most permissive classes, it's hard to get beyond "You have the right to freedom of speech (and I understand why you might want to exercise that right), but you shouldn't exercise it if you want to pass." Lu argues that there is never an option to embrace both cultures or to see the university culture changed by the new population. Instead the "nonstandard" students must conform (or perform conformity) to the university culture, which Sharon Crowley defines as "male, European American, middle- or upper-class," the only demographic that was allowed in colleges until this past century (Crowley 1998, 27, 253). The assimilation/acculturation/accommodation model is based on a sort of imagined cultural purism, in the tradition of the native/nonnative distinction Trimbur describes.

Further, Suresh Canagarajah points out that the discussions in comp/rhet have also been limited by nationalism (which is a primary force behind language normalization). He writes that SRTOL, which has formed the basis for most discussions of pedagogical alternatives to code censoring, appeals to nationalist ideas to argue for linguistic diversity. First, let's look at the actual wording of the resolution (emphasis mine):

> We affirm the students' right to their own patterns and varieties of language—the dialects of their nurture or whatever dialects in which they find their own identity and style. Language scholars long ago denied that the myth of a standard American dialect has any validity. The claim that any one dialect is unacceptable amounts to an attempt of one social group to exert its dominance over another. Such a claim leads to false advice for speakers and writers, and immoral advice for humans. *A nation proud of its diverse heritage and its cultural and racial variety will preserve its heritage of dialects.* We affirm strongly that teachers must have the experiences and training that will enable them to respect diversity and uphold the right of students to their own language. (Smitherman 1995, 21)

Canagarajah acknowledges SRTOL's radical position on language for its time, but he proposes updating it without the nationalist appeals to affirm the constant flux of language and the multilingualism and multidialectism of students. He writes in a November 4, 2010, CCCC blog post:

> SRTOL, written and adopted in 1974, was far ahead of its time in articulating the connections between language, power, and pedagogy. However, today in the twenty-first century, it is beginning to show the traces of the dominant ideologies of its original context. In terms of language, SRTOL is informed by a structuralist orientation. It focuses on systematized varieties of language, with a stabilized grammar. In this sense, languages are treated as separate and discrete entities . . . SRTOL's social vision was and continues to be circumscribed by national boundaries. It perceives the locus for policy making as the nation-state. It is for this reason that it doesn't address the language use rights of migrant and transnational groups. It is also silent about the rights of languages other than English. (Canagarajah 2010)

He argues for a revised statement, "to build from its position of strength and legacy of radical change," based on a post-structuralist understanding of language that allows for change and hybridity. (Participants of the 2011 Penn State Conference on Rhetoric and Composition collaborated to propose a revised draft.)

Conversations within the field of comp/rhet have been similarly circumscribed by nationalism, class hierarchies, and cultural purism but, according to Bourdieu, anyone teaching in schools will be complicit with language normalization to a certain extent because that is specifically what the job calls for. When the First Lady, a philanthropist, or the school board (usually populated by the most influential local businesspeople, not teachers) decides to institute new educational standards or a "back to basics" campaign, teachers adjust their pedagogies and try to normalize their students to the new "distinctive deviations" of language. Students who hope for upward mobility strive to internalize the new norms. In this way, Bourdieu (1991) writes, there is support for class inequality coming from both the top and the bottom, something he calls a process of "diffusion": "What is described as a phenomenon of diffusion is nothing other than the process resulting from the *competitive struggle* which leads each agent, through countless strategies of assimilation and dissimilation (*vis-à-vis* those who are ahead of and behind him in the social space and in time) constantly to change his substantial properties (here, pronunciation, diction, syntactic devices, etc.), while maintaining, precisely by running in the race, the disparity which underlies the race" (64). Ira Shor has joked that Bourdieu begins a sentence at breakfast and finishes it at lunch, so allow me to simplify that long sentence by stripping out all the clauses: "[E]ach agent . . . [is] maintaining . . . the disparity," led by "the competitive struggle" (personal communication). According to Bourdieu, anyone who participates in the process at any level—creating the standards, enforcing the standards, or normalizing to the standards—helps reproduce the hierarchy.

So don't blame teachers (or administrators), at least not excessively—or, as we say in SouLa, not too-too much. I agree with Bowles and Gintis when they write, "Repression, individual powerlessness, inequality of outcomes, and inequality of opportunity did not originate historically in the educational system, nor do they derive from unequal and repressive schools today. The roots of repression and inequality lie in the structure and functioning of the capitalist economy" (Bowles and Gintis 1976, 49). US inequalities were largely established during the nation-building process, as I described in chapter 2, and educational policies have followed those arrangements. Many teachers, especially the comp/rhet theorists I've named above, understand the race- and class-based discrimination of the composition course, but what else should they do? Pass every student? Then the next teacher will fail them (as well as be angry at the first teacher for passing the student), and that's not to mention the threat of losing one's job for breaking university policy. Also, most students come to college specifically to learn to imitate the "right" demographic so that they can do what it takes to get a good job (or at least hope and try). Though code censoring doesn't guarantee social mobility, it seems unethical to deny students the service they're specifically paying for. And many teachers believe in code censoring, passionately, because they believe (often rightly) that it is what allowed them to climb out of their own cultural blue-collar destinies to become members of academe. Further, there's nothing wrong with wanting to equip students for jobs in the current socioeconomy (even while disagreeing with the socioeconomic structure). Because of the complicated position of teachers, I don't fault them for equipping students to deal with the prejudices they will go on to face (and have already faced for most of their lives). But it's not necessary to teach the mandated material uncritically, as many theorists like Lu have pointed out, or to comply with the sociopedagogical function of education.

### PART TWO: ALTERNATIVES TO CODE CENSORING

One possibility for a writing policy that both equips students for current standards and challenges the hierarchy of languages is based on a growing awareness of translanguaging practices in language intersection and change (the original definition of *code switching*). In "Toward a Rhetoric of Translingual Writing," Suresh Canagarajah (2012) categorizes the many terminologies in different fields about this topic: "composition: codemeshing (Young; Canagarajah, 'Place of World Englishes'), translingual writing (Horner, Lu, Royster, and Trimbur), and transcultural literacy (Lu); new literacy studies: multiliteracies (Cope and Kalantzis), continua of biliteracy (Hornberger), and hetero-graphy (Blommaert); sociolinguistics: fluid lects (Auer), ludic Englishes (Pennycook), and poly-lingual languaging (Jørgenson); applied linguistics: translanguaging (Canagarajah, 'Translanguaging'), pluriliteracy (Garcia), and third spaces (Guttierez)" (1). In contrast to older models that portrayed language difference in classrooms as either a cognitive failure (blaming the students), a sign of incomplete acculturation (placing more of the burden on teachers), or resistance to the legitimate language (chalking it up to "student choice"), proponents of this approach recognize the normal processes of language change as well as the power issues involved in language decisions, engaging both students and teachers in a negotiation of meaning and of writing standards. Bruce Horner, Min-Zhan Lu, Jacqueline Jones Royster, and John Trimbur explain in a basic introduction to translanguaging, "This approach sees difference in language not as a barrier to overcome or as a problem to manage, but as a resource for producing meaning in writing, speaking, reading, and listening" (Horner et al. 2011, 303–4). I support this new movement; in fact, I think Canagarajah's (2013) development of the translingual lens in *Translingual Practice: Global Englishes and Cosmopolitan Relations* is almost revolutionary compared to the native/nonnative paradigm. He argues that every language and code is always already mixed, and boundaries are only put up between ways of speaking to serve nation-states, colonization, and imperialism (20). And I second these scholars' emphasis on student agency, but I caution that translingual pedagogies can be used in the same sociopedagogical way as code censoring and eradication, as I explain shortly, so it's still important to teach translanguaging critically.

The burgeoning conversation in comp/rhet around translanguaging has sometimes been discussed in terms of the pedagogical approach *code meshing*—one of many possibilities within translanguaging, but kind of a hot topic recently. There was ambiguity in the field about who coined the term, because Canagarajah wrote about it in 2006 without crediting a source, but Vershawn Young actually coined it in his 2004 article "Your Average Nigga," based on work in his dissertation dealing with African American English and Standard English. He explains in a footnote, "As an alternative to code switching, I argue, in my doctoral dissertation 'Your Average Nigga: Language, Literacy, and the Rhetoric of Blackness,' that true linguistic and identity integration would mean allowing students to do what some linguists have called *code mixing*, to combine dialects, styles, and registers. Code mixing, or what I call *code meshing*, means allowing black student to mix a black English style with an academic register (much as I do in this essay). This technique not only links literacy to black culture, it meshes them together in a way that's more in line with how people actually speak and write anyway" (Young 2004, 713). Later, in his book *Your Average Nigga*, Young writes that code meshing is "no panacea," but he also writes, "I believe that it is crucial, if beneficial, for no other reason than that it allows black students (and some teachers) from the ghetto a place in school, a site where many feel alienated" (Young 2007, 8). Though he doesn't develop any pedagogical suggestions for using or teaching code meshing yet, Young pushes for the language standards in classrooms to extend to include stigmatized ways of using English.

In "The Place of World Englishes in Composition: Pluralization Continued," Canagarajah (2006) theorizes and extends Young's theory of code meshing to create practical ways of teaching the multilingualism that Smitherman and Horner and Trimbur propose to institutionalize through policies. He writes that "teachers don't have to wait till these policies trickle down to classrooms. They have some relative autonomy to develop textual practices that challenge dominant conventions and norms before policies are programmatically implemented from the macro-level by institutions" (587). He suggests that students can use code meshing to "work from within the existing rules to transform the game" and that code meshing actually requires a higher level of sophistication from students than merely writing in the legitimate language (599, 598). Students can insert nonstandard English and even other languages into their formal academic writing with textual cues or footnotes to explain the meshings for any readers unfamiliar with the writer's codes. Canagarajah gives a textual analysis of Geneva Smitherman's writing style to show a successful model of code meshing in high-stakes writing. Other scholars have developed approaches to code meshing. Carmen Kynard (2008) compares code meshing to the meshed musical genre "the blues" and suggests playing the "trickster" in writing to "alter old conditions by rhetorically creating new possibilities and worlds" (368). In addition, the "Pedagogy" section in *Code-Meshing as World English* (2011, edited by Vershawn Ashanti Young and Aja Martinez), contains several essays on classroom approaches to teaching code meshing.

Elbow, who once advocated using home discourse in drafts only (and editing them out for the final product), cautions that a code-meshing focus can revert to a product-oriented writing class, ignoring the importance of home languages in the planning, freewriting, and revising processes. He also proposes, in keeping with his desire to help students avoid discrimination, what he calls "invisible" code meshing in *Vernacular Eloquence* (Elbow 2012): "Canagarajah and Young somewhat neglect . . . the possibilities for what might be called *'invisible'* or *'under the radar'* code meshing. That is, what I've learned from Wolfram, Adger, and Christian (earlier) is that people can use quite a lot of their comfortable spoken vernacular if they avoid certain usages that trigger the error alarm" (331). He proposes this kind of meshing for now because, he writes, it can enrich formal writing without causing students to fail gatekeeping moments. He cites the research of Geneva Smitherman to show that it can work: "Smitherman and her team . . . looked at thousands of papers on the nationwide NAEP exams and showed that 'Black expressive discourse style' correlated with *higher scores*—as long as it wasn't accompanied by the Black syntax or grammar—and this was 20 years ago" (332). Elbow suggests that, while he supports the "in your face" meshing of Young and Canagarajah, encouraging "invisible" code meshing may be a better temporary solution for students.

Horner and Lu (2011) point out that translingual pedagogies are not limited to code meshing. The primary tenet of translanguaging practices is the view of language as historically and politically situated so that students, outfitted with this perspective, can make decisions about their own language use. The purpose is to acknowledge and encourage student agency in writing decisions, in contrast to the traditional model of top-down, teacher-prescribed writing requirements. They write, "We have argued that a translingual approach identifies the issue we face not as a question of whether to teach standardized forms and meanings but, rather, the need for all of us to deliberate over how and why to do what with language in light of emergent and mutually constitutive relations of language, context, identity, and power relations" (29). Horner and Lu deal with two main concerns about translingual pedagogies: that students won't be properly "equipped" for the legitimate language and that translanguaging isn't relevant to "mainstream" students. They respond by pointing out that, whether students choose to code censor or code mesh, both are acts of agency, based on a translingual awareness of language processes: "both . . . represent rhetorical strategies in which writers exhibit agency and engage in the process of language sedimentation in light of different spatial-temporal, macro-micro contexts" (28). And they argue that this applies to "so-called 'native,' 'monolingual' 'mainstream' students" too, who can be asked to think about "how they are doing English and why" (19). The statement on translingual pedagogies by Horner et al. (2011) sketches a few ways these ideas work out in the classroom, including dealing with error and how monolingual teachers can handle translanguaging.

I agree with these theorists that translingual pedagogies have a lot of potential to help institutionalize plural (and changing) models of language in school writing and invite students to think critically about language choices—as long as these approaches aren't simply appropriated as better methods for assimilating and ushering students into their places in the economy, as Dewey's reforms were strategically appropriated. First of all, there are signs that this is a period of national reorganization. Like past correlations between shifts in capitalism and pedagogies, attention to translanguaging in classrooms is increasing at the same time that job requirements for translingual skills are increasing. As global capitalism expands and talk of "transnational markets" is increasingly common, translingual training happens to be better job training because the capitalist economy is no longer circumscribed by national boundaries. Whereas nation-states have relied on national languages to unify the markets of internally colonized and assimilated groups, the nationalist model is growing obsolete. Instead, the transnational model is on the rise, requiring a global language—a language of commerce or a "lingua franca"—to enable the circulation of capital. The British *Times Higher Education* recently addressed lingua franca studies in an article featuring Jennifer Jenkins, the director of the University of Southampton's new Centre for Global Englishes, who argues against teaching the nativeness model in favor of teaching for comprehension. She writes, "[Nonnative English speakers] use [English as a lingua franca] very successfully, but not in the ways that native speakers speak to each other. Their priority is communication rather than correctness or imitating some particular native version of English" (Reisz 2012). Under translingual pedagogies, students learn to be more tolerant of language differences and espouse more sophisticated attitudes about error. These classroom lessons easily accommodate the economic transition that will put them in contact with more speakers of other Englishes and languages. In these job encounters, they will need to know how to negotiate "error" and be more forgiving and flexible about language. This progressive attitude toward error is being institutionalized because it suits the economy.

Canagarajah has addressed the fallacy of appealing to arguments that are based on serving the economy, a position so easy to assume that even he has unintentionally done it. In his CCCC guest blog post (Canagarajah 2010) critiquing and proposing changes to SRTOL, he unwittingly appeals to newer transnational economic arrangements as the basis for arguing for transnational language policies. He writes, "The languages students from outside the U.S. bring to American classrooms are a resource that should be harnessed and promoted—if for nothing else than the good of the nation, all language, and writing instruction," and this will serve to expand the "repertoires all of us need for transnational relations." Canagarajah writes that incorporating multilingualism into one's pedagogy actually helps prepare students for future jobs, as multilingualism is a helpful resource for students in increasingly international markets. I asked in the blog comments about this issue, and Canagarajah agreed that it's a fallacy to appeal to arguments about normalizing students to the economy. He explained, "John Trimbur has pointed out to me that though we transnational scholars/students may benefit from a resources-based argument, indigenous minority groups (such as the African American and Native American communities) are more concerned about protecting their languages. So, I think, it is important to keep the rights-based discourses alive as we update SRTOL." Incorporating multilingualism and transnational perspectives in classrooms is an improvement on institutionalized nationalist-based monolingualism but, as Canagarajah agrees, even these progressive changes to pedagogy can be used in the United States as another form of class sorting, requiring students to conform to the (revised) discourse practices of the dominant "or else."

This shift to translingual pedagogies is occurring at the same time as another pedagogical shift in educational systems, another sign that the economy is shifting. Francesco Crocco argues in "Critical Gaming Pedagogy" (Crocco 2011) that there has been a great deal of interest in building digital games into K-12 school curricula to help engage and motivate students to learn, but the increased attention to gamification in classrooms directly parallels the growing trend of "business gamification." The game-based model is built on things like situated learning (more like simulations or apprenticeships than book learning), "failing forward" (low-stakes opportunities to learn from mistakes), simple-to-complex learning progression, instant feedback, and "just-in-time" information. Crocco argues that using gaming pedagogies really does help students learn better, but implementing these changes uncritically only helps students better learn their places in existing social conditions. He writes, "Game-based learning will likely inherit the work of traditional schooling, albeit with an updated pedagogy and cutting-edge technology. It will produce a more highly trained workforce without addressing the growing inequality and instability of the global capitalist economy in which this workforce must operate" (29). Indeed, gamification is being used in schools primarily for STEM fields—science, technology, engineering, and math—which have traditionally received greater attention during national wars. Crocco concludes by encouraging teachers to incorporate digital and nondigital games in ways that provoke students to reflect critically on current social conditions (using Paulo Freire's critical pedagogy) instead of simply adapting to them; he provides a modified use of the board game *Monopoly* as an example.

In the same way that the modern corporate business model is based on the military corporate model, business gamification and the gamification pedagogical trend are training and working strategies that derive from current military practices. In *War Play*, Corey Mead (2013) builds on Deborah Brandt's theory of "sponsors of literacy" to show the connections between game-based military training and game-based learning in our public schools. Mead illustrates this connection by describing how the army-developed recruitment video game *America's Army* is now being used to teach science, engineering, and mathematics in thousands of junior high and high schools in all fifty states. The military has seen impressive results in recruitment increases due to the popularity of *America's Army*, which was developed as a tool to recruit tech-savvy young people into the army. As Mead writes, "Barely one year after the game's release, 20% of incoming West Point freshmen reported having played it. By 2008, a Massachusetts Institute of Technology study noted that, '30 percent of all Americans age 16 to 24 had a more positive impression of the Army because of the game and, even more amazingly, the game had more impact on recruits than all other forms of Army advertising combined'" (75). The explicit military connections to emerging pedagogies and the US government's financial investments in them demonstrate an interest in not only a larger military but also a revised kind of labor training.

These current pedagogical shifts addressing both language normalization and sociopedagogical normalization indicate that we are in the middle of a period of national reorganization. Conditions are ripe for an economic transition, since the largest socioeconomic changes have historically been signaled by nationally reorganizing events like wars and crises, during which the most influential capitalists lobby heavily for changes in education. The last decade or so has seen tragedies (like 9/11 and Hurricane Katrina) that prompted national unification as well as crises (the "recession") that demand national redefinition; multiple wars; and civil unrest (Occupy Wall Street, for example, and dozens of protests across the country that have also been violently repressed). Another sign of socioeconomic reorganization is that there have been open critiques and discussions of the failures of capitalism in major media like the *New York Times* and the *Huffington Post*. In May 2014, representatives of the ruling class from all over the world convened at the Conference on Inclusive Capitalism to consider strategies to transition to a newer and more sustainable form of capitalism, tackling issues like environmentalism and the disappearing middle class. The conference featured speakers like Prince Charles and Bill Clinton, and organizers asked attendees to read thought pieces like "How Capitalism Can Repair Its Bruised Image," "Rewiring Capitalism: We Need a Narrative We Can Believe In," "Is There a Future for Capitalism?" and "The Capitalist Threat to Capitalism."

Meanwhile, other signs of reorganization show up in education. Influential capitalists are granting huge sums of money to redesign education by privatizing public schools (charterization), reforming community colleges (the recently proposed CUNY "Pathways," for example), and even purchasing testing industries (Rupert Murdoch recently acquired 90 percent of Wireless Generation, a student-tracking software company, for $360 million).[5] Bill Gates, who has taken an interest in social-engineering experiments like mass vaccine gassing and stealth sterilization of human males, funds one of the largest research grants available for digital pedagogy, and he has also funded an experimental community college to test a new model of education that he hopes will catch on. The New Community College at CUNY in Manhattan is, according to its Web page, "a powerful, purposeful college, specifically designed to link classroom learning to practical career experiences." Geared at improving student retention rates, this new community college model has so far been reported to have unsatisfactory faculty retention rates, with several teachers quitting due to poor labor conditions. The community college's explicit link to job training and its "sponsor" are indicative that it is part of national reorganizing.

The efforts of affluent businesspeople to reform education on all levels also extend to Louisiana: New York City mayor Michael Bloomberg contributed $100,000 "on behalf of pro-charter, anti-teacher-tenure and anti-union candidates" via his PAC, Alliance for Better Classrooms, in 2011.[6] This contribution helped secure votes in favor of Governor Bobby Jindal and big-business groups backing him in his K-12 education reforms (as well as cutting more than half of Louisiana state college funds). In the aftermath of Katrina, Jindal wrecked the already poor educational system in Louisiana by selling public schools opportunistically to private buyers and instituting "merit pay" for teachers based on the performance of their students (prompting the resignation of more than 500 teachers and creating a great deal of anxiety among those who stayed). Jindal's system of vouchers (for either public or private schools, meaning state money goes to Christian and charter schools) was ruled unconstitutional twice (in 2013 and 2014) for many reasons, including undermining the legal desegregation of schools. His damage is so well known that Brad Pitt has commented jokingly on the Bill Maher show, "What I ought to do is run for governor and save the great state of Louisiana from Bobby Jindal." Indeed, Jindal defunded nearly all public institutions in Louisiana in his efforts to prove himself a good presidential candidate for the ultra Right (he was runner-up to Sarah Palin in the 2012 election), but his 2016 presidential campaign never got off the ground. Diane Ravitch (2013), former US assistant secretary of education, writes, "Bobby Jindal is the Reverse Robin Hood of the South. Corporations should flock to Louisiana: Cheap labor! Low taxes! No unions! Big profits! A poorly educated workforce, and likely to stay that way as long as this governor is in office." All joking aside, Ravitch warns that Louisiana is intended to be a test case and "national model" of the kind of corporate reform agenda backed by the Gates, Broad, and Walton foundations.

Because of these signals of national, economic, and pedagogical reorganization, another caution I offer about code meshing and other translingual pedagogies is that, if taught uncritically, they can wind up serving the same sociopedagogical function of assimilating students into the national economy as code censoring and eradication. As Bowles and

Gintis (1976) explain, it's not the content or product (or even the writing process, I might add) being taught that normalizes students to class inequality but the sociopedagogical relationship between the teacher, the students, and the material. Like past programs intended to "help" marginalized people, code meshing can be used in just as authoritarian a way as code censoring or eradication to reinforce the sociopedagogical objective of assimilating students into the relationships of the capitalist economy. Canagarajah (2004) reports that some students have been resistant to showing their vernaculars in classrooms, indicating that it's not something every student would choose. Horner and Lu's (2011) model in "Translingual Literacy and Matters of Student Agency" avoids imitating the top-down model of past pedagogies by building in an awareness of student agency, but I'm skeptical of a kind of parallel assertion they make that translingual pedagogies are intrinsically positioned to honor student agency.

I agree with Horner and Lu (as well as Canagarajah and Elbow) when they write that it's important to honor student decisions to code censor as an act of agency and to point out the agency in these decisions to students: "[W]e need to learn to recognize, and help students learn to recognize, the production of the same in what appears to be different, the production of difference in what appears to be the same, and the agency operating in both" (Horner and Lu 2011, 29). Canagarajah (2012) provides a classroom illustration of this principle when he describes the case of one student (he calls her Buthainah) who produced code-meshed texts in class. He emphasizes the need to explain to students the impressions their writing choices can make so that they can make informed rhetorical decisions. During Buthainah's revising process, feedback from both her fellow students and Canagarajah helped her distinguish which meshes (based on several languages) were helpful for her readers (for example, nonstandard phrasings of ideas) and which were distracting in an unproductive way (like spelling variations). She then was able to make decisions about how she wanted to come across in her writing. Canagarajah writes that, though he personally would have made different decisions had it been his own text, he respected her rhetorical decisions, and he concludes that the most important part of the process for Buthainah was being equipped to make these writing decisions: "Buthainah didn't elaborate on the distinction between error, mistake, and codemeshing. However, intentionality seems to make a difference in some cases" (26). Buthainah was able to engage productively with her text, bend it and stretch it, until it communicated what she wanted it to communicate. This is the process of negotiation that a translingual approach can bring to classrooms. Students aren't forced into top-down writing molds, and they also aren't left to flounder because their writing is already "beautiful" (yet "illegitimate"), but they and the teacher work together to create texts that accomplish the students' intentions. Students must be made aware of what can look like errors, or their decisions to code mesh can't really be counted as agency.

Thus, Horner and Lu argue that a translingual approach may include code meshing, but it may also include code censoring and even "the most seemingly clichéd writing" (they cite David Bartholomae's [1997] example of the author of "White Shoes" from "Inventing the University"), based on students' various intentions (Horner and Lu 2011, 17). When students like Buthainah choose to censor some of their vernacular influence from a sentence or even an entire text, it's an informed decision. And when they break the rules, they are doing it on purpose, fully aware of the impact their decisions will have on their audiences. As a minority writer myself, I've benefited from being informed about my meshing decisions. My writing group consistently interpreted the "colorful" style of Cajun rhetoric—which is warm, humble, and engaging in speech—as sassy, grandiose, and off-putting in writing. Since I didn't want to seem grandiose, I chose to code mesh very little in my theoretical discussions and arguments. Choosing to self-censor may seem like "token" code meshing, but it's an informed decision I made in light of what I think are important rhetorical considerations. I think other minority and working-class academics should be equipped to make that choice too. As I've argued earlier, code censoring reifies sociopolitical and economic inequalities, it's just a shoddy work-around ("working the system"), and I don't think students should be required to do it. But I still teach it to students who want it. And, like Delpit, I teach it explicitly. It may sound paradoxical to argue that code censoring is terrible and that I teach it unambiguously, but this is the paradoxical position that minority and working-class academics find themselves in. Students must conform to school expectations today not for the sake of achieving upward mobility but just to avoid downward mobility, as jobs are increasingly scarce compared to their parents' job prospects (and ability to live comfortably on the wage). So I agree with Horner and Lu when they write that code censoring is also a legitimate decision.

I hesitate, however, when they argue that translingual approaches automatically enable student agency; this claim conflates pedagogy with sociopedagogy. They write, "By foregrounding the mutual interdependence of structure and language practices, a translingual approach shifts attention to matters of agency—the ways in which individual language users fashion and re-fashion standardized norms, identity, the world, and their relation to others and the world" (Horner and Lu 2011, 5). Though they state that a "translingual approach shifts attention to matters of agency," it's completely possible to separate the teaching of translingual awareness (the pedagogy) from asking for student input and decisions (the sociopedagogy). Or teachers might stress student agency in writing decisions while ignoring student agency in all other matters. As the example of the Deweyan progressive model shows, there can be an uptake of the principles that serve the economy and a rejection of the ones that don't. Elements of translingual pedagogies may be appropriated for what serves capitalism, especially since translingual pedagogies are emerging at the same time as a transition to a transnational economy, which requires a global language to enable the circulation of capital. As I wrote earlier, a more sophisticated understanding of language and error is appropriate for the current economic shift, but not necessarily a more sophisticated understanding of policy making or race and class inequality. Unfortunately, like Dewey's progressive pedagogy, even extremely democratic translingual approaches can be appropriated to sociopedagogically assimilate students into an unequal economy.

Further, though I agree that choosing to code censor is an act of agency, it's not completely voluntary (or involuntary either), so I don't think it should be presented as an *equal* option in translingual pedagogies. As Horner and Lu point out, choosing to abide by prejudiced rules is a form of agency because it's not completely involuntary, but compliance is also never fully voluntary under the threat of intimidating forces like the possibility of not being able to provide for one's children or pay rent for housing—basic physical needs, which can carry more weight than ideological decisions about asserting one's linguistic identity. Choosing in the spectrum of code censoring and meshing is not like choosing between a semicolon and a period; it's more like choosing whether or not to show one's class or ethnicity. Though Lu generally calls these "stylistic" decisions in "Professing Multiculturalism: The Politics of Style in the Contact Zone" (1994b), they are, as she acknowledges in her title, political decisions. Horner and Lu are known for encouraging student agency in their articles and talks, so I'm not questioning their own practices. But again, I'm cautious about the general uptake of translingual pedagogies—especially since there is a similar discourse of student agency surrounding the old idea of code censoring: if students *want* to succeed, they can *choose* to code censor; if they don't code censor, they are *choosing* to resist language assimilation, and teachers can respect that decision (as they fail the students). I used to espouse this position, and I know plenty of teachers who still do. I can imagine similar situations in which teachers embrace translingual pedagogies, with proper understanding of language processes and situatedness, and then require code censoring in the name of translanguaging. Any teacher can claim translingualism and still teach only code censoring by claiming that students have already mastered translanguaging or code meshing in their practices outside the classroom; the students' amateur writing might be interpreted as a need for class time dedicated entirely to the legitimate language only. Misused in this way, translanguaging could come to be another name for code censoring or even eradication. In their efforts to make translingual approaches accessible to any teacher and applicable to any student, I think Horner and Lu may lose what is truly radical about their own translingual approach if it becomes institutionalized.

That said, I'm not arguing against their pedagogy, just being cautious. It's productive to debunk the native/nonnative myth of language use, but I'm wary of what will replace it. The sociopedagogical function of school is still integrating workers into the economy, regardless of scholars' theories about language as situated and emergent. I am impressed with practitioners of translingual approaches' awareness and validation of student agency, but translingual pedagogies are not inherently critical. They require, as Crocco (2011) argues for gaming pedagogies, a critical lens. It's important for teachers to acknowledge that translingual approaches to language instruction correspond with the needs of transnational capitalism and that they can be taught either critically or uncritically. I also suggest that teachers present code censoring not as a stylistic choice but as a political choice. To continue the efforts of theorists of translingual pedagogies in inviting student agency, I suggest going one step further than asking for students' opinions and decisions about language and ask them what they want to learn/study. Instead of continuing to sociopedagogically prescribe what is in their best interests, teachers can draw on the tenets of critical pedagogy and ask students to negotiate the actual curriculum with them.

Based on the work of Paulo Freire in Brazil, critical pedagogy is a time-tested sociopedagogical approach for both conveying the material effectively and encouraging students' capacity to think critically about the material. Freire aimed to teach his adult students how to read words and how to "read the world." Ira Shor develops ways to implement Freire's theory in US classrooms in the "bible of critical pedagogy," *Empowering Education: Critical Teaching for Social Change* (Shor 1982). In it Shor explains how to use problem-posing strategies, generative pedagogy, critical dialogue, and other tools to raise students' awareness of the political context surrounding language. His ideas around the practice of *desocializing* are particularly important to me, as I explain in the next chapter. Shor's and Canagarajah's work, informed by Horner and Lu's multicultural ideas and made more accessible to working-class and minority students with Delpit's explicitness, can converge to create "critical code meshing" or "critical translanguaging." I also like Sharon Crowley's (1998) idea in *Composition in the University* of teaching the literature of comp/rhet (like Villanueva, Delpit, Lu, and so on) to our composition students. Bringing the students in on the discussions we have about them and the legitimate language can help them learn how to think critically about the policies and pedagogies being "done" to them, as well as the process and politics of policymaking in the United States, while giving them plenty of topics to practice their writing on. Whatever approach to English comp I recommend now, though, I probably won't be recommending in twenty to thirty years because the economy is ever changing, and I think our pedagogies should also be ever changing to keep up with best practices. What won't change is my recommendation to incorporate a critical sociopedagogy, which Freire stressed should be continually reinvented and adapted for each context—not just illiterate adult peasants in 1970s Brazil (Russell-Buffalo and Stanford 2014). My main concern is that anything we teach, we teach with a critical sociopedagogy, inviting students to develop and practice their agency. After all, they get plenty of practice suppressing it almost everywhere else.

## CONCLUSION

I remember that when I told Chris Schroeder I was planning to go into comp/rhet, he seriously discouraged me. I had contacted him again when I was getting my MA at University of New Orleans and realized that all that stuff he did in class was based on real literature, not just his odd whims and beliefs. He was gracious about my former judgmentalism, but he cautioned that I would wind up feeling uncomfortable being employed in a field that existed for gatekeeping reasons. Chris recommended that I read Sharon Crowley's *Composition in the University* before I signed up for the PhD (I didn't). Shortly before I packed up and moved to New York City to attend CUNY Graduate Center, he wrote, "I know all about the idealism of being a literacy worker, but the longer I do this work, the more convinced I am that a.) we can't accomplish much in a university setting; b.) the literacies we push are increasingly irrelevant to people's everyday lives (and may never have been that relevant for most); and c.) the work we do is more like intellectual masturbation than I ever thought—somewhat satisfying but not very productive." I still don't think he was right about being able to fly, but he called it when he said that working within the university system is too limiting when it comes to language inequality.

So if I seem brief on pedagogical solutions, it's because I think there's already a lot of conscientious work in this area, and I'm not really aiming to add to the pile. Obviously, I'm not proposing anything new, simply situating pedagogical considerations within the network of other pressures in linguicism. Unfortunately, changing language policies in classrooms can't truly change the linguicism that students (and teachers) face because the current standards are also a symptom of the inequality. The function of language in the socioeconomy is as a sorting mechanism that orders laborers according to which occupations they might qualify for, from Wall Street to wage labor and illegal immigrant labor too. The language hierarchy is easy to enforce because it's easy to pass off as meritocratic. Since the inequality doesn't originate in the classroom, it can't be fixed solely in the classroom. At this point, the inequality is diffused throughout the entire society, and anyone involved in the cultural markets helps reinforce it. Critical translanguaging is one way to push for more equal standards in language, but I address in the next chapter the hegemonic values and practices that underwrite the unequal language markets. After all, even if Cajun students weren't being assessed according to the standards of code censoring in classrooms, they would still normalize to the legitimate language in other contexts, as I did.

# 5
## BEYOND CLASSROOMS
*Debunking the Language Myths*

*The invader thinks, at most, about the invaded, never with them; the latter have their thinking done for them by the former.*
—Paulo Freire, *Education for Critical Consciousness*

*And because we internalize how our language has been used against us by the dominant culture, we use our language differences against each other.*
—Gloria Anzaldúa, *Borderlands/La Frontera*

It was when I was teaching English in Venezuela that I had my epiphany: Cajuns aren't backward, just different. Fresh out of college with a BA in English, I had moved to Mérida to teach entry-level and advanced conversational English classes. Each of the teachers at my institute, which hired only native English speakers, took a turn presenting about our home cultures on Fridays. When my turn arrived, I felt this funny dissonance between what I perceived as my mainstream American identity and the stuff I was describing in my presentation about my home life. Most of my favorite foods, restaurants, towns, festivals, and people had French names. Which wasn't helpful for my English as a foreign language students. The other teachers, most of whom were American, also commented on how unusual, how foreign my home sounded. And that was the first time it occurred to me that we had something cool going on, and why was I working so hard to suppress it and escape it? I had wanted to get out so badly and find something interesting, but now I realized I had left something totally interesting at home. What I had interpreted before as outdated, folksy ways, I now saw as cultural difference.

It's not that I had been ashamed of my family's Cajunness before then; I had been ashamed of our poor Americanness. I grew up identifying as mainstream American but, as I understood it, we were crummy Americans. True, all the Cajuns I knew were very patriotic and hardworking, and they were able to recognize standardized English when they heard and read it. But they spoke this mishmash that outsiders could barely understand sometimes, and they were content to hunt and fish their lives away instead of working hard to get a nicer home or car. As far as I could tell, Cajuns were nice, but they were failures. Turns out, I had internalized the hegemonic principle that is generally used to usher internally colonized groups into the US economy; we were American, but we weren't good at it, and that's why we deserved to be at the bottom of the economy. But it began to dawn on me that maybe Cajuns consistently failed at the American socioeconomic rules not because we were lazy, inferior, and backward, but because we were good at being Cajun.

It was also in Venezuela that I began owning my Cajun accent. I was working so hard on my accent in Spanish that I also began speaking English with a Venezuelan accent. It was disconcerting not to be able to remember my "normal American" accent. I tried to speak "unaccented" English, but I found myself speaking like the teacher from Prince Edward Island, Canada, who literally said *ern't* for *aren't*. It kind of freaked me out, like I had gotten lost. In the evenings, I would concentrate on trying to hear my Paw-Paw Jeff's voice in my head and practice letting that accent flow in my English. I had worked so hard to remove that accent, but now I needed it to feel like myself again.

I came to understand why my friend Esther back in the States keeps her thick Scottish accent, even though people have a hard time understanding her. I used to get frustrated with her for not being clearer—like the time we were playing a small gig at a coffee shop in New Orleans. We wound up with an extra hour after our set because the next band didn't show up, so we were jamming to anything we could think of. I had started up a cover song that we both knew when she leaned over her djembe and said in my ear something that sounded like "Let's sing a bare sea!" Stumped, I strummed through the intro again and asked her what the heck she had just said. She leaned over again and hissed, "Let's sing a bare sea!" I gave her the "Huh?" look again, to which she replied with a "Really?" look. This time she spoke with a flawless midwestern American accent: "Let's sing a *verse each*." She could have spoken like that all the time, and it would have made her life easier, but she kept her accent, she told me, because it felt like part of her identity. Raised in a sort of hippie commune in an old castle near Glasgow, she had run away when she was sixteen to live all over Europe before she finally settled in the United States in her twenties. She could imitate nearly any accent, but she needed her Scottish accent to feel grounded. After my time in Venezuela, I could relate.

Apparently, this is an old story, kind of like the traditional quest narrative. Something about the change in perspective makes you miss and value what you disdained before—even the "broken English." One Cajun I met said he set out on a tour of the United States to "find his happy." The more he traveled and saw, the more he realized how good it was back home. He returned determined to open the eyes of Cajuns and Creoles to what we have in Acadiana and never to leave again. Now he works at Vermilionville, maintaining historic Acadian homes and keeping the Vermilion River clean. Elista Istre writes about a similar experience coming to appreciate Cajun and Creole culture in the introduction to her study of Louisiana tourism: "Although born and reared in Lafayette, 'the Heart of French Louisiana,' I had little appreciation for Cajun culture until I went away and returned, thirsty to discover who my people are after discovering who other people were" (Istre 2002, 1). Since then, Istre has served in various capacities in media and cultural celebrations geared toward raising awareness and preserving Louisiana French culture.

It's the same story for many Cajun activists, according to Shane K. Bernard (2003) in *The Cajuns: Americanization of a People*. Barry Jean Ancelet had an awakening of sorts in Nice, France, when he heard a musician there play an old Cajun tune, "The Crowley Two-Step." He recognized the melody but realized he didn't know any of the musicians back home who had influenced this fellow all the way over in France. He hadn't even really liked Cajun music up till that point. Since that awakening, Ancelet has gone on to become instrumental in establishing some of the most important cultural institutions for Louisiana French speakers, including Festival International, French-immersion school programs, and the UL Lafayette archives on Cajun music and folklore. Bernard writes that there was a wave of Cajuns who had similar "exile experiences" and, because of the change in perspective, became activists guarding the disappearing Cajun culture. He writes, "By leaving their homeland and exposing themselves to new ideas and surroundings, these Cajuns were either inspired to become activists or, if already activists, were inspired with a renewed sense of mission" (108). He mentions as examples historian Carl A. Brasseaux, linguist Richard Guidry, attorney David Marcantel, and musicians Michael Doucet and Zachary Richard, who all grew up in the 1950s and 1960s "suspended between traditional and mainstream cultures" (108). In addition to these activists and several Canadian French activists and scholars (including Sylvie Dubois and Dominique Ryon), there is now a new generation of Cajun and Creole activists that grew up in the 1980s and 1990s, still feeling the same tension between the "traditional and mainstream cultures" as the last generation, including Louis Michot, Christophe Landry, Elista Istre,

Anne Laughlin, Stephen Ortego, and many others. Most of them also had the "exile experience" of moving away or traveling, then returning with a new love for SouLa. These life-changing and consciousness-changing experiences, which in some cases have driven people to become full-time activists for and experts on language, weren't connected to conventional school or family experiences. In fact, since schools and families are the primary ways that socioeconomic inequality is normalized, individuals must get outside these structures to have moments of what Paulo Freire (1993) calls *conscientization*, or coming to consciousness.[1]

As I've hung my case study on Bourdieu's framework in the last few chapters, I've argued that there is a combination of factors that lead to people's individual compliance with the legitimate language: first, during the period of national codification, nation builders determine the hierarchy of languages according to the class structure, creating a "language market" in which some ways of speaking are worth more cultural capital than others; next, this language inequality is programmed into schools, where students (under compulsory attendance laws) are normalized to the standards surrounding the legitimate (and resulting illegitimate languages) with policies such as eradication and now code censoring; then, students who have internalized this inequality reinforce the linguistic hierarchy in the markets when they police themselves and their families as well as the language of others. This compliance, of course, is never quite voluntary when the alternatives to compliance can be social ostracization and the inability to meet one's most basic needs like food and shelter. Cajuns who code censor and pressure one another to code censor have consistently reported doing so for the sake of a good job and/or to avoid shame or humiliation.

A final critical reason individuals comply with language inequalities is the inaccuracies they believe about language, the myths that circulate throughout the hegemony. I'm writing about this in the last chapter, but that doesn't mean it's the last piece of the process. What supports the very foundation of unequal language markets are intentionally deceptive ideas about language that people have internalized. Language markets in turn determine job markets, which in turn determine school normalizing policies, so these false notions are integral to producing individual collaboration throughout the whole process. Bourdieu writes, "[T]he language of authority never governs without the collaboration of those it governs, without the help of the social mechanisms capable of producing this complicity, *based on misrecognition*, which is the basis of all authority" (1991, 113; emphasis mine). Misrecognition in this case pertains to understanding possibilities for good and bad only in terms of the already existing ideology—kind of like how if you believe there's nothing on the other side of the ocean, there's no reason to look for other people. Basically, a lot of people in the United States don't know there's a way of viewing nonstandard English as anything besides a sign of laziness or even moral depravity.

## LANGUAGE MYTHS

Bourdieu refers only briefly to these language myths, but I think they're crucial to the self-policing of minority groups as well as conscientization experiences, so I expand on them and tie in other theorists to explain their impact in the United States. In the spirit of Bourdieu, linguist Geoffrey Nunberg uses an economic metaphor to explain the problem with these myths: "Indeed, to linguists who have studied these questions, most of these 'everyday common sense' ideas about language sound very much the way an appeal to 'everyday common sense' ideas about inflation would sound to an economist—they're hardly the grounds that you would want to rely on for making policy" (Nunberg 2004, xv). Nunberg invokes the idea of "common sense" as a reference to Antonio Gramsci's (1971) notion of *cultural hegemony*. Though Bourdieu does not use the word *hegemony* (instead explaining circulation of the legitimate language in terms of a market), language myths are easier to understand in terms of Gramsci's theory, which is based on the idea of "mass consent," a form of what Bourdieu often calls "collaboration." Gramsci's articulation of how these values are internalized accounts for the power of Bourdieu's language myths.

Cultural hegemony, or mass consent, is the ideological component reproducing inequalities in a capitalist society (like the United States), where violence and political coercion are less popular (though still present). Language myths are part of the "common sense" that circulates throughout the society and seems to always confirm the order of things. We quote it and pass it on without knowing the source of it. The source, Gramsci argues, is the dominant of the society, who put a lot of money and time into creating and maintaining "commonsense" ideas that reify their positions. By the "dominant" (what Gramsci calls the "ruling class"), I mean the relatively few who benefit from an economy that exploits those who do the actual labor. In Gramsci's theory, the dominant values in cultural hegemony mask as common sense, so it's difficult to discern one's beliefs from the beliefs circulating in the hegemony. He explains, "Common sense is not something rigid and stationary, but is in continuous transformation, becoming enriched with scientific notions and philosophical opinions that have entered into common circulation. 'Common sense' is the folklore of philosophy and always stands midway between folklore proper (folklore as it is normally understood) and the philosophy, science, and economics of the scientists. Common sense creates the folklore of the future, a relatively rigidified phase of popular knowledge in a given time and place" (Gramsci 1971, 421). Like common sense, the myths are part of hegemony the way that forwarded emails, Facebook reposts, and memes are a part of Internet hegemony. People pass on these blurbs, which circulate for years, often with outdated, inaccurate, and outright false information. Likewise, people pass on myths about language that often contain outdated, inaccurate, and outright false information.

The four primary language myths correspond to some of the most important US socioeconomic myths: the myth of classlessness, the laissez-faire myth, the manifest destiny myth, and the democratic process myth. I've touched on these misconceptions in previous chapters as I've explained the processes of codifying, institutionalizing, and circulating the legitimate language; here, I systematize, summarize, and critique these myths more pointedly.

*The Myth of Linguistic Classlessness*

Bourdieu criticizes linguists who treat language as a neutral medium for expression, and he refutes the idea that everyone has equal access to linguistic capital and thus an equal shot at success. Bourdieu calls it "the illusion of linguistic communism which haunts all linguistic theory," invoking the idea of having all things in common (1991, 43). He quotes Auguste Comte, the founder of sociology, as an example of someone who promoted this linguistic myth: "'Language forms a kind of wealth, which all can make use of at once without causing any diminution of the store, and which thus admits a complete community of enjoyment; for all, freely participating in the general treasure, unconsciously aid in its preservation'" (43). In fact, writes Bourdieu, language is a limited form of capital that is distributed according to class; it is not "limited" by its formal qualities (language in any usage can be recombined into infinite formulations), but rather "limited" politically and artificially by restricted access to usages of high distinction. He writes, "To speak is to incorporate one or other of the expressive styles already constituted in and through usage and objectively marked by their position in a hierarchy of styles which expresses the hierarchy of corresponding social groups" or, as he says a few sentences later, "social classes" (54).

Language-wise, it might be said that some are born on third base and think they hit a triple.

This "illusion of linguistic communism" is prevalent in the United States as well. Given our history with the c-word in this country, however, we might recognize it as the myth of "linguistic classlessness," the myth that every child has equal access to high-status linguistic capital and therefore has an equal shot at success. Anyone who doesn't want to take advantage of linguistic classlessness is lazy or undeserving because they didn't work hard enough. E. D. Hirsch Jr.'s *Cultural Literacy: What Every American Needs to Know* (Hirsch 1988) is a well-known statement of this perspective. Hirsch itemizes the cultural capital everyone needs to obtain in order to pass as upper class, from grammar to classical literary allusions to popular culture references. Social mobility, in his view, is as easy as studying his index of culturally literate references. In addition to assuming that no one will mind replacing his or her own cultural knowledge and traditions (as well as perspectives and beliefs) with an apparent Anglo cultural bent for the sake of upward mobility, Hirsch ignores the US sociopolitical system, which requires losers in order to have winners. Bourdieu writes that capitalism is a "competitive struggle" that requires differentiation between the working class, the professional and middle class, and the ruling class so that, even if working-class students learn how to work the system and sound or write like upper-class speakers and writers, a new standard will emerge to ensure differentiation. Recall, Bourdieu calls this a "strategy of assimilation and dissimilation": there are "deep mechanisms which, through surface changes, tend to reproduce the structure of distinctive deviations and to maintain the profits accruing to those who possess a rare and therefore distinctive competence" (Bourdieu 1991, 64–65). As long as the United States is a capitalist country, it is impossible to achieve linguistic or any other kind of equality. The educational system reproduces already existing class structures: "[T]he educational market is strictly dominated by the linguistic products of the dominant class and tends to sanction the pre-existing differences in capital . . . The initial disparities therefore tend to be reproduced" (62).[2] Put another way, the cultural capital needed for success circulates unequally, distributed prejudicially by birth and schooling.

Requiring students to code censor (or "code switch") is based on the myth of linguistic classlessness. Specifically within language, as I've explained in depth in chapters 3 and 4, Bourdieu identifies concepts of error and correctness in grammar as the primary linguistic-pedagogical means of preserving class hierarchy: "Grammar is endowed with real legal effectiveness via the educational system . . . because, through examinations and the qualifications which [grammar and spelling] make it possible to obtain, they govern access to jobs and social positions" (1991, 258). In this vein, Smitherman criticizes the strategy of requiring African Americans and "other minority groups and lower-class whites as well . . . to assimilate the language patterns of the dominant white middle class" (1986, 173). She writes that it actually maintains the status quo in the end: it "is an implicit acknowledgement that the system is good and valid, and all that need be done is to alter the people to fit into it" (207). The American dream isn't exactly equally accessible when one demographic speaks the legitimate code, and all other demographics must master two codes—or master only the academic code while giving up the family code, as Rodriguez did—just to have an "equal shot." Rodriguez and Villanueva both contest the idea of the "equal shot" when they point out that scholars of color often achieve academic success only because of affirmative action policies and funding.

Yet discussions about "proper," "correct," or "error-free" English are based on and reinforce the myth of linguistic classlessness. In *Our Magnificent Bastard Tongue: The Untold History of English*, John McWhorter (2008), a popular linguist, stresses the lack of science behind these beliefs: "To a linguist, if I may share, these 'rules' [of 'correct' grammar] occupy the exact same place as the notion of astrology, alchemy, and medicine being based on the four humors. The 'rules' make no logical sense in terms of the history of our language, or what languages around the world are like" (63). He writes that an actual error in language means there is a linguistic stumble that hides or loses meaning in communication, but the "rules" of "correct grammar" are the linguistic equivalents of fashion; they are not necessary for language to function. Definitions of error, arbitrary "fashions" of usage though they may be, bear very real consequences for those who write in academic settings. In *Errors and Expectations: A Guide for the Teacher of Basic Writing*, Mina Shaughnessy (1977), the first compositionist to suggest that BW errors are often simply variants of elite "refinements of usage" (9), pointed out that "most college teachers have little tolerance for the kinds of errors BW students make," interpreting them as "indicators of ineducability" (8). Further, what are deemed errors in writing can lead to academic failure and ultimately exclusion from certain jobs and social privileges, a form of academic gatekeeping.

Consequently, "error" in basic writing and first-year composition courses often winds up being more a political consideration than one of clear communication. For instance, "He like to play tennis" is understandable and, as far as anyone knows, true; it is nevertheless an erroneous sentence, because it adheres to the grammatical rules of African American English instead of Standard Written English. As in past language struggles, certain vernaculars of English are privileged over others in US gatekeeping moments (such as entrance, placement, and exit exams), not because they're inherently better for communication, but because of the political clout associated with them. Bourdieu argues that there are distinctions in language use that carry a form of social capital, either enabling speakers access to certain social privileges or excluding them. Social structures are encoded in and reified by language use, as defined by "error." Misconceptions about "error" and "correctness" in English are part of the myth of linguistic classlessness that portrays the educational system (and consequently economic access) as a meritocratic institution rewarding hard work instead of privilege and conformity.

*The Laissez-Faire Language Myth*

Along the same lines, another misconception is the "laissez-faire myth" of linguistic evolution. This myth is based on a misinterpretation of the normal process of language change, and it results in several ill-advised arguments in support of linguicism. The main problem with the laissez-faire myth is that it "forgets" the process of national codification that I described in chapter 2. According to this myth, the unseen hand of the markets has guided our language standards into the best possible scenario, and one narrow version of English has emerged as the fittest survivor in a competition of legitimate languages with no policies, no restrictions, no taxes, and no bailouts. All other languages have naturally deselected themselves from the running. They are fit for only home and street talk, not school and job talk.

But language standards under capitalism are artificially engineered during national codification and maintained as a continued function of nationalism. The legitimate language does not neutrally emerge as the most egalitarian language, nor is it the most efficient one for communication. Rather, it is selected, imposed, and preserved. As Bourdieu puts it, the legitimate language is "[p]roduced by authors who have the authority to write, fixed and codified by grammarians and teachers who are also charged with the task of inculcating its mastery" (Bourdieu 1991, 45). Stressing its political origins, John B. Thompson writes in the introduction to *Language and Symbolic Power* that the legitimate language can also be called the "victorious language" because it "has been *pre*-constructed by a set of social-historical conditions" (Thompson 1991, 5). Public language use has traditionally been politically controlled by nations and tribes that outlawed the local languages of whomever they conquered when they instituted their own languages. For instance, after the Norman invasion of 1066 and subsequent occupation of what is now England, the Normans outlawed the local Germanic dialect and required French in public, legal, and ecclesiastical settings. The conquered Anglo-Saxons continued to speak their own dialect in private but spoke Latin-derived French in public. The result today is that English has an unusually large number of synonyms that still correspond to those home/public language practices: *job* for informal settings but *occupation* for formal settings, *sheep* in the pasture and *mutton* on the table, *ask* at home but *inquire* on the cover letter, and so on. Further, as the language evolves (as all living languages do), it is controlled by the same strategy of "assimilation and dissimilation," in which the dominated assimilate to elite usages and the dominant invent new ways to dissimilate their status from everyone else. Limited in this system, language evolves only in favor of those who are already sociopolitically dominant, so even if the language shifts, the social structure is retained.

This process of class sorting by language has been the case with English. As John Trimbur (2005) points out in "Linguistic Memory and the Politics of U.S. English," the founding fathers instituted language inequalities by instituting race and class inequalities. With race and class inequalities such as the slavery of African Americans, the genocide of Native Americans, and gender-based discrimination of women woven into the socioeconomy, nation builders didn't need to declare an official language because the language markets automatically followed the already established job markets. Unlike other forming nations, the United States allowed for a "laissez-faire language policy," but it wasn't exactly a natural, "hands-free" process. Trimbur writes that this "laissez-faire language policy, despite its ostensible neutrality, may be just as programmatic as overt forms of language policy" (576). As I've stressed throughout this book, the foundation of unequal language markets is an unequal job market. Trimbur writes similarly about the "laissez-faire language policy" that "its very covert nature virtually guaranteed the inevitable Anglification of language in the United States through the workings of labor relations, the market, and civil society" (577). Like the socioeconomic inequalities that were instituted at the founding of the United States but are now often interpreted as evidence of race and class inferiority, the language hierarchy can seem like the result of natural processes.

In addition to the "covert" workings of language policy at the founding of the United States (by that I mean killing or enslaving the speakers of certain languages), Trimbur (2005) points out that there were overt efforts to suppress the circulation of African and Native American languages as well (forbidding their use, dividing speakers). Since then, English has been imposed on other immigrants and internally colonized groups like Mexican Americans, Hawaiians, and Cajuns via abusive physical and psychological punishments in US classrooms. After his experience in Kenya, Ngũgĩ wa Thiong'o writes that English has been imposed in other countries with similar levels of coercion (Ngũgĩ 1981). Even populations who assimilate to English because of economic hardships today are responding to a form of coercion created by transnational capitalism.

*The Manifest Destiny Language Myth*

On the other side of the laissez-faire myth, some people do acknowledge the nationalist origins of English, and they lobby to institute it as the only legally observed language in the United States. It's similar to the discourse of early American history, when it was the "manifest destiny" of the nation to go out and conquer land and peoples to build a divinely chosen empire. Analogously, there is a chosen language. Proponents of the manifest destiny of language myth argue that a national language is necessary for national unity in our great nation. Languages will diverge so much that communication will become difficult, if not impossible. First, though, divergence doesn't necessarily mean people can't understand each other. Americans can communicate just fine with the English, an entirely different nation from whose language we actually did try to diverge. With an ocean and national border between us for more than 200 years, we should be getting close to having two separate languages, as Webster predicted. But we don't, and what small differences there are in grammar, idiom, and vocabulary may cause initial difficulties and misunderstandings, but they are generally resolved with chuckles and good attitudes. Swedes and Norwegians can converse easily in their own respective national languages with each other, so national languages don't automatically draw boundaries for inclusion and exclusion (also proof that the difference between *language* and *dialect* is subtle).

Another reason to be suspicious of a national language is that it is often used to create an artificial sense of unity where there is none. Linguists point out that language evolves in favor of people who *want* to communicate, meaning that any divergence that impedes communication is often based on an already existing lack of communication. If the language seems to diverge repeatedly in spite of efforts to unify it, there's a good chance that the people speaking it have major political differences that cannot be reconciled with only a common language standard. When stodgy white professors complain that African American English is unintelligible to them, I wonder if the communication problems might actually be rooted in the desire or lack thereof to communicate, not national language policy. After all, many of these same professors pride themselves on the hard work they've done to be able to understand speakers of elite languages like French and Italian.

Discussions of national languages are signals that the imagined unity is threatened because of divisions within as well as from without. Drives for national linguistic unity are more likely to crop up during periods of "national reorganization"—generally when wars are imminent or being waged. And it's for this reason that I'm cautious about supporting the idea of world Englishes and other lingua franca. Global languages enable the global circulation of capital, which replaces independent subsistence economies with exploitative, export-dependent economies based on cash crops. Also, even as translingual pedagogies catch on, there is still a hierarchy of usage, and it's often based on nationalisms. Recognized world Englishes so far have been labeled by the nation-states they come from—Indian Englishes, Malaysian English, and so on. And these, I predict, will have more status than, say, CE or AAE, because of the level of power backing each one. A nation-state has more clout than a subculture, if only because of its army and navy.

One misconception arising from the manifest destiny language myth is the idea that, though English has evolved up until now (guided by the unseen hand of the markets), it shouldn't evolve anymore. Circumstances were divinely ordered specifically for this golden moment, and now the language is whole. But a sign of a healthy language is that it continues to change. Linguist Edward Finegan (1980), who charts the idea of language error in *Attitudes towards English Usage: The History of a War on Words*, explains that linguistic evolution is necessary for healthy languages: "[I]n order to have a language become fixed, it is first necessary that those who speak it should become dead" (78). And linguistic evolution is usually beneficial, enabling better communication. For example, many linguists write that the best thing that ever happened to the English language was being neglected by language guardians like scholars and political leaders for centuries after the Normans invaded England in 1066 and instituted French as the official language. During that time, English evolved for efficiency in the mouths of peasants, who simplified it by dropping most conjugations and declensions. For example, as any medievalist probably knows, the word *help* used to have the past forms *holp* and *holpen*, but has simplified to *helped*. This is one example from hundreds. The result today is that English is one of the easiest languages to conjugate and decline because it came to rely primarily on word order instead of endings to mark parts of the sentence. Note that it was the "errors" that made English clearer; it was the fact that English was put into the hands of the "illiterate" who simplified it out of disregard for the rules. They dropped declensions much like some people drop linking verbs. However, the language evolution slowed again in the late 1300s in Chaucer's time, when it was again used by academics and language critics who deemed certain usages not "effective" or "ineffective" but "right" or "wrong."

This myth is evident when people talk about "bad," "broken," or "mixed" Englishes, implying that Legitimate English is "pure" or "whole" in its present form. But McWhorter explains that the English we speak today emerged specifically from "impurities": "The real story of English is about what happened when Old English was battered by Vikings and bastardized by Celts. The real story of English shows us how English is *genuinely* weird—miscegenated, abbreviated" (McWhorter 2008, xxii). Not only is English a result of conquests, compromises, and peoples of different ethnicities living together, but a formative part of English coming to be what it is today was "adult learners screwing things up" because of the prevalence of people speaking English as a second language and passing it on (similar to a "patois") to following generations (124). As English continues to mix with other languages or diverge into other Englishes, though, it's considered "impure." Peter Elbow (2012) responds to this myth in *Vernacular Eloquence*: "It's touching when speakers of English argue for purity of language since English is probably the most impure bastardized language there's ever been. It's slept with every language it ever encountered, even casually. The strength of English comes from how many babies it's had with how many partners" (365). Though most people are aware of Old and Middle Englishes, they aren't usually aware that today's version of English is just one point on a long continuum that should continue to evolve and mix with other languages. This misconception can lead people to believe that the normal language processes of change have somehow not worked properly in the cases of illegitimate vernaculars and language meshings. They are seen as mutations of English that are not fit to survive but are strung along by liberal language policies (bilingual education programs, for instance), whereas Legitimate English is the self-evident victorious language.

*The Democratic Process Language Myth*

Another version of the laissez-faire myth is more directly related to comp/rhet. It's the democratic process language myth—the idea that, though currently there are language inequalities, given enough time and freedom, conditions will become more democratic because justice always prevails. Elbow, for instance, encourages optimism about language democracy, and he seems to suggest that we'll become more linguistically progressive if we just leave things alone and trust the process. He writes that language standards are evolving on their own to become "more democratic" (Elbow 1991, 152), and he makes a similar case again in *Vernacular Eloquence* (Elbow 2012). Pointing to developments in history like the invention of the printing press and the resulting spread of democratic ideals, he predicts that the Internet will make language more democratic. It's true that new technologies offer opportunities to disseminate uncontrolled and uncensored information for a time, but the means of production are quickly bought up by investors who impose proprietary restrictions on what information is available. Today's publishing industry, for instance, is very different from when the printing press was invented; it is owned and tightly controlled by for-profit corporations, in spite of the democratic origins that Elbow cites. Writers must be keenly aware of which are the prestigious presses; their words matter more (and are often more expensive) when they are published by more elite presses than when they are printed by a recent upstart. Even now, Internet access is being commodified by corporations that stratify what information is available and at what speeds, based on how much customers can pay.

Elbow doesn't take into account in his predictions of language democratization in *Vernacular English* (Elbow 2012) that social conditions tend to be reproduced, without resistance and even in spite of resistance, because of the structures and institutions in place to guard the socioeconomic order. Similarly, he ignores the forces of nationalism and efforts to maintain class differentiation in language change. Language does evolve, but it's a controlled evolution in favor of the dominant because the dominant are constantly organizing to remain dominant. The key is controlling the circulation of texts. Small-scale niche circulation is possible for self-selected adherents to a website or list, but mass circulation is tightly controlled through a few corporate hands determining what gets broadcast over TV and cable; what gets printed in books, newspapers, and magazines; and what narratives are represented as reality through cinema. When oppositional culture does achieve a breakthrough in hegemonic representations, it attracts enormous restrictive/suppressive attention, as in the case of the Occupy Wall Street movement after September 17, 2011. Protesters generally sought to exercise their right to free speech by peacefully assembling in public places with signs and speeches, but the movement's statements and demands were continually silenced by police brutality and extremely limited media representation. The important idea here is that those in power work extremely hard to stay in power, and that means crushing the democratic process that we are told to trust. The same applies to language.

Elbow is optimistic about recent language changes in the direction of democracy (more relaxed), but I'm cautious that the changes he notes are part of the same signals of economic shift I described in chapter 4. Language has not historically become more egalitarian under repressive conditions. He points out that white, middle-class men have taken a lot of liberties by using a relaxed, vernacular style in their professional writing (in *New York Times* articles and editorials, for example), even as he acknowledges that it's still unacceptable for minority writers to use their vernaculars in professional writing (2012, 348–57). This is another example of Bourdieu's "strategy of assimilation and dissimilation"; as language evolves, correctness is redefined so that there are still ways to sort people according to class. So, though Elbow urges readers to be patient, that positive change will come in time, I agree with Villanueva when he writes, "Time changes nothing, only people make change—the message of Martin Luther King's 'Letter from Birmingham Jail'" (Villanueva 1993, 53). Though he may never write about this, Elbow himself also agrees with my critique. After a long chat in 2012 about these things, I asked him to stop saying that things will improve on their own. "What do you want me to say instead?" he asked. "Just say *we* will," I told him. Elbow promised he would. He also said he doesn't bother with retractions, but I was welcome to write it for him. So voilà. Unfortunately, the idea still permeates much of his writing.

*Language Myths and Self-Policing*

These myths based on commonsense notions of language win the compliance of everyone participating in language markets, but they are particularly resonant for those who are in hardest pursuit of upward mobility. Bourdieu explains that working-class speakers internalize and reinforce these norms in their efforts to assimilate to higher social positions, whereas "the bourgeois and the intellectuals [exhibit] controlled hypocorrection which combines confident relaxation and lofty ignorance of pedantic rules with the exhibition of ease on the most dangerous ground" (1991, 63). Consequently, minority and working-class groups are the most likely to internalize language myths and the most likely to support language pedagogies and policies that hurt them the most. Elbow writes similarly, "The most fiercely imposed standards often come from the margins" (Elbow 2012, 370). As an example of a politically marginalized group that internalized and reinforced national language standards, he summarizes Miller's account of the seventeenth-century Scottish rhetoricians (during British nation building and language codification) who sought, after being colonized by the British, "to establish an aggressively *proper* standard for [English] rhetoric and language" (370). The style guides of rhetoricians like Hugh Blair and George Campbell were so "proper" that they persisted long into the nineteenth century.

Villanueva also writes about this dynamic in *Bootstraps: From an American Academic of Color* (Villanueva 1993), focusing on groups that have been internally colonized in the United States. He describes his surprise during his service in Vietnam when his Japanese American company commander ordered his company to speak only English, even in private, because they were in the "American Army." He writes that it was odd coming from someone who was a racial minority, who, like Villanueva and his fellow Spanish-speaking soldiers, seemed more patriotic than the monolingual English-speaking kids who were burning flags back in the United States. Villanueva couldn't understand why language alone would determine someone's loyalty. But he came to understand that his company commander had given the English-only order because he had bought into the myth of upward mobility even more ardently than nonminorities: "Now I see that the order came from one who had succeeded, one who had taken the path of racelessness, one who would impose racelessness on us all" (44). As a result of economic pressures and promises of upward mobility, marginalized groups who have bought into the idea of upward mobility can be the toughest audiences when it comes to contesting language myths. McWhorter (2008) describes the reactions he receives when he discusses basic linguistics principles that do not agree with national language myths: "Yet, in my experience, to try to get these things across to laymen often results in the person's verging on anger" (64). These language myths are deeply ingrained; they help support an entire socioeconomic structure, from poverty and crime to hope and perseverance under sometimes terrible conditions. They hide the class and race inequalities built into the US socioeconomy, winning the complicity of untold numbers of well-meaning individuals.

Most of my SouLa friends and I have very different attitudes about our accents now, but we were at our peak self-policing and self-ordering performances in college, where we gathered from several towns and had a chance to compare accents and levels of Cajunness. My friend Jerry, who grew up in the small town of St. Martinville, had a thicker accent than most of my friends at UL Lafayette. We picked on him for saying "Choosday" for *Tuesday* and something like "Ee's cawl-aside" for *It's cold outside.* He would just shrug his brawny shoulders and keep eating his lunch at the student union where we hung out, but he knew he had slim chances when it came to the American dream. He told us he had resigned to his fate—in other words, his low socioeconomic worth— when he heard somewhere that if you don't change your accent by age eighteen, you're stuck with it. The people with the thickest accents in Louisiana often wind up working offshore or in some other manual labor position. Jerry was the lead guitarist in our college rock band, and he cringed at how stupid he was going to sound when we got famous and had to do interviews on MTV. None of us disagreed, but we comforted him by reminding him that a lot of women from other states would find his accent sexy.

As Bourdieu's model predicts for working-class groups and as my friends and I experienced, Cajuns comply with linguicism because of our inaccurate beliefs about normal language processes, myths that hide the fact that US capitalism depends on extreme economic disparity to function properly. Like other assimilated groups, Cajuns have learned to talk about language in terms of its "correctness" or "brokenness." As I wrote in chapter 3, Cajuns who experienced punishments under the French ban grew up to repeat the same phrases about Louisiana French that they had learned as children ("broken French," "bastardized French," "pas le vrai français"), so parents avoided passing on Louisiana French to their children and even resisted bringing it back into schools. But Cajuns also learned inaccurate linguistics principles about basic language acquisition processes, so parents not only didn't pass on their French to their children but also made it a point to prevent bilingualism. Ann Martin Scott (1992a), a professor in the composition studies PhD program at UL Lafayette, writes in "Language Education in Acadiana" of her dismay at learning about local beliefs about language when she moved to Louisiana. "Soon after moving to Cecilia I ran into a local high school teacher at the hardware store, and in the course of the conversation he said to me, proudly, 'Me, I don't *let* my little girl learn French!' When I recovered the ability to speak, I asked why, and he replied that it would interfere with her learning 'good English.' It was obvious that he was sincere in his attempt to look out for the linguistic welfare of his daughter, but equally obvious that he knew little about the nature of language or about the language acquisition process in children. If he had, he would no doubt have made different decisions about his daughter's language education" (92). Scott's story demonstrates that this well-intentioned Cajun high school teacher misunderstood language acquisition processes; he also subscribed to the myth that there can be "good" and "bad" Englishes. Scott concludes that it will be necessary to "instill linguistic pride in our youth, and effect the unlearning of misconceptions in adults" before Cajuns will stop seeing their languages and themselves as inferior (100). The French ban was a huge factor in the loss of Louisiana French, but inaccurate ideas about language have fueled the process of eradication.

Carl Brasseaux describes another myth about language circulating among Cajuns that especially reinforces the idea that they are illiterate (Segura 1999). As the story goes, Cajun names like Boudreaux, Thibodeaux, Arceneaux, Comeaux, and Quibodeaux originally did not contain the final $x$ (as in many Parisian French names), but since Cajuns could neither read nor write, the local priests drawing up birth, death, and wedding certificates had them sign their "X" after their printed names. As records were compiled by literate officials later, Cajuns continued to go by the spellings ostensibly written on those certificates. However, Brasseaux refutes this story and the illiterate stereotype it carries. Actually, he argues, one Judge Paul Briant, an Antilles exile, decided to standardize the many different spellings of ō-sounding last names for the 1820 census, and arbitrarily chose "-eaux" when, "phonetically, he had about 12 ways to standardize [them]." Brasseaux goes on to point out the stigma inherent in the circulating myth: "It's a strong indication of the negative, internalized attitudes about our culture that so many Cajuns would naturally assume their ancestors were illiterate." These assumed hegemonic values persist, even after the Louisiana Constitution of 1974 "recognized" French (though it did not yet rescind the prohibition), and other forms of legislation opened opportunities for reclaiming "historical origins" (Ancelet 1988, 346). Brasseaux maintains that their perpetuation of their low societal position is a psychological result of Cajuns' "internalization of negative stereotypes...of a web-footed, ignorant, inbred and generally inferior ethnic group [exploited] in motion pictures, books written for mass consumption, and demeaning so-called 'Cajun humorists.'" He says Cajuns know what's expected of them and perform accordingly, "especially when the movie cameras show up" (Segura 1999). The negative stereotypes have become a part of Cajuns' oral traditions, which will persist unless new oral traditions are introduced.

Deany Marie Cheramie similarly argues that language myths are detrimental to CE in Louisiana. In her dissertation "Cajun Vernacular English and the Influence of Vernacular on Student Writing in South Louisiana" (Cheramie 1998a), she points out that teachers of composition generally aren't trained in vernaculars and linguistics principles, so they tend to pass on their own language misconceptions to students. She quotes from a background report by the committee that drafted the CCCC resolution Students' Right to Their Own Language, in which the members argue that "all teachers should, as a minimum, know the principles of modern linguistics, and something about the history and nature of the English language in its social and cultural context" (Committee on CCCC Language Statement, quoted in Cheramie 1998a, 150). Citing two studies that demonstrate that teachers consider speakers of nonstandard dialects to be "less capable," Cheramie writes that students become "obesessed [sic] with errors" because of their teachers' negative attitudes (151–52). She concludes by arguing for teachers and students to be educated about language varieties so they won't continue to see them as stigmatized. The results of my own study showed that college teachers of English in Acadiana generally no longer see language difference in terms of intelligence or ability, but as a problem with students' audience awareness—another myth hiding the reality of limited access to language capital in an unequal socioeconomy. In an echo of other language experts, Cheramie writes, "[T]he myths about language will be resistant to change" (152).

Yet the collection of language myths is one of the most important sites for opposing linguicism because these language myths underlie unequal language markets, and they keep people from supporting more progressive school policies about language—not to mention more progressive work conditions. Doing away with the myths will not make everything equal, but it will strip away the veil of meritocracy and the euphemisms for class and race inequality that keep people from seeing exactly what's going on. To answer the question I posed at the outset of this study, Bourdieu's model of the language/class correlation explains that, in spite of the recent Cajun Renaissance and the odd US fascination with Cajunness, the economy is structured in a way that pressures Cajuns to censor CE in relation to their economic aspirations. As Dubois and Horvath (2003b) have shown and my survey has confirmed, degree of code censoring does correlate with level of education, especially since the educational system is a primary means of normalizing the legitimate language. But correlation is not causation. Though level of education correlates with the disappearance of CE, and though it was the cause for individual decisions to censor Louisiana French (in the cases of the children who were schooled under the French ban), level of education is not the cause of CE disappearance today. Based on my research, I conclude that what actually determines the decision to code censor CE is pursuit of upward mobility, and this pursuit is fueled by inaccurate hegemonic myths that are tied to the American dream. Language myths are now one of the key factors in winning the compliance of Cajuns in the process of social reproduction, as they interpret poverty and poor grades not as a sign of systematic inequality but as a sign of laziness, inferiority (racially, biologically, or mentally), or lack of patriotism.

## BALANCING REPRODUCTION AND RESISTANCE

As we say back home, though, it's just a bunch of yanh-yanhing if you never do anything about it. After a book focused solely on the process of social reproduction in the educational and linguistic assimilation of Cajuns, the next step is examining possible roads out of this linguicism— for the Cajun community as well as other minority and working-class communities. During the course of my studies, I discovered, like Suresh Canagarajah (1999) in *Resisting Linguistic Imperialism in English Teaching*, that it's often necessary to turn to subaltern and marginalized groups to find resistance literature discussing language inequalities. Much of the existing literature on language inequality is based on the "reproduction model," the idea that power inequalities inevitably re-create themselves. "Reproduction models," Canagarajah writes, "explain how students are conditioned mentally and behaviorally by the practices of schooling to serve the dominant social institutions and groups; resistance theories explain how there are sufficient contradictions within institutions to help subjects gain agency, conduct critical thinking, and initiate change" (22). Canagarajah argues that the skewed perspective stressing the reproduction model is especially true of the literature coming from the "center," whereas periphery literature deals more with resistance (32). He goes on to discuss a "resistance linguistics," in which he describes the many forms of resistance already happening in the Sri Lankan community. Periphery people aren't just unthinking victims of language programs who swallow dominant values; they also make savvy decisions about language use for their own political advantage.

Like Canagarajah, I think that language debates in comp/rhet will benefit from more attention to resistance, and the voices of periphery scholars are integral to these discussions because of their perspective. As a periphery scholar who has undergone extensive normalization to center perspectives (twenty-two years of schooling, nine of those in graduate school), I draw on what postcolonial scholar Homi Bhabha (1994) calls my "in-between-ness" to discuss the myths that win individual compliance to dominant policies. As I mentioned before, I think a huge problem with creating positive changes in language markets will be the lack of popular support for more progressive language policies and pedagogies, particularly from the dominated themselves. I often hear from my own family—which has endured the punishments and humiliations of the French ban and constantly heard and shared stories of it in hushed, reverent tones—indignant complaints that they "have to press 1 for English" (shorthand for their objection to automated phone menus offering bilingual options). If they had to endure the cultural bomb of language eradication, then everyone else should too. It's a contradiction I wouldn't understand—except that I grew up with the same attitude.

I used to be an avid proponent of code switching for minority and working-class students. It was the obvious answer for upward mobility; anyone who didn't do it must be lazy or morally incompetent. I wrote my master's thesis about code switching—how Ralph Waldo Emerson changed the form of his writing according to context and why this can work for minority students too. This was not exactly a parallel argument, since Emerson wasn't switching between privileged and nonprivileged codes and also because, with his already established clout and privilege as a white male political figure, he was redefining writing during a period of national recodification (defining American literature in contrast to British literature, much like Noah Webster codified the American language). I intended to extend this research into a PhD dissertation all about the merits of code switching, but the more I learned the more I began to question the actual function of education. If languages are *supposed* to evolve and diverge, why were people, particularly those who had been internally colonized, being punished for language divergence? English has evolved since the founding of the United States but consistently not in favor of minority populations. The other thing that changed my perspective was the reaction to my accent when I moved to New York—when it crept out, people found it exotic and musical, not low class and illiterate, making me see up close how constructed and unstable our language standards are. I never anticipated focusing my graduate work on Cajuns; I was trying to distance myself from being Cajun so that I could be academic.

So I understand where my family and the friends I grew up with are coming from as they try to erase their Cajun accents and tease those who can't. Following in my grandparents' steps, much of the rest of my family has taken on the dominant culture's values against multilingualism and multidialectalism in their quest to be upwardly mobile, to identify with the winners instead of the losers. There are definitely Cajun and Creole families with different perspectives from my family's—especially culturally iconic families who benefited from their Louisiana French cultural capital—but there are a lot of families like mine too.[3] Loving to the core, one foot still in the communal family clan thing, but "making extra novenas" for anyone who disagrees about the American dream or imposed monolingualism. And this understanding makes me want to learn how to change the values of people who are no longer in school, who are beyond the reach of pedagogies and policies, who are the parents objecting to progressive language policies in their children's education and progressive legislation allowing for multilingualism, who are passing on the Internet memes that portray multilinguals as lazy mooches.

Digging into the literature of counterhegemonic movements like French Feminism, the civil rights struggle, Mahatma Gandhi's nonviolent resistance, early Christianity, the abolition movement, liberation theology, and several other postcolonial struggles, I found a great deal of theorization on the compliance of the dominated. Many writers on the margins have asked the same question I ask in this book: "Why do we comply?" In spite of the very diverse perspectives composing the huge body of counterhegemonic literature, an extraordinarily common theme is what I've described in terms of Bourdieu's "myths" and Gramsci's "common sense": ideological beliefs that keep us complying, not coercive forces standing over us. These myths are a key part of creating reproduction, so their undoing is a key part of inspiring resistance. One of William Blake's (2000) images resonates with me regarding this. Critiquing the class inequalities and exploitation created by British Empire in his poem "London," he called the internalization of hegemonic beliefs "the mind-forg'd manacles," or self-limiting beliefs. In Marxist theory it's called "false consciousness," Michel Foucault called it "regimes of truth," Simone de Beauvoir called it "mythologizing" (the "eternal feminine"), Ngũgĩ wa Thiong'o called it "colonization of the mind," the apostle Paul called it "bondage to the law," W. E. B. Du Bois called it "double consciousness," Martin Luther King Jr. called it "mental slavery," Gandhi called it "the enemy within," and Freire called it "oppressor consciousness." These writers stress that effective resistance is possible only when people can remove the "chains" or other metaphors of oppression from their minds. Reiterating what I wrote earlier, stripping away the myths will not automatically make everyone equal, but it will make it possible for people to see what's really going on and make informed choices at that point.

In addition to the theme of internalizing false ideas, another common feature among subaltern and marginalized writers is a focus on the complicity of the dominated rather than their victimization alone. Consent to inequalities is never completely voluntary, as Bourdieu writes, but these periphery writers point out that it is never completely involuntary either. Though their thoughts vary when it comes to violent or peaceful methods, subaltern writers almost universally call for noncompliance, indicating that they acknowledge that subordinated people do comply. Understanding the compliance of the dominated is essential to acknowledging their agency. Failing to acknowledge their agency—thus their ability to participate in decision making—leaves only one conclusion: the dominated *deserve* to be dominated. It may seem disrespectful to discuss the complicity of working-class and minority groups in US inequalities, but a balanced discussion will acknowledge both sides: the culpability of the center *and* the culpability of the periphery. After all, if people aren't blameworthy, they also aren't praiseworthy, and their actions can be interpreted only as childhood innocence or beast-level instincts, meaning yet again they need to be ruled by those who are capable of making moral decisions in their best interests. Failing to hold the marginalized responsible for their complicity (not necessarily for the origin or cause) with institutionalized, ongoing inequalities (not crimes done to them) is another form of domination that takes away their right to make their own decisions. The discourses of aid and victimization found in reproduction models actually reproduce domination, but subaltern writers recognize the agency of the dominated by acknowledging their complicity. As long as the center doesn't recognize that people in the peripheries are complicit in their domination, using the myths and stereotypes to their own advantage, the center will never recognize the dominated's agency but continue to make decisions for them instead of with them. So if the center wants to do anything helpful, it can stop creating policies to "help" those on the periphery and ask them what they think. In many cases, though, people who have long been subordinated aren't sure what they think because of the myths they have learned to repeat in discussions of language issues. Thus, the need for conscientization.

But those in dominant positions probably aren't planning to help those in subordinated positions explore their agency anytime soon; they are, after all, invested in keeping the dominated dominated. It's not that they see the working class as their enemy; in fact, they don't. They see the working class as a bunch of people on their side, as they wage wars against their real enemies: other capitalists threatening their holdings. So the relationship between the ruling class and the working class may be inherently antagonistic because the system requires poverty to sustain extreme wealth. But the members of the ruling class actually perceive themselves to be allied with their workers. Marx writes that, in the bourgeoisie's wars to conquer the capital of other empires, "it sees itself compelled to appeal to the proletariat, to ask for its help, and thus, to drag it into the political arena" (Marx and Engels 1978, 481). Armies are not contingent on nations; nations are contingent on armies. Without the huge supply of soldiers and workers, there can be no ruling class or nation. So members of the ruling class make policy decisions that they think are in their workers' best interests, about their health and education and working conditions. And they think things are fine and that their workers are on their side until something breaks down; then they put down the rebellion, almost as if taking an aspirin to keep the headache from interfering with work. The headache may be caused by tumors that will ultimately bring down the whole system (workers included), but for now the aspirin is enough to suppress it and keep running. For this reason, many periphery theorists argue that those of us who are marginalized and suppressed by inequalities, linguistic and otherwise, will have to initiate conscientization for both the dominated and the dominant.

Stepping off from Bourdieu's theory of the language markets, the primary way I understand conscientization is in light of Gramsci's theory of cultural hegemony. Gramsci (1971) literally wrote the book on counterhegemony, theorizing cultural hegemony in his *Prison Notebooks* during his imprisonment under Benito Mussolini's fascist regime from 1926 until his death in 1937. I find education theorist Michael Apple's (2009) discussion of hegemony and education in *Education and Power* useful for understanding the spaces for resistance in Gramsci's cultural hegemony. Like Canagarajah, Apple contests the "education as reproduction" model that became popular in the 1970s. He critiques his own work and the work of others who have leaned too far in one direction to stress the lack of agency teachers and students have in schools. Schools, according to what he calls the "mechanistic" view, exist only for capital's accumulation ("they sort, select, and certify a hierarchically organized student body") and legitimation ("they maintain an inaccurate meritocratic ideology and, therefore, legitimate the ideological forms necessary for the recreation of inequality") (13). Like Apple, I find the Marxist analyses of schools as sites of reproduction—one major example being Bowles and

Gintis's (1976) *Schooling in Capitalist America*—useful for understanding how inequalities are so readily perpetuated. But these reproduction analyses don't tell the whole story. Instead of a simple input/output model of hegemonic reproduction in which students enter school, undergo the hidden curriculum (which reproduces class inequalities), and exit as normalized labor, Apple argues that schools are also sites of *production*. He admits he has focused excessively on reproduction in the past and argues for more focus on resistances within schools.

And that's why changing pedagogies and policies is such important work. As I wrote in the introduction to this book, I support the efforts of Geneva Smitherman, Bruce Horner, John Trimbur, Suresh Canagarajah, and other education activists who push for more egalitarian language standards in schools. In addition to their work in schools, though, a critical place to fight linguicism is in the language markets—the network of forces that pressure individuals to comply even after they've finished their schooling and even in their private practices at home (where they are ostensibly allowed to use home discourses). And a primary way to address the inequalities of the language markets is to strip away the language myths that underlie it or, as Gramsci would put it, the "common sense" of the cultural hegemony.

There are a few reasons to be optimistic about changing US cultural hegemony. For one, there are many opportunities to challenge it. Since hegemony is constantly changing (because it is constantly being *produced*, as Apple argues), encountering new ideas and events that must be interpreted and absorbed, it must constantly be renegotiated according to certain power lines if inequalities are to be maintained. As Canagarajah has pointed out, "[C]ultural hegemony is an ongoing activity, a process, that can always be met by opposition" (Canagarajah 1999, 31). There is space within hegemony for resistance leading to real shifts in power because it is constantly being renegotiated and redesigned. These new negotiations are important points of potential. Another way that hegemony is unstable, and consequently changeable, is that the dominant who benefit from the state's efforts are not unified, even if allied. Apple writes, "[T]o maintain its own legitimacy the state needs gradually but continuously to integrate many of the interests of allied and even opposing groups under its banner" (Apple 2009, 26–27). The power that seeks to keep hegemony unequal isn't monolithic or impenetrable.

As hegemony is produced and reproduced, another reason I'm arguing that there is room for change is that much of what passes for hegemony is counterintuitive and even detrimental for the majority of people consenting to it. There are tons of people, for instance, who support legislation against the right to collective bargaining, who vote to privatize Medicare, who support tax cuts for the wealthiest few, who staunchly argue for English only, even when they and their own families are consequently excluded from political participation. It's easier to get people to support things that benefit them than it is to get them to support things that don't, so those who struggle for equality have the advantage of people's personal interests on their side. There are considerable efforts and actions of the subordinated in the struggle for equality, but I think it's worth acknowledging that there's a lot of hard work on the part of the dominant, too, when it comes to keeping hegemony working for them. It takes a great deal of work to maintain the US hegemony, which privileges such a small demographic over the rest of the population. In terms of numbers, the odds are in the favor of the people who get the short end of the stick.

*Consent* is the pivotal word here. While people usually don't invent and lobby for policies that aren't in their best interests (in fact, they resist when they think they're outrageous), they often grant consent for them (in a lesser-of-two-evils situation, for example), so I'm proposing that people quit consenting. It's not possible to control everyone's thoughts, as Apple (2009, 26) points out, so the state settles for consent. While the subordinated are constantly resisting, contesting, and so on, the state is conducting a "process of compromise, conflict, and active struggle to maintain hegemony" (27). Because hegemony requires consent, sometimes the values of the subordinated can actually be represented in the hegemony; these are "gains" or "wins." One might argue that these are only small concessions from the ruling class that take the wind out of the working class, tricking people into working harder and happier. I agree that some reforms actually solidify the power of the ruling class, but there are also true gains wherein the subordinated win more autonomy (as opposed to winning a gift or concession from someone(s) who continue(s) to rule them). A true win will alter the relationship between dominant and subordinated, not maintain the relationship while alleviating some of the discomfort of the subordinated.

Language has the same opportunities for change as hegemonic values. Language is constantly evolving because people are constantly challenging meaning, inventing new words, inventing new concepts that need to be named, incorporating new ways of saying things, and encountering new languages and ethnic groups. If the hierarchy is to be maintained, the dominant discourse must evolve along with the subordinated ones. It accepts new words in the dictionary, it allows some professionals to write in first person and reflective essays, and some grammar and style rules change. These changes may be part of the dissimilation process, but the fact that dissimilation is happening is a really good sign. It's an indication that holes keep appearing in the hegemony that must be patched. Language does change, and as hegemonic standards are newly produced to handle new content, the uncertain and uncodified sites of writing—for instance, the Internet, as Elbow suggests—are strategic places for dissent.

Rejecting the practice of code censoring is one way to take advantage of this constant struggle of assimilation and dissimilation in language, as I've argued in "Publishing in the Contact Zone: Strategies from the Cajun Canaille" (Stanford 2011). I think it's important for academics to use home and other discourses in publications. "None of us are 'dead white males,'" I write, "meaning each of us has something to contribute from our own Englishes and our own literacies, be it gendered, cultural, visual, multi-medial, or anything that will further communication" (134–35). Even academics who feel they don't have any distinct home discourses to bring into their writing can pick at the edges of hegemony when they are in positions to edit or review meshed manuscripts. They can focus on the content instead of the form, or they can favorably highlight language choices in their feedback to publishers. This kind of public challenge to hegemonic language standards can begin to push our language standards to evolve to accommodate today's academics, an entirely different population from that of 200 years ago. Yet I've seen very little (if any) meshing or translanguaging in the writing of some of the very scholars who are its greatest proponents for students (for example, Bruce Horner, Suresh Canagarajah, Min-Zhan Lu, and John Trimbur). If they do code mesh in their scholarship, it's only what Elbow (2012, 331) calls "hidden meshing." As a student of Suresh's, I once saw an early draft of an article he was writing and asked if a kind of archaic phrase, *sit in judgment*, was an example of Sri Lankan English, which is often marked with flowery, seemingly grandiose, old British usages. He thanked me for pointing it out and replaced the phrase with *are judgmental*, explaining that he only meshes in humanities articles. Though I understood his reasoning, I thought he may not have realized how much clout he had and just how much he could get away with bending the rules at that point in his career, as well as what kind of impact it would have on other academic writing from the periphery.

But code meshing, as Young (2007, 8) warns, is "no panacea." Even "in your face" meshing may stir up a lot of trouble by pushing English to evolve a little, only to resettle into a new pattern of dissimilation. It's an ongoing struggle. And code meshing, which is very difficult, may still have a lower status than texts written wholly in the legitimate language. In *Decolonising the Mind*, Ngũgĩ criticizes "the literary gymnastics of preying on our languages to add life and vigour to English and other foreign languages" (Ngũgĩ 1981, 8). He continues, "Why, we may ask, should an African writer, or any writer, become so obsessed by taking from his mother-tongue to enrich other tongues? Why should he see it as his particular mission?" Even after "the literary gymnastics," he writes, the colonized still don't have any more power or legitimacy of status. So, on one hand, code meshing can wind up being just one more form of submitting to the legitimate language, but with a few marks of cultural resistance on it. On the other hand, some of us no longer have mother tongues that aren't varieties of English, and the only way to express our cultural identity and resistance is through English. To code mesh in formal writing is, as Young argues, to write it like we would say it anyway. In their roles as scholars, theorists in comp/rhet can also bring this conversation to the public by writing for general audiences, as Peter Elbow and Mike Rose have striven to do as they address hegemonic myths about language and education.

Likewise, the hegemony *within* each individual who complies is constantly being revised and produced as we encounter new ideas and experiences; it takes a lot of work to keep everyone complying. So I think there are a lot of reasons to be optimistic that personal standards and values can shift as a result of Freire's (1993) theorization in *Pedagogy of the Oppressed* of conscientization—creating a critical consciousness in people by helping them distance themselves from and rethink circumstances they tend to take for granted or see as hopeless, unchangeable, or even deserved. Freire's theories are particularly appropriate in a discussion of language myths that hide structured inequality because, though his title is clearly pedagogical, he isn't writing about how to teach the required content of an academic discipline but specifically about how to make people conscious of hidden inequality. Freire was writing from the counterhegemonic position of critiquing class inequality in his home country, Brazil. He was jailed and exiled for radicalizing peasants in his work with adult literacy programs, in which he taught them to read words as well as to "read the world."

In the model that Freire proposes to explain ongoing inequalities, people who are oppressed have been dehumanized, and they must reclaim their humanity. In the process of ongoing inequality, the dominant see workers as lesser humans or beasts; they don't value them as equals. They can justify treating their workers poorly the same way the food industry justifies its horrific treatment of animals: they're brutes;

they don't truly feel pain. When workers internalize and normalize to the ideas of the dominant and perform as they are told, Freire (1993) writes, they become just like the beasts that the dominant see them as. The workers take on "oppressor consciousness" and then keep themselves in line. What Freire calls "oppressor consciousness" is another way of explaining the way people internalize the values of the dominant under Gramsci's cultural hegemony: "They are at one and the same time themselves and the oppressor whose consciousness they have internalized" (48). Their own consciousness is not replaced, just pushed down under the new perspective, so that they are divided within. People who have internalized the oppressor consciousness also keep each other in line—like my Grandmama Emma who stayed on her kids for their grammar, and my Paw-Paw Roland who tried to take her down a notch.

It's not just workers who are dehumanized by exploitation; the people doing the exploiting also lose a part of their humanity: "[T]he oppressor, who is himself dehumanized because he dehumanizes others, is unable to lead this struggle" (Freire 1993, 47). In fact, the ideology underlying the unequal system dehumanizes anyone who participates in it, and people can't be free of it until they overthrow not the oppressors but the oppressive system. In this vein, another myth in the United States is the idea that some people have to suffer for others to live well; there have to be losers for there to be winners. This idea isn't limited to capitalism; it's in all unequal sociopolitical systems. It's rooted in the misconception that what happens to one part of humanity doesn't affect the rest, that the suffering of some can somehow not affect the rest. The people suffering are affected most obviously, but the people causing the suffering and the people turning a blind eye to it are also affected because they have to give up a piece of their humanity to be able to carry on with day-to-day functions.

So in the process of conscientization, people must exercise a great deal of self-control to remember that the real enemy is the unequal system instead of the oppressors. Freire warns against trying to overthrow the oppressors, becoming like them in the process: "In order for this struggle to have meaning, the oppressed must not, in seeking to regain their humanity (which is a way to create it), become in turn oppressors of the oppressors, but rather restorers of the humanity of both. This, then, is the great humanistic and historical task of the oppressed: to liberate themselves and their oppressors as well" (Freire 1993, 44). Martin Luther King Jr. similarly denounced the US ideology that reduced working-class people, particularly African Americans, to "the status of things," and he pushed for a "revolution of values." He cautioned against simply turning the tables without addressing the value system that permits any humans at all to be mistreated: "There is the danger that those of us who have lived so long under the yoke of oppression, those of us who have been exploited and trampled over, those of us who have had to stand amid the tragic midnight of injustice and indignities will enter the new age with hate and bitterness. But if we retaliate with hate and bitterness, the new age will be nothing but a duplication of the old age" (King 1992, 21). King succinctly pointed out the limitations of reacting to inequalities in the system from within the same paradigm. To quote him again: "For through violence you may murder a murderer but you can't murder murder" (175). In order to truly end inequality, people have to overthrow oppression, not the oppressors.

Once the oppressed recognize that the real enemy is the system, not the pawns or even the kings and queens in the system, they can step away and design a new system. The only way to step outside the old system is to decide to see the oppressors as human too, even when they don't act like humans. This means making a conscious choice not to write them off as jerks who are heartless or, worse, who enjoy seeing people suffer, but understanding that they are operating according to the rules of an oppressive system, that they are doing a top-notch performance and getting high marks. That doesn't mean, however, that they're innocent victims of a repressive system that forces them to abuse others. Seeing the oppressors as human also means seeing them as blameworthy and holding them accountable for their actions, just as it's important to acknowledge that those who have been oppressed are both blameworthy and praiseworthy, not simply victims. Then, acknowledging the way the oppressors have misused their agency to oppress others, the oppressed have to resist the temptation to retaliate according to the rules of the old system and instead institute a new set of rules. Somebody has to stop the cycle of retaliation by volunteering not to exact revenge or require repayment, by offering forgiveness for old debts. It won't be the oppressors because, in general, they are too deeply invested in the system to see why it must be toppled. They need help from the oppressed. As Freire writes, "It is only the oppressed who, by freeing themselves, can free their oppressors" (Freire 1993, 56). The oppressed must refuse to be enemies any longer as well as refuse to see their oppressors as enemies. In this way, they destroy their enemies by destroying the system that pits them as enemies, like two dogs in a ring who would otherwise be in the same pack.

Applying these far-reaching theories of power and social change to language inequality in the United States, there are myths and misconceptions on many levels that underwrite and reinforce the language markets and their corresponding labor markets. In Freire's model, people must step outside of the system, which is a form of violence that dehumanizes people, and create a new one in which all are equals. Drawing on his early experiences in the adult literacy programs, Freire writes that the first step toward escaping the old system is coming to consciousness: "[P]eople must first critically recognize [the causes of inequality], so that through transforming action they can create a new situation" (1993, 47). In order to accomplish this, people must be able to differentiate between oppressor consciousness and their own consciousness. They can think critically about hegemonic common sense and myths by having new encounters with them, what Ira Shor calls "desocializing" experiences.

Shor has developed in *Empowering Education: Critical Teaching for Social Change* (Shor 1982) practical ways to apply some of the main features of Freire's critical pedagogy in US classrooms—for example, how to conduct a democratic classroom, how to foster dialogue (rather than teacher talk), and how to use problem-posing teaching methods that lead to activism. He describes what he calls a "desocializing" aspect of critical pedagogy: "When educators offer problem-posing, democratic dialogue in the classroom, they challenge socialization into the myths, values, and relations of the dominant culture" (117). As an example, he describes a teacher who presented a new perspective on Columbus's "discovery" of America by "stealing" a student's purse (with prior permission), claiming that it wasn't stealing because he "discovered" it. Students rethought the story of Columbus and the New World, concluding that Columbus "'stole' it, 'took' it, 'ripped it off,' 'invaded it' and 'conquered it'" (121). The teacher then asked the students whose interests were served by the account that portrayed Columbus's experience as a "discovery," leading them to see the racism hidden behind the official story. Similarly, people can be desocialized from language myths that portray socioeconomic position as the natural results of meritocracy.

Similar to what Bourdieu calls "myths," Freire argues that subordinated people often have fatalistic attitudes toward their conditions because they are "under the sway of magic or myth" (1993, 61). He writes that "they must first cut the umbilical cord of magic and myth which binds them to the world of oppression" (175). In order to see through the myths, the subordinated have to deal with their own oppressor consciousness, the hegemonic beliefs they have internalized. Once people have come to consciousness or have gotten rid of the deceptions—the myth and magic—that hide unequal conditions, they can see the world as it is and become agents for change: "The world—no longer something to be described with deceptive words—becomes the object of that transforming action by men and women which results in their humanization" (86). Desocializing experiences can debunk the language myths, allowing people to see class stratification for what it is and whose interests are being served by it.

This was the process for Cajuns who have become cultural activists. Their "exile experiences" gave them a desocialized view of what they had previously taken for granted in Cajuns' status and disappearing culture, inspiring them to quit complying with the hegemonic values that pressured them to code censor (and censor others). In fact, most of these Cajun activists now heavily advocate the public use of Louisiana French and CE, as well as Spanish and other local languages, as one of the most prevalent and audible forms of cultural protest.[4] Though research shows that CE disappears in relation to level of education, these statistics seem to go out the window in the face of consciousness-raising experiences about prejudice and social inequality because the greatest determining factor for compliance is the degree to which people have bought into US myths about language, education, and upward mobility.

The process of desocialization isn't limited to Cajuns and Creoles who are now activists. It was also the catalyst that reversed the shame and other negative attitudes toward Louisiana French that many Cajuns had learned from their punishments after the 1921 French ban. Grace Dupuis (b. 1935), like many other Cajuns, reported that visiting Canada was a life-changing experience for her, one that reshaped her language practices at home and in public. Dupuis was one of the children who was forced to wet her pants because she didn't know how to ask to go to the bathroom in English when she began attending school—what she described as a "total world of disbelief." She writes that she learned to be ashamed of being Cajun because "*Cajun* became a nasty word which meant I was nasty." After visiting Acadian settlements in Canada and using her language in a nonstigmatized way, though, her view of French and her own Cajunness changed: "I now speak French with a great deal of pride because of my visiting Canada and feeling 'at home.'" Dupuis didn't even need a lesson on linguistics, as Cheramie and Scott argue for, just an experience that demonstrated Louisiana French has worth in language markets. Dupuis probably didn't articulate it in terms of critical pedagogy or French theory, but she learned that the devaluing of her language in Louisiana had nothing to do with its brokenness or correctness and everything to do with socioeconomic discrimination against it.

Many other Cajuns followed the same path as Dupuis, growing up feeling ashamed of French and then realizing it was something valuable.

For a great number of Cajuns, it happened because of military service. Shane Bernard (2003) writes in *The Cajuns: Americanization of a People* that, though many French-speaking Cajuns report negative experiences in their military service, such as discrimination (often being called "coonass"), culture shock, and linguistic isolation, many others had positive experiences reinforcing their linguistic abilities. Several Cajuns came to serve vital roles as French interpreters during World War II. Robert J. LeBlanc writes, "Many times my radio operators and driver would wonder if I was coming back. My ability to speak French was crucial" (quoted in Bernard 2003, 9). Dudley J. Theriot describes his translating work: "I would ask the French people where some of the Germans were dug in the ground, or the building they were hiding in . . . They spoke very fast, but after asking them to speak slower I could understand them easily" (9). Delton J. Menard (who finished high school in 1944) writes in Shane Bernard's survey that he identified with people from other similarly stigmatized US subcultures and groups, "I had a lot in common with the Spanish speaking soldiers, because most of them had an accent and of course the people from Georgia and especially the Yankees from the Bronx." As a result of these positive experiences with their first languages, which they had previously suppressed in most cases, many Cajuns began to see Louisiana French in a different light; they became proud of their French, and they quit code censoring. Allen Simon (b. 1937), who writes that he encountered Cajuns all over Lafayette who denied speaking French for their jobs, explains that it was his military service in Europe that changed his own habit of code censoring: "I was embarrassed until I left for the service. I wish somebody would have told me a long time ago, 'It's ok; it's all right!' But I had to pass my twenty-second birthday before I found out that there was nothing wrong [with speaking French], and in Europe, if you speak [only] one language, *you're* the oddball!" Like Dupuis, these Cajuns reconceived Louisiana French in terms of its linguistic function, which varies by context, instead of its assigned class status. With a broader perspective as a result of desocializing experiences, they were able to distance themselves from the discrimination associated with the language and quit code censoring, in spite of Cajuns' overwhelming movement to censor Louisiana French at the time.

The experiences above relate to Louisiana French, but there have also been similar changes in view regarding CE. As part of my survey, I asked Cajun teachers who reported that their attitudes had changed about CE what had brought about the change with the questions "Are there any defining moments that have shaped your attitude toward

Cajun linguistic features? Explain" and "Has your attitude toward Cajun linguistic features changed since you were a child? Describe." Four of the ten Cajuns responded by describing times they began to feel more positive toward their own and others' marks of Cajunness (other Cajuns responded by describing their attitudes but not with examples). As related in the stories of the French speakers, it was desocializing experiences that led them to change their views on language. Two report that it was a change in location or community:

> Living outside of the state, I was struck with the dullness of standard English. Greater exposure to the cultural absence that marks English in other parts of the nation has resulted in a greater sense of pride.
>
> As I entered college and adulthood, I gained a new respect for my culture, accent and all.

For some it was traveling and experiencing new things; for another it was learning actual principles of linguistics in contrast to the myths of "broken" English and illiteracy circulating in the hegemony:

> Studying linguistics and learning more about dialects have made me regret my intentional loss of much of my dialect and accent. The older I get, the less I "look down" on those features that I worked so hard to get out of my speech, [and] the more I wish I hadn't done so.

The fourth respondent writes about feeling more linguistic pride after studying Cajun culture in the UL Lafayette Cajun studies program, where he or she would have studied under Barry Ancelet, Carl Brasseaux, and/or some of the other Cajun scholars who had desocializing "exile experiences" and became activists:

> Getting a degree with a specialization in Louisiana folklore certainly helped to shape my attitude. The above-mentioned degree helped to strengthen the pride that I already had in my Cajun heritage, including [CE] linguistic features.

In this last case, the desocializing experiences of a few resulted in the institution of a new degree at UL Lafayette that has helped this respondent—and most likely many others Cajuns (and non-Cajuns)—to see past some of the myths that win their complicity with class inequality. In the other reports, people who previously thought they deserved lower grades and income because of their linguistic "inferiority" realized that they were just experiencing discrimination. Again, these desocializing experiences didn't make everything equal; they just debunked the myths that hide the function of linguistic inequality in the US socioeconomy.

Though minority and working-class speakers often undergo the most extensive normalization and are therefore the most resistant to progressive standards, conscientization can change the perceptions even of people who are staunchly mainstreamed, as I was. Many activists for language and class equality already recognize this principle and dedicate their time to creating and improving pedagogies and policies designed to raise this kind of consciousness. Institutionalizing programs that conscienticize is effective, as in the case of the survey respondent I quoted above who studied in the Cajun studies program and came to have a new understanding of Cajun culture and language. I think one of the most effective desocializing situations for Cajuns is studying another similarly internally colonized group, such as Puerto Ricans or Mexican Americans. In my experience, right-wing Cajuns often think of Spanish-speaking populations as lazy, demanding, and unpatriotic, even though their histories, festivals, bilingual programs, and poverty levels are extremely similar. When Cajuns learn that we're perceived the same way as other minority groups, it helps us understand our own situation as an internally colonized group better, and it helps us understand the other internally colonized groups in terms of their political histories instead of the hegemonic conclusion that they're second-rate Americans. I also agree with Cheramie (1998a, 152) when she argues that teachers need to be educated about language varieties and language change (Smitherman and others also argue for this). That way, even if teachers continue to teach code censoring, they teach their students that it's explicitly because of US structural inequalities, not because of minority and working-class groups' inferiority. And as long as they're teaching code censoring, of course, I agree with Delpit (1997) that they should be very explicit about it.

But schools exist to normalize, so it would be difficult for teachers to do much more than teach the required curriculum critically (without being fired). Ultimately, the solution to inequality in classrooms is changing the socioeconomy, since schools are explicitly tied to labor training. Within the existing structure, enforcing much stricter laws and regulations on corporations and banning or at least heavily discouraging their offshoring practices and exploitation of workers will spur drastic changes in the educational system. Better conditions in jobs means better conditions in schooling. Ideally, a new sociopolitical system would revolutionize education. Until then, there are effective and meaningful ways to teach to current standards critically, particularly with a combination of Shor's critical pedagogy and Canagarajah's translingual practices. But that only reaches people in school. So I suggest raising the consciousness of people who find themselves in an unequal language market but who are beyond the reach of pedagogy by taking advantage of the other most important institution for normalizing the legitimate language: the family.

## LA FAMILLE

Language inequality isn't limited to schools, so language activism shouldn't be limited to schools either. In the same way that language activists are attempting to reverse institutionalized linguicism by rewriting policies and pedagogies, I'd like to think about reversing its normalization in families. Bourdieu maintains that "the two principal factors of production of the legitimate competence [for normalizing inequality are] the family and the educational system" (Bourdieu 1991, 62). And in fact, families are stronger normalizing institutions than schools are. After all, Shirley Brice Heath (1983) found that home literacy practices, not pedagogical strategies, were the most important factors in determining children's school performance. The children who performed best in schools were from the middle-class families with the most school-like literacy practices at home, so they simply assimilated more easily than the working-class children. The power of home practices is also the driving force behind the tracking system in schools; whatever literacy habits students enter with determine what kinds of treatment they'll get in school and, consequently, which postsecondary education and jobs they qualify for. Schools don't really change literacy habits; they mostly just sort students according to their already existing home literacy habits and reinforce ideas children already knew about language. Overwhelmingly, students turn out pretty much like their families. That's why the social mobility narrative—the accounts of people who so closely identified with school instead of family that they became exceptional in language studies—people like Richard Rodriguez, Keith Gilyard, Mike Rose, Victor Villanueva, Vershawn Young, and me—makes a great story. It's not the norm. The norm is that students' performance in school corresponds approximately to their families' literacy habits and competencies.

This is consonant with the experiences of Cajuns in my parents' generation and my generation who grew up with intense language normalization at *home* instead of school. Many Cajuns in my parents' generation can't speak Louisiana French because their own parents (my grandparents' generation, who were the first to be punished in schools) were deliberate about censoring it at home to protect their children from experiencing linguistic normalization in school (after their own terrible experiences). The French-speaking community in SouLa would have wound up being strongly bilingual if parents hadn't censored at home, if students simply spoke one language at school and another at home, like millions of other people in bilingual communities. Maybe the hand that rocks the cradle really is the hand that rules the world—or, in this case, enables inequality in the world.

Once established, the trend of monolingualism has continued in families. Cajuns in my own generation, as my survey results confirm, are mostly monolingual. In fact, they have very few negative experiences in school regarding CE because their families normalized them first. It's not that they entered school speaking "flawless" English as a result of home practices, but that they entered school with an understanding that "flawless" English is good and mixing is bad, so they generally reacted well to correction. Experiences can differ by parish and family, but the responses to my question "Have you ever been corrected for Cajun features in your [English] speech/writing by a teacher? If so, how did your teacher handle it? Was it effective, in your opinion?" indicated overwhelmingly that they didn't experience or don't remember experiencing linguistic normalization at school. Seven say "no," and two report having experienced normalization in school, but only one seems to have been surprised by it. The following response indicates that the respondent wasn't prepared for CE prejudice before entering school:

> Yes, when I was younger I was corrected for these things. At first, I think I was angry. Then, I was embarrassed. After I learned not to speak this way, I then learned to not speak this way around that teacher and to code switch for school/home.

The respondent above perhaps hadn't been taught about the stigma of CE at home, but the other respondent comments very minimally, possibly indicating that he or she had no emotional reactions to correction at school because correction was expected. He or she writes simply:

> Not since high school.

One respondent explains why he or she wasn't corrected for CE in school:

> I learned very early in life how to filter the Cajun features out of my writing; my mother was very instrumental in this.

As I confessed in chapter 1, I really did expect to find lots of juicy stories about innocent students being shamed by their teachers for making Cajun "errors" in writing, but I hadn't taken into account how hard families work to prepare their children for societal expectations. This form of normalization was also my experience at home and in school. Though my peers and I continued to learn to distinguish CE features from standardized English in different encounters (including school sometimes, as well as graduate studies), teachers who embraced code-censoring practices (under the name of "code switching") were only reinforcing what we already knew about the status of CE as a result of values we had learned in our homes and communities. We had already normalized to code censoring, so that any correction we received in school only helped us in our censoring efforts.

These disheartening stories about families losing their French and facts about why schools are socially immobilizing can actually be good news for parents who want their children to grow up bilingual or bicultural. Parents can teach their children at home the same things translingual teachers would teach in school: a critical awareness of prejudices and the impact their language choices will have on others, but without a sense of shame or moral wrongness. Families can continue to prepare their children for societal norms by teaching elite usages, because standardized English really does make a good impression in job interviews, like pleasant manners, punctuality, and a sharp suit. But families can teach these language choices as part of a political game we play, not as the hegemonic myths that justify poverty and prisons. I've heard of families who teach their children the difference between home and restaurant behavior by "playing restaurant" at home during some meals. Maybe the same simple strategy could work for language behavior.

The main thing, if I may generalize from my survey data and all the personal stories I've collected, seems to be the mamas. The logic that teachers and policy makers use to justify code censoring in schools is that students will freely speak the other code at home, but mothers—and, I'm sure, fathers as well—are hypercorrecting their kids every time they open their mouths, effectively prohibiting instead of promoting bilingualism. Many families in SouLa can no longer speak Louisiana French at home, but we can speak Cajun English or whatever other mixed and mixing codes we are fluent in. Cajuns have been taught the same things about Cajun English that we were taught about Louisiana French—that it's "broken," that it's "bad," that it's not "real English." I suggest we learn from the last time around and quit censoring ourselves and our children at home for speaking this healthy, strongly circulating language (which is as common as mosquitoes for us but an absolute gem for linguists). Or we can continue to self-censor and then launch campaigns in twenty years to try to revive Cajun English, as we're doing for Louisiana French now. And in the same way that home life generally determines the language capital students enter school with, families can help determine the degree that their children normalize to other values in the economy.

So an important place for language activists, comp/rhet scholars, and people who have been conscienticized to the reality of US hegemony to work to raise consciousness is in their own family networks—nuclear families, extended families, or the close ties that have come to be (or in some cases replace) family. Freire writes that this is as simple as conversations in everyday situations. Simply negating the myths in dialogue with people is a huge step: "There is no true word that is not at the same time a praxis [the interaction of action and reflection producing activism]. Thus, to speak a true word is to transform the world" (Freire 1993, 87). There is no need to create any campaigns, programs, or special circumstances to raise consciousness because "the starting point" for conscientization is, Freire writes, "the present, existential, concrete situation" (95). Dialoguing in everyday encounters is similar to Freire's "generative pedagogy," the practice of letting students (whom he calls "student-teachers" to stress their equality in the dialogue process) pose the discussion topics—like when someone says that being an English teacher must be a terrible job because everyone is so illiterate. In these encounters, Freire stresses the importance of dialoguing instead of sermonizing, and he requires anyone participating in raising critical consciousness to be humble, loving, and respectful of the other person's knowledge. Admittedly, being humble, loving, and respectful is not always easy with family members, so the family can be one of the most difficult places to protest hegemony and practice critical pedagogy.

Equally important is putting the topic in desocializing terms to give people an opportunity to think their own thoughts and arrive at their own conclusions instead of repeating the values of hegemony—like the students Shor mentions who came to describe Columbus's actions in terms of theft and conquest instead of discovery (Shor 1982, 121). In my own conversations, I've found it helpful to draw on people's prior knowledge and opinions of recent debates of the political biases of history textbooks. I've often responded to people's questions about my book with a sentence I wrote in chapter 2: "The victors wrote the history books, and then they went on to write the grammar books." I've seen some great discussions and a good deal of head nodding as people come to see that language standards can serve dominant interests. But, as Freire warns, sloganizing is not enough. It's also helpful to ask people about their own real experiences to see if they match the myths they are often willing to repeat and apply to others. It can be particularly effective to ask people to compare the way one of their family members is judged according to language standards with what they know of the family member—for instance, a brother with poor grades or a parent who speaks nonstandard English. Is that family member unintelligent or lazy or a bad member of society? The end of the conversation is usually something like, "Of course not, but other people will judge him or her that way, so he or she needs to conform." At that point, both members of the dialogue have agreed that language standards are based on discrimination, not inherent superiority or inferiority.

The other day, for example, my mother observed to me that the fax she had received from a local state worker showed that he must not have really paid attention in English class. Yeeeees, I responded, but it didn't mean he was any less equipped to do his job well. She thoughtfully asked, "But isn't it true that you can tell—maybe not their character—but you can tell someone's level of education by their language and grammar?" I agreed, of course, because distinctive usages absolutely correlate with level of education, but I asked her about her personal knowledge of speakers of nonstandard Englishes to see if she experientially believed that they can be expected to perform their jobs less well than people with elite usages. Many people would judge the language, accent, and grammar of her husband, the completely Cajun Pat Feucht from Mamou, as "illiterate" and "uneducated" and definitely unrefined. But he rocks at his job as a commercial tire salesman, which requires enormous levels of language and literacy for every client meeting and all the paperwork that goes along with it. As I said before, he doesn't even have to put on a Cajun accent for Boudreaux and Thibodeaux jokes, but he has been consistently recognized as one of the top salesmen in his industry in Louisiana. Basically, I asked my mother if the myth that people have to learn standardized English and make good grades to be equipped for a good job is true in her experience, and it's not. So she agreed that there's probably no reason to expect that state worker with nonstandard grammar to be any less proficient at his job than if he used standard grammar.

An excellent way to teach our students how to do the same thing in their families is Shor's simple but potentially significant strategy of having students interview members of their family about different topics from class. Though Margaret Mead (1943, 637) predicted in 1943 that modern education had overwhelmingly served to create discontinuity between familial generations, crises of capitalism have ensured that the family network, particularly in minority and working-class communities, remains strongly intact by reinforcing the network of social supports that enables people to survive on extremely low wages. By economic necessity, families are mini-economic units that operate on the principles of sharing and cooperation, often providing childcare, loans, transportation, meals, and even living arrangements for each other. Capitalism, which is ostensibly based on fair competition and survival of the fittest, is actually based on socialism for the wealthy capitalists who own the means of production (via corporate subsidies, estimated at $154 billion in 2013 [Rowland 2013]) and socialism for the workers (through remaining social programs and lingering precapitalist family arrangements). Federal neglect of social programs in the past few decades has possibly helped reinforce the strength of the family structure, making it a particularly effective purveyor of values today.

So asking students to dialogue about what they've learned in class with a family member or two, as Shor suggests, is a simple, low-stakes assignment that can potentially introduce counterhegemonic ideas to the *other* primary institution responsible for normalizing language inequalities, the family. Even if each student speaks to only one family member, that's double the number of people thinking about alternative language and economic arrangements. It's the compliance of individuals in everyday decisions that constitutes their consent to linguistic and—by extension—socioeconomic inequalities. These individual compliances are multiplied in families and communities and combine to form mass consent, the basis of hegemony. So the *noncompliance* of individuals in everyday situations, especially in social organizations as strong as family units, is also an important factor in creating mass *dissent*. The first step is examining our personal language beliefs and censoring practices, expanding our personal consciousness so much that there's no room for oppressor consciousness.

More is possible than we are led to believe. The exact nature of cultural hegemony and oppressor consciousness is to hide possibilities, to lead us to believe that our choices are either A or B, when they're actually A through Z. Cultural hegemonic processes also hide our own strength from us, similar to the old-fashioned way of training elephants for circus performance (before the invention of elephant farms). A baby elephant was captured and tied to a tree for days or weeks, where it fought and struggled until—hungry, tired, and bleeding—it finally gave up. After this period of breaking in, the elephant learned that any time it was tied or chained up, there was no point resisting. So a three-ton adult circus elephant, fifty times stronger than a man, could be controlled with nothing more than a chain attached to a small stake in the ground. Convinced that it wasn't strong enough to resist, the adult elephant never even tried. No matter what we've been told by family, teachers, administrators, and politicians, I want us to test the limits. We won't know what's possible until we try it—and try it with the strength of numbers.

## CONCLUSION

Before Paw-Paw Jeff died, he read an article I wrote about CE and language inequalities. "Good God but you smart!" he declared in a voicemail that I listened to at least sixteen times before my phone automatically deleted it. I thought it was funny that he assumed I was the smart one, since he was the one who had no training in my field but managed to wade through an entire scholarly article on language issues, just as he had pushed himself as a boy to read all the newspapers passed on from his city cousins before the family used them for toilet paper. But I loved watching his changing opinions on his Cajunness as I explored my own and shared them with him. Though he was already practically a third parent to me, we grew closer as we desocialized together about the place of Cajuns in the US socioeconomy.

Our last conversation was over the phone on an Easter Sunday. He was in the hospital after having major skull surgery from a buildup of several bruises that were putting too much pressure on his brain (from multiple incidents over several years). As GrandmaMona puts it, "Evidently, he wasn't as hard-headed as we all thought." I called him from the New Jersey home of my Italian in-laws, who told me to wish him "Buono Pasquale." He replied with the Cajun "Bonnes Pâques" and asked about the baby I was carrying at the time. He would never meet her; he died two months before she was born. I told him I could tell she was Cajun because I always craved Community coffee, a fixture of many Cajun households. (Don't judge me for drinking coffee while pregnant; I was writing a dissertation.) He laughed and replied with his signature phrase, "Dat's great." I could picture him doing his right hook from his hospital bed at the same time. Then, just before he passed the phone back to my mom, he added, "I know you'll be a great mother." I told him I hoped so.

If assimilation of minority groups requires the complicity of parents in censoring themselves at home, my Italian American husband and I have chosen to dissent to that practice. I can't pass on Louisiana French to my children, but I do pass on CE (easy, considering that it has a way of asserting itself in domestic contexts). My husband speaks English meshed with his Calabrese variety of Italian. We jokingly call our home culture "Cajalian," a combination of Cajun and Italian, as we mesh our languages, cooking, and cultural traditions. Our children will grow up normalized to celebrating Easter with Italian eggloaf while "paquing" eggs, eating rice and gravy as much as pasta, and equally familiar with my Cajun "Mais la!" and my husband's Italian "Aye ye yai, questa qua!" ("this one here").[5] For us, this linguistic relaxation is not the "hypocorrection" that Bourdieu ascribes to the intellectuals and bourgeoisie, but a rejection of attempts at achieving socioeconomic status through our language practices. Both disillusioned by the PhD and tenure process, the "shadow workload" of committee work and publishing requirements, enormous student debt, and the increasing corporatization of higher education, we have made a conscious decision not to pass on to our children the drive for upward mobility that our own parents instilled in us, but to encourage them simply to do what makes them happy.

Because those competitive values are built into the economy, our children will still pick up on them from their schooling, from seeing their parents unconsciously code censor in public (it's hard to undo a lifetime of practice), from hearing their Italian grandparents' apologies for their own "broken" Italian (Calabrese is a stigmatized dialect in Italy), from media representations of language and prejudice, and so on. Hegemony is constantly asserting itself, so we have to be on the lookout for it. I was working at a café the other day when I was totally annoyed to overhear the "grating" accents of a couple of Italian American women. I had to acknowledge to myself that my prejudice against their accent is probably just because of the show *Jersey Shore*, which once drove my husband to say, "This show makes me ashamed of my own people." It's going to be my turn soon enough with the debut of *Party Down South*. Our hope is that our children will understand these values but not internalize them, that they will be able to maintain a critical distance from them while internalizing our own home values based on cooperation, sharing, and mutual respect.

# ACKNOWLEDGMENTS

Many thanks to my academic mentors, whose feedback has shaped and continues to shape my writing and thinking. An overwhelming thank-you to Rebecca Mlynarczyk, former editor of *JBW*, for rigorously scrutinizing my arguments and my language. As my greatest critic, you've been my greatest friend. I know that my demanding writing schedule was challenging not just for me as the author, but also for you as my primary respondent (and editor). Your mentoring has been invaluable to me, and it's a model I'll follow if I'm ever in the same position. There are very few people I hope to be like, but at some point I realized you're one of them. And thank you to Ira Shor, who convinced me I should tell this story and made me think so hard during my graduate studies that it hurt my brain and assumptions. You are the reason I moved to New York for grad school. You are also the master problem-poser; because of your ratio of questions to pronouncements, I'm amused to note that I actually still don't know where you stand on a lot of things. Suresh Canagarajah, your work in comp/rhet and your guidance have given me access to the kinds of scholarly conversations I've been looking for since I began my graduate studies. I admire the way your heart matches your head in your writing, and I truly believe that you are prompting a huge paradigm shift in English language teaching. Thank you for letting me watch and learn from you.

I am indebted to Shane Bernard for many reasons. Not only did I rely hugely on his research in *The Cajuns: Americanization of a People* and other publications, but I have also happily drawn data from material he sent me when he found out about my area of research: dozens of his interviews with elderly Cajuns and a fat packet of letters from Cajuns who went through the French ban. He has also answered random questions and given me lots of leads in ongoing email conversations. As I am no historian but needed lots of history for this book, I'm thankful for his love of history, which overflows his books and permeates his emails and conversations. Speaking of history, thanks also to Christophe Landry, who compared notes with me several times to balance scholarly literature about Cajuns and Creoles with cultural memory and experience; your research in genealogies and other historical documents is essential to the narratives we're writing about ourselves.

Loving thanks to my husband, Frank, for volunteering to be ignored for several months so that I could finish this project. It's impossible to be a full-time academic, full-time mother, and full-time partner; one area will always suffer, and it's been yours. Meanwhile, thanks also for letting me prey on your mind when I needed inspiration; I deeply value your perspectives and our conversations. I truly hit the jackpot when I found you. Now that I'm done being married to this thing, I look forward to resuming my place in your arms and heart. No thanks at all to our bébés, who constantly seduced me away from my writing. Those darlings have been eminently more interesting than language inequalities. I'm so happy to belong to y'all again.

Also, thanks to my sister Gracie and my mother-in-law Rosina, my children's third and fourth parents, for providing the best childcare in the world. I've never heard of a mother who has succeeded in academia without outsourcing a huge portion of the mothering, and that makes me really angry at the systemic problems inherent in this career, but I'm also glad this book was a good excuse for Emma, Jacques, and now Giuseppe to get to know Aunt GiGi and Nonna.

After I wrote this book, the bungee cords really did pop back, and I am, happily, living in SouLa once more. I'm thankful for the way the community has welcomed me back, the way the sunshine has healed me, and the ways the people here still uphold our village values.

*Good God but You Smart!* is dedicated to my three departed Cajun and Creole grandparents, two of whom died during the writing of this book—I wish I could have spoken your language and known your histories long before my graduate studies. To my remaining GrandmaMona, now that I'm done with this thing, we can get back to our looooooong conversations over your perfectly dark pots of coffee. Love you big-big.

# APPENDIX
## Survey on Cajun Vernacular English in Classrooms

This appendix reports the responses to all the questions listed in the survey. I have assigned a number to each of the forty respondents who took the survey so that their additional comments can be identified beneath each question. The responses from the eleven Cajuns are italicized (respondents 1, 10, 14, 17, 18, 19, 20, 23, 24, 26, 32). One other respondent (6) also identified as Cajun, but I have not included this one in the Cajun responses, since he or she did not grow up identifying as Cajun or experiencing prejudices toward Cajuns (he or she reports having "married into" being Cajun). In addition, while 8, 15, and 33 do not identify as Cajun, they are from the Acadiana area, so their responses are also of interest when it comes to local attitudes. Please note that I've edited some of these responses for clarity and consistency in chapter discussions, but here they are presented exactly as the participants typed them.

**PARTICIPANT'S INFORMATION**

**1–3. Universities attended, degree(s), specializations:**

|   | Universities Attended | Degree(s) | Specializations |
|---|---|---|---|
| (1) | Macalester College, St. Paul, Minnsesota; USL, UL Lafayette | BA, MEd, PhD | Cognitive Science |
| (2) | Univerzita J. E. Purkyne, Usti nad Labem, Czech Republic; Emory University, Atlanta, GA | MA, English and Czech PhD, Translation Studies—in progress | translation studies, literary avant-gardes, modern and contemporary American poetry, creative writing |
| (3) | Southern University; Southeastern Oklahoma State University; Mountain State University | BA Liberal Arts —English M. ED Education (concentration in English) MA Interdisciplinary Studies (concentration in Instructional and Curriculum Leadership | English |

*continued on next page*

|  | Universities Attended | Degree(s) | Specializations |
|---|---|---|---|
| (4) | Kenyon College, Exeter University (England, Junior Year Abroad), Naropa University | MFA, Prose, & BA English/Creative Writing | Creative Writing |
| (5) | Virginia Commonwealth University | BA in English (2000) and MFA in Creative Writing | Fiction, Technical Communications |
| (6) | University of Louisiana Lafayette, Northwestern State University, McNeese State University, University of New Orleans | MA | English—Rhetoric/Comp |
| (7) | Samford, LSU | MA, ABD in History and Reading Education | English, History |
| (8) | University of Louisiana at Lafayette, Louisiana State University | Honors Baccalaureate in English MA in English | Renaissance Studies Rhetoric Pop Culture Texts |
| (9) | UNC Chapel Hill, The New School for Social Research | BA, MA | Literature |
| (10) | University of Louisiana at Lafayette, Louisiana State University | ULL, BA, 2005; LSU, MA, 2008; Working on PhD at LSU | BA: English and Spanish, History Minor; MA: English, Comparative Literature Minor; PhD: Renaissance Literature and British Women Writers |
| (11) | Louisiana State University | PhD | Adolescent Literature, Horror Fiction, Gender Studies |
| (12) | University of New Hampshire, Clark University, Louisiana State University | BA, MA, PhD (abd) | Literature (critical theory, American and British 20th century novels and film) |
| (13) | University of Louisiana at Lafayette, University of Minnesota Twin Cities, MN | MEd (English instruction, adults) | Critical thinking; teaching across disciplines |
| (14) | UL Lafayette | MA Rhet/Comp, BA English | Freshman Writing, Grammar, ESL, Pop culture, Moving Media |
| (15) | La Tech University. Our Lady of Holy Cross College, University of New Orleans, USL | Bachelor—Tech Master's—USL Post graduate work in Library Science—the other 2 colleges | Reading Specializst |
| (16) | Centenary College of Louisiana, Cerro Coso Community College, Universite de Mons-Hainaut, University of Louisiana at Lafayette, Mcneese State University, University of Colorado at Boulder, Louisiana State University | BA Interdisciplinary Language and Literature MA Comparative Literature MA Teaching, Secondary Level | French, Spanish, Francophone Vietnamese Literature, Writing |

*continued on next page*

|  | Universities Attended | Degree(s) | Specializations |
|---|---|---|---|
| (17) | Louisiana State University Eunice Louisiana State University Baton Rouge University of Louisiana at Lafayette | BA English MEd Secondary Education MA English PhD English | American Literature Creative Writing (Fiction) |
| (18) | The University of Louisiana at Lafayette | Bachelor's in Mass Communications Master's in English with a specialization in Folklore | Bachelor's in Mass Communications specialization print journalism Master's in English with a specialization in Folklore |
| (19) | University of Louisiana–Lafayette Texas A&M University | Honors BA in English MA in English PhD in English | Irish Drama Cajun/Louisiana Literature |
| (20) | University of Louisiana at Lafayette Western Kentucky University–Bowling Green, KY | BA MAE | Secondary Education British/American Literature |
| (21) | University of South Florida, PhD Colorado State University, MA California Univ. of PA, BA | PhD, MA, BA | Creative Writing; Honors |
| (22) | Southern Methodist University UT Austin UT Dallas | BA Liberal Arts MA and PhD Arts and Humanities Literary Studies | Virtual Rhetorics Evolution and Literature Twentieth-Century Theatre Theory |
| (23) | St. Joseph Seminary College, Louisiana State University, McNeese State University, University of Louisiana at Lafayette, University of Texas at Dallas | BA in English, McNeese St. MA in English, McNeese St. MFA in Creative Writing, MeNeese St. PhD in Hunmanities (Studies in Literature), UT–Dallas | poetry and poetics, playwriting and theatrical performance, American and European Modernism, 19th and 20th century European intellectual history, anti-semitism, Ezra Pound |
| (24) | UL Lafayette | BS Secondary Education MED Curriculum- Minor English | English Mathematics |
| (25) | Austin Community College, AAS New England College, BA University of Northern AZ, MA University of Louisiana at Lafayette | AAS, BA, MA, currently ABD for PhD | 19th century literature in French and English and Cajun and French folklore |
| (26) | University of Louisiana Lafayette | BA—English, BA—History, MA—English |  |
| (27) | University of California, San Diego, Northwestern State University, University of Louisiana at Lafayette | BA, MA, PhD (in progress) | Folklore and American Literature |
| (28) | Trinity University, University of York, University of Louisiana at Lafayette | BA English MA Renaissance Literature Doctoral Candidate, ABD, Rhetoric and Composition | Rhetoric and Composition, Renaissance Literature, Folklore |

*continued on next page*

Appendix    261

|  | Universities Attended | Degree(s) | Specializations |
|---|---|---|---|
| (29) | U of North Alabama, U of Tennessee (Knoxville) U of Minnesota | BA MA PhD | Rhetoric, feminist theory |
| (30) | University of Louisiana at Lafayette | BA and MA | English |
| (31) | New Mexico State University–Carlsbad, Eastern New Mexico University, University of Louisiana at Lafayette | Associate of Arts Bachelor of Science—English & History Master of Arts—English PhD—English (in progress) | sci-fi; creative writing; rhetoric |
| (32) | ULL | BA in English MA in English | Renaissance English Lit |
| (33) | Southwestern Louisiana Institute, University of Southwestern Louisiana, University of Louisiana @ Lafayette | BME (Voice)—bachelor of music education; MEd Master of Education with emphasis in English; Specialist in Reading Education | Reading, Teaching children to read, and teaching content for interpretation and understanding; English: Grammar, History/Linguistics, Modern American Lirterature, Black Literature. |
| (34) | University of South Florida, University of Louisiana at Lafayette, Manatee Community College, Florida State University | MA in English MA in International Affairs BA English BA Women's Studies AS Film and Media Studies | Victorian and Women's Literature |
| (35) | Webster College (now Webster University) St. Louis Community College at Meramec (non-degree seeking student) University of Arkansas at Fayetteville | BA Child Study MFA Creative Writing (Poetry) | Creative Writing (Poetry) Composition 16th Century Poetry and Prose (Shakespeare, etc.) |
| (36) | Bowling Green State University, Bowling Green, OH | BA, MA, PhD | Modern and contemporary American poetry and creative writing. |
| (37) | University of North Carolina at Wilmington, University of Florida | BA, MA, PhD | Modernism, Narrative Theory, Film and New Media |
| (38) | Colby-Sawyer College, Fitchburg State College, University of Louisiana at Lafayette | BA, MA, PhD in progress | Folklore, British Victorian lit, Early American lit, Children's lit, |
| (39) | Warren Wilson College, College of Charleston, University of Louisiana at Lafayette | Masters. Working on PhD | African American Literature. |
| (40) |  | Master's in Literature |  |

4. **Where are you currently teaching?**
   (1) UL
   (2) instructor at Department of English, LSU
   (3) retired but currently teaching adjunct classes at South Louisiana Community College
   (4) Louisiana State University
   (5) LSU
   (6) English composition
   (7) LSU
   (8) Louisiana State University
   (9) LSU
   (10) LSU
   (11) Advanced Comp (Environmental Writing), Gender and Popular Culture, American Literature 1865 to present
   (12) Composition First and Second Year
   (13) South Louisiana Community College
   *(14) Freshman writing courses, developmental English, Advanced Writing in the Academy*
   (15) SLCC—New Iberia
   (16) Church Point High School, Louisiana State University at Eunice
   *(17) Louisiana State University Eunice*
   *(18) Louisiana State University Eunice*
   *(19) South Louisiana Community College*
   *(20) Dual Enrollment, AP, English IV*
   (21) Louisiana State University Eunice
   (22) Louisiana State University Eunice
   *(23) Louisiana State University Eunice*
   *(24) English 1001 online, English 1002 online*
   (25) University of Louisiana at Lafayette South Louisiana Community College
   *(26) Compostion and Rhetoric, Composition and Critical Thought*
   (27) University of Louisiana at Lafayette
   (28) University of Louisiana at Lafayette
   (29) U of Louisiana at Lafayette
   (30) University of Louisiana at Lafayette
   (31) University of Lousiana at Lafayette
   *(32) ULL*
   (33) UL of Lafayette
   (34) University of Louisiana at Lafayette
   (35) ULL
   (36) UL
   (37) UL Lafayette
   (38) Lafayette LA

(39) University of Louisiana at Lafayette
(40) University of Louisiana Lafayette

5. **What classes do you typically teach?**
   *(1) Grammar, Linguistics, Honors Freshman Englsih*
   (2) English Composition 1001 and 2000
   (3) Developmental English, English 1010, English 1020, Sophomore levels
   (4) Freshman/Sophomore English Composition, Sophomore-level English literature
   (5) I teach Freshman and Sophomore Composition and a variety of engineering courses as a non-grading instructor
   (6) College freshman composition
   (7) E1001, E2000
   (8) Basic composition and argument, occasionally fiction or major British authors
   (9) Composition 1000 and 2000
   *(10) English 1001 or 2000 (writing courses). I have also taught Major British Authors, Drama, Shakespeare, and Images of Women. I will be teaching Images of Women again this summer.*
   (11) Advanced Comp, Adolescent Literature, Introduction to Women's and Gender Studies, Horror Fiction, Business Writing, Technical Writing, Zombie Fiction, and various survey courses
   (12) Composition
   (13) English 1010, 1020
   *(14) Freshman writing courses, developmental English, Advanced Writing in the Academy*
   (15) REading and Engl 92
   (16) French I, French II, English IV, Advanced Placement English IV, Dual Enrollment English IV, Remedial English 001, English Composition 1001, English Literature 1002
   *(17) Freshman Composition, English American Literature*
   *(18) composition, literature*
   *(19) English 092, English 1010*
   *(20) Dual Enrollment English IV*
   (21) English Composition I and II, Honors Classical Literature, Classical Mythology and Folklore, Survey of English Literature from 1798 to the Present, Honors Seminar III
   (22) ENGL 1001, 1002, 1003 (Honors), 0001 (Developmental), 2007 (Introduction to Writing Poetry), but have taught others
   *(23) ENGL 1001—Freshman Composition*
   *(24) English 0001, English 1001, and English 1002*
   (25) Freshman and sophmore English, American and British Literature, Advanced Rhetoric and Exposition (junior and senior level)

264   APPENDIX

(26) *development courses, composition courses, and literature courses*
(27) First Year College Writing
(28) Freshman Composition, Advanced Composition and Technical Writing
(29) English 101, English 102, graduate-level courses
(30) ENGL 101, 102, 205, 206, 304, 360, 365. Respectively, Intro to College Writing, Research and Composition, Early and Late American Lit., Vocabulary Development, Advanced Composition, and Technical Writing
(31) Freshmen English composition and Freshmen English Research
*(32) Freshman Comp, Advanced Comp, British Lit I*
(33) Usually English 101, very seldom 102
(34) Developmental English Composition (102 usually), 200-Level Surveys (American Lit I, British Lit II, Novel and Short Story, Poetry, Drama), Humanities Survey
(35) 102, 293
(36) 115, 214, 319, 496, 580, other seminar-level classes
(37) Graduate Seminars, Sophomore Surveys, Upper-Division Special Topics Courses, Freshman (Honors) English
(38) First Year writing courses (Eng 101, Eng 102), Early American Lit, British Lit, Advanced writing
(39) 101 and 102
(40) Eng 102, 101, American Lit

**6.    Where did you live for most of your early life?**

(1)   *southwest Louisiana*
(2)   Czech Republic
(3)   Franklin, LA
(4)   Southern California
(5)   Tennessee and Virginia
(6)   Southeast Louisiana (New Orleans area)
(7)   LA, AL, MS
(8)   Lafayette, LA
(9)   North Carolina
*(10)  Born and raised in Lafayette, Louisiana until I moved to Baton Rouge in 2005. I go home once or twice a month.*
(11)  outside of Chicago near Gary, Indiana
(12)  Massachusetts and Rhode Island
(13)  Brooklyn/Long Island, New York
*(14)  South La., baby! Originally from Crowley, La.*
(15)  ACADIANA
(16)  Sierra Nevada Desert, rural California
*(17)  Lawtell, Louisiana*
*(18)  Lafayette, LA*

(19) *Acadia Parish Louisiana*
(20) *rural South Louisiana*
(21) South Louisiana
(22) Pennsylvania
(23) *Dallas, TX*
(24) *Raceland, Louisiana*
(25) Wabash Valley in Southern Indiana
(26) *A very small, rural town within the geographical and cultural area identified as Acadiana*
(27) Southern California
(28) Houston, Texas
(29) Florence, AL
(30) New Orleans, Pittsburgh, Manila, Hong Kong, Honolulu, Sausalito, and back to New Orleans from 2nd grade until the end of high school.
(31) New Mexico
(32) *Acadiana*
(33) In Carencro, Louisiana, middle of Cajun Country, I spoke French before English, I have taught many Cajun students in Music and in Language Arts classrooms.
(34) St. Louis and environs
(35) Florida
(36) Wyoming, Ohio
(37) North Carolina
(38) New Hampshire.
(39) England and then South Carolina
(40) Midwest

7. **Do you code switch (use different ways of speaking/writing for different contexts, for example, family interactions compared with school situations) in either speech or writing? If so, which codes do you use?**

   (1) *Yes.*
   (2) Standard English, colloquial English (with some Southern vocabulary)
   (3) Yes. I mainly use correct grammar; however, outside of my immediate family, I may code switch just a bit in speech. I never code in writing.
   (4) Yes: different slang, political ideas, pop culture references, tone, etc.
   (5) Yes, I can converse in multiple registers: formal for presentations and other professional contexts, semi-formal for classroom interactions and day-to-day dealings, and downright goofy southern twang for friends and family.

(6) casual, formal academic
(7) No
(8) Slightly, but despite coming from a heavily Cajun area, my schools were mostly inner city, and my parents do not use much colloquial language (outside of the familiar "y'all" and a few distinct phrases). My brother (schooled on the more Cajun outskirts of Lafayette) code switches noticeably between SAE and CVE, however. He uses CVE primarily with coworkers in the oil field and shipping industries and SAE at home and elsewhere.
(9) Not really
*(10) Although my family thinks that I speak "proper English," I know that I will use some slang or contractions like "aint" when talking with family.*
(11) constantly. I use academic speech in situations where I need to assert my authority and sound professional. I use southern speech patterns with friends and neighbors and in less formal situations, I use northern speech in medium formal situations and when I am among my relatives from the north who mock me for speaking like a southerner (can't help it as I have been here since 1978).
(12) Yes. Academic and provincial New England accent shifts between professional/academic and personal situations.
*(13) No.*
*(14) Absolutely. I use Academic discourse, sometimes informal, with my students, and some Cajun vernacular does come up from time to time, but at home I curse alot more and also French Cajun expressions (for cursing and otherwise lol)*
(15) Not sure what you mean. Sometimes but try not switch from the Standard Edited English to the vernaculary. Probably do it more with family and home. Try real hard not do it in a classroom. This I feel would be confusing to the students.
(16) yes, Spanish at home with mom, English everywhere else
*(17) Speech—I say "Ya'll" instead of "you" when I'm with family. Also "gonna" instead of "going to."*
*(18) Yes. Cajun English dialect to Standard English*
*(19) [unanswered]*
*(20) Yes, most definitely. I even wrote a paper on code switching in my undergraduate journalism studies*
(21) Yes. Formal English in the classroom and in general workplace situations. A mix of formal, informal, and slang with colleagues I'm closer to. Informal, slang, and CVE including French phrases at home and with select friends and family.
(22) No
*(23) I'm not sure I understand the question. I use whatever code is appropriate to the rhetorical situation.*

(24) *At school I speak more formally than I do at home. I grew up in South Louisiana, so I have to be careful not to let things like "ya'll" slip in while I am teaching.*
(25) Yes. Hoosier, Southern and Cajun.
(26) *Very much so; my speech is much more polished and Anglicized when addressing my students, whereas my familial speech is peppered with various Cajun-French phrases and pronunciations. Some terms that I would not typically use in a classroom setting that I do use with family are "ain't," double-negatives, "cher," "beb"/"bebe," and other common Cajun-French terms.*
(27) No
(28) Of course. I am from a mixed black and white family, so I use more African-ethnic language with my black family and more white-southern vernacular with my white family. Both families are lower-middle class, so I speak differently with them than I do with my colleagues at work.
(29) no
(30) I attempt to make no distinction between academic and situational speech because it is readily understood that I am an English instructor and hold myself to a "beyond the spoken" treatment of language. For family interaction my diction tends to run the gamut from high to low brow, so as to keep understanding to a premium but, at the same time, not forsake my educational background for the sake of belonging.
(31) Yes; family interactions and my accent (Texas twang); school situations and grammar
(32) *Yes—friends, family, and academic*
(33) Yes, I do. I often speak to my family and friends in French. Whatever works. In government, shopping, driving, and other basic communications, I speak the language of the person to whom I am speaking. I definitely "dumb down" my writing for people who can't read or write very well.
(34) Formal and Less Formal (For family, I care less about grammar and use more slang expressions/speech short cuts). In the classroom I speak more formally, unless circumstances dictate otherwise.
(35) Yes. I use text speak and some southern slang while around friends/family.
(36) No
(37) Sure. Outside of simple levels of formality, I speak something of a relic dialect with my close relatives from coastal North Carolina (see Walt Wolfram's work on the Outer Banks dialect for an example).
(38) Yes. Formal and informal English, depending on the situation.

(39) No.
(40) no

## PERSONAL VIEWS OF LITERACY

1. **Students should master Standard Edited English in a composition class.**

   | | |
   |---|---|
   | **Strongly agree** | **56.4% (22)** |
   | Somewhat agree | 35.9% (14) |
   | Not sure | 2.6% (1) |
   | Somewhat disagree | 5.1% (2) |
   | Strongly disagree | 0.0% (0) |

   *ADDITIONAL COMMENTS*
   - (3) They must learn the difference between academic writing and less formal options.
   - (4) Actually, I don't have a strong interest in "standard edited English," as long as their tone/voice is appropriate to the audience and makes a strong point. Strong writing is important, but grammar/spelling can always be adjusted through peer editing. If a student's ideas and voice are strong, grammar/spelling are secondary, and I expect them to master that in high school, or at least have a basic
   - (5) We should privilege critical thinking over language use. Use of "proper English" is overrated in some academic circles, IMHO. (Note the use of a different code.)
   - (8) I believe that in spoken language we can be less exacting, but in writing, where we generally lack the immediacy of spoken dialogue, it's important to avoid extremely colloquial language or phrasing that might not make sense or be misconstrued by people unfamiliar with the vernacular. This is far more true for professional and academic writing, however.
   - (9) I think it's important for them to learn to speak at that register but I don't want them to feel like they have to abandon their own form of speaking.
   - (11) Students need to master Standard English in composition classes and in other courses because they will be judged later if they have not acquired this mastery.
   - (13) Industry requires its workers to communicate in Standard English

(15) The student needs to know standard edited English for writing purposes. May not need it as much in the speaking.

*(17) "Master" may be a strong word. As long as they know the difference b/w informal and standard English, I am happy.*

*(23) Students should at least attain competence: clear, precise, and organized communication of basic ideas and information presented with minimum errors.*

(25) The professional world can be a cruel place to those who do not conform to Standard English, and since many people from Louisiana are often judged harshly based solely on their geographical background, they may have even more difficulty proving themselves to be intelligent, thoughtful individuals. Poor language and composition skills will only hinder those aiming to be part of a larger corporate or academic community.

*(26) Needed for business and commerce. How they talk is fine in any register if they can carry on life skills, but standard written English is a must.*

(28) Students should be able to recognize Standard Edited English and participate in those conversations with competency, not mastery.

(30) There is a clear distinction between written and spoken language and a composition class is the primary location for them to understand and practice this distinction. If not in this type of setting, then where?

*(32) "master" is too strong of a term, they should be competent in it.*

(34) Grammar is something that can be worked on throughout life. I do not think that a student shoudl fail because of some problems, though they might not receive a high grade for the course. In other words, there are exceptions, in my opinion.

(40) The composition class has a goal to help students move forward. Mastery is setting students up for failure.

2. **Illiteracy is a big problem in the US.**

| | |
|---|---|
| **Strongly agree** | 48.7% (19) |
| Somewhat agree | 28.2% (11) |
| Not sure | 12.8% (5) |
| Somewhat disagree | 10.3% (4) |
| Strongly disagree | 0.0% (0) |

### ADDITIONAL COMMENTS

(3) Because we are mainly a verbal society, speakers are unaware that a difference exists between the written and spoken word.

(5) I have taught at a variety of institutions of higher ed, and I have seen brilliant students, but I have also seen students who didn't know how to punctuate a sentence. In college. What did the work of the non-college-bound students from those neighborhoods look like?

(8) I don't think we have as much outright illiteracy as unfamiliarity. This shows most often in poor spelling and simple grammar errors. Students aren't retaining what they are taught in elementary school.

(11) I have been at LSU since the days when we were an open admissions instittuion, and I taught many remedial courses. Several of the kids in those classes were functionally illiterate. We have this problem today in the public schools. A friend of mine is a high school reading coach. And there are a number of jobs at community colleges for people who can teach students how to read, so apparently students everywhere are graduating from high school unable to adequately read.

(13) Among some immigrants who have not spoken the language for 7 years or more

(15) Students have problems writing and they do NOT read. Some think that the texting they do consitutes good writing because it is caring over into writing of essays, paragraphs, etc.

(17) *Based on the freshmen at my university, I would say that 5% are functionally illiterate, and that is only the young people who try to attend college—many more never go beyond high school.*

(23) *it's impossible to make such a claim becuase the term "illiteracy" lacks a precise definition. I believe most people are capable of reading and writing, but the degree and effectiveness of these skills varies greatly. Furthermore, the purposes to which these skills are applied ought to be taken into consideration. For example, though most politicians are literate (and most likely to a higher degree than average), when the basic expectations of a freshman composition class are applied to it, much political rhetoric can only be called "illiterate."*

(25) Many people may know how to read words, but the comprehension level and vocabulary of many individuals is far below par.

(26) *Especially here—as much experience in and out of school has shown.*

(28) Any illiteracy in a nation as developed and weathly as the US is a major problem.

(30) Semi-literacy is almost worse than complete illiteracy because at least the illiterate do not make a pretense of understanding what they read instead of actually understanding what they read. As King says, "Lukewarm indifference is worse than outright and vociferous rejection." This semi-literacy is the academic equivalent of going through the motions with a noticeable lack of substance. This is the struggle that most composition teachers are fighting because, yes, the students are in college, therefore display at least a modicum of literacy, but the real issue is to take that semi-literacy and mold it into constructive literacy, not just the bare minimum of literacy required to "pass," which is a misnomer because it doesn't prepare them for the very non-pass/fail-oriented real world.

(32) *Too many cell phones and too much mindless entertainment (music, tv, film)*

(40) I don't feel students are illiterate, unprepared would be a better term.

3. **Standard Edited English is correct English.**

| | |
|---|---|
| Strongly agree | 20.5% (8) |
| Somewhat agree | 17.9% (7) |
| Not sure | 23.1% (9) |
| **Somewhat disagree** | 25.6% (10) |
| Strongly disagree | 12.8% (5) |

**ADDITIONAL COMMENTS**

(2) but it's not the only correct way to speak or write English.

(4) I don't find such generalizations useful.

(5) It depends on audience, purpose, and conventional expectations. All rhetoric is situational.

(8) I believe SEE or SAE is the "standard" that the professional world generally demands for upwardly mobile employees. Vernaculars are just as "correct" in their context, but American society demands a uniform language for upper levels of business and academia, and that language happens to be SAE. A student who masters SAE has a wider range of options for employment than one who does not.

(11) There is no correct English. However, I recognize the value in our having a common version of the English language that we use to communicate in professional situations, and students need to learn to be compentent in this English. Students from the south really need to master this English as their speech patterns (and writing patterns) can caused them to be judged as less intelligent than their northern counterparts.

(12) It is correct in a formal sense . . . but not in a cultural sense.

(15) Not necessary

*(18) This is entirely dependent upon the context. In some settings, standard English is preferred and advantageous. In others, it is not necessary.*

*(19) "Correct" is a dicey word. It is the correct English for business, academics, etc. but as far as the correct English for home use, that can and does vary.*

*(23) The point is not whether it is correct, but whether one's ignorance of it will limit one's future. In other words, the question is not one of correctness, but of preceptions and expectations over which academica has very little control.*

*(25) I'm not familiar with Standard Edited English.*

*(26) There is no such thing as "correct" or "perfect" English, but in written English standard form is preferred for Business and commerce.*

(28) "Correctness" has been in debate far too long to speak with any certainty now. "Correct" for me is ultimately a judgement claim, the value/assessment of which usually depends on ones audience. However, it is also a power issue with the people in power determining which usages are "correct." So, there is some practical sense to the claim that Standard Edited English is the (hegemonic) "correct" version.

(30) Once the distinction between spoken and written language is explained, spoken is indicated as more "open" and nearly infinitely improvisable compared to written language, which is infinitely revisable and adheres to conventions of formality. Insofar as this caveat is concerned, these are the "correct" parameters of language usage. I eschew the purist/absolutist notion of language purity, unlike the French proper.

(34) There are many Englishes, as I tell my students. You may not need all of them. But you need to know how and when to use Standard Edited English (usually for workplace situations and school).

Appendix    273

(35) I do believe in using different ways to communicate in different situations. Writing a perfect text message, for instance, seems a bit over the top.
(36) Question does not make sense without defining "correct." I take it that you're looking for prejudices of participants. Not a good question.
(37) I reject the premise of this question, as I understand it.
(38) Standard Edited English is the language of the academy. In the context of a college classroom it is the expected language. Outside of this context, such as spoken English, other forms of English are acceptable.
(40) Different genres require different language choices. To tell students that all writing must follow Standard Edited English is a disservice to the students. Teaching them to analyze the writing situation and determine what is appropriate will serve them in and beyond the University.

**4.    Nonstandard French constructions in English, such as "get down from the car" and "save the dishes," are incorrect.**

| | |
|---|---|
| Strongly agree | 5.1% (2) |
| Somewhat agree | 23.1% (9) |
| Not sure | 15.4% (6) |
| Somewhat disagree | 23.1% (9) |
| **Strongly disagree** | **33.3% (13)** |

### ADDITIONAL COMMENTS

(3) In informal conversations, these may be acceptable.
(4) They are regional dialects/slang and I find them endearing. At the same time, I discourage all students from using regionalisms in formal academic papers because of the chance it may alienate the reader. In other words, if they reference something the reader doesn't understand, then the reader is left out in the cold. But such phrases, as above, would be wonderful for more creative/narrative/personal essay types of writing because of how they contribute to tone/voice.
(5) "Incorrect" implies a single set of criteria for all rhetorical situations. See above for comment on that.
(8) As stated previously, these are phrases that are "incorrect" for SAE but are perfectly correct given the linguistic development of CVE. French constructions are no less correct than English constructions—they just bear a different historical and cultural context.

(13) I do not know what those constructions are. I do hear, however, omissions of certain verbs [Where she at?]
(15) If you are not from the area and have not grown up with this, then you might think the person saying it is not smart, but this may not be the case.
(16) I think we should maintain Cajunisms . . . the French is dying so we need to keep any heritage we have left.
*(17) They are incorrect in the professional world.*
*(18) Again, context is everything. See answer for #3 above.*
*(19) They aren't incorrect, they're local and in many cases, they are literal translations from French. Losing the local vernacular isn't necessary. Learning to code switch, well that's another matter.*
(21) Again, I refer to my point above. Also, since "get down from the car" is the only way I know to indicate exiting an automobile, I'm not sure I'm the right person to be asked this question.
(22) They are, perhaps, translations from the French or just have long term old Southern connections; "get down" pertains to the horse and buggy days, for instance; students can rephrase such points or put quotations around them to show their recognition of the local color phrases.
*(23) In what context?*
*(24) They are fine when speaking, but they are not okay in writing.*
(25) Truthfully, I have always used the term "get down" when referring to exiting a vehicle. My mother has fought the use of this term my whole life. Finally, as an adult, I researched the origin of the phrase and found that it dates back to carriage days when people physically had to descend from, or "get down from" the carriage. I hold that some of these terms, while possibly antiquated and not always correct, do have interesting origins, even if they are outdated. (P.S.—I'm very short, so I really do have to "get down from" most vehicles.)
*(26) Simple local Cajun English is clearly understood here, but will not be understood as well if the person moves to another region.*
(30) It illuminated Twain's vernacular characters and gave them a "realness" or verisimilitude that would have been lost had the diction/dialogue been sanitized or "made proper." In this context, nonstandard French constructions keep the mother language in its "sponge-like" state that keeps it vital and ever-adapting to differing cultural treatments.
*(32) Like most issues, it's a matter of context. If those lines succeed in communicating information between two people who both*

understand them, then they're acceptable in such a context and are correct. If they fail to do so in a different context, then theye are incorrect.
- (34) Depends on context
- (36) Ditto. Be direct with questions. It's beginning to sound like you have an agenda and are not after objective discovery.
- (37) Wouldn't be appropriate in what you're referring to as SEE.
- (38) It depends on the context. Spoken and informal situations, these phrases are acceptable. In academic writing they are not.
- (40) See comment above.

5. **The Cajun accent sounds backwards and illiterate.**

| | |
|---|---|
| Strongly agree | 0.0% (0) |
| Somewhat agree | 7.7% (3) |
| Not sure | 17.9% (7) |
| Somewhat disagree | 25.6% (10) |
| **Strongly disagree** | **48.7% (19)** |

*ADDITIONAL COMMENTS*

- (4) I enjoy regional dialects of all types and find them fascinating.
- (5) It doesn't make a good impression in all situations, but no accent does that I know of.
- (8) In the same way that AAVE is often accused of sounding "backwards and illiterate," so is CVE. I've grown up with SAE, and I'm a strong supporter of proper grammar and conjugation, so at times I feel myself resistant to CVE constructions and conjugations, but just because a culture speaks a certain way doesn't make them stupid or illiterate.
- (13) Here no. Elsewhere, maybe.
- (15) Some persons who have advanced degrees have that accent but it does not make them backwards or illiterate.
- (16) I think we need to protect out language and lifestyle
- (17) *It's not the accent that sounds backwards and illiterate—many educated Cajuns sound "Cajun" but speak almost perfect English. The reason some people think a Cajun accent sounds illiterate is because there are too many illiterate (or uneducated) Cajuns. However, the accent itself does not sound backwards or illiterate. To me, that would be like assuming anyone with an Irish accent was backwards and illiterate—which is certainly not true.*

(18) *To which Cajun accent are you referring? There isn't only one Cajun accent. Additionally, you need to clarify if you are referring to Cajun accented English or Cajun accented French. And in what context?*
(19) The Cajun accent is part of what makes this area of Louisiana distinct and interesting.
(21) This is a matter of perspecive. I don't think anyone would vote for a presidential candidate who had one.
(23) *It merely sounds French, but once you have lived with them for a long time, it is no longer evident to you.*
(25) I am certainly biased because I grew up surrounded by Cajun accents, but it can sound very beautiful, especially when the speaker uses many French terms throughout their speech. On the other hand, having "learned" how a "proper" accent should sound, some Cajun accents can make the speaker sound a bit uneducated
(26) *But it does say "country" doesn't it?*
(30) Maybe to the ignorant.
(32) *How can an accent alone be backwards or illiterate? It seems that it would only be through mistaken association that this could occur.*
(34) I personally enjoy the local color aspects of it, but I do know that many people would consider it backwards and illiterate (and when used in certain contexts, it could actually create an impression of illiteracy for more than just the individual speaker).
(35) However, I do have a hard time understanding it. For instance, when a student said "around" once, I heard "Ryan" and was very confused.
(36) Here's where I get off.
(37) This question is not phrased well.
(38) The media has considerable influence on the way accents are perceived. For instance, the Disney Film The Princess and the Frog portrays those with Cajun accent as backwards an illiterate. However, this perception is not necessarily accurate, simply commonly reinforced.
(40) I think this is the perception of many.

6. **All vernaculars of English are broken and/or incorrect.**
   
   | | |
   |---|---|
   | Strongly agree | 0.0% (0) |
   | Somewhat agree | 23.7% (9) |
   | Not sure | 15.8% (6) |
   | Somewhat disagree | 21.1% (8) |
   | **Strongly disagree** | **39.5% (15)** |

## ADDITIONAL COMMENTS

(5) Only if you like living atop an ivory tower.

(8) No one speaks SAE the exact same way, and I don't think anyone should. Language evolves, and part of the way it does that is through vernacular diversity. Plus, cultural diversity is what makes language so interesting. Accents are the same way. But I do think that we need to be able to code switch well enough to communicate across vernaculars, and the easiest way to do that is an accepted "standard" form of English.

(16) Regional dialects are important parts of American culture!

*(23) These questions are beginning to reveal an agenda that is more political than scientific.*

(25) If the standard is not being spoken or written 100% precisely, then it would serve to reason that all vernaculars are somewhat incorrect.

*(26) If you can carry on your life in it, it is fine. If it gets in the way of that, it must be modified for success.*

(30) Regionalism clearly illustrates that there are varying treatments of the mother language based on locale, personality types, and cultural history. It is a main theme on which to creatively embellish. Again, these vernaculars are "real" manifestations of the language and should not be derided because of it.

*(32) See above comments about context.*

(35) Some vernaculars are actually more regular in their constructions than Standard English.

(37) Neither is this one.

(38) Again, the perception of vernacular is influenced by the way media presents it. This can be traced back to the construction of characters who speak in vernacular. Compare the Artful Dodger with Oliver Twist. As the protagonist, Oliver speaks in Standard English; his foil, The Artful Dodger speaks in the vernacular, which symbolizes his character.

(40) Again, I think we overlook the value of the vernacular. Is the use of the vernacular appropriate in my History 101 research paper on World War II, no. Was it appropriate in Twain's "Jumping Frog," I would argue yes.

## CAJUNS' EXPERIENCES WITH CAJUN VERNACULAR ENGLISH

**1. Do you identify as Cajun? If not, you may skip this page.**
Yes 36.4% (12)
No 63.6% (21)

### ADDITIONAL COMMENTS

(16) (No.) I moved here to raise my children in a french-speaking environment.
*(17) Both of my parents are Cajun.*
*(23) My father grew up in Rayne during the Depression. He did not speak English until he began attending school.*
*(24) My mom was a Boudreaux!*
*(32) Both of my parents are from Acadiana. My father's family was part of the second generation of French immigrants who came to the area after Le Grand Dérangement and intermarried with the original Cajuns.*

**2. I speak Cajun French.**

| | |
|---|---|
| Not at all. | 26.7% (4) |
| **A little.** | **46.7% (7)** |
| I don't speak it, but I understand a lot. | 13.3% (2) |
| I am fluent. | 13.3% (2) |

### ADDITIONAL COMMENTS

*(10) My grandparents spoke/speak Cajun French. One aunt speaks it, and another understands. Otherwise, it hasn't been passed down.*
*(17) My parents never taught me, nor did they speak to me in French, because they were punished for speaking French when they were in school.*
*(23) My father never taught me French, but he was very insistent that I speak English correctly.*
*(26) I understand a significant amount, and I can say several words and short phrases.*
*(32) I picked up a little from working with my father at his business when I was younger as he spoke it with his friends and customers who were locals.*

3. **My parents/grandparents were punished for or prohibited from speaking Cajun French in school.**
   Yes (please explain below)   71.4% (10)
   No                           28.6% (4)

*ADDITIONAL COMMENTS*
   *(1)   My mother was required to see a speech therapist and was punished (spanked) for speaking French.*
   *(10)  I remember my maternal grandmother talking about her elementary school experiences. She and other students would get paddled/punished for speaking in French in the classroom.*
   *(14)  And so was I! Although I began kindergarten in the early 80s, I spoke fluent Cajun French at that age and was disciplined for using it in school.*
   (16)  not from here
   *(17)  My father, who was in grade school in the 1940s, told me that he and his brother would be "put on their knees" by teachers who heard them speaking French.*
   *(18)  My father claims that this was not the case, but I am inclined to think he was for reasons too difficult to elaborate on here.*
   *(20)  Not that I'm aware of*
   *(23)  My father was forbidden to speak French in school. He was punished if he uttered one word in French.*
   *(24)  My mom's grandparents were punished if they spoke Cajun French at school.*
   *(26)  My paternal grandfather was made to kneel on rice for speaking Cajun-French.*
   *(32)  My father (who was born in 1938) was punished for speaking it, but (at least in his case) it was not as severe as some stories made it out to be.*

4. **My parents/grandparents think speaking with Cajun features is illiterate.**
   Yes                      0.0% (0)
   **No**                   **66.7% (10)**
   Other (please specify)   33.3% (5)

*ADDITIONAL COMMENTS (RESPONSES TO "OTHER")*
   *(14)  To some degree, my parents' generation (early 50s now) was indoctrinated to thinking Cajun was "bad" and it wasn't good to be different so they never used it in the home when I was growing up although my grandparents sure did, especially when fighting and/or cursing.*

(16) not applicable
*(19) This is too complex an issue for a blanket Yes/No answer. First off, what are "Cajun features?" Second, are you referring to "Cajun features" in French or English? This survey also needs to account for regional variation. Within this culture, the language (let's use French in this example) of one community is sometimes judged "better" than the French of other communities. As an example, many individuals consider the French of the Henderson/Cecilia area to be inferior to the French of the Opelousas/Eunice area. Others do not make such distinctions.*
*(23) It would depend on the features and the social context.*
(39) They haven't really been exposed to it.

5. **Cajun features in speech (click all that apply).**
   I speak English with a Cajun accent. 20.0% (3)
   I try to filter out Cajun words and accent in professional settings such as teaching, job interviews, and public speaking. 46.7% (7)
   I am proud of my Cajun accent. 40.0% (6)
   I am embarrassed when others call attention to nonstandard, Cajun features in my speech (give examples below). 0.0% (0)
   **I don't really have an accent; I speak Standard English. 53.3% (8)**
   Sometimes I exaggerate my Cajun accent. 20.0% (3)

   *ADDITIONAL COMMENTS*
   (16) I have worked hard for it!
   *(18) For the most part I speak Standard English but at home with my family, I do have a Cajun accent and this is fine.*
   *(32) I filter my word selection when it would not generally be understood—in an academic setting, with non-local professionals. I don't turn off the accent, though it's not strong in the first place and generally understandable to non-locals.*

6. **Cajun features in writing (click all that apply):**
   I use nonstandard Cajun features in my high-stakes writing (e.g. for a grade or publication). 0.0% (0)
   I was embarrassed when the nonstandard, Cajun features of my writing were pointed out to me. 0.0% (0)
   **I use nonstandard Cajun features in my low-stakes writing (e.g. personal emails or letters). 100.0% (7)**

7. **Have you ever been corrected for Cajun features in your speech/writing by a teacher? If so, how did your teacher handle it? Was it effective, in your opinion?**
   *(1) Not since high school.*
   (4) no

(6) No
*(10) I have never been corrected for this.*
*(14) No.*
*(18) If so, it happened too long ago for me to recall.*
*(19) Yes, when I was younger I was corrected for these things. At first, I think I was angry. Then, I was embarrassed. After I learned not to speak this way, I then learned to not speak this way around that teacher and to code switch for school/home.*
*(20) Never*
*(24) No.*
*(26) I learned very early in life how to filter the Cajun features out of my writing; my mother was very instrumental in this.*
*(32) Nope.*

8. **Are there any defining moments that have shaped your attitude toward Cajun linguistic features? Explain.**

*(1) Studying linguistics and learning more about dialect have made me regret my intentional loss of much of my dialect and accent.*
*(4) no*
(6) I am not a native Cajun speaker—I acquired Cajun French conversational skills as an adult. I was drawn to the language first by hearing and enjoying traditional Cajun folk music.
*(14) Times when I realized someone didn't know what I was talking about because they weren't from here.*
*(17) When I entered college, my freshman year, I realized that most professionals (in this case, my professors) pronounced the "th" sound, and I often did not. I remember hearing myself say, "I'm going to da store," and thinking, "My professors would never say 'da store'." That's when I really began to force myself to remove "Cajun-speak" from my writing and speaking.*
*(18) Living outside of the state, I was struck with the dullness of standard English.*
*(19) Getting a degree with a specialization in Louisiana folklore certainly helped to shape my attitude.*
*(24) No.*
*(26) Throughout school, engaging in extracurricular activities that often involved public speaking made me acutely aware of how Cajun accents affected attitudes toward those speakers. Many people believe that the Cajun accent sounds unintelligent and uneducated, so I fought to develop a more "Anglicized" accent, especially in professional and public matters. My personal attitude toward the accent and features of the Cajun language is still one of pride, but I do recognize the stigma associated with those features.*
*(32) Nothing specific.*

282  APPENDIX

9. **Has your attitude toward Cajun linguistic features changed since you were a child? Describe.**

(1) *The older I get, the less I "look down" on those features that I worked so hard to get out of my speech, the more I wish I hadn't done so.*

(4) *not really*

(14) *Yes, I am more proud of it know as an adult that when I was a child.*

(17) *I was never embarassed, really, but my Cajun accent. And as I grow older, I am more and more proud of it. I'm just careful to keep some of the "Cajun slang" in check when I'm in a professional setting.*

(18) *Yes. Greater exposure to the cultural absence that marks English in other parts of the nation has resulted in a greater sense of pride. But, again, this question is too vague. What is a "Cajun linguistic feature?"*

(19) *The above-mentioned degree helped to strenghten the pride that I already had in my Cajun heritage, including these linguistic features.*

(24) *Since becoming a teacher of composition, I am more careful when writing.*

(26) *As a child, I didn't realize that the accent was different; I was living within a society that consisted of nothing but Cajun accents. As I became a young adult, I did become a bit more ashamed of my accent and those of my family members, but only because I was learning that people associated that accent with a lack of intelligence. As I entered college and adulthood, I gained a new respect for my culture, accent and all. Althought I do speak differently given the situation and company, I am very proud of my heritage, and the accent is a huge part of that.*

(32) *Nope. I've always been proud of it and have suffered no persecution because of it.*

### PEDAGOGICAL STRATEGIES REGARDING CVE

1. **I have, or have had, students with Cajun linguistic features.**

    Yes                              91.7% (33)
    No (you may skip to #6 below)    8.3% (3)

### ADDITIONAL COMMENTS

(8) I have not had distinctly Cajun students, but I do have friends with whom I've discussed some of these elements, particularly the ones that seem to linger after code switching to SAE/SEE.

(9) I'm not familiar enough with Cajun English to know

(10) Since I teach at LSU and most LSU undergraduates are from Louisiana, I have taught many students who speak with a "cajun" accent. There are also many from New Orleans who have that accent.

(14) Mon dieu! I do teach in south LA.

(16) these students teach me more about rural Louisiana then any book!!!

*(17) I teach in Acadiana, so I get Cajun students every semester, some of whom have thick accents and use lost of Cajun vernacular.*

*(19) As much as I know what you mean by a "Cajun linguistic feature," I'll answer yes.*

(25) And some very bright ones too.

2. **Select Cajun linguistic features you have encountered in your students' SPEECH. Some of the following are not necessarily always CVE, but select them if you think they are examples of Cajun Vernacular influence (click all that apply):**

- **Cajun accent ("clipped" or "flat" vowels, lack of "th" sound, etc.) 88.2% (30)**
- Cajun cadence (sometimes described as more "musical" than Standard English) 73.5% (25)
- double pronoun usage (e.g. "I don't know, me") 58.8% (20)
- deleting final consonant (e.g. "las" for "last," "dis" for "disk," "barb" for "barbed") 70.6% (24)
- dropping linking verbs (e.g. "we leaving") 79.4% (27)
- using "go" as a linking verb (e.g. "we went eat") 70.6% (24)
- using French words (e.g. *cher, lagniappe, couillion, envie*) 64.7% (22)
- a preference for story telling over logic or argument 52.9% (18)
- nonstandard French constructions (e.g. "pass a good time," "save the dishes," "make a B+") 55.9% (19)
- French interrogative constructions (e.g. "you like that, yeah?" and "why you like that?") 58.8% (20)
- other (please specify) 14.7% (5)

*ADDITIONAL COMMENTS (RESPONSES TO "OTHER")*

(3) I'm going to prom. I don't want you to fuss me. or Don't fuss me.

(8) One of the most common elements of CVE I see is "axe" instead of "ask." Several people I know from Cajun families (or who started school in more Cajun districts) bear very little evidence of it in their speech except for this. Also, outside of Cajun society, this pronunciation tends to be corrected by ridicule, taking the pronunciation as a literal "axe."

(29) I've heard a lot of students and teachers use "y'all" in a sort of French construction, with a dropped possessive, like "get out y'all books" or "get in y'all groups."

(34) See previous.
(37) How is "make a B+" a French construction? Do you mean as opposed to "earn?" This is not a Gallicism, I don't think. I'm also not sure on what basis you're making the distinction between story-telling and argument.

3. Have you ever addressed any of the above features in your students' SPEECH? If so, please explain.

4. Select Cajun linguistic features you have encountered in your students' WRITING. Some of the following are not necessarily always CVE, but select them if you think they're the result of Cajun Vernacular influence (click all that apply):
   - misspellings based on CVE pronunciations (e.g. deleting final consonant, wrong vowel) 44.4% (12)
   - **dropping linking verbs (e.g. "we leaving")** 55.6% (15)
   - using "go" as a linking verb (e.g. "we went eat") 51.9% (14)
   - using French words (e.g. *cher, lagniappe, couillion, envie*) 37.0% (10)
   - a preference for story telling over logic or argument 51.9% (14)
   - nonstandard French constructions (e.g. "pass a good time," "save the dishes," "make a B+") 48.1% (13)
   - double pronoun usage (e.g. "I don't know, me") 25.9% (7)
   - a preference for story telling over logic or argument 25.9% (7)
   - French interrogative constructions (e.g. "you like that, yeah?" and "why you like that?") 18.5% (5)
   - other (please specify) 11.1% (3)

**ADDITIONAL COMMENTS (RESPONSES TO "OTHER")**
(13) where he at? We arrived to; And then add to all of these unique patterns, the new tendency to text in the essay. (So you could invent text language for unique linguistic features—just as easily as you can for Standard English features.)
*(19) It would be a logical jump to connect writing errors such as these to "Cajun linguistic features." Many—if not most—of the same issues were present in students I've taught in Texas and Missouri.*
(25) Much black English constructions of verb to be used in black English.

5. Have you ever addressed any of the above in your students' WRITING? If so, explain as thoroughly as possible your pedagogical strategy for dealing with CVE in your students' writing:

(1) *It's no different than what I do for students who have other dialects, explicitly point out the difference between the grammar of the dialect and the grammar of the Standard dialect and ask that they use the Standard in writing.*

(3) I provide examples of correct options; however, since many of these are the result of family background and regionalism, not much changes. There are some students who wish to excel in their writing, so they work harder are affecting a change.

(4) For the most part, many French Cajun words (like lagniappe), I consider so integrated into everyday speech that they are no longer even slang, for readers/academics in South Louisiana. If anything, as an outsider, I had to learn some of them just to participate in normal conversation, so I was the one adapting my speech for this community. I have encouraged particularities in speech for some assignments, like personal essay/narrative/profile, because it helps establish character and forces students to pay attention to language use.

(5) Usually, the students correct the issues themselves in peer response groups focused on editing.

(6) I frequently point CVE features out because many students don't realize the uniqueness of their idiom or usage. I never represent their vernacular as sub-standard or incorrect—The school system did enough of that two generations ago, greatly aiding and abeting the demise of the language and, in some ways, the culture. Actually, I would never demean speakers of any regional or ethnic dialect, including BVE or the Southern US Scotch-Irish, but I do explain to students the reasons for appreciating their language, for understanding levels of usage, and for adapting usage to a variety of audiences.

(7) Yes, Try to explain street vs formal in language

(10) *I have not seen this as much in student writing. More often, I see standard grammar and punctuation mistakes.*

(11) I don't see the CVE problems in my students writing, or I do so rarely. However, several of the things you have identified as characteristic of CVE are also things I see in black and white students, particularly from the New Orleans area. Since we have raised our standards substantially at LSU over the past decade, I rarely see these problems in student writing, and when I do, I see them most frequently in the writing of African-American students. I don't really have a strategy for addressing these problems though. I just identify why they are deviations from standard English and tell them to cut it out.

(13) No stragegy. My rubric for all writing is based on the same three standards: Form (the essay proper), Function (carry out the

assignment as given), and Use (all mechanics). I use Word's comment feature and make corrections/comments on individual issues in balloons to the right. My explanation will be centered on whichever standard applies—assuming Standard English

(14) *Yes, because my job is to teach formal academic english.*

(15) I have not had any one recently.

(16) I have included assignments specifically to ALLOW students a creative space to use their colloquialisms and find most do not use them in their formal work.

(17) *I find the best way is to model the correct grammar/construction for them. I simply re-word their sentence, then they must write it down correctly in their revision. Later, when we have one-on-one conferences, I discuss the error with the student in greater detail.*

(19) In what context? As errors, yes. As cultural elements, no.

(21) I will mark them and then show them how to say that phrase in standardized English.

(22) No. The worked in the context they were used.

(24) *Yes. I simply mark the mistakes without addressing possible reasons for the mistake.*

(25) I definitely address these issues in students' writing, usually simply by writing "colloquialism" near the error, followed by an explanation of why it doesn't fit Standard English guidelines. Most students don't realize that these features are not commonplace in other vernaculars until they are pointed out to them.

(26) See above.

(27) No

(28) I do not address the vernacular in writing unless it adds nothing to the essay being written. I may not have enough knowledge to know when grammatical errors are CVE errors and so may not know that I have corrected these.

(29) it hasn't been widespread enough for me to really call attention to it. Most students, everywhere I've taught, prefer story telling over argument, and I've always chalked that up to being just an early stage in their intellectual development.

(31) It has been very limited in my students' writing, even from locals (the bulk of my students). I don't make a big deal out of it as I understand where it's coming from. I simply correct it as it comes up in papers.

(32) *showing proper useage of Standard American English; discussing the issues of written language and why they need to know the difference.*

(34) The features I associate with CVE are not ones I usually find in written work, and that's the only place I would deal with it. I never address it when students are speaking to me. There are some items on your list that I do see in writing, but I don't

particularly associate those features with CVE (leaving out a verb, for example, or preferring story telling over logic or argument).
(35) Yes. I usually suggest a more stand usage. I do stress argument over storytelling. However, I do not comment on the use of cajun words, such as lagniappe, in writing. I have not come across the use of "cher" in writing.
(37) I've never seen any of those issues in students' writing, at least not any that could be tied to CVE specifically.
(38) I spend a considerable time working on sentence structure, particularly subject verb agreement, and proper verb selection. I also go over how to use foreign words within academic language.
(39) Yes, I have just written "nonstandard" or explained that one cannot write as one talks.

6. **My pedagogy can best be summed up as:**
   - eradication (teaching students never to use the vernacular) 0.0% (0)
   - multiculturalism (teaching students to use the vernacular everywhere, including the classroom) 5.7% (2)
   - **code switching (teaching students to use Standard Edited English in classrooms and vernaculars at home) 62.9% (22)**
   - code meshing (teaching students to use a blend of Standard Edited English and vernacular everywhere, including the classroom) 11.4% (4)
   - other (please specify) 20.0% (7)

*ADDITIONAL COMMENTS (RESPONSES TO "OTHER")*
(4) Multiculturalism (in general) with Code Meshing when necessary
(8) I work in between code meshing and code switching, encouraging students to consider word choice (in vernaculars and also informal/formal language) based on audience and context/rhetorical situation.
(11) not sure how to answer this question. I do require that students write in standard English in their formal writing assignments, but since I teach composition, that's my job. I don't, however, make comments about their spoken English usually unless they are giving an oral presentation and honesty, I've not really had problems with students' dialects when they make oral presentations.
(13) Standard English in their writing; vernaculars wherever else they wish

(21) Eradication or quotation marks to show their recognition of the phrases, but I only do such correcting as it pertains to writing . . .
(37) I believe that teaching what you're calling SEE for writing in composition classes is necessary, though I would call attention to the arbitrary and constructed nature of it while doing so.
(40) Teaching students to assess when CVE is appropriate.

7. **I learned my pedagogy for dealing with vernaculars from (click all that apply):**
   - my own teachers 58.3% (21)
   - my teacher education/certification 30.6% (11)
   - reading literature on the topic 36.1% (13)
   - trial and error 41.7% (15)
   - my parents or other family member 27.8% (10)
   - **personal reflection** 72.2% (26)
   - other (please specify) 13.9% (5)

*ADDITIONAL COMMENTS (RESPONSES TO "OTHER")*

(6) marrying into the Cajun culture: "If you marry a Cajun, you become a Cajun":)
(13) actual classroom experience—and 30 years of experience in industry before that.
(21) As it came up in written work...
(25) I've been here since 1995 and I'm kinda' "Cajunized."
(38) I spend a lot of time communicating with my students about their needs and expectations for our First Year writing courses. Most students want to learn to use Standard English in their academic papers.

*CONTACT INFO*

1. **May I contact you for further information or an interview regarding your thoughts, opinions, and experiences?**
   **Yes** (79%)
   No (21%)

2. **Additional thoughts about the survey:**
   (6) I'm happy to see this study. I did a linguistics project on CVE in grad school (years ago) and have always been fascinated by the issues.
   (13) You probably could add a question or two that deals with texting in the vernacular.

*(14) This was fun! Good luck with your project, you. :)*

*(18) Honestly, I've had less problems with language from my Cajun students and/or because of Cajun vernacular than I have had with current slang vernacular and with my African American students this semester. This could be because I have, I'd say 60% of the class that is African American right now. But I've never really noticed a particularly strong problem with people putting local regional accents/regional speaking into their writing.*

*(19) This survey seems to need additional refinement. In particular, the blanket assumptions of a homogenized Cajun culture are resulting in problems. There is no, single, Cajun identity or accent. In addition, any consideration of this area needs to address the influences of Creole French as well.*

(25) I wish more instructors knew about code switching and do not tell Cajun students that they "speak poor English."

*(32) Interesting project.*

(34) Very interesting study. I would like to read it when it is finished—it might help me with my students.

(36) Any sociology undergraduate would call this a poor instrument.

# NOTES

## INTRODUCTION

1. The difference between immigrants and minorities may not be as clear-cut as Villanueva portrays in this quotation. Immigrant groups also express resistance to assimilation, both culturally and linguistically.
2. Ira Shor points out that the enforcement of an elite standard in schools on children who can't or won't normalize is a means of producing a "structured failure" that supports other unacknowledged functions of the state, such as supplying recruits for the military (personal communication). For this reason, Paulo Freire advocated teaching standard usage to low-income students as one measure against this structured failure.

## CHAPTER 1

1. To avoid confusion, I have changed references to *Cajun Vernacular English* and *CVE*, respectively, to *Cajun English* and *CE* in this quotation and throughout the rest of the book.
2. One other participant identified as Cajun as well, but I switched him to "non-Cajun" because he reported that he wasn't raised Cajun, just married into it and claimed it for himself.
3. Judging the elite *r* as "correct" is also an example of something Bourdieu calls *misrecognition*, insofar as the usage of distinction is perceived as superior because of normalization, while it is actually only *different* from nonelite usage. I expand on this in chapter 5.
4. I know this from personal communication with several relatives and acquaintances who have worked offshore.
5. Further, the flooding has increased in Louisiana as a result of business developments in northern Mississippi River states, according to a Rutgers University expert on US flood policy, Karen O'Neill: "Every time someone builds a shopping mall in Illinois or Missouri, water drains to the river that would have formerly filtered into the groundwater locally" (quoted in Llanos 2011).
6. Funny story. Prudhomme is from my hometown (Opelousas), where we pronounce his family's name something like "Prood'm" in English, but he changed the pronunciation to "Proo-DOM" when he opened his restaurant. Chachere is also from Opelousas. In fact, he lived in my neighborhood and I grew up calling him, with his grandkids, "Paw-caw." Had no idea he was famous until late in high school when I asked about the mirrors on his kitchen ceiling (for his cooking show).
7. *Cajun Justice*, a reality show on A&E following Terrebonne Parish sheriff's deputies portrays Cajuns in a typical postcolonial light; it "investigate[s] thousands of violent crimes every year in the creepy, eerie bayou. And with the personalities of the local Cajuns, no police call is routine" (Heisig 2011, 2). And *Cajun Pawn Stars?* Puh-lease. First of all, they're in Alexandria, and everybody knows that anything north of Bunkee is not French, much less Cajun. Plus, my stepsister told me she knows that

crew, and they're actually Italian. They're just buying into the Cajun craze because, as successful pawn businesspeople, they know Cajunness turns a profit.

## CHAPTER 2

1. Many conservatives support these policies because they want the freedom to enjoy their wealth in the very rare event that they rise above the middle class (an aspiration that is generally unsupported by US history). This is how hegemony operates; workers take on the perspective of capitalists. But as long as workers are doing unto others as they would have others do unto them, they can hold capitalists accountable for their unfair hiring and firing practices, bad stewardship of the earth, and manufactured financial (and other) crises by boycotting them and voting to support regulations that enforce consequences for unbridled greed and exploitation. Federal regulation shouldn't be a problem at all for conservatives, who are willing to ban gay marriage "out of love" (because they don't want to support homosexuals' "destruction" of their own lives). Likewise, conservatives can hold corporations accountable "out of love," since the decisions of corporations affect everyone, sometimes entire communities of workers and national education policies, whereas gay marriage has not so far caused many people to marry their pets or leave their straight spouses.
2. G. William Domhoff (2010) suggests in *Who Rules America?* a rubric for identifying the US ruling class. Similar to Brandt's theory of "sponsors of literacy," he asks the questions "Who benefits?, Who governs?, and Who wins?" If one question doesn't fit the situation, another will, and they all point to who organizes political policies in their own interests. Based on his rubric, he identifies the US ruling class as "the owners and managers of large income-producing properties; i.e., corporations, banks, other financial institutions, and agri-businesses. But they have plenty of help from the managers and experts they hire" (Domhoff 2012). The Koch brothers, the third-richest Americans who founded and funded the Tea Party Movement under the guise of anti-immigration and other libertarian policies (but actually want to do away with corporate regulations), are a great example of Domhoff's rubric. Who wins or benefits most from the Tea Party Movement? Not the thousands of people taking a day off from work to go picket but the extremely wealthy corporations that will be freer to exploit the people picketing for them.
3. And you too can buy your own politicians, if you just work hard enough and save your money!
4. In fact, the Acadians who stayed in Canada (from whom Cajuns are descended, as I explain later) claim the purist blood of the Acadian diaspora, whereas Cajuns are known to be very mixed.
5. Most past representations in literature have either sentimentalized and romanticized Acadians/Cajuns or depicted them as low-class trash (in keeping with the traditionally classed terminology surrounding Cajuns). Elista Istre (2002) writes in her thesis, "Laissez les Bon Temps Rouler! Cajun Stereotypes and the Development of Cultural Tourism in South Louisiana" that there have been two primary representations of Cajuns in literature—the gentle, romanticized "angel" and the dirty, ignorant, violent, and backwards masses. She writes, "Authors like Longfellow and De la Houssaye [who wrote *Pouponne and Balthazar* (1888)] isolated their [Acadian] heroines from the [Acadian] people around them, perhaps because of Victorian America's rejection of the *real* Acadian stereotypes. In glamorizing the Acadian experience, both writers presented a surreal stereotypical figure that had little basis in fact. While praising the simplicity of Acadian life, Longfellow exaggerated the harmony and tranquility of their pastoral existence. De la Houssaye, on the

other hand, was careful to distinguish between the poor, uncouth, violent 'Cajuns' and the genteel, upper-class French Creoles" (25). Cajun scholars characterize Longfellow's story as sentimentalized, romanticized, and an inaccurate depiction of Acadians. The Cajun movement beginning in the 1970s criticizes the genteel Acadians' attempts to appeal to US audiences by rewriting their history to conform to their Anglo expectations (created by Longfellow in *Evangeline*).

6. An alternative version suggests that Giovanni Verrazano named the encampment after Arcadia, which eventually evolved into Acadie. Jacques Henry supports this theory with official maps from 1548 to 1575 that "named the area corresponding to Nova Scotia *Larcadia, Larcadie* or *Arcadia*" (1998, 32). John Mack Faragher concludes that, regardless of the origin, the settlement's name came to favor the Mikmawísimk word, indicating the level of "intercultural conversations between Mikmaw hunters and French traders" (2005, 6).

7. Brasseaux draws this conclusion by contrasting Acadians with "the Englishmen at Plymouth and Jamestown and the Normans and Picards in the St. Lawrence Valley" (3).

8. Faragher writes that the Acadian dike system improved upon other existing dikes: "Its key feature, the *aboiteau*—a sluice fitted with a clapet that was forced shut by the rising tide on the seaward side, then pushed open as the tide fell by water draining from the fields—is found neither on *saunier* dikes nor in the drainage systems of Poitou, and the word *aboiteau* itself has no equivalent in continental French. The colonists developed this system during the 1640s, and it was in full operation by the early 1650s, when Nicolas Denys was impressed with the 'great extent of meadows which the sea used to cover and which the Sieur d'Aulnay has drained'" (2005, 49).

9. LeBlanc's information is from one of many letters to Shane Bernard in response to survey questions he posted in several local newspapers. Bernard shared these letters with me when I told him about my research.

10. Incidentally, one of the Cajuns who gives an interview about the French ban (which I use in the next chapter) notes that he had a "beautiful German teacher from Mamou" named Ms. Feucht—this was my great-aunt Ella (Billadeaux n.d.).

## CHAPTER 3

1. I would qualify this assertion by saying that small waves of immigrants experience assimilation and hybridity, but large waves of immigrants (for example, at the turn of the twentieth century) experienced deculturalization and cultural genocide in their schooling, just like internally colonized groups. There are reports of Jewish and Italian children experiencing treatments similar to what I describe later in this chapter for Cajun children. Additionally, the status of immigrants depends on where they're from and the color of their skin.

2. You would never know from looking at it, but this city's name is pronounced "Nack-a-dish."

3. Jean Arceneaux is the pen name of Barry Jean Ancelet, a prominent activist and folklorist in Cajun studies.

4. One more note on representing the stories of these Cajuns. It wasn't possible to standardize how I represented the ages of the respondents. As much as was possible, I tried to list the year they were born, but other times the only information I had was the year they entered first grade or the year they graduated. Students generally entered school at the age of five.

## CHAPTER 4

1. Bowles and Gintis (1976) accurately use the term *corporate capitalism* for this period, but their use of *corporate* is different from the way it is generally discussed today (under what David Harvey [2007] and other economic theorists call "finance capitalism").
2. Despite the progress of the field, attitudes were still very traditional when it came to women, who were not even considered in professional contexts. In the article "The Use of 'Mr.,'" the titles *Professor, Dr.*, and *Mr.* are clarified. Wyld (1967) recommended *Mr.* for every situation, making no mention of female faculty.
3. Elbow (2012) adds that it's not just minority groups who must code censor but also white males from the dominant group, just because general language has changed so much more than written English.
4. As I wrote in chapter 3, Annette Lareau (2003) confirms this idea in *Unequal Childhoods: Class, Race, and Family Life*. Her ethnographic study reveals that literacy practices are passed on in home and family encounters, not in schools. Schools do not equalize; they simply assess already existing literacy practices and sort students accordingly. Once the students are sorted into their (generally) class- and race-based categories, pedagogical differences like the ones Anyon (1980) describes reinforce that categorization as well as the idea that students who wind up near the vocational end of the educational spectrum are either lazy or less intelligent.
5. More information is available in the *Huffington Post* article "Murdoch-Owned Wireless Generation's Contract Should Be Scratched, Teachers' Union Leader Writes" (2011).
6. Mikhail Zinshteyn (2011) reports the details in "Mayor Bloomberg Trust Donated Big to Louisiana Education Board Elections" in the *American Independent* online. Though Governor Jindal initiated a series of anticorruption campaigns to "clean up" Louisiana politics (for instance, making the IRS records of all state employees public, triggering a mass early retirement), he has essentially flushed out a substantial number of Democrats and established a new set of corrupt practices (Zinshteyn focuses on the efforts of brother-system team Chas and Caroline Roemer) as he pushes for the privatization of Louisiana schools and other social programs.

## CHAPTER 5

1. His term is originally the Portuguese *conscientizao*, but many scholars simply use *conscientization*.
2. In *Ways with Words* Shirley Brice Heath (1983) researched literacy development in three Carolina communities and found that only the white middle-class kids thrived academically because their home-based literacy events mirrored preferred usage and rhetoric in the schools, while both African American and white working-class kids performed academically at a lower level as a result of their different socializations at home into literacy and rhetoric.
3. In particular, the families of well-known Cajun musicians are still respected in SouLa as they uphold these traditions—the Michots and the Balfas, for instance.
4. Louisiana's Iberia Parish began efforts in 2011 to erect trilingual public signs (English, French, and Spanish) in recognition of "all three languages as part of SouLa's culture" (Kline 2011).
5. "Paquing" eggs (from the French word for Easter, Pâques) is the Cajun term for the friendly competition of knocking dyed eggs together to see whose egg is the strongest.

# REFERENCES

"About Louisiana." 2012. *Louisiana.gov.* Accessed April 15, 2012. http://louisiana.gov/Explore/About_Louisiana/.
Allen, Harold B. 1957. "Communication and General Education." *College Composition and Communication* 8 (1): 33–35. http://dx.doi.org/10.2307/354414.
Alpert, Bruce. 2011. "Sen. Mary Landrieu's Oil Revenue Sharing Amendment Denied a Vote by Senate Energy Committee." *Times-Picayune,* July 21. Accessed April 15, 2012. http://www.nola.com/politics/index.ssf/2011/07/sen_mary_landrieus_oil_revenue.html.
Ames, Don. 2012. "Cajun Characters Swamp Casting Call." *WWL.com.* Accessed May 1, 2012. http://www.wwl.com/pages/11221890.php?
Ancelet, Barry Jean. 1988. "A Perspective on Teaching the 'Problem Language' in Louisiana." *French Review (Deddington)* 61 (3): 345–56.
Ancelet, Barry Jean. 1996. "From Evangeline Hot Sauce to Cajun Ice: Signs of Ethnicity in South Louisiana." *Folklife in Louisiana.* Accessed May 24, 2009. http://www.louisianafolklife.org/LT/Articles_Essays/main_misc_hot_sauce.html.
Anderson, Benedict. 1991. *Imagined Communities: Reflections on the Origin and Spread of Nationalism.* Rev. ed. London: Verso.
Anyon, Jean. 1980. "Social Class and the Hidden Curriculum of Work." *Journal of Education* 162 (1): 67–92.
Apple, Michael. 2009. *Education and Power.* 2nd ed. New York: Routledge.
Barkan, Joanne. 2011. "Got Dough? How Billionaires Rule Our Schools." *Dissent Magazine,* Winter. Accessed May 26, 2014. https://www.dissentmagazine.org/article/got-dough-how-billionaires-rule-our-schools.
Bartholomae, David. 1997. "Inventing the University." In *Cross-Talk in Comp Theory,* ed. Victor Villanueva, 589–619. Urbana, IL: NCTE.
Baugh, Albert C., and Thomas Cable. 2007. *History of the English Language.* 5th ed. London: Routledge.
Baum, Bernard. 1967. "Some Thoughts on Teaching Grammar to Improve Writing." *College Composition and Communication* 18 (1): 2–6. http://dx.doi.org/10.2307/354486.
Bernard, Shane K. 2003. *The Cajuns: Americanization of a People.* Jackson: University Press of Mississippi.
Bernard, Shane K. 2008. *Cajuns and Their Acadian Ancestors: A Young Reader's History.* Jackson: University Press of Mississippi.
Bernard, Shane K. n.d. Audio interview with Elmo Authement. BE1.063. University of Louisiana at Lafayette Archives, University of Louisiana, Lafayette.
Bernard, Shane, and Kara Bernard. 1999. "French Language." In *Encyclopedia of Cajun Culture, 1997.* Updated February 14. Accessed November 22, 2006. http://www.cajunculture.com.
Bhabha, Homi K. 1994. *The Location of Culture.* London: Routledge.
Bienvenu, Marcelle, Carl A. Brasseaux, and Ryan A. Brasseaux. 2005. *Stir the Pot: The History of Cajun Cuisine.* New York: Hippocrene.
Billadeaux, Lionel Clayton. n.d. Audio interview with unidentified student. ST1.037. University of Louisiana at Lafayette Archives, University of Louisiana, Lafayette.

Blake, William. 2000. "London." In *The Norton Anthology of English Literature: The Romantic Period*, ed. M. H. Abrams et al., 56. New York: Norton.
Bloom, Lynn Z. 1996. "Freshman Composition as a Middle-Class Enterprise." *College English* 58 (6): 654–75. http://dx.doi.org/10.2307/378392.
Bourdieu, Pierre. (Original work published 1979) 1984. *Distinction: A Social Critique of the Judgement of Taste*. Trans. Richard Nice. Cambridge, MA: Harvard University Press.
Bourdieu, Pierre. 1991. *Language and Symbolic Power*. Ed. John B. Thompson. Trans. Gino Raymond and Matthew Adamson. Cambridge, MA: Harvard University Press.
Bowles, Samuel, and Herbert Gintis. 1976. *Schooling in Capitalist America: Education Reform and the Contradictions of Economic Life*. New York: Basic Books.
"BP Oil Spill: The 'Horribly Mutated' Creatures Living in the Gulf." 2012. *Theweek.com*, April 19. Accessed April 30, 2012. http://theweek.com/articles/476264/bp-oil-spill-horribly-mutated-creatures-living-gulf.
Brandt, Deborah. 2001. *Literacy in American Lives*. New York: Cambridge University Press. http://dx.doi.org/10.1017/CBO9780511810237.
Brandt, Deborah. 2004. "Drafting U.S. Literacy." *College English* 66 (5): 485–502. http://dx.doi.org/10.2307/4140731.
Brasseaux, Carl A. 1978. "Acadian Education: From Cultural Isolation to Mainstream America." In *The Cajuns: Essays on Their History and Culture*, ed. Glenn R. Conrad, 221–24. Lafayette: University of Louisiana at Lafayette Center for Louisiana Studies.
Brasseaux, Carl A. 1987. *The Founding of New Acadia: The Beginnings of Acadian Life in Louisiana, 1765–1803*. Baton Rouge: Louisiana State University Press.
Brasseaux, Carl A. 1991. *Scattered to the Wind: Dispersal and Wandering of the Acadians, 1755–1809*. Lafayette: University of Southwest Louisiana.
Brasseaux, Carl A. 1992. *Acadian to Cajun: Transformation of a People, 1803–1877*. Jackson: University Press of Mississippi.
Broussard, Earl Paul. n.d. Audio interview with unidentified student. ST1.023. University of Louisiana at Lafayette Archives, University of Louisiana, Lafayette.
Brown, Richard A. 1999. "Bulwark of Revolutionary Liberty: Thomas Jefferson's and John Adams's Programs for an Informed Citizenry." In *Thomas Jefferson and the Education of a Citizen*, ed. James Gilreath, 91–102. London: University Press of New England.
Burnet, MacCurdy. 1957. "Vowel Contrasts in Student Speech." *College Composition and Communication* 8 (1): 22–26. http://dx.doi.org/10.2307/354412.
Burns, Gerald T. 1990. "Class, Language, and Power in Franklin's Idea of the English School and Other Early Texts of Vernacular Advocacy: A Perspective on the Social Origins of English." In *Bringing English to Order: The History and Politics of a School Subject*, ed. Ivor Goodson and Peter Medway, 87–134. London: Falmer.
Canagarajah, A. Suresh. 1999. *Resisting Linguistic Imperialism in English Teaching*. Oxford: Oxford University Press.
Canagarajah, A. Suresh. 2004. "Subversive Identities, Pedagogical Safe Houses, and Critical Learning." In *Critical Pedagogies and Language Learning*, ed. B. Norton and K. Toohey, 116–37. Cambridge: Cambridge University Press. http://dx.doi.org/10.1017/CBO9781139524834.007.
Canagarajah, A. Suresh. 2006. "The Place of World Englishes in Composition: Pluralization Continued." *College Composition and Communication* 57 (4): 586–619.
Canagarajah, A. Suresh. 2010. "An Updated SRTOL?" *cccc-blog*, November 4. Accessed November 10, 2010. http://cccc-blog.blogspot.com/2010/11/updated-srtol.html.
Canagarajah, A. Suresh. 2011. "Afterword: World Englishes as Code-Meshing." In *Code-Meshing as World English: Policies, Pedagogy, and Performance*, ed. Vershawn Ashanti Young and Aja Martinez, 273–81. Urbana, IL: National Council of Teachers of English.
Canagarajah, A. Suresh. 2012. "Toward a Rhetoric of Translingual Writing." Paper # 1. *Working Papers on Negotiating Language and Literacy: Practices and Pedagogies*. Accessed May 16, 2012. http://louisville.edu/workingpapers/copy_of_working-papers.

Canagarajah, A. Suresh. 2013. *Translingual Practice: Global Englishes and Cosmopolitan Relations*. New York: Routledge.
Cart, Julie. 2013. "A Strong Voice in Louisiana's Cancer Alley." *Latimes.com*, August 27. Accessed July 2, 2014. http://www.latimes.com/local/great-reads/la-me-c1-subra-enviro-20130827-dto-htmlstory.html.
Cheramie, Deany Marie. 1998a. "Cajun Vernacular English and the Influence of Vernacular on Student Writing in South Louisiana." PhD diss., University of Southwestern Louisiana. *Dissertation Abstracts International A: The Humanities and Social Sciences* 60 (2).
Cheramie, Deany Marie. 1998b. "'Glad You Axed': A Teacher's Guide to Cajun English." *Louisiana English Journal* 5 (1): 72–81.
Cheramie, Deany M., and Donald A. Gill. 1992. "Lexical Choice in Cajun Vernacular English." In "Cajun Vernacular English: Informal English in French Louisiana." Special issue, *Louisiana English Journal*: 38–55.
Chomsky, Noam. 2003. *Understanding Power: The Indispensable Chomsky*. Ed. Peter R. Mitchell and John Schoeffel. London: Vintage.
Cixous, Hélène. 1986. "Sorties." In *The Newly Borne Woman*, ed. Hélène Cixous and Catherine Clément, trans. Betsy Wing, 63–129. Minneapolis: University of Minnesota Press.
Cole, Mike, ed. 1988. *Bowles and Gintis Revisited: Correspondence and Contradiction in Educational Theory*. London: Falmer.
"Comparison of State and Local Government Revenue and Debt in the United States (2010)." 2010. *Usgovernmentrevenue.com*. Accessed April 15, 2012.
Condon, Sherri L., and Pamela T. Pittman. 1992. "Language Attitudes in Acadiana." In "Cajun Vernacular English: Informal English in French Louisiana." Special issue, *Louisiana English Journal*: 56–72.
Conniff, John R. 1925. "Aims, Materials, and Methods for the Teaching of Oral and Written Composition." *Journal of the Louisiana Teachers' Association* 3 (3): 11–16.
Crocco, Francesco. 2011. "Critical Gaming Pedagogy." *Radical Teacher* 91 (91): 26–41. http://dx.doi.org/10.5406/radicalteacher.91.0026.
Crowley, Sharon. 1998. *Composition in the University: Historical and Polemical Essays*. Pittsburgh: University of Pittsburgh Press.
de Beauvoir, Simone. (Original work published 1949) 1972. *The Second Sex*. Trans. H. M. Parshley. New York: Penguin.
Delpit, Lisa. 1997. "The Silenced Dialogue: Power and Pedagogy in Educating Other People's Children." In *Cross-Talk in Comp Theory*, ed. Victor Villanueva, 565–88. Urbana, IL: National Council of Teachers of English.
Deutsch, Leonard. 1979. "Cajun Culture—an Interview." *Melus* 6 (1): 81–89. http://dx.doi.org/10.2307/467522.
Dharwadker, Vinay. 2004. "The Formation of Indian-English Literature." In *Literary Cultures in History: Reconstructions of South Asia*, ed. Sheldon Pollack, 199–267. New Delhi: Oxford University Press.
Domhoff, G. William. 2010. *Who Rules America? Challenges to Corporate and Class Dominance*. 6th ed. Boston: McGraw-Hill.
Domhoff, G. William. 2012. "Who Rules America.net: Power, Politics, & Social Change." *Who Rules America?* Accessed May 24, 2012. http://www2.ucsc.edu/whorulesamerica/.
Donald, James. 1983. "How Illiteracy Became a Problem (and Literacy Stopped Being One)." *JAC* 165 (1): 35–52.
Dubois, Sylvie, and Barbara M. Horvath. 2002. "Sounding Cajun: The Rhetorical Use of Dialect in Speech and Writing." *American Speech* 77 (3): 264–87. http://dx.doi.org/10.1215/00031283-77-3-264.
Dubois, Sylvie, and Barbara M. Horvath. 2003a. "Creoles and Cajuns: A Portrait in Black and White." *American Speech* 78 (2): 192–207. http://dx.doi.org/10.1215/00031283-78-2-192.

Dubois, Sylvie, and Barbara M. Horvath. 2003b. "Verbal Morphology in Cajun Vernacular English: A Comparison with Other Varieties of Southern English." *Journal of the English Language* 31 (1): 34–59.

Dubois, Sylvie, and Megan Melançon. 2000. "Creole Is, Creole Ain't: Diachronic and Synchronic Attitudes toward Creole Identity in Southern Louisiana." *Language in Society* 29 (2): 237–58. http://dx.doi.org/10.1017/S0047404500002037.

Du Bois, W.E.B. (Original work published 1903) 1994. *The Souls of Black Folk.* New York: Gramercy Books.

Elbow, Peter. 1991. "Reflections on Academic Discourse: How It Relates to Freshmen and Colleagues." *College English* 53 (2): 135–55. http://dx.doi.org/10.2307/378193.

Elbow, Peter. 1999. "Inviting the Mother Tongue: Beyond 'Mistakes,' 'Bad English,' and 'Wrong Language.'" *Journal of Advanced Composition* 19 (2): 359–88.

Elbow, Peter. 2012. *Vernacular Eloquence: What Speech Can Bring to Writing.* Oxford: Oxford University Press. http://dx.doi.org/10.1093/acprof:osobl/9780199782505.001.0001.

Faragher, John Mack. 2005. *A Great and Noble Scheme: The Tragic Story of the Expulsion of the French Acadians from Their American Homeland.* New York: Norton.

Finegan, Edward. 1980. *Attitudes toward English Usage: The History of a War on Words.* New York: Teachers College Press.

Fletcher, Joel. (Original work published 1941) 1958. *Louisiana Education since Colonial Days.* Lafayette: Southwestern Louisiana Institute.

Foucault, Michel. (Original work published 1975) 1977. *Discipline and Punish: The Birth of the Prison.* Trans. Alan Sheridan. New York: Pantheon Books.

Foucault, Michel. 1980. *Power/Knowledge: Selected Interviews and Other Writings, 1972–1977.* Ed. and trans. Colin Gordon. New York: Pantheon.

Franklin, Benjamin. 1993. *The Autobiography of Benjamin Franklin.* Boston: Bed Books.

Franklin, Benjamin. (Original work published 1747) 2015. "Proposals relating to the Education of Youth of Pensilvania." *National Humanities Center.* Accessed August 28, 2015. http://nationalhumanitiescenter.org/pds/becomingamer/ideas/text4/franklinproposals.pdf.

Freire, Paulo. 1993. *Pedagogy of the Oppressed.* New York: Continuum.

Gaudet, Marcia. 2003. "Introduction." In *Mardi Gras, Gumbo, and Zydeco: Readings in Louisiana Culture*, ed. Marcia Gaudet and James McDonald, vii–xv. Jackson: University Press of Mississippi.

Gilreath, James. 1999. "Introduction." In *Thomas Jefferson and the Education of a Citizen*, ed. James Gilreath. London: University Press of New England.

Gilyard, Keith. 1991. *Voices of the Self: A Study of Language Competence.* Detroit: Wayne State University Press.

Giovo, Jack, I. Bruce Turner, and Linda Parker Langley. 2000. *Jefferson Davis Parish: An Oral History.* Jennings, LA: Jefferson Davis Arts Council.

Gobry, Pascal-Emmanuel. 2014. "Want to Know the Language of the Future? The Data Suggests It Could Be...French." *Forbes,* March 21. http://www.forbes.com/sites/pascalemmanuelgobry/2014/03/21/want-to-know-the-language-of-the-future-the-data-suggests-it-could-be-french/#11a503b33933.

Graff, Harvey J. 1990. *The Literacy Myth: Literacy and Social Structure in the Nineteenth-Century City.* New York: Bedford/St. Martin's.

Gramsci, Antonio. 1971. *Selections from "The Prison Notebooks."* Ed. and trans. Quintin Hoare and Geoffrey Nowell Smith. New York: International.

Grinde, Donald A., Jr. 1999. "Thomas Jefferson's Dualistic Perceptions of Native Americans." In *Thomas Jefferson and the Education of a Citizen*, ed. James Gilreath, 193–208. London: University Press of New England.

Harden, Blaine. 2002. "Born on the Bayou and Barely Feeling Any Urge to Roam." *NYTimes.com,* September 30. Accessed May 24, 2012. http://www.nytimes.com/2002/09/30/us/born-on-the-bayou-and-barely-feeling-any-urge-to-roam.html.

Harris, T. H. 1914. "Live-Wire Arguments from State Superintendents of Education." In *Educational Foundations: A Monthly Magazine of Pedagogy*, 183–84. Collected September 1913–June 1914. New York: Educational Magazine.

Harris, T. H. 1923. *Annual Report of the Louisiana State Department of Education for the Session 1921–1922*. Baton Rouge: Ramires-Jones.

Harris, T. H. n.d.a. "Adult Illiterates." Box 1–15. *Memoirs*. Collection 52: Thomas H. Harris Papers. University Archives and Acadiana Manuscripts Collections, University of Louisiana, Lafayette.

Harris, T. H. n.d.b. "The High School Division (1908)." Box 1–29. *Memoirs*. Collection 52: Thomas H. Harris Papers. University Archives and Acadiana Manuscripts Collections, University of Louisiana, Lafayette.

Harris, T. H. n.d.c. "Parish Superintendents." Box 1–37. *Memoirs*. Collection 52: Thomas H. Harris Papers. University Archives and Acadiana Manuscripts Collections, University of Louisiana, Lafayette.

Harris, T. H. n.d.d. "Public Opinion." Box 1–40. *Memoirs*. Collection 52: Thomas H. Harris Papers. University Archives and Acadiana Manuscripts Collections, University of Louisiana, Lafayette.

Hartwell, Patrick. 1997. "Grammar, Grammars, and the Teaching of Grammar." In *Cross-Talk in Comp Theory: A Reader*, ed. Victor Villanueva, 183–212. Urbana, IL: National Council of Teachers of English.

Harvey, David. 2007. *Brief History of Neoliberalism*. Oxford: Oxford University Press.

Heath, Shirley Brice. 1983. *Ways with Words: Language, Life, and Work in Communities and Classrooms*. New York: Cambridge University Press.

Hechter, Michael. 1975. *Internal Colonialism: The Celtic Fringe in British National Development*. Berkeley: University of California Press.

Heisig, Eric. 2011. "'Cajun Blue': A TV Show without a Contract." *Houmatoday.com*, November 26. Accessed April 15, 2012. http://www.houmatoday.com/article/20111126/ARTICLES/111129737.

Henry, Jacques. 1998. "From *Acadien* to *Cajun* to *Cadien*: Ethnic Labelization and Construction of Identity." *Journal of American Ethnic History* 17 (4): 29–63.

Hirsch, E. D., Jr. 1988. *Cultural Literacy: What Every American Needs to Know*. New York: Vintage Books.

Hollister, Archie S. 1947. "The Use of French in the Language Class." *Journal of Louisiana Teachers' Association* 15 (8): 23, 26–28.

Horner, Bruce, and Min-Zhan Lu. 2011. "Translingual Literacy and Matters of Student Agency." Plenary address presented at the Penn State Conference on Rhetoric and Composition: Rhetoric and Writing across Language Boundaries, State College, PA, July 11. Collected in the Working Papers Series on Negotiating Differences in Language & Literacy, University of Louisville, Louisville, KY, 2012. Accessed May 20, 2012. http://writing.uncc.edu/sites/writing.uncc.edu/files/media/docs/Min-Zhan_Lu_and_Bruce_Horner_Translingual_Literacy_and_Matters_of_Agency(1).pdf.

Horner, Bruce, Min-Zhan Lu, Jacqueline Jones Royster, and John Trimbur. 2011. "Language Difference in Writing: Toward a Translingual Approach." *College English* 73 (3): 303–21.

Horner, Bruce, and John Trimbur. 2002. "English Only and U.S. College Composition." *College Composition and Communication* 53 (4): 594–630. http://dx.doi.org/10.2307/1512118.

Hull, Glynda, Mike Rose, Kay Losey Fraser, and Marisa Castellano. 1991. "Remediation as Social Construct: Perspectives from an Analysis of Classroom Discourse." *College Composition and Communication* 42 (3): 299–329. http://dx.doi.org/10.2307/358073.

Istre, Elista. 2002. "Laissez les Bon Temps Rouler! Cajun Stereotypes and the Development of Cultural Tourism in South Louisiana." MA thesis, University of Louisiana, Lafayette.

Kaplan, Erin Aubrey. 2003. "Black Like I Thought I Was." *LA Weekly*, October 2. Accessed November 14, 2003. http://www.laweekly.com/calendar/black-like-i-thought-i-was-2137114.

Kaplan, Robert B. 1966. "Cultural Thought Patterns in Intercultural Education." *Language Learning* 16 (1 2): 1–20. http://dx.doi.org/10.1111/j.1467-1770.1966.tb00804.x.

Kepler, Adam W. 2011. "'Swamp People' Haul in Big Ratings." *NYTimes.com*, July 26. Accessed May 10, 2012. http://artsbeat.blogs.nytimes.com/2011/07/26/swamp-people-haul-in-big-ratings/?_r=0.

King, Martin Luther, Jr. 1992. *I Have a Dream: Writings and Speeches That Changed the World*. Ed. James M. Washington. San Francisco: Harper.

Kline, Shawn. 2011. "Spanish Becoming 'Just as Influential' as French." *KATC.com*, August 10. Accessed May 18, 2012.

Knabb, Richard D., Jamie R. Rhome, and Daniel P. Brown. 2006. "Tropical Cyclone Report: Hurricane Katrina: 23–30 August 2005." *National Hurricane Center*, December 20, 2005. Updated August 10, 2006. Accessed April 15, 2012. http://www.nhc.noaa.gov/data/tcr/AL122005_Katrina.pdf.

Kynard, Carmen. 2008. "'The Blues Playingest Dog You Ever Heard Of': (Re)positioning Literacy through African American Blues Rhetoric." *Reading Research Quarterly* 43 (4): 356–73. http://dx.doi.org/10.1598/RRQ.43.4.3.

Labov, William. 1972. *Language in the Inner City: Studies in the Black English Vernacular*. Philadelphia: University of Pennsylvania Press.

Landry, Christophe. 2011. "Cajuns & Louisiana Creoles: Really a Difference?" *Christophelandry.com*, February 4. Accessed April 15, 2012.

Landry, Christophe. Forthcoming. *Multilingualism and Language Politics in Post-war Creole Louisiana*.

Lareau, Annette. 2003. *Unequal Childhoods: Class, Race, and Family Life*. Berkeley: University of California Press.

Leger, Charlene. 2013. "'White' Doesn't Define Me. I'm Cajun." *The Race Card Project*. Accessed June 26, 2014. http://theracecardproject.com/white-doesnt-define-me-im-cajun/.

Llanos, Miguel. 2011. "Cajuns to Blame for Their Own Flood Misery? Not So Fast." *Nbcnews.com*, May 20. Accessed May 21, 2011. http://www.nbcnews.com/id/43067898/ns/us_news-environment/t/cajuns-blame-their-own-flood-misery-not-so-fast/#.VeCOJbTN6lY.

Longfellow, Henry Wadsworth. 2004. *Evangeline: A Tale of Acadie*. Coral Springs, FL: Lumina.

Lu, Min-Zhan. 1992. "Conflict and Struggle: The Enemies or Preconditions of Basic Writing?" *College English* 54 (8): 887–913. http://dx.doi.org/10.2307/378444.

Lu, Min-Zhan. 1994a. "From Silence to Words: Writing as Struggle." In *Landmark Essays on Writing Process*, ed. Sondra Perl, 165–76. Davis, CA: Hermagoras.

Lu, Min-Zhan. 1994b. "Professing Multiculturalism: The Politics of Style in the Contact Zone." *College Composition and Communication* 45 (4): 442–58. http://dx.doi.org/10.2307/358759.

Macafee, Caroline. 2004. "Scots and Scottish English." In *Legacies of Colonial English: Studies in Transported Dialects*, ed. Raymond Hickey, 59–81. Cambridge: Cambridge University Press.

Mao, LuMing. 2002. "Re-clustering Traditional Academic Discourse: Alternating with Confucian Discourse." In *ALTDis: Alternative Discourses and the Academy*, ed. Christopher Schroeder, Helen Fox, and Patricia Bizzell, 112–25. Portsmouth, NH: Boynton/Cook.

Marx, Karl, and Frederick Engels. (Original work published 1848) 1978. "Manifesto of the Communist Party." In *The Marx-Engels Reader*, 2nd ed., ed. Robert C. Tucker, 469–500. New York: Norton.

McDowell, Jody. 1984. Letter to the editors of *Louisiana Magazine*, February 1,. Box 4–10. Collection 206: Council for the Development of French in Louisiana (CODOFIL), 1966–2001. University Archives and Acadiana Manuscripts Collections, University of Louisiana, Lafayette.

McWhorter, John. 2008. *Our Magnificent Bastard Tongue: The Untold History of English*. New York: Gotham Books.

Mead, Corey. 2013. *War Play: Video Games and the Future of Armed Conflict*. Boston: Houghton Mifflin Harcourt.

Mead, Margaret. 1943. "Our Educational Emphases in Primitive Perspective." *American Journal of Sociology* 48.

Melancon, Megan. 2005. "American Varieties: Cajun English." *Do You Speak American? From Sea to Shining Sea*. Accessed November 22, 2006. https://www.pbs.org/speak/seatosea/americanvarieties/cajun/.

Mufwene, Salikoko S. 2008. *Language Evolution: Contact, Competition and Change*. London: Continuum.

"Murdoch-Owned Wireless Generation's Contract Should Be Scratched, Teachers' Union Leader Writes." 2011. *Huffington Post*, August 5. Accessed May 24, 2012. http://www.huffingtonpost.com/2011/08/05/murdoch-wireless-generation-contract-teachers-union_n_919325.html.

Ngũgĩ wa Thiong'o. 1981. *Decolonising the Mind: The Politics of Language in African Literature*. London: James Currey.

Nunberg, Geoffrey. 2004. "Foreword." In *Language in the USA: Themes for the Twenty-First Century*, ed. Edward Finegan and John R. Rickford, xiii–xvi. Cambridge: Cambridge University Press. http://dx.doi.org/10.1017/CBO9780511809880.001.

Oakes, Jeannie. 1986. *Keeping Track: How Schools Structure Inequality*. New Haven: Yale University Press.

Omisore, Bolanle. 2010. "Cajun Speakers Try to Breathe New Life into Dying Language." *Nola10.nytimesinstitute.com*, May 24. Accessed May 24, 2011.

Parks, Stephen. 2000. *Class Politics: The Movement for the Students' Right to Their Own Language; Refiguring English Studies*. Urbana, IL: National Council of Teachers of English.

Perl, Sondra. Forthcoming. *Making a Place for the Personal*.

Perrin, Warren. 2012. "History Channel Has Backed Preservation of French Culture." *Theadvertiser.com*, January 18. Accessed January 18, 2012.

Phillipson, Robert. 1992. *Linguistic Imperialism*. Oxford: Oxford University Press.

Post, Lauren C. 1962. "Some Notes on the Attakapas Indians of Southwest Louisiana." *Louisiana History* 3 (3): 221–42.

"Poverty on the Rise in Louisiana." 2011. *Louisiana Budget Project*, September 22. Accessed September 22, 2011.

Powell, Malea. 2002. "Listening to Ghosts: An Alternative (Non)argument." In *ALTDis: Alternative Discourses in the Academy*, ed. Christopher Schroeder, Helen Fox, and Patricia Bizzell, 11–22. Portsmouth, NH: Boynton/Cook.

Prendergast, Catherine. 2009. "The Fighting Style: Reading the Unabomber's Strunk and White." *College English* 72 (1): 10–28.

Ramanathan, Vaidehi. 2005. *The English-Vernacular Divide: Postcolonial Language Politics and Practice*. Clevedon, UK: Multilingual Matters.

Ravitch, Diane. 2013. "Bobby Jindal Admits a Mistake." *Diane Ravitch's Blog: A Site to Discuss Better Education for All*, April 9. Accessed May 26, 2014. http://dianeravitch.net/2013/04/09/bobby-jindal-admits-a-mistake/.

Reisz, Matthew. 2012. "A Word of Advices: Let Speakers of Englishes Do It Their Way, UK Told." *Timeshighereducation.com*, May 17. Accessed May 18, 2012. https://www.timeshighereducation.co.uk/news/a-word-of-advices-let-speakers-of-englishes-do-it-their-way-uk-told/419935.article.

Rodriguez, Richard. 1982. *Hunger for Memory: The Education of Richard Rodriguez; An Autobiography*. New York: Dial.

Rose, Mike. 1987. *Lives on the Boundary: A Moving Account of the Struggles and Achievements of America's Educationally Underprepared*. New York: Penguin Books.

Rose, Mike. 2008. "The Language of Exclusion: Writing Instruction at the University." In *Negotiating Academic Literacies: Teaching and Learning across Languages and Cultures*, ed. Vivian Zamel and Ruth Spack, 9–30. New York: Routledge.

Rowland, Christopher. 2013. "Tax Lobbyists Help Businesses Reap Windfalls." *Bostonglobe.com*, March 17. Accessed September 10, 2015. http://www.bostonglobe.com/news/politics/2013/03/16/corporations-record-huge-returns-from-tax-lobbying-gridlock-congress-stalls-reform/omgZvDPa37DNlSqi0G95YK/story.html.

Rushton, William Faulkner. 1979. *The Cajuns: From Acadia to Louisiana*. New York: Farrar Straus Giraux.

Russell-Buffalo, Gail, and Nichole E. Stanford. 2014. "Pedagogy of Reinvention: Paulo Freire in 20th and 21st Century Education." In *Educating about Social Issues in the 20th and 21st Centuries: Critical Pedagogues and Their Pedagogical Theories, vol. 4 in Research in Curriculum and Instruction*, ed. Samuel Totten and Jon E. Pedersen, 71–93. Charlotte, NC: Information Age.

Ryon, Dominique. 2005. "Language Death Studies and Local Knowledge: The Case of Cajun French." In *Reclaiming the Local in Language Policy and Practice*, ed. Suresh Canagarajah, 55–72. Mahwah, NJ: Lawrence Erlbaum.

Sabia, Dan. 2011. "Democratic/Utopian Education." Paper presented at the Society for Utopian Studies Annual Conference, State College, PA, October.

Sacks, Peter. 2007. *Tearing Down the Gates: Confronting the Class Divide in American Education*. Berkeley: University of California Press.

Said, Edward. 1978. *Orientalism*. New York: Vintage Books.

Sasser, Bill. 2010. "Despite BP Oil Spill Louisiana Still Loves Big Oil." *Csmonitor.com*, May 24. Accessed May 24, 2011. http://www.csmonitor.com/USA/2010/0524/Despite-BP-oil-spill-Louisiana-still-loves-Big-Oil.

Schroeder, Christopher. 2002. "From the Inside Out (or the Outside In, Depending)." In *ALTDis: Alternative Discourses and the Academy*, ed. Christopher Schroeder, Helen Fox, and Patricia Bizzell, 178–90. Portsmouth, NH: Boynton/Cook.

Schroeder, Christopher, Helen Fox, and Patricia Bizzell, eds. 2002. *ALTDis: Alternative Discourses and the Academy*. Portsmouth, NH: Boynton/Cook.

Scott, Ann Martin. 1992a. "Language Education in Acadiana." In "Cajun Vernacular English: Informal English in French Louisiana." Special issue, *Louisiana English Journal* 92–101.

Scott, Ann Martin. 1992b. Preface to "Cajun Vernacular English: Informal English in French Louisiana." Special issue, *Louisiana English Journal* i–iii.

Scott, Ann Martin. 1992c. "Some Phonological and Syntactic Characteristics of Cajun Vernacular English." In "Cajun Vernacular English: Informal English in French Louisiana." Special issue, *Louisiana English Journal* 26–36.

Scott, James C. 1990. *Domination and the Arts of Resistance: Hidden Transcripts*. New Haven: Yale University Press.

Scribner, Sylvia. 1984. "Literacy in Three Metaphors." *American Journal of Education* 93 (1): 6–21. http://dx.doi.org/10.1086/443783.

Segura, Chris. 1999. "Speaker Takes Mystery out of Cajun X-factor [in] Cajun Surnames." *Acadian-Cajun*, August 5. Accessed December 2, 2006. http://www.acadian-cajun.com/cmanew5e.htm.

Shaughnessy, Mina. 1977. *Errors and Expectations: A Guide for the Teacher of Basic Writing*. New York: Oxford.

Shor, Ira. 1982. *Empowering Education: Critical Teaching for Social Change*. Chicago: University of Chicago Press.

Simon, Allen. n.d. Audio interview by Shane Bernard. BE1.060–BE1.061. University of Louisiana at Lafayette Archives, Lafayette.

Skutnabb-Kangas, Tove. 1988. "Multilingualism and the Education of Minority Children." In *Minority Education: From Shame to Struggle*, ed. Tove Skutnabb-Kangas and Jim Cummins, 9–44. Clevedon, UK: Multilingual Matters.

Smith, Griffin, Jr. 1990. "The Cajuns: Still Loving Life." *National Geographic Magazine*, October. Accessed July 2, 2014. http://zachary.waiting-forthe-sun.net/Pages/Archives/CajunsLoveLife.html.

Smitherman, Geneva. (Original work published 1977) 1986. *Talkin and Testifyin: The Language of Black America.* Detroit: Wayne State University Press.

Smitherman, Geneva. 1987. "Opinion: Toward a National Public Policy on Language." *College English* 49 (1): 29–36. http://dx.doi.org/10.2307/377787.

Smitherman, Geneva. 1995. "'Students' Right to Their Own Language': A Retrospective." *English Journal* 84 (1): 21–27. http://dx.doi.org/10.2307/820470.

Sohn, Katherine Kelleher. 2006. *Whistlin' and Crowin' Women of Appalachia: Literacy Practices since College.* Carbondale: Southern Illinois University Press.

Sohn, Katherine Kelleher. 2011. "Language Awareness in an Appalachian Composition Classroom." In *Code-Meshing as World English: Policies, Pedagogy, and Performance,* ed. Vershawn Ashanti Young and Aja Martinez, 79–93. Urbana, IL: National Council of Teachers of English.

Spring, Joel H. 2010. *Deculturalization and the Struggle for Equality: A Brief History of the Education of Dominated Cultures in the United States.* 6th ed. Boston: McGraw-Hill Higher Education.

Stanford, Nichole E. 2011. "Publishing in the Contact Zone: Strategies from the Cajun Canaille." In *Code-Meshing as World English: Policies, Pedagogy, and Performance,* ed. Vershawn Ashanti Young and Aja Martinez, 115–42. Urbana, IL: National Council of Teachers of English.

Stephens, Edwin Lewis. 1933. "Education in Louisiana in the Closing Decades of the Nineteenth Century." *Louisiana Historical Quarterly* 16 (1): 38–56.

Stephens, Edwin Lewis. 1935. "The Story of Acadian Education in Louisiana." *Louisiana Historical Quarterly* 18:397–410.

Strickland, Donna. 1998. "How to Compose a Capitalist: The Predicament of Required Writing in a Free Market Curriculum." *Composition Forum* 9 (1): 25–38.

Stuckey, J. Elspeth. 1991. *The Violence of Literacy.* Portsmouth, NH: Boynton/Cook.

Suarez, Raleigh A. 1971. "Chronicle of a Failure: Public Education in Antebellum Louisiana." *Louisiana History* 12 (2): 109–22.

Sullivan, Paul. 2010. "As Private Tutoring Booms, Parents Look at the Returns." *Nytimes.com*, August 8. Accessed April 15, 2012. http://www.nytimes.com/2010/08/21/your-money/21wealth.html.

Sullivan, Paul R., Robert Lado, Garland H. Cannon, Burnet MacCurdy, and Edith Crowell Trager. 1957. "English as Second Language—Potential Applications to Teaching the Freshman Course." *College Composition and Communication* 8 (1): 10–33. http://dx.doi.org/10.2307/354409.

Tentchoff, Dorice. 1980. "Ethnic Survival under Anglo-American Hegemony: The Louisiana Cajuns." *Anthropological Quarterly* 53 (4): 229–41. http://dx.doi.org/10.2307/3318106.

Thier, Dave. 2014. "Sorry, Louisiana Is Not Actually Made of Magic." *Esquire.com*, March 11. Accessed March 13, 2014. http://www.esquire.com/entertainment/tv/a27742/louisiana-is-not-magic/.

Thompson, John B. 1991. "Introduction." In *Language and Symbolic Power,* ed. John B. Thompson, trans. Gino Raymond and Matthew Adamson, 1–31. Cambridge, MA: Harvard University Press.

Tidwell, Mike. 2004. *Bayou Farewell: The Rich Life and Tragic Death of Louisiana's Cajun Coast.* London: Vintage.

Timmerman, John. 1957. "Do Illiterate A.B.'s Disgrace Us All?" *College Composition and Communication* 8 (1): 50–55. http://dx.doi.org/10.2307/354421.

Torgovnick, Marianna. 2001. "Experimental Critical Writing." In *The Fourth Genre: Contemporary Writers of/on Creative Nonfiction,* ed. Robert L. Root Jr. and Michael Steinberg, 409–14. New York: Longman.

Trépanier, Cécycle. 1991. "The Cajunization of French Louisiana: Forging a Regional Identity." *Geographical Journal* 157 (2): 161–71. http://dx.doi.org/10.2307/635273.

Trimbur, John. 2005. "Linguistic Memory and the Politics of U.S. English." *College English* 68:574–88.
Trimbur, John. 2008. "The Dartmouth Conference and the Geohistory of the Native Speaker." *College English* 71 (2): 142–69.
Truss, Lynne. 2004. *Eats, Shoots and Leaves: Why, Commas Really Do Make a Difference!* New York: Gotham Books.
Unger, Harlow Giles. 1998. *Noah Webster: The Life and Times of an American Patriot.* New York: John Wiley & Sons.
Valdman, Albert, Kevin J. Rottet, Barry Jean Ancelet, Richard Guidry, Thomas A. Klinger, Amanda LaFleur, Tamara Lindner, Michael D. Picone, and Dominique Ryon, eds. 2010. *Dictionary of Louisiana French: As Spoken by Cajun, Creole, and American Indian Communities.* Jackson: University Press of Mississippi.
Vergano, Dan, Rick Jervis, and Elizabeth Weise. 2011. "Measuring Full Damage from BP Oil Spill Is Still Hard." *Usatoday.com*, April 17. Updated April 18. Accessed April 15, 2012. http://usatoday30.usatoday.com/news/nation/2011-04-17-bp-oil-spill-annive rsary.htm.
Villanueva, Victor, Jr. 1993. *Bootstraps: From an American Academic of Color.* Urbana, IL: National Council of Teachers of English.
Voss, Albert L. 1928. "Problems in the Teaching of English." *Journal of Louisiana Teachers Association* 5 (9): 26–31.
Walton, Shana. 2004. "Not with a Southern Accent: Cajun English and Ethnic Identity." In *Linguistic Diversity in the South: Changing Codes, Practices, and Ideology*, ed. Margaret Bender, 104–19. Athens: University of Georgia Press.
Worsham, Lynn. 1991. "Writing against Writing: The Predicament of *Ecriture Féminine* in Composition Studies." In *Contending with Words: Composition and Rhetoric in a Postmodern Age*, ed. Patricia Harkin and John Schilb, 82–104. New York: Modern Language Association.
Wyld, Lionel D. 1967. "The Use of 'Mr.'" *College Composition and Communication* 18 (1): 14–15. http://dx.doi.org/10.2307/354488.
Young, Vershawn Ashanti. 2004. "Your Average Nigga." *College Composition and Communication* 55 (4): 693–715. http://dx.doi.org/10.2307/4140667.
Young, Vershawn Ashanti. 2007. *Your Average Nigga: Performing Race, Literacy, and Masculinity.* Detroit: Wayne State University Press.
Young, Vershawn Ashanti, and Aja Martinez, eds. 2011. *Code-Meshing as World English: Policies, Pedagogy, and Performance.* Urbana, IL: National Council of Teachers of English.
Young, Vershawn Ashanti, Aja Martinez, and Julie Ann Naviaux. 2011. "Introduction: Code-Meshing as World English." In *Code-Meshing as World English: Policies, Pedagogy, and Performance*, ed. Vershawn Ashanti Young and Aja Martinez, xix–xxxi. Urbana, IL: National Council of Teachers of English.
Zinshteyn, Mikhail. 2011. "Mayor Bloomberg Trust Donated Big to Louisiana Education Board Elections." *American Independent Online*, October 25. Accessed May 24, 2012.

# ABOUT THE AUTHOR

**NICHOLE E. STANFORD** is a writer in composition and rhetoric focusing on Cajun English, minority academics, and prevalent language myths in the United States for general audiences.

# INDEX

Acadian diaspora, 30, 68, 104–6, 291n4 (chap. 2)
Achebe, Chinua, 14
African American English (AAE), 7, 9, 14, 15, 29, 40, 45, 62, 78, 178, 221, 224
Ancelet, Barry Jean, 38, 57, 215, 298n3 (chap. 3)
Anderson, Benedict, 79, 99
Anyon, Jean, 126–28
Appalachian English, 8, 11, 72, 78, 194
Apple, Michael, 236–38
Aristocracy, 86–87, 192
assimilation, 99, 102, 103, 110, 112, 116, 118, 120, 123, 132, 156, 292n2 (chap. 3); and
dissimilation, 219, 222, 227, 239; forced linguistic, 4, 6, 30, 35, 50, 76, 87, 91, 117, 130–33, 143–44, 194, 223; pedagogy designed to enable, 172, 177, 195–96, 206, 207; resistance to, 110, 141, 254, 290n1 (intro)

Bernard, Shane K., 64–65, 124, 130, 215
Bloom, Lynn Z., 92–93
Bourdieu, Pierre, 8–9, 13, 47, 48–54, 71, 76–77, 79–85, 88–89, 91–92, 94, 95, 98, 117, 121, 123, 124–25, 129–30, 143–45, 153, 155, 164, 166, 191, 194, 197–98, 216, 217–21, 227, 231, 236, 248, 255, 290n3 (chap. 1)
Bowles, Samuel, and Herbert Gintis, 125–26, 173–207
Brandt, Deborah, 163–64
Brasseaux, Carl, 64–65, 76, 142; on Acadian history, 100–112, 292n7 (chap. 2); and the Cajun x, 230; on education of Cajuns, 141

Cajun English (including CE), 232, 298n1 (chap. 1); attitudes toward, 3, 45–47, 61–63, 181–82, 187, 250; changed attitude toward, 245–46; and family, 249–50; history and codification of, 39–45; and pedagogy, 180–89, 231
Cajun Renaissance, 38–39, 45, 239

Cajuns who self-censor, 6–7, 45–48, 52–53, 119–20, 143–44, 154–57, 229–30, 248; author's personal experience as, 3, 19, 23, 29–30, 44, 63–64, 68, 112, 114–15, 117–18, 153, 185, 190, 213–14, 228–29, 232–34, 254–55; education of, 120, 128, 130–52, 179, 188–92, 249; "exile experience" of, 213–16, 244–47; geography of, 36–38; history of, 7, 34–35, 38–39, 55–58, 108–16, 130–52; popular culture portrayals and stereotypes of, 31–35, 58–63, 72–73, 116, 129, 141, 187, 213–14, 229–30, 291n5 (chap. 2); race and ethnicity of, 64–71, 78, 291n4 (chap. 2); and social class, 75–77, 81–83, 100, 109–17, 122–23
Canagarajah, A. Suresh: on code meshing and translanguaging, 11–13, 199–201; critique of, 203, 207, 239; on error, 98; on resistance, 4–6, 232, 237; on SRTOL, 196–97; on standard English, 78
capitalism, 27, 52, 116–17; connection to language myths, 221–27; connection to pedagogy, 167–76, 202, 209–10; discussion of, 81–83, 95–96, 205, 252–53
Cheramie, Deany Marie, 41–45, 231
code censoring, 185–94, 219
code meshing, 11–12, 199–11, 239–40
code switching, 19, 28, 178–80; problems with, 184–94, 233
codification, 49, 79–92, 221
CODOFIL, 30, 39, 72, 165–66
Condon, Sherri, 43, 61–63
conscientization, 236, 240–41, 247, 293n1 (chap. 5)
corporate pedagogy, 171–74
counterhegemony, 174–75, 226–27, 234–40
Crocco, Francesco, 204
Crowley, Sharon, 92–96, 173, 177, 211
cultural hegemony. *See* hegemony

Dartmouth Conference, 175
deculturalization, 128–29

Delpit, Lisa, 189–91
democracy, 85
desocialization, 243–47, 251
Dharwadker, Vinay, 4
dissimilation, 95–99, 198, 219–25, 239
*Distinction: A Social Critique of the Judgement of Taste* (Bourdieu), 49, 53
Donald, James, 169–70
Dubois, Sylvie, 40, 45, 64

Elbow, Peter: on code censoring, 187, 293n3 (chap. 4); on code meshing, 11–13, 201; critique of, 226–27; on standardized English, 78–79, 94, 96, 99
English-only policies, 9, 174, 246
error, 196, 201, 219–21; as arbitrary constructs, 81, 97–100, 178; Cajun "errors," 44–45; evolving, 202–3
exile experience, 215–16, 244, 246

factory pedagogy, 168–71
family as an economic arrangement, 58, 100, 105–9, 116–18, 252–53; and class, 82, 143, 191–93, 293n4 (chap. 4); as a normalizing institution, 121, 124, 127–28, 153–56, 248–52
Faraghar, John Mack, 101–4, 292n6 (chap. 2), 292n8 (chap. 2)
Foucault, Michel, 234; on normalization, 121, 153; on teachers, 165
Franklin, Benjamin, 87, 91, 92
Freire, Paulo, 210–11, 240–43, 290n2 (intro); and banking model, 170–71; and conscientization, 216, 240, 251
French ban, 121–57, 237–38

Gilyard, Keith, 15–16, 192–93
Graff, Harvey J., 170
grammar, 88–89, 124–25, 137, 191
Gramsci, Antonio, 50–51, 167, 217–18, 236–37
Grand Dérangement, 34–35, 103–6

habitus, 53–54
Harris, T. H., 132–41
Hartwell, Patrick, 171
Hawaiian Americans, 7, 78, 128, 223
Heath, Shirley Brice, 84, 125, 248, 293n2 (chap. 5)
hegemony, 12–13, 17, 291(n1) (chap. 2); challenging, 234–47, 250–53; and "correctness," 182–83; definition of, 50–54; and language prejudice, 216–18; reorganization of, 167; and teachers, 129–30. *See also* counterhegemony
hidden curriculum, 125–26, 237

Horner, Bruce on multilingualism, 99, 173–74; on translanguaging, 199–202, 207–11

Indian English, 5, 224

Jefferson, Thomas, 85–87

Kaplan, Robert B., 178
King, Martin Luther, Jr., 227, 241–42

Labov, William, 54, 98
Landry, Christophe, 65, 215
language myths, 216–32
language policing, 92
language prejudice, 48–49, 77–78, 188
Lareau, Annette, 127–28, 293n4 (chap. 4)
legitimate language, 8–9, 48–54
Linguicism, 4. *See also* language prejudice
linguistics, 4–5, 37–45, 48–49; "code switching," in 186; inaccurate understanding of, 228–31, 246
literacy practices (at home), 125–28, 192, 248, 293n4 (chap. 4)
literacy standards, 13, 96–99, 163–79
Longfellow, Henry Wadsworth, 69, 103, 299–300(n5) (chap. 2)
Louisiana, 28, 290n5 (chap. 1), 293n6 (chap. 4); in Cajun history, 106–18; economic exploitation in of, 55–60, 206; education in, 130–59; in popular culture, 31–39; race in, 63–72
Louisiana Creoles, 37–38, 57, 64–70, 100, 118–20, 291n5 (chap. 2)
Louisiana French, 3, 35–39, 76, 111, 116, 144–45; reviving, 157–58. *See also* French ban
Lu, Min-Zhan, 10, 195–96, 247; on translanguaging, 199, 201–2, 207–10

Macafee, Caroline, 8
Mao, LuMing, 8
Mead, Corey, 204–5
Mexican Americans, 7, 223, 247
misrecognition, 224, 290n3 (chap. 1)
Mufwene, Salikoko, 4
multicultural pedagogy, 175–79

nationalism, 30; and composition, 92–95, 174–75, 181; and language elitism, 80, 84; and national language, 89–90, 99, 221, 223–27; and SRTOL, 196–97; and Villanueva, 17
nation builders (and building), 49, 79–80, 83–88, 222–23; and reorganizing, 166–69, 172

Native Americans, 7, 36, 66, 67; and Acadians/Cajuns, 102, 112; languages, 8, 129, 222–23
native English speakers, 99, 154, 175–78, 218; who speak nonprivileged dialects, 7–8, 202–3
Ngũgĩ wa Thiong'o, 5–6, 223, 240; on self-censorship, 145–48
normalization, 49–50, 121, 124–30, 216, 241, 255; and families, 153–56, 191–92, 248–50, 253; among Louisiana French speakers, 143–57; and pedagogy, 162, 197–98; and sociopedagogy, 165–72, 184, 205, 207

Oakes, Jeannie, 126–27
orientalism, 33, 63, 195. *See also* southern orientalism

Phillipson, Robert, 4–6
postcolonial, 78, 195, 234; and Cajuns, 33–35, 55–60
Powell, Malea, 8
Prendergast, Catherine, 94–95

Ramanathan, Vaidehi, 8
reproduction model, 4–6, 232–37
resistance model, 4–6, 232–37
resistance (of Cajuns to assimilation), 38, 40, 77, 108, 117, 138–41; of Cajuns to French immersion, 157; ineffective, 51; in language, 240; of students, 196
Rodriguez, Richard, 14–15, 19, 192–93, 220, 248
Rose, Mike, 191, 196; on error, 97; literacy narrative of, 14–16, 19, 25, 248; on native English speakers, 177
Rushton, William Faulkner, 105
Ryon, Dominique, 144–45

Sacks, Peter, 127–28
self-censor, 3, 6–7, 45–47, 53, 71–72, 144–53, 208. *See also* Cajuns who self-censor

Schroeder, Christopher, 93, 161–62, 167–68, 177, 211–12
Scott, Ann Martin, 41, 229–30
Scott, James C., 51
Scottish English, 8
Scribner, Sylvia, 98
Shaughnessy, Mina, 97, 191, 196, 220
Shor, Ira, 210–11, 243, 252–53
Skuttnab-Kangas, Tove, 4
Smitherman, Geneva, 7, 9–10, 200–201; on code switching, 178–79, 193–94, 220
sociopedagogy, 163–79, 194–99, 208–11
Sohn, Katherine Kelleher, 8, 72, 78, 195
southern orientalism, 34
Spring, Joel, 128–29
standardized English, 77–79, 92–93, 252
Strickland, Donna, 173
Stuckey, J. Elspeth, 95–96, 99
Students' Right to Their Own Language (SRTOL), 9–10, 175, 196–97

Tidwell, Mike, 63–64
tracking, 126–28
translanguaging, 27–28, 199–212, 239
Trimbur, John, 9, 84, 90–91, 99, 222–23, 239; on native English speakers, 173–76; on translanguaging, 199–203

Villanueva, Victor, 7, 195, 220, 227, 248, 298n1 (intro); on language prejudice, 78, 228; literacy narrative of, 14–19, 25, 193; on teachers, 165–66

Webster, Noah, 80, 88–92
white (whiteness), 3, 7, 17, 25–26, 29, 64–71, 78, 111, 125, 141, 190, 194, 220, 224, 293n3 (chap. 4), 293n2 (chap. 5)

Young, Vershawn Ashanti, 14, 29; on code switching/meshing, 18, 179, 199, 200–201, 239–40; literacy narrative of, 17–18, 19, 25

www.ingramcontent.com/pod-product-compliance
Lightning Source LLC
Chambersburg PA
CBHW020355080526
44584CB00014B/1025